FLORIDA STATE
UNIVERSITY LIBRARIES

JUL 11 1995

TALLAHASSEE, FLORIDA

LATINOS IN THE UNITED STATES

History, Law and Perspective

Series Editor
ANTOINETTE SEDILLO LÓPEZ
University of New Mexico
School of Law

Advisory Panel

Tobias Duran, Ph.D.
Cecelia M. Espenoza, J.D.
Paul Finkelman, Ph.D.
Christian Fritz, J.D., Ph.D.
F. Chris Garcia, Ph.D.
Placido Gomez, J.D., LL.M.
Richard Gonzales, J.D.
Emlen Hall, J.D.
Berta Hernandez, J.D.
Eduardo Hernandez-Chavez, Ph.D.
Victor Lopez, J.D.
Jose Martinez, J.D.
Margaret Montoya, J.D.
Michael Olivas, Ph.D., J.D.
Leo Romero, J.D., LL.M.
Christine M. Sierra, Ph.D.
Gloria Valencia-Weber, J.D.

A GARLAND SERIES

SERIES CONTENTS

HISTORICAL THEMES AND IDENTITY
Mestizaje and Labels

LATINA ISSUES
Fragments of Historia(ella)
(Herstory)

CRIMINAL JUSTICE AND
LATINO COMMUNITIES

LATINO EMPLOYMENT, LABOR
ORGANIZATIONS AND IMMIGRATION

LATINO LANGUAGE AND EDUCATION
Communication and the Dream Deferred

LAND GRANTS, HOUSING
AND POLITICAL POWER

VOLUME

6

LAND GRANTS, HOUSING AND POLITICAL POWER

Edited with an introduction by
ANTOINETTE SEDILLO LÓPEZ

GARLAND PUBLISHING, INC.
New York & London
1995

Introduction copyright © 1995 Antoinette Sedillo López
All rights reserved

Library of Congress Cataloging-in-Publication Data

Land grants, housing and political power / edited with an introduction by Antoinette Sedillo López.
    p.   cm. — (Latinos in the United States ; v. 6)
    Includes bibliographical references.
    ISBN 0-8153-1800-6 (alk. paper)
    1. Hispanic Americans—Southwest, New—Politics and government. 2. Hispanic Americans—Suffrage—Southwest, New.
3. Hispanic Americans—Housing—Southwest, New. 4. Hispanic Americans—Southwest, New—Land tenure. 5. Southwest, New—Politics and government. I. López, Antoinette Sedillo.
II. Series.
F790.S75L36   1995
305.868'079—dc20   94-36779
                                                                             CIP

Printed on acid-free, 250-year-life paper
Manufactured in the United States of America

To my children, Victor Francisco and Graciela Raquel.
Esta colección es tu historia y tu herencia.

CONTENTS

Introduction	ix
Fair Housing and Latinos *Herminia L. Cubillos*	1
The Demise of "Jim Crow" *David Montejano*	14
Housing Price Inequalities: A Comparison of Anglos, Blacks, and Spanish-Origin Populations *Lauren J. Krivo*	43
Housing Segregation of a Predominantly Middle Class Population: Residential Patterns Developed by the Cuban Immigration into Miami, 1950–74 *Morton D. Winsberg*	61
The Voting Rights Act and Hispanic Political Representation in the Southwest *John A. Garcia*	77
A New Remedy for an Old Ailment: Cumulative Voting as an Alternative to the Single Member District in Minority Voting Rights *Maurilio E. Vigil*	96
Voting Rights and the Constitution: The Disenfranchisement of Non-English Speaking Citizens *Sandra Guerra*	105
An Analysis of Chicano and Anglo Electoral Patterns in School Board Elections *John A. Garcia*	124
Minority Population Proportion and Black and Hispanic Congressional Success in the 1970s and 1980s *Bernard Grofman and Lisa Handley*	140
Ethnic Officeholders in Los Angeles County *Fernando J. Guerra*	151
Toward an Understanding of the Role of the Mass Media in Latino Political Life *Federico A. Subervi-Velez, Richard Herrera and Michael Begay*	157

Gárza v. County of Los Angeles: Preservation of Minority
Group Voting Strength as Justification for Deviation
from One Person-One Vote Standard
  Robert G. Retana   169
Case Note Addendum: Gárza v. County of Los Angeles
  Robert G. Retana   202
The Election of Hispanics in City Government:
An Examination of the Election of Federico Peña
as Mayor of Denver
  Rodney Hero   207
A Gender Gap Among Hispanics? A Comparison
with Blacks and Anglos
  Susan Welch and Lee Sigelman   221
A Longitudinal Examination of Political Participation
Rates of Mexican American Females
  Susan A. MacManus, Charles S. Bullock III
  and Barbara P. Grothe   240
A Comparison of Black and Mexican American Voters in
Denver: Assertive versus Acquiescent Political
Orientations and Voting Behavior in an Urban Electorate
  Nicholas P. Lovrich, Jr. and Otwin Marenin   250
Ethnicity and Electoral Choice: Mexican American Voting
Behavior in the California 30th Congressional District
  Bruce E. Cain and D. Roderick Kiewiet   261
Hispanics Gain Seats in the 98th Congress
After Reapportionment
  Maurilio E. Vigil   274
Land Policy in the Spanish Southwest, 1846–1891:
A Study in Contrasts
  Howard R. Lamar   286
Land, Water, and Ethnic Identity in Taos
  Sylvia Rodríguez   305
Acknowledgments   397

INTRODUCTION

The adjusted 1990 Census counted 22.3 million Latinos in the United States. People who trace their origins to Mexico represent the largest group (13.5 million people: 60 percent of all Latinos in the United States). About 2.7 million are of Puerto Rican origin. About one million are of Cuban origin and 5.1 million are of other Spanish origin including Central Americans, Spaniards and others who come from families who lived in the Southwest before it was annexed into the United States.[1] Thus, consideration of subgroups is necessary in surveying land issues, housing and voting. Many Mexican Americans in California and the Southwest are descendants of Mexicans who found themselves citizens of the United States when Mexico ceded the territory to the United States after the Mexican-American War. Many of them have lost their land and some are in the process of being displaced by further Anglo encroachment. Puerto Ricans are concentrated on the East Coast and experience substandard housing. The majority of Cubans live in Florida in predominantly Cuban communities. Land issues, housing and voting are all related to economic and political power.

Housing

Housing has been a critical contemporary issue for Latino people in that many live in substandard housing or have experienced segregated housing conditions. There is also evidence that Latinos pay more than Anglos for comparable housing. The articles in this section look at the issue from empirical, legal and social perspectives.

Herminia L. Cubillos writes on housing conditions of Latinos in the United States and how fair housing policies affect the Latino community. She discusses the economic conditions of Latinos and examines the impact of discrimination in the sale and rental of housing to Latinos. She reviews the historical development of federal housing legislation and argues that fair housing legislation should be strengthened and that HUD should establish a

Latino-focused fair housing initiative. The article is important in that it provides a framework for working on the housing problems of Latinos.

David Montejano's essay describes the factors leading up to the gradual dismantling of social, educational and residential segregation in Texas. He examines changes in economic and political subcultures as well as the impact of the civil rights movement. The article is a fascinating social history of Mexican Americans in Texas.

Lauren Krivo analyzes data from the Annual Housing Survey to look at housing price and rental price inequalities among Anglos, Blacks and Latinos. She found that African Americans, Mexican Americans and Puerto Ricans frequently pay higher rent than Anglos for the same quality housing although the Cuban population does not. She did not find significant differences in price paid for housing.

Morton Winsberg's article describes the processes of urban ethnic residential segregation in Miami. He found that Cubans, despite having upper and middle class backgrounds, did not "assimilate" into the city but lived in close proximity to one another. The article is interesting in its obvious negative slant on the issue. For example, he calls Latin immigrants an "invasion." He does not seem to understand how preserving their culture might be important to Cubans in establishing their communities.

Political Power

The traditional path to self-determination in this country is access to the political process. Federal, state and local legislation, community assistance and control of education all depend on political power. Traditionally, Anglo Americans have experienced the privileges associated with political power and cultural dominance. Minority groups are beginning to develop a political sophistication that can make a difference. Minority political action is a riveting game in a majority-rule democracy. Ensuring that Latinos have a voice in their future is a challenge for Latino community and political leaders.

Andrew Hernandez of the Southwest Voter Registration Project has pointed out that the areas in which Hispanics are concentrated give them national political clout. The ten states with high Hispanic populations account for more than three-fourths of the electoral votes needed to decide a presidential election. President Clinton appointed two Hispanics to cabinet positions in 1993.

Introduction

Hispanics make up 38 percent of the population in New Mexico, 26 percent in California and 26 percent in Texas. Currently there are Hispanic mayors in Miami, Florida, Sacramento and Oxnard, California, Albuquerque and Las Cruces, New Mexico, and Laredo and Brownsville, Texas. According to the National Association of Latino Elected Officials (NALEO) Education Fund there have been significant increases in the number of Hispanic municipal officials. In 1992, NALEO counted 1,358 Hispanic municipal officials. Thus Latinos are gaining political strength nationally, statewide and locally.[1]

Of course, numbers alone do not translate into political power. Our political process is much too complex for such an easy analysis. Geographic lines, reapportionment, voting patterns, language barriers, political sophistication, media coverage, gender issues and political orientation are all factors to think about in gauging Hispanic political clout. I have selected a variety of articles that address these issues.

John Garcia examines the changes in numbers of Mexican American and other Hispanic elected officials in five southwestern states for federal, state and local offices during the period from 1973 to 1984. He measures the impact of the extension of the Voting Rights Act to expand coverage to the southwestern part of the United States to include provisions for non-English-speaking minority groups. He concludes that the Voting Rights Act removed the more blatant obstacles to electoral participation and resulted in uneven gains across the southwestern states.

Maurilio Vigil analyzes a little known court case in Alamogordo, New Mexico, in which a federal district judge approved a unique method of cumulative voting to be used in the election of city commissioners. Allowing voters to cast more than one ballot for a candidate resulted in a Mexican-American woman winning and becoming the first Mexican American to sit on the Commission because her support base, which was primarily Mexican American, could concentrate their votes for her.

Sandra Guerra develops the argument that as a fundamental right, voting and access to the ballot should be available to non-English-speaking minorities. She argues that, without compelling justification, states should not provide voting assistance to English speakers unless they provide equivalent assistance to non-English speakers in order to make voting available to both groups on an equal basis.

John Garcia analyzes Anglo electoral patterns in school board elections in urban Arizona to discern the degree of voter polarization, the sociopolitical factors affecting voters' preferences and the distinctiveness of Anglo and Chicano bloc voting. Chicanos indicated a slightly greater degree of support for Chicano candidates than Anglos for Anglo candidates. However, each group voted for candidates of their own ethnic background in discernible patterns. A winning strategy for a Chicano candidate effectively mobilizes the Chicano community, restricts the field of Chicano candidates for each office and either neutralizes or obtains a reasonable share of Anglo votes.

Bernard Grofman and Lisa Handley focus on congressional success and the role of combined minority (black plus Hispanic) populations in achieving that success. They conclude that for blacks, a black plurality and a combined (black and Hispanic) minority population above 50 percent is enough to create a congressional district in which a black candidate will eventually succeed. For Hispanics, the combined minority population should exceed 63 percent to offer a Hispanic candidate a realistic opportunity of success. It is important for Latinos and blacks to think about the potential for coalition building to achieve political success.

Fernando J. Guerra looks historically at Black, Latino and Jewish elected officials in Los Angeles County. He found that minorities who won office did so in minority districts that either became vacant or were recently reapportioned or both. When a minority candidate won a position it tended to remain in minority control.

Federico Subervi-Velez, Richard Herrera and Michael Begay analyze the characteristics of the Republican party's multimillion dollar effort to use the broadcast media to attract Latino voters to Ronald Reagan in the 1984 election. The article describes the type of advertising and the ways in which they were used to successfully attract Hispanic voters.

Robert Retana wrote a case study and an addendum on the *Garza v. County of Los Angeles* reapportionment case. In this landmark case, the court found evidence of past discrimination against Latinos. The court further found that the 1982 redistricting was calculated at least in part to retain the effect of the prior discriminatory redistricting and to prevent Latinos from attaining a majority in any district.

Rodney Hero wrote a case study of the election of Federico Peña as mayor of Denver. He analyzes the campaign themes and Peña's successful attempt to increase participation and to develop a liberal coalition.

Susan Welch and Lee Sigelman explore whether the differences between male and female white voters also occur among

Black and Hispanic voters. They analyze data from six election day exit polls conducted in 1980, 1984 and 1988 for differences between Hispanic men and women in ideological and partisan identification and in vote choice. The data reveal that Hispanic women are more liberal and more prodemocratic than Hispanic men. The magnitude of these differences is essentially similar among Hispanic, Black and Anglo Americans.

Susan MacManus, Charles Bullock and Barbara Grothe examine changes between 1974 and 1984 in the registration and voter turnout rates of Mexican-American women in Sutton County West Texas and found a sharp increase in rates as well as an increase in political sophistication.

Nicholas P. Lovrich and Otwin Marenin compare Black and Mexican-American voters in Denver. They believe that Hispanics lag behind African Americans in their ability to use the electoral process to their advantage. They believe that Mexican Americans do not share the same reactions to their oppressed situation and thus have not developed a sense of ethnic cohesion and political consciousness to the same extent as Blacks. Bruce Cain and D. Roderick Kiewiet, on the other hand, studied racial bloc voting in California's 30th Congressional District and found a high degree of Mexican-American support for the Mexican-American candidate and a high degree of party loyalty.

Maurilio Vigil examines the effect of reapportionment after the 1980 Census and the increase in Hispanic office holders. He finds a direct causal link between the redrawing of congressional districts and increased Latino representation in the Sunbelt. He describes the electoral process that enabled Hispanics to capture four seats in Congress.

Land Grants

How Mexican Americans have fared in the legal treatment of their land grant claims is a case study in Anglo hegemony after the Mexican-American War. The available articles on land grants could fill a six volume anthology; the complex legal issues have generated volumes of commentary. The two articles in this volume represent an overview of the Spanish colonial land grant process, the American takeover and adjudication of the claims and a contemporary case study of the displacement of rural landowning Latino peoples.

Howard Lamar studied land policy in the Spanish Southwest between 1846 and 1891 at the time the United States acquired the territories. He describes the vast differences between the American land system and the older Spanish-Mexican one. The culture clash and the clash of legal systems ultimately resulted in the loss of large parcels of land belonging to the Mexican-American colonists and settlers at the hands of the Anglo Americans.

Sylvia Rodríguez describes contemporary land issues. She demonstrates that the historic process of land expropriation described by land grant scholars continues today, while rural Hispanos resist further Anglo encroachment and cling to their shrinking parcels of land. Rural Hispanic cultural identity is closely linked to their relationship to their land; thus such displacement effectively effaces cultural identity.

The articles in this volume demonstrate increasing political sophistication and power. Hopefully, Latinos will use this power to address the land and housing issues documented in this volume as well as the other critical issues facing the Latino communities that have been documented in this series.

NOTES

1. Jesus M. Garcia, "The Hispanic Population in the United States: March 1992" Current Population Reports, P20-465RV, July 1993.

FURTHER READING

Bannon, John Francis, *Spanish Borderlands Frontier, 1513–1821.* Albuquerque: University of New Mexico Press, 1974.

Ebright, Malcolm, "The Embudo Grant: A Case Study of Justice and the Court of Private Land Claims," 19 *Journal of the West* 74 (1980).

Forment, Carlos A., "Political Practice and the Rise of an Ethnic Enclave: The Cuban American Case, 1959–1979," 18 *Theory and Society* 47 (1989).

Garcia, F. Chris, ed., *Latinos and the Political System.* Notre Dame, Ind.: University of Notre Dame Press, 1988.

Gates, Paul, "The California Land Act of 1851," 50 *California Historical Quarterly* 395 (1971).

Gomez, Placido, "The History and Adjudication of the Common Lands of Spanish and Mexican Land Claims," 25 *Natural Resources Journal* 1039–1080 (1985).

Hall, G. Emlen, *Four Leagues of Pecos: A Legal History of the Pecos Grant, 1800–1933*. Albuquerque: University of New Mexico Press, 1984.

———, "Landholding: The Spanish Borderlands," *Encyclopedia of the North American Colonies*, 669. New York: Charles Scribner's Sons, 1993.

Hornbeck, David, "Land Tenure and Rancho Expansion in Alta California, 1784–1846," 4 *Journal of Historical Geography*, 371 (1978).

Krivo, Lauren J., "Home Ownership Differences Between Hispanics and Anglos in the United States" 33 (No. 4) *Social Problems* 319 (April 1986).

Villarreal, Roberto E., Howard E. Neighbor and Norma G. Hernandez, *Latino Empowerment: Progress, Problems and Prospects*. New York: Greenwood Press, 1988.

Weber, David, *The Mexican Frontier, 1821–1846: The American Southwest under Mexico*. Albuquerque: University of New Mexico Press, 1982.

Westphall, Victor, *Mercedes Reales: Hispanic Land Grants of the Upper Rio Grande Region*. Albuquerque: University of New Mexico Press, 1983.

FAIR HOUSING AND LATINOS

Herminia L. Cubillos*

National attention has recently focused on problems associated with homelessness resulting in emergency measures, blue-ribbon panels and other responses. However, insufficient attention and analysis has been directed to the critical status of Latinos regarding housing and housing discrimination. This article focuses on the housing conditions of Latinos in the United States and how fair housing policies affect the Latino community.

Part I is a review of the data demonstrating the economic and living conditions of Latinos. Part II examines the impact of discrimination in the sale and rental of housing to Latinos. Part III surveys the federal legislation designed to counteract the socio-economic and discriminatory factors affecting the availability and adequacy of housing. Part IV examines the shortcoming of current federal fair housing laws and how they are enforced. Finally, Part V offers recommendations to ensure fair and adequate housing for Latinos.

I.
Latino Housing Status and Problems

To understand the importance of comprehensive and effective fair housing legislation, a review of the severe housing problems facing Latinos is essential. The Latino population is one of the fastest growing groups in the country.[1] A recently released report from the Bureau of the Census showed that between 1980 and 1987 the Latino population grew from 14.5 million to 18.8 million.[2] In 1987, Latinos accounted for 7.9% of the population, compared with 6.4% in 1980.[3] A study by Cushing N. Dolbeare for the National Council of La Raza demonstrated that in 1983 more than three-quarters (78%) of Latino households lived in metropolitan areas and 83% lived in areas classified as "urban" by the Census Bureau. About 41% of Latinos lived in the West compared with

---

* The author was the legislative director and senior policy analyst for the Policy Analysis Center, National Council of La Raza, Washington D.C., from 1986 until 1988. The National Council of La Raza is a private, non-profit, tax-exempt corporation dedicated to promoting the social and economic well-being of Americans of Hispanic descent.
 1. Bureau of the Census, U.S. Dep't of Commerce, Current Population Reports, Series P-20, No. 416, The Hispanic Population in the United States: March 1986 and 1987 (Advance Reports).
 2. *Id.* at 8.
 3. *Id.* at 9.

32% in the South, 19% in the Northeast, and 8% in the Midwest.[4]

Latinos suffer from lower incomes and from higher poverty rates than non-Latinos. In 1986, 27.3% of Latino families lived below the poverty level, compared with 11% of white families and 31.1% of black families. Median Latino family income was only 65% that of whites.

The most recent comprehensive data on Latino housing status comes from the 1983 Annual Housing Survey. The survey found that Latinos were less likely than either whites or blacks to be homeowners; 57% of Latinos were renters and 43% were homeowners.[5] In comparison, 69% of whites and 45% of blacks were homeowners. In 1983, about 79% of all Latino households lived in housing that was built before 1970.[6]

Housing conditions for much of the Latino community are inadequate.[7] An unpublished Housing and Urban Development (HUD) study showed that approximately one-third of all Latino households live in physically inadequate or overcrowded housing, compared with only one-tenth of white households.[8]

The affordability of housing is a more critical problem for Latinos than housing quality. According to the National Council of La Raza study, low income households typically spend over half their incomes for shelter, including utilities.[9] This leaves insufficient resources for other necessities such as food or clothing.

In 1983, the median income of all Latino households was below the poverty level and the income of one household in ten was less than half the poverty level. As a result, more than one Latino household in ten paid more than 70% of their income for housing, and two in five spent more than 30%.[10]

One factor which contributes to Latino housing problems is the lack of adequate rental housing for families with children and large families. In 1986, 26.6% of Latino families had five or more members, compared with 13.9% of non-Latino families.[11] The 1985 Current Population Survey shows that over 75% of Latino families had three or more persons compared with less than 60% of non-Latino families.[12]

---

4. Policy Analysis Center, Nat'l Council of La Raza, The Hispanic Housing Crisis 5 (1988).
5. *Id.* at 5.
6. *Id.*
7. Office of Policy Development and Research, U.S. Dep't of Housing and Urban Development, Housing the Hispanic Population: Are Special Programs and Policies Needed? (Unpublished 1983) (unpublished manuscript available at the National Council of La Raza).
8. *Id.* at 6.
9. Policy Analysis Center, National Council of La Raza, *supra* note 4, at 7.
10. *Id.* at 8.
11. Bureau of the Census, U.S. Dep't of Commerce, *supra* note 1.
12. *Fair Housing Amendments Act of 1987: Hearings on S. 558 Before the Subcomm. on the*

A 1980 HUD study found that 25.5% of all rental units in the United States did not allow children. Another 50% had policies which restricted the ability of families with children to rent. Restrictions included limits on the number of units in an apartment complex where families with children could reside, limits on the age of child occupants, and prohibitions on children of the opposite sex sharing the same bedroom.[13] The housing problems faced by Latinos correlate directly to family size.

II.
Housing Discrimination Against Latinos

A. Overview

Latinos are both disproportionately poor and inadequately housed, but low income alone cannot fully explain poor housing conditions. According to a 1983 internal HUD study:

> When common factors contributing to housing deprivation are taken into account, differences in housing conditions among Whites, Blacks, and Hispanics are narrowed somewhat, but sizeable differences still remain . . . Blacks and Hispanics are twice as likely as whites to be either inadequately housed or overcrowded, even when they have similar financial resources.[14]

It is clear that factors other than income are partially responsible for poor Latino housing conditions. One of these factors is housing discrimination. While there has been considerably less research on the nature and extent of housing discrimination against Latinos than discrimination against blacks, the available data shows that housing discrimination against Latinos is pervasive. The following subsections describe research findings on housing discrimination and Latinos in selected urban areas.

B. Dallas

Most studies of housing discrimination have focused on the housing experiences of blacks. Far less is known about the nature and extent of housing discrimination against other minorities. A 1979 HUD "audit" in Dallas was the first HUD research to focus on the extent of housing discrimination against Latinos.[15] It had often been assumed that Latinos

---

Constitution of the United States of the Senate Comm. on the Judiciary, 100th Cong., 1st Sess. 79-80 (1987) (statement of Raul Yzaguirre, Pres. of Nat'l Council of La Raza).

13. *Fair Housing Amendments Act of 1987: Hearings on H.R. 1158 Before the Subcomm. on Civil and Constitutional Rights of the House Comm. on the Judiciary*, 100th Cong., 1st Sess. 182-183 (1987) (statement of James B. Morales, staff atty., Nat'l Center for Youth Law).

14. Office of Policy Development and Research, U.S. Dep't of Housing and Urban Development, supra note 7 at 7.

15. Office of Policy Development and Research, U.S. Dep't of Housing and Urban Develop-

would suffer less than blacks from housing discrimination for two reasons: (1) Latinos were a smaller population, and (2) the income of Latino renters was substantially greater than that of black renters.[16] The HUD audit showed otherwise.

The Dallas study found that 42% of dark-skinned Mexican-Americans and 16% of light-skinned Mexican-Americans were given false information on the availability of rental units.[17] The chance of dark-skinned Mexican-Americans experiencing at least one instance of discrimination in a typical housing search was 96%. The probability of light-skinned Mexican-Americans experiencing similar discrimination was about 65%.[18] The incidence of discriminatory treatment against dark-skinned Mexican-Americans was far greater than that against either blacks or light-skinned Mexican-Americans. Discriminatory treatment against dark-skinned Mexican-Americans regarding the availability of a unit was two and one-half times as great as that against either blacks or light-skinned Mexican-Americans. Furthermore, discriminatory treatment against dark-skinned Mexican-Americans on terms and conditions of the rental contract was also far greater.[19]

C. Denver

A 1982 HUD funded study in Denver also found evidence of housing discrimination against Latinos. When teams of white, black and Latino auditors were sent to homes that were advertised for sale, the white auditors received considerably more information than black or Latino auditors. One in three Latino auditors were told there were no homes available which were similar to the advertised home in the same general area, compared with one in five white auditors. Furthermore, 60% of Latino auditors were told of no similar homes in other areas, compared with 31% of white auditors. These differences in the degree to which Latino and white auditors were informed of housing alternatives were sizeable and statistically significant.[20]

---

ment, Discrimination Against Chicanos in the Dallas Housing Rental Market: An Experimental Extension of the Housing Market Practices Survey (1979).
    16. Office of Policy Development & Research, U.S. Dep't of Housing and Urban Development, *supra* note 15.
    17. *Id.* at 2.
    18. *Id.* at Forward.
    19. *Id.* at 33.
    20. Colorado Civil Rights Division, Discrimination, Segregation, and Minority Housing Conditions in Sun Belt Cities: A Study of Denver, Houston, Phoenix (1983).

D. Boston

In a 1981 Boston HUD funded study,[21] a telephone survey was done of selected realtors who were advertising units for rent. The test teams consisted of three persons: one that would normally be identified by voice as white, one as black, and one as Latino. In all tests, the white surveyors were invited to come to the office to be shown a unit, while the black and Latino surveyors were informed that no units were available 31 times.

Site visits were carried out on 17 firms including those that were already covered by the telephone survey and continued to advertise units for rent. In 23 of 47 test visits, only white testers were shown units. Black and Latino testers were told nothing was available.[22]

E. Other Studies

A 1986 HUD funded study in Phoenix found evidence of discriminatory rental practices against both blacks and Latinos. In 13% of the audits, blacks and Latinos were asked to pay higher rents and deposits while whites were given a variety of rental inducements.[23]

Surveys in Houston and San Jose found evidence of housing discrimination. In both surveys, blacks encountered more discrimination than Latinos. In 1973, the Houston survey found that at "white-occupied" apartment complexes, black surveyors encountered at least one form of discriminatory treatment in 42% of their visits, compared with 10% of Latino surveyors.[24] The 1978 San Jose study found that black surveyors encountered some form of discriminatory treatment in 58% of their visits, compared with 20% of Latino surveyors.

III.
FAIR HOUSING LAWS

A. History of Fair Housing Legislation

Before 1962, there were no federal laws or policies prohibiting housing discrimination. For the most part, local elected officials and influential members of the housing industry dictated housing policies.[25] As blacks migrated to urban centers, some cities adopted zoning laws designed to prohibit blacks from purchasing or occupying property in a

---

21. Office of Policy Development and Research, U.S. Dep't of Housing and Urban Development, The Fair Housing Enforcement Demonstration (1983).
22. *Id.* at 25.
23. Equal Opportunity Dep't, City of Phoenix, Housing Discrimination in Phoenix: 1985 (1986).
24. Office of Policy Development and Research, U.S. Dep't of Housing and Urban Development, *supra* note 15.
25. *See, e.g.,* Buchanan v. Warley, 245 U.S. 60 (1917).

manner that would destroy the "racial purity" of a given area.[26]

In urban centers which did not adopt such zoning laws and in other cities where zoning laws were eventually struck down as unconstitutional, racially restrictive covenants[27] and other tactics of the real estate industry were used to achieve the same results.[28]

"Racial redlining" and "racial steering" maintained rigidly segregated neighborhoods in many areas. Originally, "racial redlining" referred to a practice used by lenders to delineate areas of a city or town in which they would not extend credit because of the racial make-up.[29] Insurance companies began to follow the same practice.[30] If a neighborhood was all minority, appraisers often considered it to be "unstable" or otherwise a poor financial risk.[31] The result was an appraisal below the fair market value, which led to a denial of the mortgage request.[32]

Another common technique used to promote segregated housing was "steering" in which homeseekers were shown homes only in certain parts of town where persons of their race or ethnicity were in the majority.[33]

Another technique used to promote segregated housing was "blockbusting." This occurred when a real estate broker went into a white community and sold a house to a minority family and then advised the neighbors that they should sell their homes before the area became "undesirable."[34] This often led to panic selling and re-segregation, as a neighborhood quickly became all minority.

During the Great Depression, the federal government entered the

---

26. Citizens' Commission on Civil Rights, A Decent Home . . . A Report on the Continuing Failure of the Federal Government to Provide Equal Housing Opportunity (1983).

27. See Shelley v. Kraemer, 334 U.S. 1, 20 (1948). Under *Shelley*, while a private agreement restricting the sale of property only to persons of "the Caucasian race" does not violate the Fourteenth Amendment, state court enforcement of such a racially restrictive covenant violates the Equal Protection Clause of the Fourteenth Amendment.

28. Citizens' Commission on Civil Rights, *supra* note 26.

29. See Laufman v. Oakley Bldg. and Loan Co., 408 F. Supp. 489 (S.D. Ohio 1976). The *Laufman* court rejected plaintiff's claim that when a lender views a racially integrated neighborhood as per se, a declining neighborhood, and therefore a bad credit risk, it is unconstitutional "redlining" in the absence of "legitimate business criteria" such as credit worthiness, marketability of the security property, and diversity of the lender's assets. *Id.* at 501.

30. See, e.g., Dunn v. Midwestern Indemnity, 472 F. Supp. 1106 (S.D. Ohio 1979). Plaintiff was a black homeowner and successfully brought an action to prevent defendant from denying renewal of his homeowner's policy. Defendant's had not renewed an entire portfolio of policies because a significant portion of them were issued to persons living in predominantly black neighborhoods.

31. *See* note 29.

32. Citizens' Commission on Civil rights, *supra* note 26.

33. Chicago Real Estate Board v. City of Chicago, Ill. 2d 530, 536, 224 N.E.2d 793, 798 (1967). "[I]t has been the practice of the [real estate] industry for many years not to lease to Negro families in certain areas of Chicago."

34. Summer v. Teaneck, 53 N.J. 548, 551, 251 A.2d 761, 762-3 (1969).

housing arena to prevent the collapse of the housing industry and to protect the investments of homeowners.[35] Federal housing entities like the Federal Housing Administration (FHA), the Federal Home Loan Bank Board (FHLBB), and the Federal National Mortgage Association (FNMA) were created to help safeguard and facilitate home ownership but did not address the problems faced by minorities in securing decent housing.[36] Public housing projects were the only programs which recognized the right of participation by minorities—and only by segregating blacks from whites. Federal housing policy at the time largely mirrored the assumptions of local governments and the housing industry regarding the desirability of racially dual markets.[37] Federal policy continued to support segregated public housing and discriminatory practices in FHA and Veterans Administration (VA) programs even after the 1948 Supreme Court decision of *Shelley v. Kraemer*, which outlawed the enforcement of racially restrictive covenants.[38]

After World War II, the federal government began taking an active role in aiding the housing industry to meet the demand for new homes. The Housing Act of 1949 established a series of programs designed to promote growth in the housing industry. The federal government underwrote the development of large subdivisions of single-family homes in areas outside the central cities by insuring home mortgages of middle-income home buyers and guaranteeing mortgages for veterans under the G.I. Bill of Rights. Yet federal policy did nothing to ensure that minorities would share in the new housing boom.[39]

While the suburbs developed as white and middle class, the cities remained a patchwork of minority and white neighborhoods.[40] Ghettos and barrios—largely segregated neighborhoods in which minorities lived—expanded into white neighborhoods, which experienced "blockbusting" caused by unscrupulous real estate brokers.[41] Often minorities paid prices above market value for their housing, yet were denied the benefits of the low- or no-down payment mortgage loans that lenders made when federal insurance was available.[42] Discrimination and segregation in housing continued through the decade of the 1950's often with the support of the federal government.[43]

---

35. Citizens' Commission on Civil Rights, *supra* note 26.
36. *Id.*
37. *Id.*
38. *Id.*
39. Shelley v. Kraemer, 334 U.S. at 20.
40. Citizens' Commission on Civil Rights, *supra* note 26, at 14.
41. *Id.*
42. U.S. Fed. Housing Admin., Underwriting Manual, Valuation Procedure under Title II of the National Housing Act, Para. 228 (1936).
43. Citizens' Commission on Civil Rights, *supra* note 26, at 14.

Discrimination in federally-subsidized housing emerged as a public issue during the 1960 presidential campaign. John F. Kennedy stated that, if elected, he would issue an executive order to eliminate this injustice with "a stroke of a pen."[44] On November 20, 1962, Executive Order 11063 on Equal Opportunity in Housing was signed by President Kennedy. Although the Executive Order represented the first national policy supporting equal housing opportunity, it was narrowly constructed to cover only prospective federally assisted housing. Severe sanctions were imposed upon violators, including cutting off funding and barring housing developers and realtors from future participation in federal housing programs.[45] However, the inadequacy of the Order soon became apparent. Discrimination was barred in federally subsidized housing, but the law did not cover the private market.[46]

Generally, the private housing industry did not adopt non-discriminatory policies. In fact, many in the private sales and rental industry believed that adopting such a policy would place them at a competitive disadvantage.[47]

In 1965, fair housing legislation was introduced by President Lyndon Johnson.[48] A far-reaching fair housing bill was approved in the House of Representatives the following year, but a Senate filibuster killed it.[49]

In 1968, three major developments changed the political landscape of the fair housing issue. First, responding to the grief and anger caused by the assassination of the Reverend Martin Luther King, Congress enacted Title VIII of the Civil Rights Act of 1968 which broadly prohibited discrimination in both private and public housing markets based on race, color, religion, sex, or national origin.[50] Title VIII was passed only after extensive and bitter debate culminated in legislative compromises which limited the bill's enforcement provisions.

Second, through *Jones v. Mayer*, the Supreme Court re-examined the coverage of the Reconstruction Civil Rights Act of 1866 and concluded that it was broad enough to provide black citizens with redress against private as well as government discrimination in housing transactions.[51] Third, Congress passed a Housing and Urban Development Act authorizing new housing programs for low income and moderate income

---

44. *See id.* at 14.
45. *Id.* at 17.
46. *Id.*
47. *Id.*
48. *Id.* at 22.
49. *Id.*
50. *Id.* at 26.
51. *Id.*

families that would provide volume and choice of location.[52]

Title VIII provided certain enforcement mechanisms designed to achieve fair housing goals. First, a victim of housing discrimination could seek relief by filing a complaint with HUD. Second, it created a private right of action for victims of discrimination. Third, it gave the Attorney General the authority to initiate litigation in cases where there was a "pattern or practice" of discrimination.

As regulations were adopted and HUD began to implement the law, deficiencies became evident. Under the law, a victim of housing discrimination can report a violation to HUD. The Department will then investigate and try to bring the two parties together to conciliate their differences. HUD does not have the authority to issue "cease and desist" orders to those found guilty of violating the law or the power to otherwise enforce its conciliation efforts. Accordingly, HUD has been largely unsuccessful in getting landlords and sellers of housing to take the process seriously.

The 1968 law provides another alternative to a victim of housing discrimination. A victim can initiate a private lawsuit against the landlord or seller. However, this takes considerable time and money. Besides having to hire an attorney and taking time off from work to appear for depositions and to appear in court, the victim must go through a lengthy litigation process which is often further delayed by overcrowded court calendars.

The Justice Department can also sue to enforce fair housing laws, but only where the Attorney General believes there is a "pattern or practice" of housing discrimination, or in cases raising an issue of general public importance. This provision of the law has little impact on practices in the housing market. From November 1, 1983 to January 31, 1987, the Justice Department filed a total of 53 lawsuits, fewer than 18 per year.[53]

B. *The Fair Housing Amendments Act*

At the beginning of the 100th Congress, Senators Edward M. Kennedy (D-Mass.) and Arlen Specter (R-Pa) and representatives Don Edwards (D-Ca.) and Hamilton Fish, Jr. (R-NY) introduced the Fair Housing Amendments Act (HR 1158). The bill won House and Senate approval and was signed into law by President Reagan on September 13, 1988.[54] The amendments will strengthen the Fair Housing Act of 1968 in two ways: (1) by strengthening the enforcement provisions of the act,

---

52. Housing and Urban Development Act of 1968, 12 U.S.C. § 1715(1) (1976).
53. Leadership Conference Education Fund, Civil Rights Monitor, Vol. 2, No. 4, Washington, D.C., June-July 1987.
54. H.R. 6491, 100th Cong., 2d Sess., 134 Cong. Rec. 117 (1988).

and (2) by expanding protected classes to include disabled persons and families with children.

The amendments increase HUD's ability to enforce fair housing laws. Where HUD's conciliation process fails, victims are entitled to a determinative hearing before an administrative law judge. Furthermore, the complainant has the right to intervene in the proceeding, and the decision of the administrative law judge can be appealed to the federal court of appeals for the circuit in which the discriminatory practice was alleged to have occurred.

Under the amendments, when the administrative law judge finds discrimination, equitable and declaratory relief (including orders requiring the respondent to sell or rent the house to the complainant) as well as compensatory and punitive damages can be awarded (similar administrative enforcement procedures are currently used by 28 other federal agencies and departments). The Fair Housing Amendments Act also permits an application to be made to a federal court for an order to hold a house or apartment off the market while a case is being decided.[55]

IV.
NEED FOR LATINO FOCUSED EFFORTS

Federal fair housing laws need more effective enforcement mechanisms to resolve housing discrimination complaints overall. However, additional efforts focused on Latinos are also essential to effectively address housing discrimination against Latinos.

Current legislation is limited to improving the effectiveness of the enforcement process after a complaint is filed. It does not address the need to increase the likelihood that Latinos encountering housing discrimination will file complaints. Despite evidence of pervasive housing discrimination against Latinos, HUD data reveal that Latinos tend to file very few complaints. According to the data:

* From Fiscal Year 1980 through Fiscal Year 1985, formal complaints filed with HUD-certified fair housing state and local agencies by blacks alleging discrimination totaled 14,172. Such complaints by Latinos totaled 1,328; yet the black population is only about 37% larger than the Latino population.[56]
* This pattern was consistent over the six-year period. The ratio of black-to-Latino complaints exceeded 10:1 in every year except Fiscal Year 1983 (9:1).[57]

---

55. Leadership Conference on Civil Rights, Some Questions and Answers on the Fair Housing Amendments Act of 1987 (1987).

56. *Fair Housing Amendments Act of 1987: Hearings on S.558 Before the Subcomm. on the Constitution of the United States of the Senate Comm. on the Judiciary*, 100th Cong., 1st Sess. 79-80 (1987) (statement of Raul Yzaquirre, Pres. of Nat'l Council of La Raza).

57. *Id.*

* During the same period, complaints from Latinos as a percentage of total complaints ranged from 5.4% to 7.2%, and exceeded 7% in only one year.[58]

There are several possible reasons for this differential. The black population is larger, and the above-cited studies suggest that in some markets, blacks are more likely to encounter discrimination than Latinos. It is also possible that blacks are more likely to encounter overt forms of discrimination than Latinos and are therefore more likely to know that they have been discriminated against. However, these factors do not fully explain the extent of the difference in complaints.

Latinos are less likely to file civil right complaints in general and fair housing complaints in particular. Several reasons have been suggested. First, many Latinos may not have a complete understanding of their rights. Second, all but the most blatant forms of housing discrimination frequently are not recognized as illegal discrimination by the victims. Some forms of housing discrimination for example, "steering," false information on the availability of rental units, and differential treatment in lending practices are difficult, if not impossible, for a victim to identify.

Furthermore, the weak enforcement mechanism in the present fair housing laws may contribute to the low numbers of complaints filed by Latinos. The lengthy period required to reach conciliation and the lack of any real redress to the victim may deter Latino victims from filing complaints. In addition, rental agents and realtors are aware that they are not likely to be penalized for practicing illegal housing discrimination and, therefore, are not often deterred from discriminating. These factors may limit confidence within the Latino community in the HUD conciliation process, thus reducing the number of complaints.

Language differences may exacerbate the above cited factors. HUD no longer publishes brochures explaining fair housing laws in languages other than English. This reduces the ability of limited English proficient persons to understand their rights under the law. Limited English proficiency may hinder Latinos from fully understanding what realtors or rental agents are telling them, thus limiting their ability to detect discrimination.

Additionally, a review of HUD grants to public and private fair housing groups reveals that very few grants have gone to groups emphasizing services to the Latino community. Moreover, HUD has not carried out a single fair housing initiative focusing on Latinos since the 1979 Dallas survey.[59] To the extent that building the capacity of state and local groups is at least partially a function of the availability of resources,

---

58. *Id.*
59. *Id.*

it is not surprising that there are few strong local fair housing groups focusing on the needs of Latinos.

While HUD has not focused on Latino fair housing needs, potentially effective mechanisms for addressing housing discrimination against Latinos do exist. The Fair Housing Enforcement Development Project, sponsored by HUD and the National Committee Against Discrimination in Housing (NCDH), provides some insight into ways in which increased anti-discrimination activity can be generated. Under the 1981 Demonstration Project, small grants were provided to nine local fair housing groups to conduct fair housing testing and a limited amount of outreach and public information.

The Demonstration Project was successful. This project resulted in a series of impressive achievements:

* In each geographic area participating in the project, complaints rose dramatically. There was also a relatively high rate of success in complaint resolution.[60]
* During the two-year period of the project, HUD reported a dramatic increase in complaints (from 4,000 to 5,300); over 50% of this increase occurred in areas where the demonstration was being conducted.[61]
* A modest amount of federal funding generated an extremely high level of activity. It is estimated that each dollar of project funding generated two to three dollars in activity by the local groups.[62]

At least one of the demonstration groups, the Greater Dallas Housing Opportunity Council, carried out Latino focused activities. Its effort resulted in increased complaints by Latinos, although this data did not permit precise quantification of Latino-specific effects.

The activities carried out under the demonstration project clearly address many of the factors contributing to the low level of fair housing complaints by Latinos. The local groups increased awareness of housing discrimination, provided counseling and technical assistance in filing complaints, and established a strong institutional presence in their respective communities.

V.
CONCLUSIONS

Strengthening the effectiveness of fair housing laws in protecting the rights of Latinos requires two major policy initiatives. First, the strengthening of existing fair housing laws is crucial. There is a need for expansion of coverage and the establishment of more effective enforcement mechanisms to resolve complaints. Latinos, particularly families

---

60. *Id.*
61. *Id.*
62. *Id.*

with children, need effective enforcement mechanisms for complaints because they cannot afford remedies which require them to take individual legal action.

Second, publication and outreach is needed to increase the capacity of Latinos to assert their own rights. Both of these policy objectives have been partially advanced through the Fair Housing Amendments of 1987.

However, this new legislation alone will not be sufficient. The unique issues confronting Latinos in the housing market require the establishment of a Latino focused fair housing initiative within HUD. This initiative should include the following:

* Systematic testing including Latino, white and black teams, in various locations, to provide more solid data on Latinos and the housing discrimination they face,
* Funding to Latino organizations involved in fair housing activities, to support outreach and public education,
* Receiving and recording of complaints,
* Conducting of tests,
* Referral of documented complaints to HUD, and
* Provision for all necessary bilingual materials and training required to inform the Latino community of equal housing rights, opportunities, and complaint procedures.

The data shows that housing discrimination is not an occasional incident; it is too often the norm. Responsible and active federal, state, and local policies are needed to protect the civil rights of Latinos in this country in their search for decent housing.

12. The Demise of "Jim Crow"

GREAT STRIDES in dismantling the segregationist order have occurred since the 1940s, but we—the generations that have lived through these decades—may not have a clear comprehension of the events we have witnessed. The more activist and "younger" of us may emphasize the critical place of the civil rights movement, believing that struggle and organization alone brought the old racial patterns down. Those with a more detached and "older" view may point to basic changes in economic and political structures as a primary cause. Both views contain persuasive elements but remain inadequate as separate explanations. A full understanding of the changes in race patterns must weave together the elements of social protest and structural change into one cloth, into one argument. The following chapter attempts to do this. Put in its barest, the argument is that, yes, we "living generations" have indeed made history but not in a world of our choosing. The demise of segregation was not a simple reflex reaction to an opposition movement; it was also the result of fundamental shifts in economic and political conditions.

"Jim Crow" may appear to be an odd description of the situation of Mexicans in Texas. There was no constitutionally sanctioned "separate but equal" provision for Mexicans as there was for blacks. According to the prevailing jurisprudence, Mexicans were "Caucasian."[1] But in political and sociological terms, blacks and Mexicans were basically seen as different aspects of the same race problem. In the farm areas of South and West Texas, the Caucasian schools were nearly always divided into "Anglo schools" and "Mexican schools," the towns into "white towns" and "little Mexicos," and even the churches and cemeteries followed this seemingly natural division of people. This was not a natural phenomenon, however, but the cumulative effect of local administrative policies. In the farm districts, the result was a separation as complete—and as "de jure"—as any in the Jim Crow South. To emphasize these commonalities, I use "Jim Crow" to refer to a situation of nearly complete separation and control of blacks or Mexicans. This use of Jim Crow also serves as a reminder that this demise was regional in nature. Throughout the South, the movement of people from farms to cities and industries was accompanied by the collapse of the South's rigid race segregation. The institutional supports of southern conservatism, as V. O. Key identified them—the one-party structure, malapportionment of state legislatures, and disfranchisement of blacks—all crumbled.² A similar institutional collapse occurred along the greater Texas border region.

What caused the demise of Jim Crow for Mexicans? The segregated order was based ultimately on the political influence of the farmers, and herein lay the weaknesses of segregation in Texas and, by extension, the Southwest. Already by World War II, growers had begun to give way to urban commercial interests as a social and political force in Texas. Agribusiness itself gradually became "urbanized" as resident farm ownership passed into corporate hands. The bottom layer of the segregated order also collapsed as farm workers emigrated to the cities or to the fields of other states.

For their part, the new urban elites, in spite of their conservatism, constituted a weakened foundation for Jim Crow. Financiers, industrialists, and merchants had never been as dependent as growers on labor repression. In the absence of repression, an element of competition characterized the posture of Anglo merchants in their relations with Mexicans. Such competition signified vulnerable points in the racial order, points that Texas Mexicans leveraged (as workers, consumers, and voters) to secure concessions and "rights." Mexicans in the cities remained second-class citizens, but Anglos were more cautious and respectful. Thus, the character of Mexican-Anglo relations in recent memory has manifested a clear rural-urban dichotomy: segregation and repression in the countryside; partial integration and patronage in the cities. These differences were evident in the 1940s but would become increasingly sharper over the following two decades.

Such contrasts lent hope to liberal Texas intellectuals of the 1940s and 1950s that industrialization and urbanization would weaken the inefficient and counterproductive system of race segregation. Pauline Kibbe, executive director of the first Good Neighbor Commission, for example, recognized that a primary cause of anti-Mexican discrimination stemmed from the state's agricultural character. The solution to the Mexican problem, reasoned Kibbe, lay in the expectation that capital would be "liberal and progressive" and labor "cooperative" in industrial society.³

Change in Mexican-Anglo relations did occur during the period of industrialization, but not because of progressive capital or cooperative labor. Likewise, the flexibility of the racial order in the cities could not be attributed to some special "assimilative" quality in urbanization; the fact that Texas cities in the 1940s were major "leaks" through which the Mexican escaped from the rural "caste system" has to be explained in the context of the various competing interests of local class groups.[4]

Social conflict and national crises provided the necessary impulse for the decline of old race arrangements. World War II, in particular, initiated dramatic changes on the domestic front. The need for soldiers and workers, and for positive international relations with Latin America, meant that the counterproductive and embarrassing customs of Jim Crow had to be shelved, at least for the duration of the emergency. In more lasting terms, the war created a generation of Mexican American veterans prepared to press for their rights and privileges. The cracks in the segregated order proved to be irreparable.

The cracks did not rupture, however, until blacks in the South and Mexican Americans in the Southwest mobilized to present a sharp challenge from below in the 1960s. In Texas the protest activity among all segments of the Mexican American community—farm workers, factory workers, students, professionals, businessmen—was unprecedented. This complex movement accelerated the decline of race restrictions in the cities and initiated a similar process in the rural areas.

The following discussion highlights, in overlapping sketches, four important events of recent Texas history: the emergency of World War II, the mechanization of labor-intensive agriculture, the emergence of urban-based political power, and pressure from below and outside—the civil rights struggle of the 1960s.

War and Industrialization

The industrial and urban revolution came to Texas abruptly under the "forced march" of World War II. The number of manufacturing establishments increased from 5,085 in 1940 to 7,128 in 1950; the number employed in these plants increased from 163,978 to 328,980. As a result of the building of a great war industry, nearly half a million people migrated from rural counties to industrial centers. Two hundred Texas counties lost population to the remaining fifty-four counties. The census figures suggest the remarkable growth in the urban population: from 2,911,389 or 45.4 percent of the state population in 1940 to 4,834,000 or 62.7 percent in 1950.[5]

Along with this sweeping transformation came a momentary relaxation of race segregation. This was not due, however, to "industrialization" or "urbanization" but rather to the war emergency. What makes this evident is that, prior to the war, industrialization and urbanization had merely incorporated the previous patterns of race exclusion.

In the prewar period, the urban situation for the majority of Mexicans was not vastly different from that found in the rural areas, in spite of some concessions. The urban Mexicans of Corpus Christi, San Antonio, and the bigger towns of South Texas, for example, attended school in relatively high proportions compared to rural Mexicans. Nonetheless, the public schools in these cities were segregated, businesses refused to serve Mexicans in places patronized by Anglos, and the Catholic churches conducted special services to prevent contact between Mexicans and Anglos. "Urbanization" merely signified the geographic expansion of segregation. Thus, as the "Mexican town" of San Antonio grew in the 1930s, new subdivisions on the Anglo side (such as the Jefferson and Harlandale areas) began to adopt restrictive covenants prohibiting the sale or rental of properties to persons other than of the Caucasian race—"implicitly excluding the Mexicans."[6]

Generally speaking, during the 1930s Anglo businessmen and skilled labor in the cities and big towns reproduced the prevailing racial practices of the countryside. The exceptions to this pattern were the border cities (El Paso, Laredo, Brownsville), where ethnic relations were flexible and pragmatic, that is, more a matter of class than of race. Away from the border, however, Mexicans were as a rule confronted with general discrimination. According to Kibbe, Mexicans experienced four kinds of discrimination: refusal of service in public places, real estate restrictions, police brutality, and employment barriers.[7] Of these, the employment barriers pointed most clearly to the castelike position of the urban Mexican.

Racial segmentation characterized the urban and industrial labor market across the state. In the oil industry, both Mexican and black workers received a lower wage (of several cents per hour) than did Anglo Americans in the same classification. The "Latin American" and black workers were not permitted to use the drinking fountains or the toilets and bathing facilities provided for Anglos. Nor were they permitted to punch the same time clock or receive their pay through the same window used by Anglos. A similar situation was to be found in the railroad industry.[8]

In San Antonio, according to a 1927 survey by the Texas Agricultural and Mechanical College, Mexican workers were limited to the unskilled labor market, while skilled occupations were nearly completely dominated by Anglos. Of twenty-eight skilled categories, Mexican employees had a significant presence in only three—structural iron (132 of 217), blacksmith (45 of 119), and automotive

Above left: Legal exhibit in school segregation case; modern school in Mathis, 1954 (courtesy George I. Sanchez Collection, Benson Latin American Collection, University of Texas at Austin). *Below left:* Legal exhibit in school segregation case: Mexican school in Mathis, 1954 (courtesy George I. Sanchez Collection, Benson Latin American Collection, University of Texas at Austin). *Above:* Executive Committee meeting of the School Improvement League, 1948; young man seated at far right is future Congressman Henry B. Gonzalez (courtesy E. Escobar Collection, Benson Latin American Collection, University of Texas at Austin).

painting (128 of 336). Among the categories that Mexicans were excluded from were retail sales, commercial trades (bookkeeping, general clerks, stenographic), and airplane and engine repair; and Mexicans were barely present in the printing and building trades; for example, of 2,551 carpenters only 150 were Mexicans. The same condition prevailed in employment by the city and the public utilities, where Mexicans were found only in common labor positions until World War II.[9]

In many cases job discrimination was not the result of management policy but of union policy. During the 1930s the great majority of labor unions (especially the skilled crafts) refused to admit Mexicans and blacks to membership, thus making their employment by management virtually impossible. The only unions readily open to Mexicans in the early 1930s were "Mexican unions" like the Hod Carriers and Common Laborers Union.[10]

In short, neither urbanization nor industrialization brought about the relaxing of race restrictions in the 1940s. Such relaxation as occurred had to do with the war emergency—with the need for soldiers and workers. Labor shortages opened job opportunities, military service presented many with training and experience, the need for stable relations with Mexico stimulated a drive to minimize discrimination, and the war emergency sanctioned such experimental measures as the Fair Employment Practices Committee.

These war-related necessities, however, did not require any real consensus, much less commitment, about a policy of nondiscrimination. The war years, in fact, saw a worsening of relations between Anglos and Mexicans in the Southwest. Increased discrimination, growing friction (including pogroms and police raids of barrios), and Mexican government irritation all reached new heights by 1945.

In rural Texas, Jim Crow conditions remained virtually unaffected by the war against Hitler and race supremacy, a situation that prompted Mexico to exclude the state from its international agreement regarding guest workers (*braceros*). The ban was not a "blacklist," as Mexican Consul General Miguel Calderón politely put it, but "merely exceptional measures for protecting Mexican Nationals in view of exceptional circumstances prevailing [in] this State." In 1943, in response to Mexico's blacklisting, Gov. Coke Stevenson established the Good Neighbor Commission (GNC) and had the legislature approve a "Caucasian Race Resolution," which forbade discrimination against "Caucasians." Pauline Kibbe, the first executive director of the GNC, called on Texans to remember that the state constituted "a living laboratory experiment in American unity" on which the eyes of the Americas were focused; that Texas was "a test case to prove or disprove the validity of the Good Neighbor policy."¹¹

Such exhortations and other neighborly rhetoric did little to alter the shape of things. The Mexican government wanted "positive action and not bureaucratic lip service," as one GNC official put it. The strongest antidiscrimination plans devised by Texas authorities were based on voluntary cooperation. Nonetheless, Consul General Calderón noted, such steps would be "constructive and helpful in eliminating discrimination." In reference to a proposed "Stilley Plan," Calderón suggested to Texas representatives that they "experiment the Stilley Plan with American citizens of Mexican origin in order to appreciate its good results."¹²

In the cities, it also seemed that the war crisis would accommodate itself to previous employment patterns. According to one estimate, less than 5 percent of the Mexican American community in Texas was employed in war industry in the early 1940s. Those industries that did provide employment to Mexicans restricted them to common or unskilled labor jobs regardless of their ability or training. At San Antonio's Kelly Field, where approximately 10,000 of 35,000 civilian employees were Mexican Americans, none had a position above that of a laborer or a mechanic's helper. This pattern was common throughout the Southwest. Federal investigations in the mining, oil, ship, and aircraft industries in 1943–1944 revealed that in a good many cases "Latin Americans" classified as common laborers and semiskilled workers were in fact performing skilled jobs at the lower rate of pay.¹³

The weakening of labor barriers was due to direct federal intervention in the form of the Fair Employment Practices Committee (FEPC). Created by executive order, the FEPC was charged with the task of seeing that no federal agency or company doing business with the government discriminated against any person because of race, color, creed, or national origin. Field operations did not begin in the Southwest until 1943, and only then did Mexican labor begin to be integrated into the industrial plants. Carlos Castañeda, FEPC regional director for Texas, New Mexico, and Louisiana, stated that "the shipyards, the airship factories, the oil industry, the mines, the munition factories, and the numerous military and naval installations slowly, reluctantly, and with much misgivings, began to give the Mexican American a trial in semiskilled positions, and eventually in some skilled jobs."

These trials and experiments met general opposition from Anglo employees during the war years. In one dramatic episode in 1945, the oil union at Shell's Deer Park Refinery responded to the FEPC-ordered upgrading of three "Latin Americans" by going out on a wildcat strike in protest. Even within the FEPC administration, resistance to FEPC policy surfaced. Many staff members told Castañeda that when the war "was over the Mexican American would be put in his place."[14]

Whatever appearance of "fair employment" and unity existed during wartime rapidly evaporated during peacetime. One Sam Smith of Sonora expressed the opinion of many in West Texas when he complained to Texas officials that he and his fellow veterans did not fight for "ill-smelling Mexicans" who were overrunning movie houses and would soon probably move into swimming pools, dancing places, schools, and cafés; they were even taking veterans' jobs. Thus, with the return of the normal labor supply and the withdrawal of such controversial wartime agencies as the federal FEPC, job discrimination against Mexican Americans returned in force. When the United States employment offices were turned back to the states in November of 1946, they (in Castañeda's words) "relapsed to the discriminatory practices in general use before the war." Mexican Americans who registered for skilled jobs were never referred to the employers calling for such skills. The only openings to which the former U.S. Employment Service referred Mexican Americans were common labor jobs.[15]

Some observers saw an overall attempt to destroy any economic or social gains made by Mexican Americans during the war years. The South Texas newspapers had begun a steady campaign against the Mexican and his "lawlessness." And every attempt by Sen. J. Franklin Spears of San Antonio to check anti-Mexican discrimination was defeated. With the entry of thousands of "wetbacks" in the mid-1940s, the ineffective Mexican ban and the accommodating Good Neighbor Policy no longer mattered. When the matter of funding the GNC came up, the legislature refused to give the commission any power other than that of research. After a few years of further emasculation, the GNC devolved into the international public relations arm of Texas government.[16]

It was too late, however, to turn the tide back. World War II had accelerated industrialization and the flight to the cities and generally had shifted the principal arena of Mexican and Anglo relations to the urban areas. The war had also exposed Texas Mexican soldiers to a world of greater freedoms and equalities, an experience that became especially important on the return home. According to Kibbe, "Latin Americans" who for years had tolerated discrimination "have acquired a new courage, have become more vocal in protesting the restrictions and inequalities with which they are confronted." A "new consciousness," to use Kibbe's words, was evident.[17]

Factories in the Field

Despite the apparent intransigence of Jim Crow in the rural areas, its social base began a gradual erosion before the repercussions of the war crisis. The massive migrations to the cities were the clearest sign of change—for these represented a displacement of two major classes, migrant laborers and small farmers. In their stead emerged the highly mechanized corporate farm, the basis of modern agribusiness.

After the war industrial capital and techniques "spilled over" into agriculture, intensifying a trend toward corporate ownership. In the Winter Garden, for example, several of the largest farms were branches of urban-based corporations that had similar operations in Florida, California, and Mexico. The modern basis of the corporate farm was "scientific farming," a loose term referring to mechanization, frequent agricultural research, and the development of highly integrated production systems. Del Monte, a branch of the California Packing Corporation, set the pattern, "the model which many area farmers were quick to imitate." Purchasing 3,200 acres of choice land around Crystal City, Del Monte established a highly mechanized farm, a cannery, and shipping facilities in 1946. In this fashion, Del Monte quickly became not only the leading scientific farming operation but also the region's most important economic institution.[18]

The small vegetable farmer, on the other hand, continued to operate on a marginal basis. In addition to increased operating costs, the small farmer had to contend with an unfavorable marketing situation. Because of limited acreages and a lack of facilities, small growers were forced to sell their produce through local sheds owned and operated by the area's larger growers. Marketing the produce of the small farmer was thus of secondary importance to that of the shed owner. As important, the packing sheds began to determine planting policies. Because sheds financed most Winter Garden growers, the vegetable acreage planted was largely determined by what individual shippers felt would be needed to satisfy their particular markets. The farmers of the Winter Garden's Northern District planted over 50 percent of the area's cabbage, carrot, lettuce, and onion acreage, a fact attributed almost exclusively to the planting policies of the local packing sheds. In the Southern District, the demand of Del Monte's cannery was the most significant factor influencing vegetable plantings. Del Monte itself produced virtually all of the Winter Garden's beet crop and grew or contracted over 50 percent of the spinach acreage in the southern area.[19]

In short, the postwar period saw the decline of the small owner-occupied farm. The drought of the 1950s, combined with marketing problems and rising costs, eliminated most of the smaller vegetable-farming operations in the Winter Garden. By the 1960s, the same was true of the Lower Rio Grande Valley. A report on the "swift changes" in Valley agribusiness described the matter in a straightforward manner: "The small grower is virtually out of the game. The medium-sized operator is beginning to have king-sized troubles. And the era of the giant, vertically-integrated farm operations, usually corporate, seems to be at hand." As in the Winter Garden, the reasons for these changes reflected sharpening competition with Florida and California vegetables as well as with a booming Mexican vegetable industry. Another factor concerned the marketing practices developed with the age of supermarket chains. By linking consumer demand with planting policies and crop price, the new market practices had greatly weakened the bargaining position of independent growers.[20]

A few local families in the Valley and the Winter Garden weathered the shift to corporate farming through the development of integrated production systems that controlled the growing, packing, shipping, and marketing of produce. But whether organized by "native sons" or outside investors, the trend favored corporate farming. Agricultural statistics suggest the pattern. Between 1954 and 1959, the number of farms in Texas decreased at a record pace, from 292,947 to 227,054, a 22.5 percent decrease. At the same time, the size of the average farm increased by more than 25 percent, from 497.7 acres to 629.5 acres.[21]

Accompanying the decline in the number of small farmers was a decline in the size of the agricultural work force. During the 1940s and 1950s, competition for labor and labor flight to the cities continued to plague the farmer. For the farm worker, better wages and working conditions were sufficient motivation for migration to the cities or to fields in other states. On occasion, the excesses of Jim Crow moved Texas Mexican laborers to avoid entire counties, forcing federal and state farm officials to intercede in order to get the harvest picked. A farm labor official, for example, spent the entire month of October 1944 in Big Spring straightening out "difficulties." On the highway leading into the town, a constable had flagged down all migrant-filled trucks, instructing them not to stop in town under threat of arrest. The result was that the majority of the trucks did not stop in Big Spring; they didn't even stop in Howard County, and the farmers in that region experienced great difficulty in harvesting their crops.[22] Such were the contradictions between economic needs and the social divisions of the farm order.

The farmers responded to these contradictions in ways that further accelerated the exodus of Texas Mexican laborers. On the one hand, farmers shifted to Mexican nationals who, unlike Texas Mexicans, could be recruited and removed at will. Thus, thousands were imported in the early fifties; thousands were deported during "Operation Wetback" in the mid-fifties; and thousands were imported again as *braceros* in the early sixties. This shift in the labor source also made for more complicated migratory patterns. As Mexican nationals migrated into rural Texas, Texas Mexicans migrated to the West and the Midwest. In a sense, there was a "domino effect," as one migration reinforced the other.

On the other hand, farmers turned increasingly to mechanization as the solution to the labor situation. This trend had started in the 1930s and was accelerated by the unsettled labor market of the war and postwar periods. Thus, in spite of near-chronic labor shortages, extensive mechanization and improved techniques enabled farmers to increase productivity. Agricultural reports indicate that farm output increased nearly 40 percent between the mid-thirties and the late forties, while the number of farm laborers declined 40 percent for the same period. Only 550,000 laborers worked on Texas farms in 1949 compared to approximately 981,000 laborers in 1934. The number of tractors, on the other hand, increased from 98,923 units in 1940 to more than 250,000 in 1951.[23]

These trends—increasing mechanization and out-migration of Texas Mexicans—characterized the rural setting through the 1960s. The termination of the Mexican guest worker agreement (commonly known as the Bracero Program) in 1964, ironically, intensified these patterns. The repeal removed the supply of contract workers for midwestern and western agriculture. As a result, out-of-state growers and processors, faced with the prospect of labor shortages, concentrated their recruiting efforts in Texas. The number of interstate migrants swelled from 95,000 in 1963 to 129,500 in 1966, while the number of intrastate migrants declined in the same period from 36,800 to 32,500.[24]

By the 1960s, migration to the cities and large-scale mechanization had transformed the old Jim Crow order into a thin shell. In statistical terms, between 1950 and 1970 the number of Texas farms decreased from 332,000 to 214,000, a loss of one in every three farms. The number of those gainfully employed in agriculture declined even more sharply, from 446,000 to 195,000, or less than half of the work force in 1950. The "qualitative" changes were also apparent. In the Winter Garden, as Foley and his co-authors note in their study of Frio County, local farm workers had been replaced by *braceros* and machines, whereas local grower *patrones* had been replaced by absentee owners and manager-lease operators. Few permanent workers were left on the farms and ranches, and those with permanent work in the canneries and packing sheds were under a very different wage-labor system, with much of the earlier paternalism and labor controls absent. Most of the new owners had few personal relationships with their workers and did not expect to develop them. Moreover, the new absentee landlords had altered "the structure and solidarity of the Anglo community." The outsiders had little interest in running the local community or in solving ethnic conflicts.[25]

In short, with the widespread acceptance of scientific techniques and substantial corporate investment, the social base for agricultural production was no longer characterized by a society of "resident growers" and "cheap tractable labor." The most dramatic symptoms of these structural changes surfaced in the 1960s with wildcat strikes in the Lower Valley and aggressive political challenges in the Winter Garden. Other signs were a number of basic setbacks to rural interests—the shift in legislative power to the urban areas, the termination of the *bracero* program, the passage of a dollar-per-hour minimum wage in agriculture, and, finally, the enfranchisement of Mexican Americans. These acts fundamentally altered, to the dismay of growers, the region's "traditionally low-cost labor." Corporate farmers, as the manager of La Casita farms in Starr County commented, could live with a one-dollar-per-hour wage and restrictions on the supply of Mexican nationals, but he was less sure about the small grower. The minimum wage merely forced growers to eliminate many of their preharvest labor requirements through more extensive use of chemical pesticides and mechanical devices. As a consequence, migrants returning to the Winter Garden and the Valley have found fewer job opportunities awaiting them.[26] In the age of corporate farming, every advance for rural laborers merely hastened their eventual displacement.

Political Pluralism and the Urban Vote

In the 1940s, the increasing economic power of urban-based interests was not readily translated into political power. The emerging corporate elite were content to maintain a mutually beneficial relationship with growers. The growers controlled both houses of the

Texas Legislature, while the executive branch was virtually indistinguishable from the oil-insurance-banking-construction elite. In terms of political philosophy, the corporate leaders were not very different from their rural counterparts. In the pointed summation of Texas historian George Green, the corporate elite of the 1940s and 1950s were committed to upholding a regressive tax structure, antilabor laws, oppression of blacks and Mexican Americans, and alleged states' rights.[27] The state Democratic Party, under the firm control of growers and their corporate friends, embodied these positions.

Thus, for awhile the rapid urbanization of the state did not matter, since conservatism, like so much else, left the countryside for a place in the cities. Jim Crow, in fact, seemed to be strengthened through "urbanization." Why not? Even as the businessmen began to take charge over economic and social matters, the conservative coalition remained intact. In the thirties and forties the new urban elite were busy, as one representative noted, making their first "ten or twenty million dollars." Then, in the fifties, "this Communist business burst" on them. Hugh Roy Cullen, H. L. Hunt, Sid Richardson, Clint Murchison, to name a few, became the financiers of militantly conservative causes. They became, along with other prominent businessmen, ardent supporters of Texas' "third Senator"—Joe McCarthy—whom they saw as ridding government and universities of radical New Dealers.[28] McCarthyism, in fact, swept Texas with the fervor of a religious revival. The major cities proved to be fertile ground for a score of archconservative organizations—minutemen, patriotic committees, citizen councils—all of which were dedicated to guarding against communists, atheists, and desegregationists.

In such climate, the reaction to the Supreme Court's overturning of the "separate but equal" principle (*Brown* v. *Board of Education*) in 1954 was predictably furious. The preservation of Jim Crow against federal intrusion was clothed in patriotic and religious dress. Preachers, retired generals, and politicians all railed against the evils of desegregation. A petition of 165,000 signatures of people objecting to desegregation was presented to Gov. Allen Shivers. In response, Shivers placed three segregationist referenda (preserving school segregation, strengthening laws against intermarriage, and supporting local rule over federal "intrusion") on the ballot for the state Democratic primary (July 1956). These passed by an overwhelming four-to-one margin in the state.[29] Sentiment in counties with large Mexican American populations, however, was sharply divided. Bexar, Kleberg, and Uvalde counties refused to put the referenda on their ballots; Webb County voted against the measures by an eight-to-one margin; and twelve of the sixteen counties where the referenda passed less convincingly (less than 60 percent approval) had significant Mexican American populations.[30]

Encouraged by the overwhelming support of segregation, East Texas legislators introduced a dozen bills in 1956–57 that, among other things, would withhold state funds from integrated schools, would require integrationists to register with the secretary of state (known as the "thought permit" bill), and would prohibit interracial sporting events. South and West Texas members of the House, whose school districts were partly integrated, fought a delaying action in the 150-member House. But the first nine bills rolled through by votes in the neighborhood of 85 ayes to 50 nays, with some members abstaining. When the bills reached the Senate, the senators from the major Mexican American districts (San Antonio, Laredo, Brownsville, El Paso) with support from the senators from Austin and Seguin began a filibuster to block the bills. Led by Henry B. Gonzalez of San Antonio and Abraham Kazen of Laredo, the "*filibusteros*" managed to mobilize sufficient support to block all but two of the bills. Newly elected Gov. Price Daniel, who had campaigned on the promise that he would use all lawful means to avert integration, signed the segregationist legislation. Despite his signing, Daniel attempted to assure his South Texas "Spanish-speaking supporters" that the new laws could not be used to segregate children of Mexican ancestry.[31]

After 1956 the race problem ceased to be a statewide factor in political campaigns and elections. In part this was due to the change in political guard that took place that year. Although supported by the same corporate interests, the new leaders—Lyndon Johnson, Sam Rayburn, and Price Daniel—were not as interested as the "Shivercrats" had been in maintaining a "red scare" mentality.

The renewed consolidation of a liberal wing within the Democratic Party (after its breakup during the McCarthy years) also helped to moderate the racist rhetoric in politics. A coalition of urban liberals, church groups, labor unionists, and minorities constituted the core of this faction. By the mid-1950s the "labor liberals," as they were commonly called, had developed a full-time leadership cadre, a fairly effective propaganda machine, an internal communications network, and a membership that thought it could win elections on occasion. Liberals began to challenge conservatives aggressively, if not always successfully. The election of Ralph Yarborough to the U.S. Senate in 1957 (after Yarborough had repeatedly lost the gubernatorial race) was a sign of liberal tenacity and influence. Another serious challenge was mounted in 1960 when the Kennedy campaign, antagonized by the hostile Texas party establishment, turned to groups excluded from the party machinery—Mexican Americans, blacks, labor, and liberals. Kennedy's narrow victory in Texas (50.5 percent of the vote) demonstrated the strength of this urban coalition.[32]

In spite of the rapid urbanization of Texas and the emergence of an important liberal Democratic faction, the rural conservatives were able to maintain tight control of the legislature. The key to such control was based on state constitutional limits on the number of representatives allowable per county and on pro forma redistricting, which had not significantly changed legislative boundaries since 1921. By the early 1960s, the counties containing the major metropolitan areas—Harris (Houston), Dallas, Bexar (San Antonio), and Tarrant (Fort Worth)—were grossly underrepresented. They were limited to 35 House representatives and 4 senators, when equal representation on the basis of population would have yielded them 54 House members and 10 senators.[33] In this manner, the rural conservative bloc was able to contain repeated liberal challenges in the fifties and sixties.

The entrenched position of the conservative bloc was abruptly upset in 1965 when the U.S. Supreme Court (*Kilgarlin* v. *Martin*) invalidated the districting schemas for both legislative houses as well as the limiting provisions of the Texas Constitution. The stakes were clear. As the *Texas Observer* put it, "the country boys stand to lose out, but they still had the most power in the 1965 legislature and juggled everything that would juggle with purposes as transparent as a country boy's leer."[34]

In the Senate, a split among rural representatives facilitated the transfer of 6 seats to the urban districts at the expense of the rural-based "old guard." Rural areas were reduced to 14 seats, urban-rural areas maintained their 7 seats, and urban areas increased their number to 10. In the House, the conservative leadership was able to delay the impact of reapportionment for a few years. The 1965 plan, which gave the cities 16 members at the expense of rural independents, was thrown out in federal court in 1967. In turn, the 1967 legislature, more urban oriented than the previous House, accelerated the breakup of rural control by distributing 9 more rural seats among urban and mixed urban-rural areas.[35]

A review of changes in the House composition illustrates the shift in power to the urban and urban-rural areas.[36] In 1961 the rural areas had 85 seats, compared to 35 for the four major urban areas. By 1967 the rural seats had been reduced to 63, a loss of 22 seats, while the

Table 15. *Texas House Redistricting, 1951–1967 (150 Seats)*

	Urban[a]	Urban/Rural[b]	Rural
1951	29	26	95
1961	35	30	85
1965	51	27	72
1967	52	35	63

Source: Based on *Texas Almanac*, 1958–1959, 1964–1965, 1966–1967, 1968–1969.

[a] Urban: counties with 300,000+ population in 1950: Dallas, Harris (Houston), Bexar (San Antonio), and Tarrant (Fort Worth).

[b] Urban/rural: counties with 100,000–300,000 population in 1950: El Paso, Jefferson (Beaumont), Galveston, Travis (Austin), Nueces (Corpus Christi), Hidalgo (McAllen), Cameron (Brownsville), and Lubbock.

major urban centers had gained 17 seats for a total of 52. In addition, the eight urban-rural areas increased their representation from 30 seats to 35 (see Table 15).

In terms of legislation, the impact of reapportionment has been clear. After 1967, there were fewer legislators to support what urbanites consider rural prejudices. Legislation favorable to the urban areas has passed: the optional municipal sales tax, the creation of a state Department of Community Affairs, the location of new colleges and state courts in metropolitan areas, to mention a few examples. Farm-to-market roads have become less popular subjects of legislation while state highway programs have become more urban oriented. With the increase of political power of organized labor in urban areas, the Texas Legislature enacted a minimum-wage law. Another way of summarizing the impact: in 1956 the House passed nine segregationist bills by comfortable margins. In 1969 the House rescinded the legislation with no vocal opposition.[37]

In sum, reapportionment was a major blow to the political strength of rural conservatives. Conservatism was by no means defeated—rather, the battle between conservatives and liberals had simply shifted to the urban front.

Pressure from Below, from the Cities

Commentators have suggested that the political "awakening" of the Texas Mexican in the late 1960s stemmed from the rise and development of a Mexican American business and professional class.[38] While this was certainly a significant factor, the urban class structure de-

The Demise of "Jim Crow" 279

serves the primary attention. Two particular events created an opening for the Mexican American middle class: the defeat of the old city machines by Anglo business leaders in the fifties and a momentary militance resulting from the joint efforts of middle- and working-class activists in the early sixties.

The first event brought about the initial incorporation of middle-class Mexican Americans into city government and resulted in the defeat of Jim Crow in the cities. Prior to the war, the Mexican American vote in Texas cities was largely controlled and manipulated by political bosses. Various Mexican American organizations (like LULAC) had attempted to develop a voice independent of the *patrones* but, on failing this, eventually found themselves vying for machine patronage. Laborers were controlled by job patronage and the middle class by symbolic appointments and honors. The break in the cities, despite some short periods of reform, did not come until the machines were deposed in the immediate postwar period by prodevelopment business groups. In San Antonio, for instance, the Kilday machine was undermined by a council-manager movement financed by prominent Anglo business leaders in 1949.[39]

The formation of numerous veteran organizations was also an important factor in the death of city machines. World War II and the Korean Conflict created a group of politically conscious Mexican American veterans who launched vigorous protests against segregation. In San Antonio the Mexican American veteran organizations included the Loyal American Democrats, the West Side Voters League, the Alamo Democrats, and the School Improvement League. From Corpus Christi came the most prominent new organization, the G.I. Forum, which rapidly formed chapters throughout the Southwest. The G.I. Forum had gained national recognition with its protest against a Three Rivers (Texas) funeral home that had refused to handle the body of a decorated Mexican American soldier.[40]

In general, these groups were oriented to mobilizing Mexican American poll tax registration and voting. In the early fifties, Spanish-speaking leaders were talking of organizing a "mass movement of over a million voters to the Texas ballot boxes." Such efforts did take place in the Rio Grande Valley in campaigns organized by the G.I. Forum and the CIO. Anglo-Texans reacted in fashion typical of the times by calling these efforts "Communist-inspired." The veterans' organizations, however, were able to withstand the "fifth columnist" slander commonly used against activists. As veteran activist J. Luz Saenz noted in speaking of racial discrimination, their "synopsis of The Number One Problem in Texas . . . might look Red-Hot due to the spirit that moves us to express it, but there is nothing of Red-

Communism in it as our enemies might presuppose or imply." Unlike previous community organizations, the postwar organizations were not defensive but aggressively sought the due owed to American veterans.[41]

In structural terms, the returning veterans, via the GI Bill of Rights and college degrees, formed the base for the expanding middle and skilled working classes among Texas Mexicans. The GI Bill of Rights, the compensation for WWII and Korean service, proved to be a most significant avenue for upward mobility for Mexicans and blacks. Its contribution, direct and indirect, has yet to be fully assessed. Although no figures are readily available, enrollment in state and private colleges increased substantially. Home ownership by Mexican Americans was facilitated by VA loans in the late forties and early fifties. The "military industrial complex," to use President Dwight Eisenhower's well-known phrase, provided permanent well-paying employment, thus laying a foundation for stable middle and working classes.[42]

These structural changes, evident in the growth of a profitable Mexican American consumer market, began to attract the attention of merchants, with moderating consequences for race relations. In 1955 the *Texas Business Review,* in a special issue on the Mexican American consumer market, noted that retailers who deal most successfully with Latin Americans tolerate no discrimination. "Latin American Texans" respond to fair and exceptional treatment in business and appreciate the efforts of only those who manifest a genuine interest in their welfare and comfort. A "haughty, lordly, or unfriendly attitude," on the other hand, "may be effectively dealt with by a group boycott of the guilty. Both favorable and unfavorable information travels amazingly fast by word of mouth." This, of course, was old advice for the political and economic elite of the border cities (Brownsville, Laredo, El Paso). Economically dependent on trade with Mexico and politically dependent on Mexican American voters, border city elites did not permit prejudicial expressions or practices that could antagonize their customers, clients, and voters.[43]

In San Antonio, the implications of a politically active Mexican American community were recognized by the reform-oriented Anglo businessmen and professionals who formed the Good Government League (GGL). The GGL leaders were primarily interested in economic growth and desired "an environment free of political and social conflict." To this end, the conservative business element was convinced by the liberals within the reform coalition that all groups in the city—specifically, blacks and Mexicans—must progress together if San Antonio was to progress in general. Accordingly, black and Mexican American representatives were regularly recruited to run on GGL-sponsored tickets. It was a means of allowing the minorities to have "visibility and ego input," as one GGLer put it. In San Antonio of the early 1950s, this was a notable departure from political tradition. For El Paso and other border cities, the symbolic inclusion of "successful" Mexican Americans on school board and city council slates had been the practice for some time. Pressure from the Mexican American community of El Paso, nonetheless, resulted in additional progress: El Paso elected its first Mexican American mayor, Raymond Telles, in 1957.[44]

In the urban areas, these changed political conditions steadily eroded the Jim Crow structure within a decade after the war. All types of discrimination were fought—restrictions in real estate, in voting, in access to public facilities and schools, and so on. San Antonio passed a desegregation ordinance of city facilities in the mid-1950s, and the same result was accomplished in Corpus Christi. These victories reflected the presence of a politically active Mexican American community. As prosperity and upward mobility occurred, the militancy of the veteran challenge gradually diminished.[45]

Urban ethnic relations stood in sharp contrast with the situation in the farm areas, which, as late as 1959, remained "blacklisted" by the Mexican government from any participation in the "guest worker" (bracero) program because of discrimination and abuse. South Texas farm towns, as William Madsen observed in 1961, were "separated residential districts divided by highway or railroad tracks." "Virtually the only relationship" between Anglos and Mexican Americans, noted Madsen, was that of "an employer to an unskilled employee."[46]

Through the 1950s and 1960s, despite some gains in the cities, the reign of Jim Crow in the rural areas stigmatized all Mexican Americans as second-class citizens. As long as Texas Mexicans in the countryside and the city, of working-class and middle-class backgrounds, followed unrelated and independent strategies, no major challenge to the entire segregationist edifice developed. In the cities, middle-class organizations were not sufficiently powerful to gain more than symbolic rewards. Their isolation, moreover, was reinforced by condescending attitudes toward working-class Mexicans. On the other hand, labor activism without outside support tended to be easily suppressed. The record is filled with episodes of repression by employers and authorities and of lack of support (and sometimes open antagonism) from Anglo unionists, middle-class Mexican Americans, and Catholic clergy. So long as these divisions remained, and middle-class and working-class organizations worked separately, nothing substantial was gained. What changed, on the urban side, was the emergence of an impatient middle-class organization willing to work with labor union activists. This "event" accelerated the demise of Jim Crow and introduced the process to the rural areas.

In 1960 the Viva Kennedy campaign, responsible for the John Kennedy victory in Texas, demonstrated the pivotal significance of the Mexican American vote. Just as important, the campaign demonstrated to Mexican American activists that the hold of conservative Democrats on local South Texas politics could be broken. As an organizational attempt to continue the momentum of the Kennedy victory, the Viva Kennedy campaign was transformed into a political coalition composed of Mexican American leaders from the established organizations (G.I. Forum, LULAC, and so on). The coalition was called the Political Association of Spanish-speaking Organizations (PASSO).[47]

From its founding, PASSO was split along moderate-militant lines, a tension that frequently erupted into open conflict at meetings. The moderates and conservatives favored gradual progress using established avenues, whereas the liberals urged more direct action and involvement in local issues. After a brief and inauspicious year of moderation, PASSO regrouped in 1963 under the aggressive liberal leadership of Albert Peña, Jr.

PASSO, along with the Teamsters, became involved in Crystal City in 1962–1963 in what eventually became known as the "first uprising." In 1963 the Mexican Americans of Crystal City organized and elected an all–Mexican American slate to the city council, a feat that attracted statewide and national attention. Teamster and PASSO strategy, which called for utilizing the large base of cannery and farm laborers through the small Teamsters union at the Del Monte cannery, was successful in turning the political structure of Crystal City upside down. To a large degree this success lay in the fact that the local elite no longer controlled the main economic strings of the local economy; rather, these now lay in the hands of corporate agribusiness, such as Del Monte. Local management did attempt to intimidate Del Monte workers active in the campaign but these were blocked by the local union with the help of high Teamster officials. One of the more dramatic incidents came on election day when Del Monte suddenly announced that it was going into overtime and that its workers would not have time to vote. Unable to change the company's decision, Teamster organizers placed an urgent call to their national president, Jimmy Hoffa, who in turn notified Del Monte headquarters in San Francisco that there would be action against the company. Management assented, and the Del Monte workers were

Community meeting of the Liga Pro Defensa Escolar (School Improvement League), San Antonio, 1948 (courtesy E. Escobar Collection, Benson Latin American Collection, University of Texas at Austin).

allowed time to vote. The mobilized Mexican American majority defeated— "overthrew" is not an excessive term—the long-established rule of the Anglo minority. As a symbol of what was possible in South Texas, the event far outweighed the takeover of a community of 9,000. It symbolized the overthrow of Jim Crow.[48]

The repercussions of Crystal City widened the division between moderates and militants within PASSO. In general the moderates were against the Crystal City involvement and against working with labor unions. By 1965 PASSO's middle-class membership, dissatisfied with its militancy, had largely dissipated. This defection by the moderates permitted the remaining PASSO members to take a further step and become directly involved in labor organizing.

PASSO members in Starr County had been talking about a farm worker strike for years when Cesar Chavez and the National Farm Workers Association struck the Delano (California) grape vineyards in 1965. The result was a wildcat melon strike in June 1966 against eight major Starr County growers. Virtually all of the picketing and boycott activity was aimed at La Casita farms, a huge integrated corporate operation that strikers called the "General Motors" of Valley agribusiness. The wildcat strike appeared doomed from the start. The general lack of preparation and coordination was a serious problem, but what made this a moot point was the breaking of the strike by Texas Rangers, Starr County deputies, and imported Mexican labor. In an insightful comment, a Valley banker suggested that the labor organizing efforts would have been more effective and strategic if they had been directed at shed workers, for the shed operators, not the growers, controlled the marketing of produce.[49] Shed workers could also be an efficient point for mobilizing farm workers, as the Crystal City "uprising" had demonstrated.

Although the Valley strike failed, it succeeded in catalyzing the Chicano civil rights movement in Texas. The farm worker cause, while the lead element in this movement, was for most of the urban Mexican American population important in a symbolic sense; it ignited a broad resentment among all classes of the Mexican American community. Different agendas and energies were set off, some moderate, some militant. The high school youth boycotted their schools in Del Rio, Uvalde, Kingsville, Alice, Abilene, Pharr–San Juan–Alamo, Laredo, and Robstown, to mention only a few places. College students organized countless protest marches and meetings and provided new ideas and directions as well as energy and impatience. Even the usually proper middle class became radicalized, as they protested employment practices, boycotted companies (at one meeting they burned their Humble Oil credit cards), and filed lawsuits against social inequities.

By the late 1960s, this movement was seriously challenging the dual structure of rural society. While the protest of the 1950s had focused on the cities, that of the 1960s was centered in the countryside. The major political events of a decade revolved around the farm worker strikes in the Lower Rio Grande Valley and the formation of a populist-nationalist party known as El Partido Raza Unida (The United People Party) in the Winter Garden region. The electoral take-over by Raza Unida of Crystal City and Zavala County in 1970—the "second uprising"—stunned the state, frightened the Anglo residents of South Texas, and prompted Gov. Dolph Briscoe to denounce Zavala County as a "little Cuba."[50]

In short, the social movement of the 1960s and 1970s accelerated the dismantling of the repressive social order known as Jim Crow. In its place were planted the seeds of a new ethnic order, one that is still being defined and molded. Much remains to be studied, for the Chicano movement was a complex collection of groups with various agendas and strategies, some of which were carried out with partial success. One of its more successful goals—one that the League of United Latin American Citizens (LULAC) had articulated in the 1920s—was the "opening up" of universities for Mexican American youth. LULAC had long called for this action, arguing that the Latin American people would be "uplifted" once they had more doctors, teachers, lawyers, and professionals of all types. The strategy essentially called for an expanded middle class. Such expansion may prove to be one of the more significant results of the great unrest of the sixties and seventies. Even the student activists were, in a sense, the cutting edge of a middle class frustrated by the narrow ethnic limits of the old Southwest. The militants among them succeeded and thus disappeared; in their wake, they left a modest booty of business and professional opportunities, the very stuff of LULAC dreams.

A Concluding Note

In the 1970s the legacy of segregation was still evident, especially in rural areas. The town of Ozona in West Texas illustrates the stubborn and uneven career of Jim Crow for Mexicans. In this town, drugstores were closed to Mexicans until the late 1940s; restaurants and movie houses did not open to Mexicans until the early 1950s; hotels were exclusively reserved for Anglo patrons until about 1958; barber and beauty shops were segregated until 1969; and in the early

1970s, the bowling alley, cemeteries, and swimming pools still remained segregated. Ozona, unfortunately, was somewhat typical of the Texas pattern. According to a mid-sixties study, nine of the eleven southwestern cities in which Mexican Americans were most rigidly segregated were in Texas. In descending order of magnitude, these were Odessa, Corpus Christi, Dallas, Lubbock, San Angelo, Houston, Wichita Falls, San Antonio, and Austin.[51]

The civil rights movement, nevertheless, was making some headway. In 1968 San Antonio and Corpus Christi joined Austin in adopting an open housing ordinance. And in the following year, the legislature set about the task of erasing the segregationist laws passed in 1957. In May 1969, the House and Senate passed five bills and sent them to Gov. Preston Smith with little dissent. The bills, introduced by San Antonio Representative David Evans and carried in the Senate by Joe Bernal, also of San Antonio, removed statutes that had provided for segregated schools, had empowered cities to enact segregation ordinances, had required railroads to provide separate coaches and facilities, and had banned sports events between persons of different races.[52] De jure segregation had ended in Texas.

In the meantime, a great social movement worked to eradicate de facto segregation and inequalities. The most dramatic successes occurred in the rural areas, a fact that, at first glance, may appear to weaken my argument about the ascendancy of urban commercial interests and the Mexican American middle class. On the contrary, these victories underscore one argument I have advanced—that local growers were no longer the dominant political force they had once been and that insurgent movements could be organized and sustained with urban support. The focus of the movement was on the countryside, but it emanated from the cities. It was a movement largely directed from the cities, decided in the cities. The strategy of key organizations—PASSO and later the Raza Unida Party (RUP), the Mexican American Legal Defense and Educational Fund (MALDEF), the Southwest Voter Registration Education Project (SVREP), to mention a few—consisted in large part of organizing "forays" into the countryside to accomplish some destructive mission among the remnants of Jim Crow. In the military jargon of the Vietnam era, these missions were basically "mopping up" operations.

Important questions remain to be addressed. What does the demise of Jim Crow signify for ethnic politics in the South and the Southwest? More to the point, what new forms of accommodation and control exist today? The answers rest, as this sketch has suggested, in a new order where Anglo business interests and those of the Mexican American middle class constitute the major political axis shaping contemporary ethnic relations. As political intermediary and broker for the Mexican American community as a whole, the Mexican American middle class has secured the role it has always aspired to. Anglo-Americans have by no means retired from political activity but, as Clark Knowlton suggests for El Paso, the pattern of race and ethnic relationships is beginning to resemble that of some eastern cities where the old Yankees, although retreating from local politics, still retain economic control.[53]

12. The Demise of "Jim Crow"

1. For a legal discussion, see Rangel and Alcala, "De Jure Segregation," pp. 307–391.

2. See Jack Bass and Walter DeVries, *The Transformation of Southern Politics.*

3. Kibbe, *Latin Americans,* pp. 208–209, 240.

4. Grebler et al., *Mexican American People,* pp. 322–325.

5. See Edwin Caldwell, "Highlights of Development of Manufacturing in Texas, 1900–1960," *Southwestern Historical Quarterly* 68, no. 4 (April 1965): 418; also Seth S. McKay, *Texas and the Fair Deal, 1945–1952,* pp. 1–2.

6. McCain, "Mexican Labor"; P. S. Taylor, *American-Mexican Frontier.*

7. See Kibbe, *Latin Americans;* also Alonso Perales, *Are We Good Neighbors?;* M. T. García, *Desert Immigrants;* Clark Knowlton, "Changing Patterns of Segregation and Discrimination Affecting the Mexican Americans of El Paso" and "Patterns of Accommodation of Mexican Americans in El Paso, Texas," in *Politics and Society in the Southwest,* ed. Z. Anthony Krusewski et al., pp. 131–154, 215–236.

8. Kibbe, *Latin Americans,* pp. 160, 162.

9. Texas Agricultural and Mechanical College, Department of Industrial Education, *An Occupational Survey of San Antonio, Texas* (1929), p. 22, as cited by McCain, "Mexican Labor," pp. 18–19; for a discussion of the "segmentation" of Mexicans as common laborers in industry, see Kibbe, *Latin Americans,* pp. 157–166.

10. Kibbe, *Latin Americans,* p. 245; McCain, "Mexican Labor," pp. 16–17; Nelson-Cisneros, "La clase trabajadora," pp. 239–265.

11. Kibbe, *Latin Americans,* p. 35; correspondence of the Texas Cotton Ginners' Association; also see Will Alexander, "Aliens in War Industries," *Annals of the American Academy of Political and Social Science* 223 (September 1942): 138–143.

12. The "Stilley Plan" was named after its author and chief advocate, Jay C. Stilley, executive secretary of the Texas Cotton Ginners' Association. According to the plan, members of the ginners' association in every town would monitor and mediate cases of discrimination (see correspondence to the Texas Cotton Ginners' Association).

13. Carlos E. Castañeda, statements, in Perales, *Good Neighbors?,* pp. 59–61, 95, 117; Kibbe, *Latin Americans,* pp. 163–164.

14. Castañeda in Perales, *Good Neighbors?,* pp. 59–61.

15. Ibid., pp. 60–61; Kibbe, *Latin Americans,* p. 161; McKay, *Texas and the Fair Deal,* p. 44; also letter from Sam Smith to Lt. Gov. John Lee Smith, June 4, 1945, cited by George Green, *The Establishment in Texas Politics,* pp. 256–257 n. 37.

16. See Green, *The Establishment,* pp. 80–81, 139–140; also Everett Ross Cluichy, Jr., "Equality of Opportunity for Latin-Americans in Texas" (Ph.D. diss.), pp. 45, 74–89, 180–184.

17. Kibbe, *Latin Americans,* pp. 222–223.

18. Tiller, *Texas Winter Garden*, p. 36.

19. Ibid., pp. 41, 79, 89.

20. Kemper Diehl, "Swift Changes Taking Place in Agribusiness," *San Antonio Express and News*, May 13, 1967.

21. Foley et al., *Peones to Politicos*, pp. 78–79; Fredolin J. Kaderli, "Changing Face of Texas Agriculture," *Texas Business Review* 35, no. 6 (June 1961): 8–11.

22. See Kibbe, *Latin Americans*, p. 179.

23. *Texas Business Review* 26, no. 6 (July 1952): 15; McKay, *Texas and the Fair Deal*, p. 6; Green, *The Establishment*, pp. 8–9.

24. Tiller, *Texas Winter Garden*, pp. 76–79, 89.

25. Bass and DeVries, *Southern Politics*, pp. 498–504; Foley et al., *Peones to Politicos*, pp. 83, 132.

26. Diehl, "Swift Changes"; Tiller, *Texas Winter Garden*, pp. 76–79, 89.

27. Green, *The Establishment*, pp. 16–20; Bass and DeVries, *Southern Politics*, p. 307.

28. Charles Murphy, "Texas Business and McCarthy," *Fortune* 49 (May 1954): 100–101.

29. See *Texas Almanac*, 1958–1959, pp. 455–456.

30. For county returns, see ibid.

31. See Stuart Long, "White Supremacy and the 'Filibusteros,'" *Reporter*, June 27, 1957, p. 15.

32. Green, *The Establishment*, pp. 190, 192, 199; also Robert Cuéllar, *A Social and Political History of the Mexican American Population of Texas, 1929–1963*, pp. 36–37.

33. Clifton McCleskey et al., *The Government and Politics of Texas*, esp. pp. 125–133.

34. *Texas Observer*, June 11, 1965, p. 8.

35. Ibid., pp. 7–14; Wilbourn E. Benton, *Texas*, esp. pp. 96–97; McCleskey et al., *Government and Politics*, pp. 125–133.

36. For the raw data, see *Texas Almanac*, 1958–1959, pp. 359–363; 1964–1965, pp. 534–539; 1966–1967, pp. 625–629; 1968–1969, pp. 624–627.

37. Benton, *Texas*, p. 97; McCleskey et al., *Government and Politics*, p. 132; *Texas Observer*, May 9, 1969, p. 9.

38. Knowlton, "Changing Patterns," p. 145; Foley et al., *Peones to Politicos*, pp. 136–137.

39. See Luther L. Sanders, "Nonpartisanism: Its Use as a Campaign Appeal in San Antonio, Texas, 1961–1971" (M.A. thesis), p. 51; Albert Peña, Jr., "A Marshall Plan for Mexican-Americans," *Texas Observer*, April 15, 1966, pp. 1, 4.

40. O'Lene Stone et al., "Life and Death of Mexican American Organizations," *San Antonio Light*, December 14, 1980; Carl Allsup, *The American G.I. Forum*.

41. In Perales, *Good Neighbors?*, p. 29.

42. For college attendance, see Herschel T. Manuel, *Spanish-Speaking Children of the Southwest*, pp. 57–62; for home ownership, see "Texas' Big-

gest Untapped Market: 1,000,000 Latin Americans," *Texas Business Review* 29, no. 12 (December 1955): 15–17; for the military industry, see *Texas Observer*, May 4, 1984.

43. "Texas' Biggest Untapped Market," pp. 15–17; Knowlton, "Patterns of Accommodation," pp. 215–216.

44. Sanders, "Nonpartisanism," p. 51; Knowlton, "Patterns of Accommodation," pp. 216–217.

45. *Texas Observer*, October 28, 1966, August 23, 1968; Knowlton, "Patterns of Accommodation," pp. 216, 218–219; also Rodolfo Alvarez, "The Psycho-Historical and Socioeconomic Development of the Chicano Community," *Social Science Quarterly* 53, no. 4 (March 1973): 520–542.

46. William Madsen, *Society and Health in the Lower Rio Grande*, p. 6; Meinig, *Imperial Texas*, p. 99.

47. Charles R. Chandler, "The Mexican American Protest Movement in Texas" (Ph.D. diss.), pp. 153–208; Cuéllar, *Social and Political History*, pp. 43–51.

48. John S. Shockley, *Chicano Revolt in a Texas Town*, pp. 24–41.

49. See *Texas Observer*, December 9, 1966, pp. 19–20; Cuéllar, *Social and Political History*, pp. 55–66.

50. Chandler, "Mexican American Protest Movement," pp. 231–252; see the following issues of *Texas Observer*: April 11, 1969; January 2, 1970; October 15, 1976.

51. Rangel and Alcala, "De Jure Segregation," p. 308; Grebler et al., *Mexican American People*, pp. 274–280.

52. *Texas Observer*, May 9, 1969.

53. Knowlton, "Patterns of Accommodation," p. 223.

This article analyzes data from the Annual Housing Survey on the black and Spanish-origin populations in a sample of U.S. standard metropolitan statistical areas to determine whether these minorities pay more than Anglos for comparable housing. These data demonstrate that both the black and Spanish-origin populations as a whole pay more than Anglos for the same quality housing in the rental market while no group pays significantly more than Anglos in the owners' market. Separate analyses of Puerto Ricans, Cubans, and Mexican Americans highlight some differences among the minority groups. Most important is the finding that Cubans are equally or less likely than Anglos to obtain low-quality housing at most levels of rent.

HOUSING PRICE INEQUALITIES
A Comparison of Anglos, Blacks, and Spanish-Origin Populations

LAUREN J. KRIVO
University of Texas at Austin

Sociologists and economists have long been interested in price inequalities in the housing market. Numerous studies have reported that blacks pay more than whites for equal quality housing in urban areas in the United States (Duncan and Hauser, 1960; Kain and Quigley, 1975; Rapkin, 1966; Von Furstenberg et al., 1974). Duncan and Hauser (1960), for example, found that in Chicago in the 1950s, more nonwhites than whites obtained substandard dwellings at every level of gross monthly rent. Recent case studies (Kain and Quigley, 1975; Von Furstenberg et al., 1974) have confirmed these findings. But, not all agree with these analyses. Lampham (1971) has found no statistically significant difference between black and white housing costs in Dallas, and Muth (1969)

AUTHOR'S NOTE: *I would like to thank W. Parker Frisbie, Robert L. Kaufman, and Dudley L. Poston for their comments on previous versions of this article.*

has reported inconsistent results, suggesting that the price differential in the rental market is, at most, very small. Still, the cumulative results on this subject most frequently support racial inequality in housing price.

There are, however, two major deficiencies in this research on housing price inequality. First, most of the studies have examined single cities (for exceptions, see Rapkin, 1966, and Wilson, 1979). This severely limits the generalizability of the findings. Second, research on housing price inequality focuses almost exclusively on the black population, thereby ignoring the large and perhaps similarly disadvantaged Spanish-origin minority. An examination of Spanish surname households in four southwestern cities (Grebler et al., 1970: 262-265) showed that, like blacks, these minority-group members also lived in lower-quality dwellings than Anglos at all levels of income and rent. But again, the small sample limits the generalizability of these findings. In addition, the data presented for those cities are now 20 years old.

The present article attempts to remedy these deficiencies by analyzing recent data for the black and Spanish-origin populations in a sample of U.S. metropolitan areas to determine whether these minorities pay more than Anglos for the same quality housing. No previous study has examined Spanish-origin/Anglo housing price differentials in a number of metropolitan areas. Thus, for the first time, levels of black/Anglo housing price inequality can be compared with levels of this inequality for another large minority population in metropolitan areas across the United States.

DATA AND METHODS

Extensive housing data on Anglo, black, and Spanish-origin households are available for a sample of standard metropolitan statistical areas in the 1975 and 1976 Annual Housing Surveys (U.S. Bureau of the Census, 1977-1978). The survey includes information on housing quality cross-classified by both gross monthly rent and value of owner-occupied homes. Of the SMSAs in the survey, 19 have sufficient numbers of Anglo, black, and Spanish-origin households living in them to provide all of the relevant data for all three populations. These 19 SMSAs are examined in this analysis.[1]

The Anglo population is obtained by subtracting black and Spanish-origin persons from the total sample. Defining the Anglo population in this manner could create distortions in the findings if large numbers of other racial groups (e.g., American Indians, Japanese, Chinese, Filipinos, or other races) reside in the SMSAs being studied. However, such groups comprised only very small proportions of the population in each of these metropolitan areas in 1970.[2]

The Spanish-origin population is defined by a self-identification question[3] which includes Spanish-origin persons who might not otherwise be listed in a more limited definition but who are clearly part of the large Spanish American population (Hernandez et al., 1973). However, it has been argued that persons who identify as Spanish in origin do not comprise a single homogeneous ethnic group, since Mexicans, Cubans, Puerto Ricans, and other Spanish-origin persons differ with regard to certain social and demographic attributes (cf. Ellis, 1976; Sullivan, 1978). Yet, these groups do have common characteristics; they share language, religion, and some forms of Hispanic culture. Hence, there is good reason to consider the various Spanish-origin populations as a single group.

However, separate analyses will also be performed for Puerto Rican, Mexican American, and Cuban households in a very small number of SMSAs to determine whether there are significant differences between the various Spanish-origin groups with regard to patterns of housing price inequality which are not accurately reflected in the total comparison. This can be done quite simply since these subpopulations tend to live in different SMSAs, with Mexican Americans concentrated in the Southwest, Puerto Ricans in the Northeast (especially in New York), and Cubans in Florida (U.S. Bureau of the Census, 1973). In this sample, there are five SMSAs in the Southwest in which at least three-fourths of the Spanish-origin population identified itself as Mexican in descent (U.S. Bureau of the Census, 1973).[4] Because almost 80% of the Spanish-origin population in Miami identified as Cuban and nearly 70% of the Spanish-origin population in New York identified as Puerto Rican (U.S. Bureau of the Census, 1973), each of these two metropolitan areas is also examined alone. In addition, approximately 40% of the persons in the United States who identified as Cuban live in Miami; slightly over 60% of the persons in the United States who identified themselves as Puerto Rican live in New York (U.S. Bureau of the Census, 1973).[5]

Housing quality is measured by the following seven structural deficiencies: (1) some or all of the electric wiring is exposed, (2) lacks working outlets in some or all rooms, (3) water leakage in the roof, (4) open cracks or holes in interior walls and ceilings, (5) broken plaster in interior walls and ceilings, (6) peeling paint in interior walls and ceilings, and (7) holes in interior floors. In each SMSA, the number of housing units which possesses each of these seven deficiencies is reported for each of the three subpopulations.[6] Since, for each deficiency, these data consist of the aggregate number of households with any given defect, they do not distinguish between individual units in the extent to which they are structurally defective. Summing across the types of deficiencies, however, does indicate the extent to which a given population resides in poor-quality housing. Obviously, there are other indicators of housing quality that might be of interest. But the measure employed here is closely related to other indicators of housing quality such as housing age and the number of persons per room (e.g., Bianchi et al., 1980). In addition, similar measures of housing quality have frequently been used in national studies of housing (Bianchi et al., 1980; Grebler et al., 1970; Rapkin, 1966).

Housing price is measured by gross monthly rent and home value. Gross monthly rent includes utilities (electricity, gas, water) and fuels (oils, coal, kerosene, wood, and so on).[7] Therefore, this measure is superior to monthly contract rent which may either include or exclude these goods. The value of owner-occupied homes is the respondent's estimated selling value of the property on the market at the time of the survey. Studies which have compared owners' estimates of housing values with those of professional appraisers have found individual discrepancies between the two estimates to be large, but these errors were offsetting in the aggregate. While many individuals overestimate the value of their homes, many others underestimate it to a similar degree and therefore the two errors cancel each other out (Kain and Quigley, 1972; Kish and Lansing, 1954). Thus, when using aggregated responses, as in this research, owners' estimates are adequate assessments of home values.

To determine whether the three subpopulations receive different quality housing for the same price, the average SMSA number of structural defects per 100 housing units within each housing price is compared. This measure is calculated separately for each price by race/ethnicity category as follows:

$$RD = \left\{ \sum_{j=1}^{N} \left[\left(\sum_{i=1}^{7} x_{ij} \right) / n_j \right] / N \right\} \times 100$$

where RD is the average rate of structural defects, x_{ij} is the number of units in the j_{th} SMSA with the i_{th} type of deficiency in the price x race/ethnicity category, n_j is the number of housing units in the j_{th} SMSA in the price x race/ethnicity category, and N is the total number of SMSAs (i.e., 19 in this case).

After examining these means, a two-way analysis of variance is performed to assess the statistical significance of any between-race/ethnicity differences. For this part of the analysis, the number of structural defects per 100 housing units in the SMSA is the dependent variable. Rent or value of home divided in six value categories [8] is the first independent variable. The second independent variable is race/ethnicity categorized as (1) anglo, (2) black, and (3) Spanish origin. The purpose of this analysis is not to compare the relative magnitude of the effects of housing costs and race/ethnicity but to assess whether race/ethnicity has any effect on the rate of structural deficiencies net of housing costs. Obviously, the amount paid for housing should always have a highly significant effect on the rates of structural defects for any population and it should also explain a substantial portion of the variance in this dependent variable. If race/ethnicity explains a statistically significant amount of the variation in the rates of housing defects in addition to that accounted for by housing costs, the influence of race/ethnicity is quite important.

HOUSING PRICE INEQUALITIES

THE RENTAL MARKET

In the rental market, black and Spanish-origin households clearly tend to live in lower-quality dwellings than Anglos (Table 1). On the average, Anglos have only 24 defects per 100 housing units while both black and Spanish-origin households average 42 deficiencies per 100 units. And although Anglos generally have the financial potential to pay more and thus obtain better quality housing than the black and Spanish-origin minorities, the differentials in the quality of units received remain when the value of rent paid is controlled. Both minorities have higher average rates of structural defects than Anglos in all but the lowest category of rent. The unexpectedly small numbers of deficiencies found for minorities at the lowest rent level may be due to their inability to find very low priced housing in a market where there is discrimination. The few minority households who do locate such dwellings may be tightly connected with relatives or friends who provide higher-quality "housing bargains" to them. Alternatively, the findings

TABLE 1
Average Rates of Structural Defects for the Anglo, Black, and Spanish Origin Populations Within Each Rent Category for the Total Sample of 19 SMSAs

Rent	Anglos	Blacks	Spanish Origin
Less than $70	40	27	24
$70-100	42	51	59
$100-150	32	54	53
$150-200	24	39	34
$200-250	21	33	27
Greater than $250	17	24	24
Total	24	42	42
N	19	19	19

SOURCE: See text.

based on the small numbers of households in this rent category may result from sampling error.

As suggested above, one must be cautious about generalizing these findings to all Spanish-origin groups because the patterns of overall Spanish-origin/Anglo housing inequality may not be the same as those within each of the three major Spanish-origin subpopulations. However, an examination of Mexican American renters in the southwestern SMSAs (Table 2a) finds similar patterns to those displayed by the Spanish-origin population in all 19 SMSAs; blacks and Mexican Americans have higher average rates of deficiencies than Anglos both overall and at most rent levels. The low rates of structural defects found for black households paying very low or high rent and for Mexican Americans paying very low rent are again probably due to sampling error, fluctuations in summary statistics which result when the number of cases is small, or the unusual nature of the few households who pay these rents.

Differences in housing quality among Anglo, black, and Puerto Rican households in New York (Table 2b) also show a pattern similar to that found for all SMSAs in the sample, although overall levels of structural deficiencies are much higher in this metropolitan area. The total Anglo population lives in housing with 46 defects per 100 units as opposed to 98 and 92 deficiencies per 100 dwellings for black and Puerto Rican households, respectively. Anglos also live in dwellings with fewer deficiencies per 100 units than either minority group within every rent level that is greater than $70.

TABLE 2
Rates of Structural Defects in the Rental Market for Anglo, Black, and Selected Spanish Origin Subpopulations

TABLE 2a. Average Rates of Structural Defects for the Anglo, Black, and Mexican American Populations Within Each Rent Category for the Sample of 5 Southwestern SMSA's

Rent	Anglos	Blacks	Mexican Americans
Less than $70	57	31	47
$70-100	37	52	70
$100-150	30	51	52
$150-200	20	26	25
$200-250	19	24	29
Greater than $250	14	12	36
Total	22	38	45
N	5	5	5

TABLE 2b. Rates of Structural Defects for the Anglo, Black, and Puerto Rican Populations Within Each Rent Category in the New York SMSA

Rent	Anglos	Blacks	Puerto Ricans
Less than $70	93	23	56
$70-100	74	90	134
$100-150	63	126	102
$150-200	53	98	96
$200-250	38	98	91
Greater than $250	30	82	66
Total	46	98	92

(continued)

TABLE 2 (Continued)

TABLE 2c. Rates of Structural Defects for the Anglo, Black, and Cuban Populations Within Each Rent Category in the Miami SMSA

Rent	Anglos	Blacks	Cuban
Less than $70	32	33	12
$70-100	46	46	24
$100-150	24	52	21
$150-200	17	44	10
$200-250	9	17	18
Greater than $250	11	21	10
Total	14	40	14

SOURCE: See text.

Thus, when comparing Mexican American/Anglo housing inequality with Puerto Rican/Anglo housing inequality, one finds that both Spanish-origin minorities, along with the black population, consistently receive lower-quality dwellings than Anglos for the same money. Cuban households (Table 2c), on the other hand, do not appear to suffer the deleterious effects of minority status in the rental housing market.[9] In five of six rental categories, the Cuban population has a lower rate of structural defects than the Anglo population, although rates are quite similar in two cases. These differences are most pronounced at the two lowest rent levels. (The sample size is particularly small only for Cubans paying less than $70 in rent.)

One might argue that Cubans frequently receive the same or better quality rental units than Anglos for the same money because Cuban immigrants to the United States, at least until 1980, were mainly middle- to upper-class persons fleeing the Castro regime. As a result, this group should not be considered a minority with low status and limited access to power. However, the results presented here suggest that this may be, at least, an incomplete explanation of the relative position of Cubans in the housing market, since Cuban households tend to obtain somewhat better quality housing than Anglos *for the same price* at some levels of rent. A more likely explanation is that the Cuban population is highly unified, possibly based on an anti-Castro ideology, and hence they

TABLE 3
Results of Analyses of Variance for Rates of Structural Defects in the Rental Market for the Total Sample of 19 SMSAs and the Subsample of 5 Southwestern SMSAs: Three Group and Two Group Comparisons

Variable	df	All 19 SMSA's		5 Southwestern SMSA's	
		Anglo-Black-Spanish Origin		Anglo-Black-Mexican American	
		F	Proportion of Variance Explained	F	Proportion of Variance Explained
Rent	5	12.45***	.15	6.80***	.27
Race/Ethnicity	2	4.49*	.02	3.52*	.06
Rent x Race/Ethnicity	10	1.82	.04	1.20	.10
Eta Squared			.22		.42
		Anglo-Black		Anglo-Black	
		F	Proportion of Variance Explained	F	Proportion of Variance Explained
Rent	5	8.12***	.14	4.12**	.27
Race/Ethnicity	1	10.24**	.04	.36	.00
Rent x Race/Ethnicity	5	3.03*	.05	1.51	.10
Eta Squared			.23		.37
		Anglo-Spanish Origin		Anglo-Mexican American	
		F	Proportion of Variance Explained	F	Proportion of Variance Explained
Rent	5	9.20***	.16	7.34***	.35
Race/Ethnicity	1	6.04*	.02	9.85**	.09
Rent x Race/Ethnicity	5	3.08**	.05	2.13	.10
Eta Squared			.24		.54
		Black-Spanish Origin		Black-Mexican American	
		F	Proportion of Variance Explained	F	Proportion of Variance Explained
Rent	5	9.15***	.17	4.37**	.29
Race/Ethnicity	1	.15	.00	2.87	.04
Rent x Race/Ethnicity	5	.27	.01	.48	.03
Eta Squared			.18		.36

*p < .05; **p < .01; ***p < .001

support a very tight housing network in which they locate and pass down high-quality and fairly priced housing units to each other.

Table 3 reports the two-way analysis-of-variance results which show the effects of rent value, race/ethnicity, and the interaction between these two variables for the total sample of 19 SMSAs and for the small subsample of SMSAs in the Southwest. In order to determine whether the patterns of structural defects are significantly different among all three populations or only between Anglos and each of the minority groups, three-group and all possible two-group comparisons are made. F statistics and the proportion of variance in the rate of structural defects explained by each of the three variables—rent, race/ethnicity, and the rent x race/ethnicity interaction—are reported.[10] These findings almost fully support those discussed above. In every case, the main effect for rent is significant in both SMSA samples. In addition, the race/ethnicity main effect for the total sample of SMSAs is significant for all except the black/Spanish-origin comparison. Thus, black and Spanish-origin renters do receive significantly different quality housing from Anglo renters for the same price. However, the minority groups do not obtain significantly different quality housing from each other. The significant interactions in the Anglo/black and Anglo/Spanish-origin comparisons for the total sample indicate that each of the minorities also has different patterns of housing defects from Anglos across rent levels. It is likely that as rent increases, the rate of deficiencies does not decline as rapidly for the minority groups as it does for Anglos. Rent explains the largest proportion of the variance in the rate of structural defects, as would be expected due to the size of its effect and the larger number of categories (i.e., degrees of freedom) relative to the race/ethnicity variable.

The right side of Table 3 suggests similar results for Mexican American and black households in the Southwest. The significant main effect of race/ethnicity in the three-group comparison for this sample appears to be due to significant differences only between the Anglo and Mexican American populations. Black households do not tend to receive significantly different quality housing from either Anglos or Mexican Americans in these southwestern SMSAs. None of the interactions is significant in this sample. As expected, rent also explains the largest proportion of the variance in the rate of structural defects in the sample of southwestern SMSAs. Unfortunately, similar statistical analyses cannot be performed for either the Cuban or Puerto Rican populations since data are utilized for only a single case.

THE HOME OWNERS' MARKET

The pattern for the three populations in the home owners' market is considerably different from that in the rental market (Table 4). As

TABLE 4
Average Rates of Structural Defects for the Anglo, Black, and
Spanish Origin Populations Within Each Home Value Category for
the Total Sample of 19 SMSAs

Home Value	Anglos	Blacks	Spanish Origin
Less than $10,000	69	41	18
$10,000– 19,999	25	27	19
$20,000– 24,999	14	17	13
$25,000– 29,999	11	13	10
$30,000– 34,999	10	12	12
Greater than $35,000	9	11	14
Total	11	19	17
N	19	19	19

SOURCE: See text.

would be expected, levels of the deficiency rates are generally lower for all three groups than in the rental market. In addition, differences in the rates of defects among the groups are also smaller. The total Anglo population in the 19 SMSAs has an average of 11 defects per 100 housing units, whereas the black and Spanish-origin populations have an average of 19 and 17 deficiencies per 100 units, respectively. Within every home-value category except the lowest, blacks have higher mean rates of deficiencies than either Anglo or Spanish-origin households although the differences are always very small. Spanish-origin households have even smaller average rates of structural defects than Anglos in four of the six home-value categories. But again these differences are small except at the lowest home value, where the small number of cases distorts the findings in the ways discussed previously. In the two value categories where the Spanish-origin population receives poorer-quality housing than the Anglo population, the differences in average housing received are of little importance.

These patterns indicate that although the black and Spanish-origin minority groups pay more for lower-quality rental housing than Anglos, the minorities do not have similar experiences in all sectors of the housing market. In fact, when purchasing a home, neither minority group tends to obtain very different quality housing than the Anglo population at almost all values. Furthermore, separate analyses of Mexican Americans in five southwestern SMSAs and Cubans in Miami suggest that there are few significant differences between the housing patterns of these Spanish-origin subpopulations. Because 92.8% of the Puerto Rican and 87.8% of the black households in New York live in rental units, it is not possible to perform a meaningful analysis of housing inequality for these minority groups in the owners' market.

As Table 5a demonstrates, the total Mexican American and black populations in the southwestern SMSAs both bought homes with higher average rates of structural deficiencies than the Anglo population: a mean of 13 defects per 100 units for Anglos as opposed to 23 and 22 deficiencies for blacks and Mexican Americans, respectively. Mexican Americans also receive somewhat more defects on the average than Anglos within four of the six home-value categories. The same is true for the black households; they own homes which tend to have the same or more structural deficiencies per 100 units than Anglo households within four of the six price levels. Still, the most striking finding is the relative similarity in the levels of housing quality that all three groups of owners obtain for the same price.

The situation for Cuban and black home owners in Miami is slightly different from that of the minority groups in the Southwest (Table 5b). Blacks do have higher levels of housing defects than Anglos within most value categories and these differences are not always small. Cuban home owners, on the other hand, have a tendency to live in homes with lower levels of structural deficiencies than Anglos in four of the six home-value categories. However, the differences between Anglo and Cuban households appear to be insignificant for the most part.

The two-way analysis-of-variance results reported in Table 6 support all of these findings for the home owners' market in the total sample and in the subsample of southwestern SMSAs. In every case of either two-group or three-group comparisons, the main effect for home value but not for race/ethnicity is significant. Thus, none of the three populations examined here obtains significantly different levels of housing quality for the same value when purchasing homes. Home value explains the largest proportion of the variance in the rate of structural defects as would be expected, due to the magnitude of the race/ethnicity effects. To reiterate, this finding holds for the total sample of 19 SMSAs and for the subsample of SMSAs in the Southwest where the Spanish-origin

TABLE 5
Rates of Structural Defects in the Owner's Market for Anglo, Black, and Selected Spanish Origin Subpopulations

TABLE 5a. Average Rates of Structural Defects for the Anglo, Black, and Mexican American Populations Within Each Home Value Category for the Sample of 5 Southwestern SMSA's.

Home Value	Anglos	Blacks	Mexican Americans
Less than $10,000	76	31	45
$10,000-19,999	22	31	22
$20,000-24,999	11	20	15
$25,000-29,999	13	11	18
$30,000-34,999	8	9	18
Greater than $35,000	10	10	13
Total	13	23	22
N	5	5	5

TABLE 5b. Rates of Structural Defects for the Anglo, Black, and Cuban Populations Within Each Home Value Category in the Miami SMSA.

Home Value	Anglos	Blacks	Spanish Origin
Less than $10,000	0	83	0
$10,000-19,999	26	13	0
$20,000-24,999	8	10	0
$25,000-29,999	3	18	2
$30,000-34,999	4	24	5
Greater than $35,000	10	14	4
Total	9	19	4

SOURCE: See text.

TABLE 6
Results of Analyses of Variance for Rates of Structural Defects in the Owners' Market for the Total Sample of 19 SMSAs and the Subsample of 5 Southwestern SMSAs: Three Group and Two Group Comparisons

Variable	df	All 19 SMSA's		5 Southwestern SMSA's	
		Anglo-Black-Spanish Origin		Anglo-Black-Mexican American	
		F	Proportion of Variance Explained	F	Proportion of Variance Explained
Home Value	5	8.95***	.11	8.79***	.33
Race/Ethnicity	2	2.14	.01	.46	.01
Home Value x Race/Ethnicity	10	2.16*	.05	1.51	.11
Eta Squared			.18		.45
		Anglo-Black		Anglo-Black	
		F	Proportion of Variance Explained	F	Proportion of Variance Explained
Home Value	5	8.81***	.17	6.68***	.35
Race/Ethnicity	1	.33	.00	.81	.01
Home Value x Race/Ethnicity	5	1.09	.02	2.38	.13
Eta Squared			.19		.49
		Anglo-Spanish Origin		Anglo-Mexican American	
		F	Proportion of Variance Explained	F	Proportion of Variance Explained
Home Value	5	5.81***	.11	10.29***	.48
Race/Ethnicity	1	3.75	.01	.12	.00
Home Value x Race/Ethnicity	5	3.85**	.07	1.60	.07
Eta Squared			.19		.55
		Black-Spanish Origin		Black-Mexican American	
		F	Proportion of Variance Explained	F	Proportion of Variance Explained
Home Value	5	3.55**	.07	2.59*	.20
Race/Ethnicity	1	3.19	.01	.38	.01
Home Value x Race/Ethnicity	5	1.38	.03	.47	.04
Eta Squared			.11		.25

*p < .05; **p < .01; ***p < .001

population is comprised mainly of Mexican American persons. Once again, statistical analyses of the Cuban population cannot be made since only a single case is examined.

It seems likely that the difficulty that minority groups have in getting into the home owners' market may explain the finding reported here that they do not, on the average, receive lower-quality housing in this housing market than the Anglo majority for the same price. It has been shown in previous research that black households must have higher income than comparable whites to purchase homes (Jackman and Jackman, 1980; Wilson, 1979). The findings of this study suggest that once blacks are able to enter this segment of the housing market, they are also likely to obtain relatively comparable housing to Anglos. The similarity between the results reported for Spanish-origin and black households indicates that an analogous process may take place in the Spanish-origin population. In other words, once Spanish-origin households have high enough incomes to buy homes, they are unlikely to obtain poorer-quality housing than Anglos.

CONCLUSION

This article provides evidence that the black, Mexican American, and Puerto Rican populations frequently pay higher rent than Anglos for the same quality housing although the Cuban population does not. This is not an inconsequential finding in light of the large numbers of persons in these minority populations and the high percentage of these persons that live in rental housing.[11] Sizable numbers of already disadvantaged households appear to incur additional financial costs for poorer physical home environments than the Anglo majority. In contrast, however, none of the minority groups examined in this article appears to pay higher prices than Anglos for the same quality housing when purchasing homes. This finding highlights the fact that there are, indeed, significant differences between the experiences of minority groups in the rental and owners' housing markets.

The above analyses raise many questions for future research. Of particular interest are explanations of the various rental price inequalities. Most important is the possibility that the minority groups studied here might sacrifice housing quality for other amenities such as housing size or location. Households obtain a bundle of physical and locational qualities along with neighborhood services when they buy or rent a housing unit. Differences in the sizes of dwellings, neighborhood amenities, distances from other minority enclaves, and local services received by the racial and ethnic groups examined in the present analysis may account for the housing price inequality located here. Alternatively, the minorities may pay more than the majority because of residential segregation which limits their supply relative to their demand and thus dictates higher prices or because of housing market discrimination. Other city characteristics which influence various types of inequality, such as minority proportion or industrial structure, may also help produce the price inequalities. All of these explanations are subjects for further investigation.

Finally, since the results presented differ slightly by race/ethnicity and differ drastically by housing market, they also suggest important cautions which must be taken in analyses of minority relations, particularly within the housing market. Specifically, findings which pertain to the black population should not be generalized to all Spanish-origin populations; findings which pertain to the total Spanish-origin population should not be generalized to each of the major Spanish-origin subpopulations; and findings relevant to minorities in the rental market should not be generalized to the owners' market.

NOTES

1. The 1975 and 1976 Annual Housing Surveys include a combined sample of 41 SMSAs. However, 2 of these SMSAs have insufficient numbers of both black and Spanish-origin persons in the sample to publish the cross-tabulations used in the present analysis. In an additional 19 SMSAs, no data are available for Spanish-origin households because very small numbers of Spanish-origin persons reside in these areas. Honolulu was also excluded from the analysis since over half of its population consists of persons of races other than white or black. The 19 SMSAs which are examined are Atlanta, Chicago, Colorado Springs, Denver, Hartford, Houston, Las Vegas, Miami, New Orleans, New York, Patterson-Clifton-Passaic, Philadelphia, Sacramento, San Antonio, San Bernardino-Riverside-Ontario, San Diego, San Francisco, Seattle-Everett, and Springfield-Chicopee-Holyoke.

2. In 14 of the SMSAs, other races comprised less than 2% of the total 1970 population. In San Bernardino, San Diego, and Seattle-Everett, other races comprised between 2% and 4% of the population. The largest percentages of other races were in Sacramento, 4.3% and San Francisco, 6.6%. Thus, even in San Francisco, the relative weight of the inclusion of other races in the Anglo population would be minimal when compared to the component which is white.

3. Each respondent was asked whether the head of the household was Mexican American, Chicano, Mexican, Mexicano, Puerto Rican, Cuban, Central or South American, or other Spanish origin.

4. These five SMSAs are as follows: (1) Houston, (2) Sacramento, (3) San Antonio, (4) San Bernardino, and (5) San Diego. All households in these SMSAs which identified as Spanish origin are treated as Mexican American, since the published data do not allow for finer distinctions within SMSAs.

5. All households in New York and Miami who identified as Spanish origin were treated as Puerto Rican and Cuban, respectively.

6. These data were obtained from self-reports by respondents.

7. Estimates of the costs of utilities and fuels are reported by the respondents and then added to the contracted rent to obtain the gross rent.

8. The rent value categories are (1) less than $70, (2) $70-$100, (3) $100-$150, (4) $150-$200, (5) $200-$250, and (6) greater than $250. The home value categories are (1) less than $10,000, (2) $10,000-$19,999 (3) $20,000-$24,999, (4) $25,000-$29,999, (5) $30,000-$34,999, and (6) greater than $35,000.

9. Of course, these data were compiled prior to the 1980 influx of Cuban immigrants.

10. In the case in which contingency table for the analysis of variance has equal cell frequencies, the two nominal scale variables are always orthogonal. Because these variables are independent, the proportion of variance explained by each can be separated in an unambiguous manner. Since the present analysis has equal cell frequencies, I am able to partition the explained variance in that manner.

11. In the 19 SMSAs analyzed in the article, 67.3% of the black households lived in rental housing and 71.7% of the Spanish-origin households rented dwellings.

REFERENCES

BIANCHI, M. S., R. FARLEY, and D. SPAIN (1980) "Racial inequalities in housing: an examination of recent trends." Presented at the meeting of the Population Association of America, Denver, April 10-12.

DUNCAN, B. and P. HAUSER (1960) Housing a Metropolis. New York: Macmillan.

ELLIS, B. (1976) "An investigation of the utility of broadly enumerated census data for Spanish heritage populations in the United States." Master's Thesis, University of Texas at Austin.

GREBLER, L., J. W. MOORE, and R. C. GUZMAN (1970) The Mexican American People. New York: Macmillan.

HERNANDEZ, J., L. ESTRADA, and D. ALVIREZ (1973) "Census data and the problem of conceptually defining the Mexican American population." Social Sci. Q. 53: 671-687.

JACKMAN, M. R. and R. W. JACKMAN (1980) "Racial inequalities in home ownership." Social Forces 58: 1221-1234.

KAIN, J. F. and J. M. QUIGLEY (1975) Housing Markets and Racial Discrimination: A Microeconomic Analysis. New York: National Bureau of Economic Research.

——— (1972) "Note on owner's estimate of housing value." J. of Amer. Stat. Assn. 67: 803-806.

KISH, L. and J. B. LANSING (1954) "Response errors in estimating the value of homes." J. of Amer. Stat. Assn. 49: 520-538.

LAMPHAM, V. (1971) "Do blacks pay more for housing?" J. of Pol. Economy 79: 1244-1257.

MUTH, R. F. (1969) Cities and Housing. Chicago: Univ. of Chicago Press.

RAPKIN, C. (1966) "Price discrimination against Negroes in the rental housing market," pp. 33-45 in C. Rapkin (ed.) Essays in Urban Land Economics. Los Angeles: Regents of the University of California.

SULLIVAN, T. A. (1978) "Racial-ethnic differences in labor force participation: an ethnic stratification perspective," pp. 165-87 in F. D. Bean and W. P. Frisbie (eds.) The Demography of Racial and Ethnic Groups. New York: Academic Press.

U.S. Bureau of the Census (1977-1978) Annual Housing Survey: 1975-1976. Section F, Tables A-6, A-10, A-18, A-22, A-30, & A-34. Washington, DC: Government Printing Office.

——— (1973) 1970 Census of Population: Persons of Spanish Ancestry. PC (S1)-30. Washington, DC: Government Printing Office.

VON FURSTENBERG, G. M., B. HARRISON, and A. R. HOROWITZ (1974) Patterns of Racial Discrimination Volume 1: Housing. Lexington, MA: D. C. Heath.

WILSON, F. D. (1979) Residential Consumption, Economic Opportunity, and Race. New York: Academic Press.

Lauren J. Krivo is a Ph.D. candidate, Department of Sociology and Population Research Center at the University of Texas at Austin. She is studying the causes and effects of the housing structure of black and Spanish-origin minorities in metropolitan areas. She is also involved in research on various aspects of suburbanization.

Housing Segregation of a Predominantly Middle Class Population:

Residential Patterns Developed by the Cuban Immigration Into Miami, 1950-74

By Morton D. Winsberg

ABSTRACT. *Latin Americans*, principally *Cubans*, have entered *Miami* in large numbers since 1950. Although most who arrive have both urban and middle class backgrounds, which greatly facilitate their economic *assimilation* within the city, they have come in such large numbers that they are not becoming residentially assimilated with the non-Latin population. Instead, through *invasion* and *succession* they are creating their own ethnic *ghettoes*, a fact which is proven in this study through use of the *location quotient* and *indexes of dissimilarity*. Miami's *Black population* has always been isolated from both the Latin and non-Latin *White populations*. The city's major ethnic and family-cycle groups, however, have steadily become more isolated from the Latins since 1950. Furthermore, following the departure of these groups from neighborhoods invaded by Latins, they have relocated throughout the city in a way so that they are becoming increasingly more isolated from each other.

I

INTRODUCTION

THE IMMIGRATION of Latin Americans, principally Cubans, into Miami, Florida, since 1950 affords an unusual opportunity to study the processes of urban ethnic residential segregation in a contemporary social and economic environment (1). Although the immigrants have primarily urban and middle class backgrounds, which greatly facilitate their assimilation into the culture of their new homeland, they come in such large numbers that Latin areas of concentration are in the process of forming throughout the city (2). Furthermore, although the rapid growth of the Latin population is only one of several contributing factors, albeit the most important, the residential pattern of the city's large Jewish population, as well as that of the Blacks, young non-Latin White families and the White non-Latin elderly all are becoming more geographically polarized, not only from the Latins but from each other.

In the first stage of the analysis, that part of Miami is defined in which Latin Americans had achieved a significantly higher than average share of the total population in 1950, the first year in which tract data

Table 1

POPULATIONS WITHIN DADE COUNTY AND THEIR RELATIVE IMPORTANCE

Group	1940	1950	1960	1970	1974[5]
Latin American Born	1,768 (0.6%)	6,200[1] (1.3%)	62,940 (6.7%)[6]	263,429 (20.8%)	430,385 (30.5%)[6]
Black	49,518 (18.4%)	65,392 (13.2%)	137,299 (14.7%)	189,666 (14.9%)	206,960 (14.7%)
Jewish[2]	7,500[3] (2.8%)	45,000 (9.0%)	80,000 (8.6%)	187,500 (14.8%)	225,000 (16.0%)
Non-Latin Whites 0-9 years of age	26,020 (9.7%)	67,495 (13.6%)	132,848 (14.2%)[4]	146,043 (11.5%)	ND
Non-Latin Whites 65 years and older	16,336 (6.1%)	35,456 (7.1%)	89,924 (9.6%)[4]	163,600 (12.9%)	ND
Total	267,739	495,084	935,047	1,267,792	1,410,039

1. Population for Metropolitan Miami
2. Estimates calculated by American Jewish Committee
3. 1937 estimates
4. Latin population included
5. Estimates of Spanish-speaking, black and total populations provided by the Community Analysis Division, County Manager's Office, Dade County
6. Spanish speaking population

ND No Data

are available for the city. Next, the diffusion of the Latin American population throughout the city between 1950 and 1974 is discussed (3). At this point in the study is ascertained the degree the group has concentrated. The concentration of ethnic and racial groups normally is accompanied by the process of invasion and succession (4). Since the Latin American population is establishing discrete areas within Miami in which it is of overwhelming numerical importance, it is determined here which groups the Latins have replaced, and to what degree. Finally, the effect of the growth of the city's Latin American population on the residential integration of other groups within the city is examined.

II
BACKGROUND

THE ETHNIC AND RACIAL COMPOSITION of Dade County, in which Miami is the principal city, has altered greatly over time (Table 1). In 1940 the city had many of the demographic characteristics of a typical southern city. Over 18 percent of the population were Black, who were living in enclaves throughout the city. Miami had not experienced an appreciable direct foreign migration by 1940, and even the Latin American-born population was numerically minuscule, greatly exceeded by that of the Jews, then the city's largest ethnic minority. Many of the latter group were foreign-born, but had immigrated first to northern cities before coming to Miami. As early as the 1920s a growing number of Jews had begun to choose Miami, first as a vacation center and later as either a retirement city or a place in which to establish a business (5).

In January, 1959, when Fidel Castro, a pro-Soviet Communist, assumed control of the Cuban government, a radical change began in that nation's economic, social and political systems, precipitating an emigration from the island of many who were in disagreement with these policies. Many who chose to emigrate to this country selected Miami as their home. Others who had gone elsewhere in the United States to live abandoned their first homes in exile and moved to South Florida's growing center of exile activity. The Spanish-American atmosphere within Miami so intensified in this period that numerous other Latin Americans, principally from elsewhere in the Caribbean, also were attracted. By 1970 the census enumerated 263,429 Latin American-born residents in the county, or 21 percent of the total population. The Spanish-speaking population was even more impressive, 24 percent.

Although direct emigration from Cuba ceased in 1973, movement of Cubans to Miami from elsewhere in the United States, a growing emigration from other Latin American nations, and higher than city average birth rates among the Latin Americans already resident in the county, have meant that the population continues to increase. In 1974 it was estimated that 430,385 Latins were living in Dade County, 30 percent of the population (6).

The net in-migration of Blacks into Miami during the 1960s was much smaller than during that of the 1950s, a reflection of their reduced employment opportunities in a city rapidly being populated by Latin Americans (7). Since 1950, although there has been an absolute population growth within the Black community, its relative share of the total population has remained stable. Jews, however, have continued to enter the city in large numbers, and despite the massive immigration of Latin Americans they have been able to increase steadily their share of the city's total population. Actually, in 1977 the city had the fifth largest Jewish population of any metropolitan area in the nation. To fully appreciate the importance of the Latin, Black and Jewish populations within the total population of Dade County, it is revealing to note that the three together have increased their relative share of the total population from 22 percent in 1940 to an estimated 61 percent in 1974.

III
DATA

INCONSISTENCIES in enumerating Latins in various censuses have made it difficult to establish their numbers in Miami's population. Data by country of birth are available by tract for both 1950 and 1970, and the Spanish-speaking population data are available by census tract for 1970. Tract estimates of the Spanish-speaking population for 1974 are also available. To extend the study temporally back to 1950, those born in Latin America were used to identify the Latin American population. Unfortunately, data for 1960 are only available for the Mexican and Puerto Rican populations, and the problem of obtaining data for Latin American-born in that year had to be solved by estimation (8).

Religion is not now included in U.S. Censuses, and estimates of the Jewish population are only available for Dade County. We can, however, identify areas of ethnic Jewish concentration with considerable confidence through use of data for Russian and Polish-born inhabitants, since Jews have constituted so large a percentage of the immigration from those nations (9). Furthermore, there are no recognized neighborhoods within Miami with large concentrations of Christians born in either nation.

Miami has a large White, non-Latin population which does not identify strongly with any ethnic group. Among them are many Jews as well as people of Latin American ancestry who have been assimilated within the majority culture. It was therefore considered appropriate to examine the effects of the spread of Latin American areas of concentration throughout the city upon those areas of concentration of non-ethnic Whites. To do this the non-Latin White group was divided into "family-cycle" categories, and their areas of concentration were determined (10). In 1970, the non-Latin elderly could be isolated from the Latin, and in this study they are people 65 years of age and older. Non-Latin young families could not be identified, but since children under ten years of age normally would be members of a young family, they were used as surrogates. The 1950 U.S. Census of Miami did not separate Latins from non-Latin Whites. In that year, however, the city's total population was only one percent Latin. For the purpose of this study total population 65 years of age and older in that year, as well as those below the age of ten, were considered non-Latin. By 1960 the share of Latins in the city's total population had risen to the point where one could no longer use total population by age with any confidence to identify non-Latin family-cycle groups.

IV
METHODOLOGY

THE AREA OF CONCENTRATION within Miami of people born in Latin America, as well as the area of concentration of the other groups whose interrelationship with the Latins was explored, have been identified for each census year since 1950 by calculating a location quotient for each tract. In this study the location quotient is defined as a measure which compares a census tract's share of a certain group within the population with that group's share of the total population (11). Thus, if a tract has a Latin quotient of 2.00, the tract's percentage of the city's Latin population is twice that of its percentage of the city's total population. This measure facilitates comparisons of sets of data from one census with that of another. Although arbitrarily established, henceforth all tracts in which a group's location quotient is 1.11 or higher will be considered to be a part of that group's area of concentration.

Changes in the pattern of distribution of the Latin American-born population of Miami over time have been measured by use of regression analysis (Maps 1a-c). A so-called deviational change was calculated for each census tract. The resultant figures are residuals around a line of best fit between a plot of observations at two census years (12). These residuals measure how much a tract has overchanged or underchanged relative to the changes of all tracts, and in this study refer to the amount of overchange or underchange of the Latin American-born population relative to their change in all the city's tracts. The dependent variable in each regression was the most recent year.

To calculate over time the interrelationship between the various groups used in this study, the index of dissimilarity was used. This index provides a summary statistic which compares the percentage of two groups across census tracts, and measures how equal or unequal the groups are distributed in relation to each other (Table 3) (13). The resultant figure is the percentage of people within the two groups which must change tracts in order for both groups to have the same distribution throughout the city.

V

ANALYSIS

THE TRACTS of Miami in which the Latin American-born population in 1950 was present in concentrations significantly higher than the average for the city covered an extensive area (Map 1a). Although the share of Latins in the total population of Metropolitan Miami in that year barely exceeded one percent, the tracts in which their location quotient had reached 1.11 or higher extended both to the north and the south of the central business district (CBD) almost three miles, and west to the city's residential limits. Within that large area, which at that time was primarily occupied by medium and low-cost single unit dwellings, the Latins were spatially well integrated with other elements of Miami's White population. In 1950 the tract with the highest Latin American-born location quotient was situated approximately two miles southwest of the CBD center. Although only four percent of its population was Latin, indicative of the growing importance of Cubans in the city's Latin population, the area in which it was situated had acquired the name "Little Havana" among the non-Latins. Typical of ethnic minorities who have recently arrived in United States cities, the Miami Latin population was highly centralized; 70 percent lived within a three mile semi-circle on the western side of the city's CBD. The group showed a considerably higher degree of centrality than the non-Latin

Housing Segregation

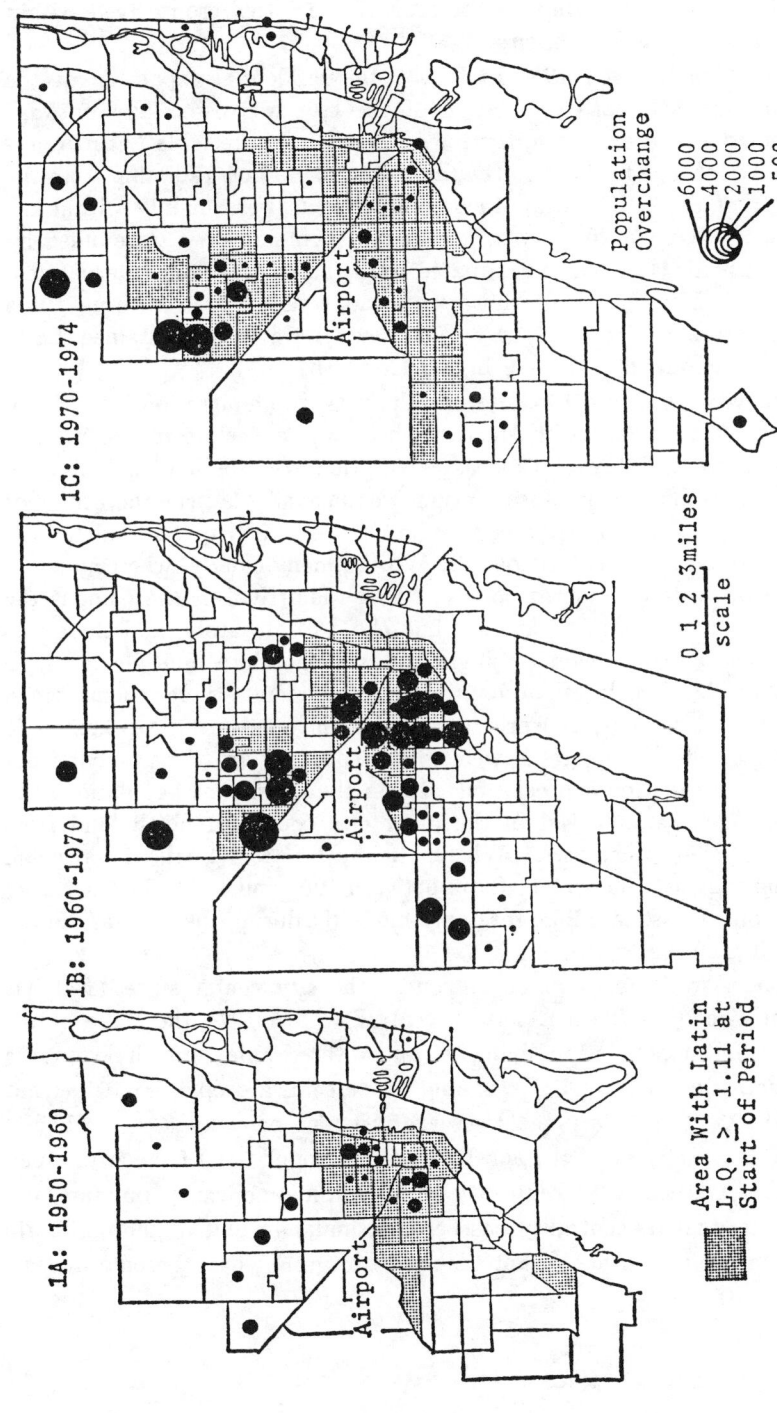

Map 1a-c. Changes in Latin American Populations Within Miami, Florida.

White population. Only 48 percent of the latter group lived within the same three mile semi-circle.

Although between 1950 and 1960 the residential expansion of the Latin American-born population of the city was essentially outward from its central core area, there were tracts of appreciable Latin American overchange far beyond the three mile semi-circle radiating from the center of the CBD (Map 1a). These tracts were mainly within the Hialeah-Miami Springs area, a center of light industry surrounded by lower middle class housing, situated to the north of Miami International Airport. Here many of those who had recently arrived from Cuba found work in factories. By 1960 several tracts had attained Latin location quotients of 1.11 or higher (Map 1b).

Between 1950 and 1960, despite the massive immigration into Miami of people born in Latin America, there was a decline in the relative importance of Little Havana as a reception area for new arrivals. In great part this was because housing was unavailable near the center of the city, where it is situated. Prior to the arrival of the Cubans the area had largely been occupied by Whites, many elderly, who commonly lived in modest detached homes. With the arrival of the Cubans the number of people in an average household rose sharply, and there was considerable conversion of single family homes into multiple units, as well as the demolition of houses to make room for new apartments. Zoning restrictions, however, regulated the conversion of homes to multiple unit dwellings as well as the construction of new apartment houses, preventing a precipitous rise in the density of population. In addition, urban renewal in the inner city converted much land from residential to other uses. Whereas many tracts in Little Havana had become almost 100 percent Latin between 1960 and 1974, their densities of people per square mile rose only modestly during the 14-year period, and in some cases fell.

The slow increase in housing near the city center since 1960 has greatly reduced Latin American centrality. In 1974 the share of the city's Latin population living within a three mile semi-circle on the western side of the CBD was only 28 percent, a drop from 70 percent in 1950. The 1974 percentage was just nine percentage points higher than the centrality of the non-Latin White population of the city. Yet, neither the decline in centrality of the Latin American population, nor the fact that its centrality has become similar to that of the non-Latin White population has meant that the two groups have become increasingly residentially integrated throughout the rest of the city. By 1974 there actually were twelve tracts five miles or more from the CBD in which Latins exceeded 60 percent of the total population, twice the average for the city.

The small expansion in housing units in most inner city tracts in which Latins had earlier settled forced many members of the group to seek housing elsewhere in the urban area during the 1960s. The success of many members of the group in finding housing in older middle class neighborhoods throughout the city is tribute to their will to reestablish their middle class status in the United States. Their personal efforts, however, were greatly facilitated by numerous programs designed to integrate them into the city's social and economic life. More importantly, the large population growth of Miami during the 1960s and early 1970s stimulated a building boom, which brought great economic prosperity to the city until the boom collapsed in 1973.

Despite the fact that Map 1c shows the overchange of Spanish-speaking population, and not Latin American-born, comparisons can be made between it and Maps 1a and 1b. Between 1970 and 1974, within the area of Latin concentration in 1970, most overchange was in tracts to the north of the airport, but there also were a number on the city's west side, immediately to the south of the airport. Outside of the area of concentration in 1970, tracts with large overchange of Latins were primarily in the extreme northwestern portion of the city, an area of new middle income housing. Of note is the high frequency of tracts in northern and northeastern Miami which between 1970 and 1974 had begun to experience a growth in the group more rapid than the city average. Three tracts on Miami Beach, noted for their high percentage of Jews, had even experienced overchange. Clearly, the Latin area of concentration was still in expansion.

The expansion of the Latin community throughout the city differs from the typical ethnic expansion which occurred in large cities in the United States between 1880 and 1914, or the more recent formation of Black ghettoes. The group has diffused far more widely throughout the urban area, in a much shorter period, a reflection of the size of the immigration as well as the rapid economic integration of the immigrants into the community. Since 1950 Miami's Black population also has grown in absolute numbers, though not so rapidly as that of the Latins. The tracts in which Blacks have experienced a population overchange, however, are generally conterminous to those in which the group already constituted a large percentage of the total population. Tracts of Latin overchange frequently are far from those in which the group already is heavily represented in the population.

Despite the geographical diffusion of the Latin population throughout the city, there is ample evidence of ghetto formation within the community. In fact, in each census year since 1950 there has been an increase in the share of the total Latin population living in tracts with high location quotients of the group (L.Q. 2.00+). In 1950 the share of Latins in tracts of this location quotient or higher was 40 percent, by 1960 it had risen to 45 percent, and in 1970 it had reached 56 percent. Estimates for 1974 show a small diminution in concentration, down to 51 percent of their total numbers in the city.

Further evidence of the increased segregation of the Latins can be found through use of the index of dissimilarity to compare that group's distribution throughout the city with that of the non-Latin White population. In 1950 the index was 31, that is 31 percent of the people within the two groups would have to change tracts for both to achieve the same pattern of residence throughout the city. In 1960 the index had risen to 44 and by 1970 it had reached 52. Using the 1974 tract estimates there was little change between that year and 1970, the index being 53.

Despite an earlier acceptance of Latins in non-Latin neighborhoods, the process of population invasion followed by the replacement of earlier residents is today very much in evidence in Miami, as the Latins spread throughout the city. Actually, there were living in the 1970 area of Latin concentration 111,268 fewer non-Latin Whites in that year than in 1960. The departure of young, non-Latin White couples has been most dramatic. Using the surrogate of children under the age of ten, it can be seen from Table 2 that the group not only suffered a relative decline in its share of the population within the Latin area of concentration between 1950 and 1970, but a numerical decline as well. There was a relative decline in the share of the Russian and Polish-born population in the total population of Latin areas of concentration between those years, as well as that of the non-Latin Whites 65 years of age and older. Only the Blacks actually increased their percentage, the result of a small Latin invasion of areas in which there were large concentrations of Blacks.

In 1950 the Latins were well integrated with other sub-populations of Miami, and it can be seen from Map 2a that their area of concentra-

Housing Segregation

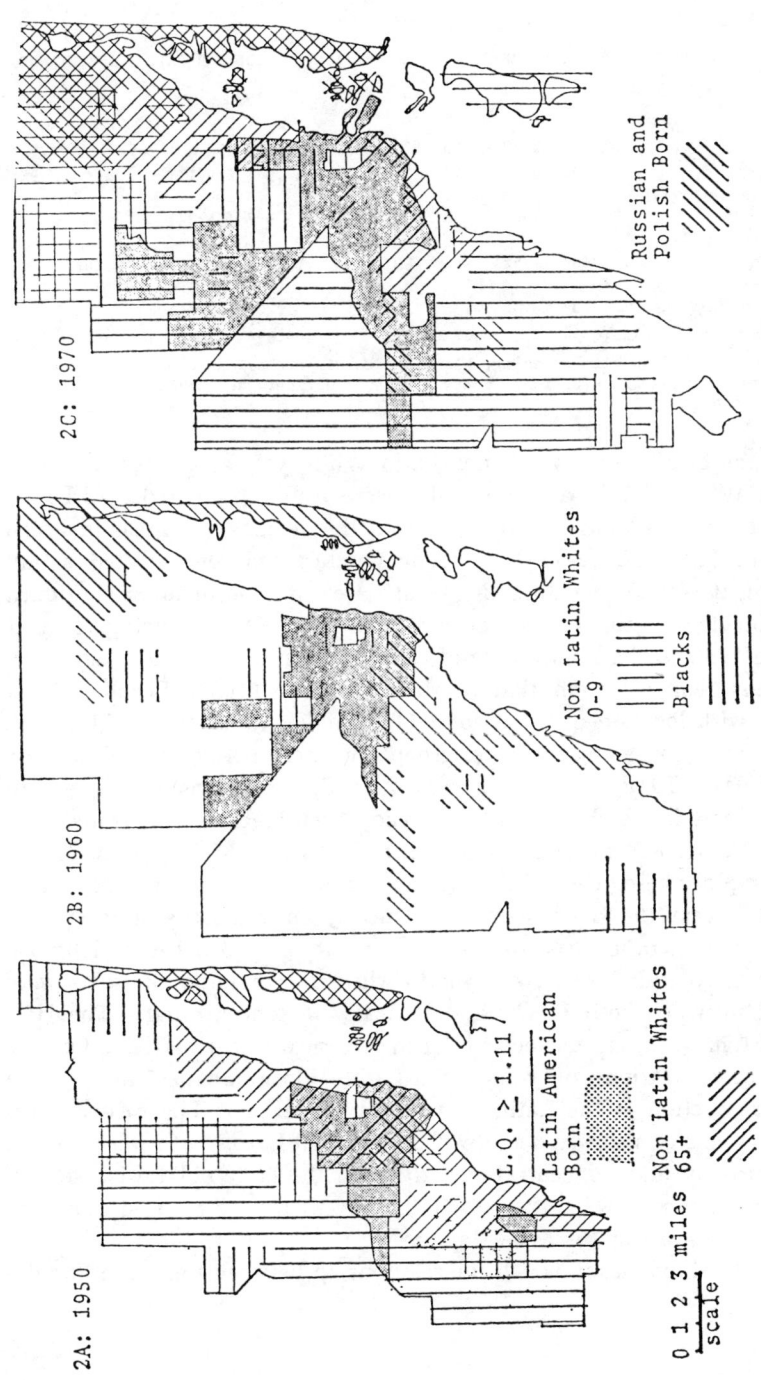

Map 2a-c. Changes in Concentration of Important Sub-Populations Within Miami, Florida, 1950-1970

Table 2

POPULATIONS WITHIN LATIN AREAS OF CONCENTRATION AND THEIR RELATIVE IMPORTANCE

Group	1950	1960	1970	1974[1]
Latin American Born	3,795 (2.8%)	35,567 (16.1%)	196,989 (48.5%)	299.516 (64.9%)
Black	528 (0.4%)	23,786 (10.7%)	36,946 (9.1%)	27,433 (5.9%)
Russian or Polish Born	3,512 (2.6%)	8,663 (3.9%)	5,392 (1.3%)	ND
Non-Latin Whites 0-9 years of age	16,768 (12.5%)	ND	10,131 (2.5%)	ND
Non-Latin Whites 65+ years of age	13,383 (10.0%)	ND	31,209 (7.7%)	ND
Total	133,904	221,403	406,494	461,360

1. Estimates of Spanish-speaking, black and total populations provided by the Community Analysis Division, County Manager's Office, Dade County
ND No Data

tion was also one in which non-Latin White young families, the non-Latin White elderly and Jews also were well represented. Although no data are available for 1960 to permit the definition of areas in which the non-Latin White aged or young families had concentrated within Miami, it can be seen that the Jewish area of concentration continued to coincide with that of the Latins in approximately the same place as it did in 1950. The largest area of concentration of this group, however, was far removed from that of the Latins on Miami Beach. Black tracts with location quotients of 1.11 or higher in 1960 coincided with those for Latins along the latter group's northern border, as well as near the CBD. Here, as previously mentioned, the Latins had begun to enter tracts in which Blacks had already been highly concentrated.

By 1970 the Latin areas of concentration within Metropolitan Miami were rapidly being cleared of concentrations of other groups (Map 2c). By that year the Latin section had nearly encircled the large area of Black concentration east of Hialeah, and it continued to be along the perimeter of this large Black ghetto where the majority of tracts were found in which both Blacks and Latins were concentrated. The Hialeah-Miami Springs nucleus of Latin Americans still had significantly high concentrations of young non-Latin White families, as did the western section of the Latin area of concentration. The western portion of the city also was one in which Jews and Latins both were present in unusually high concentrations, although the large old Jewish section immediately southwest of the CBD had by then been reduced in size to a small area along Biscayne Bay.

The final manner in which the relationship between the Latin population of Miami and other defined groups was explored was through use of the index of dissimilarity. Already it has been established that since 1950 the index has increased sharply between the Latin and the total non-Latin White population. It can be seen from Table 3 that since 1950 three of the four groups used in this study have also become increasingly more dissimilar to the Latin group. The one exception is the Blacks, who already had a high level of dissimilarity with the Latins in 1950, and since that date the index has fluctuated only slightly.

The Large Latin immigration into Miami has had a profound effect upon the interrelationship between non-Latin groups, although the degree cannot be established. Factors other than the movement of Latin Americans into the city have also been operative. Whatever the causes, neighborhood heterogeneity appears to have been markedly reduced since 1950, and there has been a geographical polarization of non-Latin groups within the city. This is particularly true of ethnic Jews, who have largely abandoned the southwestern and western portions of the inner city and have concentrated on Miami Beach and in northeastern Miami. Young non-Latin White families have become highly concentrated in the suburban southwestern and northwestern portions of the metropolitan area.

VI
CONCLUSION

THE MOST OBVIOUS CONCLUSION one can draw from this study is that since 1950 the Latin American community of Miami has grown so rapidly in population that it has dramatically affected the residential space of other groups within the city. The rapid economic assimilation of Latins, in addition to zoning regulations which prevented excessively high densities of population within the inner city, has meant the Latin minority has quickly spread throughout the older middle class residential areas of the city. As older residents of these neighborhoods moved out, different population sub-groups tended to resettle in discrete sections of the city. Since 1950 there not only has been an increased segregation of Latins from the rest of the population, but major sub-groups are now more separated from each other. Due to so large a Latin community forming in Miami there appears to be population polarization on a larger scale. Many non-Latin White immigrants to South Florida are rejecting Dade County, and seek homes in the two counties to the north (Broward and Palm Beach) (14). The decrease in the importance of

Table 3

DISSIMILARITY INDEXES FOR MIAMI[1] 1950, 1960 and 1970

Group Year	Latin American Born	Black	Born in Russia and Poland	Non-Latin Whites[2] 0-9 Years of Age	Non-Latin Whites[2] 65+ Years of Age	Total
	50 60 70	50 60 70	50 60 70	50 60 70	50 60 70	50 60 70
Latin American Born	x	87 81 86	55 58 72	36 49 60	28 41 55	34 37 41
Black		x	93 94 94	78 89 85	86 91 88	72 76 72
Born in Russia or Poland			x	36 55 81	46 36 78	54 49 57
Non-Latin Whites 0-9 Years of Age				x	31 45 55	20 25 36
Non-Latin Whites 65+ Years of Age					x	31 33 39
Total						x

1. 1950= 77 tracts, 1960= 177 tracts, 1970= 210 tracts
2. Non-Latin in 1970, Primarily Non-Latin in 1950, Numerous Latins included in 1960.

the non-Latin in-migration into Miami indirectly contributes to the growth in relative importance of the Latins within the metropolitan area.

Latin America today is the cultural area of the world which sends the largest number of immigrants to the United States, and it will continue to do so for the foreseeable future. Many Latin immigrants will choose to come to Miami, where they will join a community which already has a natural increase higher than any other major White group in the city. If present trends continue Miami will become increasingly geographically compartmentalized into a menage of different ethnic, racial and family-cycle groups, and not conform to the idealized, though not necessarily appropriate model of the American city, of being a cultural melting pot.

Florida State University
Tallahassee, Fla. 32306

1. An early and important inquiry into this question was made by F. Peirce Eichelberger, *The Cubans in Miami: Residential Movement and Ethnic Group Differentiation* (unpublished thesis, Department of Geography, University of Cincinnati, 1974).
2. A work which discusses the rapid economic assimilation of Cubans within Miami is A. J. Jaffe, Ruth M. Cullen and Thomas D. Boswell, *Spanish Americans in the United States: Changing Demographic Characteristics* (New York: Arno Press, in press). See Chap. 8, "The Cuban Americans."
3. Unless otherwise noted, the city is here defined as Metropolitan Miami. In 1950 this was a portion of Dade County; in 1960, 1970 and 1974 it included the entire county.
4. R. L. Johnston, *Urban Residential Patterns: An Introductory Review* (New York: Praeger Publishing Co., 1971), p. 243.
5. Estimates of the Jewish population of Dade County are available for a number of years from annual editions of the *Yearbook, American Jewish Committee* (Philadelphia: Jewish Publication Board).
6. Data obtained from the unpublished report *Ethnic Breakdown by Census Tract, April 1, 1970 and January 1, 1974* (Miami, Fla.: Community Analysis Division, County Manager's Office, 1976).
7. U.S. Department of Agriculture, Economic Research Service, *Net Migration of the Population 1950–60 by Age, Sex and Color* and a more recent publication of the same agency entitled *Net Migration of the Population 1960–1970 by Age, Sex and Color*.
8. It was possible to calculate that 57 percent of the county's foreign-born population which could not be identified by country of birth were from Latin America. This percentage of each tract's unidentified foreign population served as the figure for the remainder of its Latin American-born population, and was added to its Puerto Rican and Mexican populations.
9. Support for the use of the Russian-born as surrogates for Jews is offered by Erich Rosenthal in "The Equivalence of United States Census Data for Persons of Russian Stock or Descent with American Jews," *Demography*, Vol. 12 (1975), pp. 275–99.
10. It is acknowledged that a person could be both of Russian or Polish birth as well as belong to one of the family-cycle categories. Actually, a large percentage of people born in Russia or Poland living within Miami are 65 years of age or older.

11. For a full explanation of the location quotient and an interesting use by a geographer see Trevor R. Lee, *Race and Residence: The Concentration and Dispersal of Immigrants in London* (New York: Oxford Univ. Press, 1977).

12. This technique was used to define the diffusion of West Indian Blacks within London between 1961 and 1971. *Ibid*, p. 80.

13. O. D. Duncan and B. Duncan, "A Methodological Analysis of Segregation Indexes," *American Sociological Review*, Vol. 20 (1955), pp. 210–17.

14. Although there are no data to prove it, there is widespread belief among Miamians that many long-time non-Latin White residents are abandoning the city, principally to relocate in Broward or Palm Beach counties, but also places as far as the west coast of Florida and the Cape Canaveral area.

The Voting Rights Act and Hispanic Political Representation in the Southwest

John A. Garcia
University of Arizona

Extensions of the Voting Rights Act (VRA) in 1970 and 1975 expanded coverage to the southwestern United States and included provisions for non-English speaking minorities. In the South, the VRA had the effect of increasing the number of black voters and elected officials. In this article, we examine the changes in numbers of Mexican American and other Hispanic elected officials in the five southwestern states for federal, state, and local offices during the eleven-year period of 1973-1984. Gains occurred during the period, although they were uneven across the states and for different types of offices. The VRA served to remove the more blatant obstacles to electoral participation, but the law's fullest impact has also required effective political mobilization by Hispanic organizations to increase voter registration and produce a conducive environment for Hispanics to seek and win elective positions.

The Voting Rights Act (VRA) of 1965 and its subsequent extensions were intended to eliminate discrimination in voting. Originally, the scope and focus of the act dealt with black citizens in the South. Ten years after the VRA, noticeable effects were discernible, especially increased levels of voter registration among blacks and gains in the number of black officeholders.[1] Extensions of the VRA in 1970 and 1975 expanded coverage to parts of the Southwest and to non-English speaking minorities. A key question, then, is whether the VRA has had a comparable effect on Hispanic electoral participation and representation.

This article will examine the patterns of political representation for Hispanics in the southwestern United States from 1973 to 1984. Coverage of the VRA was extended to parts of the Southwest (primarily Texas and Arizona) in 1970. The inclusion of bilingual provisions in the act also widened its coverage in California and Arizona. Coverage is "triggered" where levels of voter turnout are less than 50 percent for minority groups for presidential

AUTHOR'S NOTE: Partial support for this endeavor was made possible by a grant from the Mexican American Legal Defense Fund. Janice K. Tulloss served as research assistant on this project, particularly with the compilation of officeholders' lists. In addition, I also wish to acknowledge my colleagues, Fernando Padilla (Washington State University); Charles Cotrell (St. Mary's University); Arturo Martinez (Western New Mexico University); and Harry Pachon (Executive Director of the National Association of Latino Elected Officials) for sharing their documents on Hispanic elected and appointed officials.
[1] U.S. Commission on Civil Rights, *The Voting Rights Act: Ten Years Later* (Washington, D.C.: U.S. Government Printing Office, 1975).

elections and/or where literacy tests have been used in the past.

Additional bilingual provisions and "triggers" for their coverage of non-English speaking minorities have specific effects on Spanish-origin citizens. Their presence in a political jurisdiction (at a level of 5 percent or more of the population) requires officials to make available bilingual materials and personnel to assist in the electoral process. This provision is intended primarily to enable minority citizens to gain access to the political process and to the influence that can come from greater participation.

A series of assumptions underlies the VRA's provisions. We will identify four major assumptions. 1) Historical patterns of discrimination against minority populations have minimized their levels of political participation. These barriers have included the poll tax, literacy tests, annual registration, and political and economic intimidation. 2) Direct federal action to monitor all phases of the electoral process will reduce or eliminate such barriers to participation. In particular, the provisions for preclearance of election-related changes by the U.S. Department of Justice should remove structural conditions that limit participation. 3) Opening the electoral process will result in significant gains in minority voter registrants and, subsequently, voter turnout. 4) Finally, with more eligible voters, there will be more members of minority groups running for elective office, winning political office, and influencing the political outcomes of decisionmaking bodies.

VRA AND BLACK PARTICIPATION IN THE SOUTH

Noticeable impacts of the VRA for blacks in the South have been major gains in numbers of registered voters and public officeholders. An increase of 100 percent occurred between 1960 and 1975 in the percentage of black voters registered in the South (i.e., 29 percent to 59 percent).[2] The black vote has become important, especially in presidential elections, in part, because it is concentrated in major urban states. The level of black voter turnout in the 1980 presidential election was about 61.3 percent, with the vast majority of black voters supporting Democratic candidates.[3]

With more black voters, a similar gain in the number of black elected officials was evident. Attempts to assess gains since enactment of the VRA have been difficult, however, because systematic and reliable information on black elected officials did not become available until the late 1960s. It is estimated that before the VRA, only about 100 blacks held elective office in the South.[4] Another source reported 280 black elected officials (6 congressmen,

---

[2] James Coyners and Walter Wallace, *Black Elected Officials* (New York: Russell Sage Foundation, 1975).

[3] Eddie N. Williams, "Black Political Progress in the 1970's: The Electoral Arena," *The New Black Politics*, eds. M. Preston, L. Henderson, and P. Punyear (New York: Longman, 1982), pp. 73-108.

[4] U.S. Commission on Civil Rights, *Political Participation* (Washington, D.C.: U.S. Government Printing Office, 1968).

90 state legislators, and 184 state/local officials) in 1964.[5]

Since 1970, the Joint Center for Political Studies has collected data on black elected officials.[6] Their number had increased to 2,991 by 1974. By 1980, the number of black elected officials came to 4,912, with one-fourth of them being members of education boards. Yet, despite significant absolute increases, blacks still represent only about 0.6 percent of all elected officials in the United States. Clearly, a "loosening up" of the political system has occurred, but blacks have had great difficulty winning statewide offices. Their most substantial gains have been made in winning local offices.

One-half of all the black state legislators in the South are found in Alabama and Georgia. However, they are found predominantly in the state house of representatives rather than in the state senate. Local offices have been won primarily in small communities, areas of significant black concentration, and central cities. The presence of single-member districts has been a positive structural factor making elected positions more accessible to minorities. Despite limited relative gains, a black presence in more political institutions has resulted, along with greater citizen participation in the political system. Increased political representation has facilitated greater issue articulation and agenda building for black Americans.

HISPANICS AND THE VRA

Data on voter registration of Mexican Americans, Puerto Ricans, and native Americans still remain scarce. Another provision of the VRA instructs the Bureau of the Census to estimate levels of voter registration and turnout in national elections. The Bureau's 1972 survey found that 46.0 percent of Mexican Americans and 52.7 percent of Puerto Ricans were registered to vote. By 1980, the level of Mexican Americans and Puerto Ricans registered to vote was 51 percent and 57 percent respectively.

Additional factors more specific to Hispanics and their voting participation involve language, nativity, and nationality diversity. The persistence of Spanish as a primary or secondary language, as well as minority status, has created problems of access to the political process. Levels of voter registration are also affected significantly by the presence of substantial numbers of foreign-born Hispanic persons. It is estimated that 30 percent of the Hispanic population is foreign-born. For the Mexican, Cuban, and Central and South American populations, foreign birth requires an additional step to secure voting rights—naturalization. Low rates of naturalization, especially among the Mexican-origin population,[7] reduces the eligible voting population. Finally, the Hispanic population encompasses a wide range of nationality

---

[5]A. Pinckney, *Black Americans* (Englewood Cliffs, N.J.: Prentice-Hall, 1969).
[6]Joint Center for Political Studies, *National Roster of Black Elected Officials*, vol. 1 (Washington, D.C.: Joint Center for Political Studies, 1971).
[7]John A. Garcia, "Political Integration of Mexican Immigrants: Explanations into the Naturalization Process," *International Migration Review* 15 (1981): 608-625.

TABLE 1
Change in Number of Black Elected Officials by Category of Office, 1970-1985

Year	Total black elected officials		Federal		State		Substate/regional		County		Municipal		Judicial/law enforcement		Education	
	N	% Change	N	% Change	N	% Change	N	% Change	N	% Change	N	% Change	N	% Change	N	% Change
1970	1,469	—	10	—	169	—	—	—	92	—	623	—	213	—	362	—
1971	1,860	26.6	14	40.0	202	19.5	—	—	120	30.4	785	26.0	274	28.6	465	28.5
1972	2,264	21.7	14	0.0	210	4.0	—	—	176	46.7	932	18.7	263	-4.0	669	43.9
1973	2,621	15.8	16	14.3	240	14.3	—	—	211	19.9	1,053	13.0	334	27.0	767	14.6
1974	2,991	14.1	17	6.3	239	-0.4	—	—	247	14.7	1,360	29.2	341	1.8	703	3.4
1975	3,508	13.1	18	5.9	281	17.6	—	—	305	26.0	1,573	15.7	387	13.0	939	18.4
1976	3,973	13.6	18	0.0	281	0.0	30	—	355	16.4	1,889	20.1	412	6.5	994	5.9
1977	4,311	8.3	17	-5.6	299	6.4	33	10.0	381	7.3	2,083	10.3	447	8.5	1,051	5.7
1978	4,503	4.5	17	0.0	299	0.0	26	-21.2	410	7.6	2,159	3.6	454	1.6	1,138	8.3
1979	4,607	2.3	17	0.0	313	4.7	25	-3.8	398	-2.9	2,224	3.0	486	7.0	1,144	0.5
1980	4,912	6.6	17	0.0	323	3.2	25	0.0	451	13.3	2,356	5.9	526	8.2	1,214	6.1
1981	5,038	2.6	18	5.9	341	5.6	30	20.0	449	-0.4	2,384	1.2	549	4.4	1,267	4.4
1982	5,160	2.4	18	0.0	336	-1.5	35	16.7	465	3.6	2,477	3.4	563	2.6	1,266	-0.1
1983	5,606	8.6	21	16.7	379	12.8	29	-17.1	496	6.7	2,697	10.0	607	7.8	1,377	8.8
1984[a]	5,700	1.7	21	0.0	389	2.6	30	3.4	518	4.4	2,735	1.4	636	4.8	1,371	-0.4
1985	6,056	6.2	20	-4.8	396	1.8	32	6.7	553	18.0	2,898	6.0	661	4.0	1,438	4.9

SOURCE: Joint Center for Political Studies, *Black Elected Officials: A National Roster*, New York, UNIPUB, 1985.
[a]The 1984 figures reflect blacks who took office during the seven-month period between 1 July 1983 and 30 January 1984.

groups (e.g., Mexicans, Cubans, Puerto Ricans, El Salvadorans). These different nationalities represent a wide range of political socialization experiences.

Only a few systematic examinations of Mexican American officeholders have been conducted. The U.S. Commission on Civil Rights and its state advisory commissions have been more active than academics in tracking minority officeholders. For example, the Texas Advisory Committee examined the state of civil rights in Texas (1968-1978) in the areas of employment, education, political representation, and judicial administration.[8] This report highlighted an extensive history of legal barriers to effective participation and representation for Mexican Americans, blacks, and women. Although minorities constitute over 30 percent of the state's population, levels of political representation are significantly lower than that percentage. Within the executive branch, no minority person was elected to any office during the 1968-1978 period.[9] Some slight gains were made in the state legislature, but real gains took place with the change to single-member districts in the mid-1970s. Nineteen Mexican American legislators served in the state house out of a total membership of 150 in 1978. Consistently less than 3 percent of the officeholders at all levels of political office have been Mexican Americans. Some slightly higher percentages exist for justices of the peace and judges on county commissioners' courts.

Despite some increases (primarily in local officeholding), there has been little change in political representation in Texas since 1978. Charles Cotrell's study of political participation in Texas concluded that changes in political representation were tied to single-member districts and a heightened sense of group pride and identity. The political culture of the state is still not conducive to full and effective political participation for Hispanics.

Texas is second only to New Mexico in number of elected officials in the Southwest. Significant factors for Texas are the large Mexican American population, the greater number of counties and municipalities, and the regional concentration of Mexican Americans. Fifty-two percent of the population of South Texas is of Mexican origin, as is 31.4 percent of West Texas. The concentration of Mexican Americans in these regions helps to account for a good percentage of Mexican American elected officials. Before-and-after changes in the number of Mexican American elected officials have been difficult to assess, however, because there is no comprehensive listing of Mexican American officials prior to 1970. In addition, more visible elected offices (i.e., U.S. congressperson, governor) have received better accounting than other offices.

---

[8]Charles Cotrell, *Status of Civil Rights: Report on Participation of Mexican Americans, Blacks and Females in Political Institutions and Processes in Texas, 1968-1978*, vol. 1 (Washington, D.C.: U.S. Government Printing Office, 1980).

[9]Ibid., pp. 110-125.

DATA SOURCES

Despite problems in collecting reliable data on Hispanic elected officials, we have attempted to compile such a longitudinal summary for all five southwestern states (Arizona, California, Colorado, New Mexico, and Texas). These states represent the region with the largest concentration of Mexican-origin population. These states have also been partially or entirely covered by the VRA. Since no one organization, agency, or individual compiles complete information on all Mexican American and other Hispanic elected officials, our compilation utilizes eight different sources of information to develop a chronological profile of Hispanic political representation.

The only general pre-1975 listing of Spanish-surnamed officials is that based on Frank Lemus' work. Data for subsequent years were obtained from Arturo Martinez's *Who's Who: Chicano Officeholders*.[10] Martinez has published biannual directories of Mexican American officeholders since 1975-1976. A 1982-1983 directory was published in December 1983. Another source is a preliminary directory of Spanish-surnamed elected officials for southwestern states (1974-1979) compiled by the Southwest Voter Registration and Education Project (SWVREP) in San Antonio.

Five additional sources of data were utilized as well. Fernando Padilla has done extensive longitudinal studies (covering 1900-1978) of Mexican American political representation in southwestern state legislatures. Cotrell's study of the political representation of Mexican Americans, blacks, and women in Texas provides extensive information for this state for all elected and appointed offices.[11] The information on local elected officials is particularly valuable. Another source is the *1981 National Directory of Hispanic Elected and Appointed Officials* compiled by the Congressional Hispanic Caucus. Again, the information here is most complete for federal and state officeholders. The *Official Roster of State Officials of New Mexico, 1981-1982* compiled by the Secretary of State is an additional data source. Finally, the most recent information is provided by the *National Roster of Hispanic Elected Officials* compiled by the National Association of Latino Elected Officials (NALEO). This represents the first comprehensive effort to identify Hispanic elected officials throughout the U.S. and for all public offices. The first roster was produced in 1985.

Obviously, drawing upon as many sources as possible is both an asset and a problem. Several lists cover the same time periods, resulting in some discrepancies as to the number of Hispanic elected officials by position in particular years. These discrepancies are more noticeable for county and municipal officeholders. For the following tables, some lists were combined or listed separately. Where discrepancies exist as to the number of elected

---

[10]Arturo Martinez, *Who's Who: Chicano Officeholders 1975-1976* (Silver City, N.M., 1976); Arturo Martinez, *Who's Who: Chicano Officeholders 1977-1978* (Silver City, N.M., 1978); and Arturo Martinez, *Who's Who: Chicano Officeholders 1979-1980* (Silver City, N.M., 1980).

[11]Cotrell, *Status of Civil Rights*.

officials for any given year, contacts with knowledgeable informants in the state were made to reach a correct or best approximate determination of Mexican American officeholders.

MEXICAN AMERICAN ELECTED OFFICIALS: FEDERAL AND STATE

The paucity of systematic and reliable information on Mexican American officials has influenced our decision to limit the scope of this study to elected officials and certain public offices. We begin with 1973 because it is the earliest starting point available, and it predates the period of post-1975 VRA coverage. The provisions for bilingual assistance and expanded coverage in the Southwest mark a good point from which to examine the possible effects of the VRA on Mexican American political representation.

Our initial focus will be on the number of federal and state Hispanic elected officials. For Arizona, as will be seen for almost all of the other states, representation in federal offices is very small. In Arizona, no Hispanic has served in the U.S. House or Senate. This state added a congressional district in 1982 because of reapportionment. There have been ongoing political discussions about the possibility of creating a district with a major concentration of Hispanic voters; however, the immediate prospects of electing an Hispanic representative to the Congress are not very promising.[12]

Two Hispanics have served in state executive offices. One served a term as governor (Raul Castro, 1974-1978); the other served as a corporation commissioner in 1973. Since 1978, no Hispanic has served in a state executive office. Representation in the Arizona legislature hardly changed at all during 1973-1984. On the other hand, Hispanics represented 16.2 percent of the 1980 state population, and 11.6 and 16.7 percent, respectively, of the House and Senate seats in 1982. Slight percentage gains have been made in the Senate, but a disproportionate number of representatives come from predominantly minority legislative districts. Although information is scarce, low penetration of judgeships and district attorney offices is quite evident until 1984. Overall gains and losses for all state offices have—with the exception of judgeships and district attorney positions—resulted in an essentially unchanged situation over the eight-year period.

The track record for state and federal officeholding in California has not been very promising for Hispanics. In 1980 Hispanics comprised 20 percent of the state's population. These Hispanics, in excess of 4.5 million, represent the greatest number in any single state. One U.S. Congressman (Edward Roybal) has been a member of the California delegation since the late 1960s. As did Arizona, California received two more congressional seats due to reapportionment; this resulted in two more Hispanic congressmen being

---

[12]John A. Garcia, "Reapportionment in the Eighties: The Case of Arizona and Chicanos," *The Hispanic Community and Redistricting*, vol. 2, ed. R. Santillan (Claremont, Cal.: Rose Institute of State and Local Government, 1984).

TABLE 2
Number of Federal Hispanic Elected Officials in the Southwestern States, 1973-1984

	1973[a]	1975-1976[b]	1977-1978[c]	1979-1980[d]	1979-1980[e]	1981[f]	1984[g]
Senators							
Arizona	0	0	0	0	0	0	0
California	0	0	0	0	0	0	0
Colorado	0	0	0	0	0	0	0
New Mexico	1	1	0	0	0	0	0
Texas	0	0	0	0	0	0	0
Representatives							
Arizona	0	0	0	0	0	0	0
California	1	1	1	1	1	1	3
Colorado	0	0	0	0	0	0	0
New Mexico	1	1	1	1	1	1	2
Texas	2	2	2	2	2	2	4

SOURCES:
[a] Frank C. Lamus, "National Roster of Spanish Surnamed Elected Officials, 1973," *Aztlan* 5 (nos. 1 and 2).
[b] Arthur D. Martinez, *Who's Who: Chicano Officeholders 1975-1976* (Silver City, N.M.: P.O. Box 2271, 1976).
[c] Ibid., 1977-1978.
[d] Ibid., 1979-1980.
[e] Annette A. Avina, *Preliminary Directory of Spanish Surnamed Elected Officials For Southwest States* (Southwest Voter Registration Education Project, San Antonio, Texas).
[f] Congressional Hispanic Caucus (House Annex II), *1981 National Directory of Hispanic Elected and Appointed Officials* (Washington, D.C.).
[g] National Association of Latino Elected Officials (NALC), *1984 National Roster of Hispanic Elected Officials* (Washington, D.C.).

elected in 1982. Some gains have been made in the state legislature (80 House seats and 40 Senate seats) since 1975. There were three Hispanic senators (7.5 percent of the Senate) and four representatives (5.0 percent of the House) in 1984. California does differ from three of the other southwestern states in having lower numbers of state judges, with the number declining since 1973. Thus, Hispanic political representation in California has increased slightly in the U.S. House but remained virtually unchanged for state offices. The change in congressional representation was directly related to reapportionment in 1981-1982.[13]

An almost identical situation exists for Mexican Americans in Colorado. Hispanics constitute about 11.7 percent of the state's population. No Hispanic has served in the U.S. Congress from Colorado, nor did any Hispanic serve in a state executive position during 1973-1984. One area of note since 1975

---
[13] Richard Santillan, ed., *The Hispanic Community and Redistricting*, vol. 2 (Claremont, Cal.: Rose Institute of State and Local Government, 1984).

has been in the state legislature, which has 35 senators and 65 representatives. The number of Hispanic legislators reached a high of nine in 1979-1981, but declined to six in 1984. Information is so scarce on state judges and district attorneys that it is difficult to make any assessment of Hispanic penetration of these offices. Thus modest gains appear to have been made by Hispanics only in the legislature.

New Mexico is one state where higher rates of political participation and substantial numbers of Hispanic elected officials have been something of a political tradition. During this time period (1973-1984), New Mexico was the only Southwest state with a Hispanic senator (Montoya) who retired from the Senate in 1976. Since 1972, Martin Lujan has served as a congressman from New Mexico. New Mexico also received one more congressional district with reapportionment, the outcome of which was the 1982 election of Bill Richardson, a Hispanic. As for state offices, a Hispanic served as governor and lieutenant governor during this period. Lt. Governor Roberto Mondragon held office in 1978-1982. Toney Anaya was elected governor in 1982. Currently, three Hispanics serve in state executive offices as auditor, commissioner of public lands, and corporation commissioner. Thus, except for 1979-1980, Hispanics did hold a few executive positions during 1973-1984.

Hispanics comprised 36.6 percent of New Mexico's population in 1980. In the state legislature, there has been no significant change in Hispanic representation since 1973. Currently, there are ten Hispanic state senators (23.8 percent) and twenty-two state representatives (30 percent). This represents some decline for Hispanics in the Senate and a rather steady level of representation in the House. New Mexico, like most of the southwestern states, has experienced significant interregional migration. This in-migration has been selective socioeconomically and racially, with many professional, higher-educated Anglos moving into the Sunbelt states.[14] One possible reason for the decline of Hispanic representatives is some dilution of the Hispanic population and an altering of the state's political culture and tradition. New Mexico continues to have the greatest number of Hispanic federal and state elected officials of any of the southwestern states, but that number has not increased significantly in recent years.

Hispanics comprise about 21 percent of the population of Texas, and have gained three new congressional districts due to reapportionment in 1982. As a result, two more Hispanics have joined the Texas congressional delegation. Hispanics have had the same two congressmen (Henry Gonzalez and Eligio "Kiki" de la Garza) since the late 1960s. A new Hispanic congressman, Solomon Ortiz, was elected in 1982. Hence, the five southwestern states picked up *eight* new congressional seats after 1980, which resulted in *four* new Hispanic representatives being elected to the Congress. In 1984, another Hispanic (the fifth since 1982) was elected to the U.S. House of Representatives from south central Texas.

[14]John A. Garcia, "Hispanic Migration: Where Are They Moving and Why," *Agenda* 11 (1981).

TABLE 3
Number of State Hispanic Elected Officials in the Southwestern States, 1973-1984

States and offices	1973[a]	1975-1976[b]	1977-1978[c]	1979-1980[d]	1979-1980[e]	1981[f]	1984[g]
Arizona							
Governor/Lt. Governor	0	1	1	0	0	0	0
Other State Executive	1	0	0	0	0	0	0
State Legislature	11	10	10	10	11	12	11
Judges/District Attorney	1	1	1	5	—	—	26
California							
Governor/Lt. Governor	0	0	0	0	0	0	0
Other State Executive	0	0	0	0	0	0	0
State Legislature	5	7	8	8	9	7	7
Judges/District Attorney	13	8	9	9	—	—	12
Colorado							
Governor/Lt. Governor	0	0	0	0	0	0	0
Other State Executive	0	0	0	0	0	0	0
State Legislature	4	6	7	8	9	9	6
Judges/District Attorney	1	1	1	1	—	—	6
New Mexico							
Governor/Lt. Governor	1	1	1	1	1	1	1
Other State Executive	1	2	2	0	3	3	5
State Legislature	33	29	32	30	32	31	32
Judges/District Attorney	11	15	18	17	—	5	—
Texas							
Governor/Lt. Governor	0	0	0	0	0	0	0
Other State Executive	0	0	2	0	0	0	0
State Legislature	14	15	19	21	22	21	25
Judges/District Attorney	3	12	16	24	—	—	—

SOURCES: Same as Table 2.

As mentioned previously, Hispanics in Texas have not enjoyed much success in statewide executive offices.[15] Only two Hispanics served in any state executive office during 1973-1984. Slight increases have been made by Hispanics in the Texas legislature, however, more so than in the other four states. The legislature has 31 senators and 150 representatives. In 1983-1984 there were twenty-four Hispanic legislators, four in the Senate (12.9 percent) and twenty in the House (11.3 percent). This represents modest gains in both the House and Senate since 1973, and especially since 1975. A similar pattern appears to be occurring for judges, although information is limited. Conversions to single-member districts incurred by litigation proved to be a major contributing factor in opening more offices for Hispanics. At the same time, the VRA enabled Mexican American organizations to utilize "legal handles" to raise issues of equal protection for Hispanics in specific political jurisdictions. Despite these noticeable gains, as in most of the southwestern states, the gains in an absolute sense were still small.

LOCAL GOVERNMENT OFFICIALS

The other offices to be examined are those of counties and municipalities where the possibilities for successful office attainment can often be greater because of smaller geographic jurisdictions and substantial concentrations of Mexican American voters. However, one difficulty in assessing changes in local political representation lies in the scarcity of information about local officeholding. Table 4 presents the available data on county and municipal officials for Arizona, California, and Colorado. Major gaps exist in the data. The available data suggest that Hispanic representation in county positions has remained relatively constant in Arizona and Colorado, though with slight gains in judgeship positions. In California, county office representation appears to have increased significantly since 1978, this increase being accounted for primarily by the substantial gain in the number of Hispanic judges. Overall, however, except for county judges in California, there has not been a marked increase in the number of Hispanic county officials in these three states.

For all practical purposes, the only information available for local officials is for mayors and councilmembers. Data on Hispanic school board members have been more difficult to find; yet this area has been a major policy concern for most Hispanics. The most recent NALEO survey of Hispanic elected officials shows some dramatic increases in local officeholding. In Arizona and California, the number of Hispanic local officeholders more than doubled from 1979 to 1984. The most dramatic gains have clearly occurred in school board memberships. However, these gains are due partly to better data collection in 1984. Thus, while there have been gains in local officeholding, it is impossible to calculate the real rate of increase. The number of Hispanic

---

[15]U.S. Commission on Civil Rights, *Texas: State of Civil Rights Ten Years Later, 1968-1978* (Washington, D.C.: U.S. Government Printing Office, 1980).

TABLE 4
Number of City and County Hispanic Elected Officials in Arizona, California, and Colorado, 1973-1984

	Commissioners	Other county officials	Judges	Total county	Council-persons	Mayors	School board members	Total city
Arizona								
1973	8	4	0	12	46	9	2	57
1975-1976	7	3	0	10	—	—	—	—
1977-1978	6	7	3	16	—	—	—	—
1979-1980	7	7	3	17	68	9	—	77
1979-1980	—	—	—	—			—	
1984	—	—	—	13	107[a]		84	191
California								
1973	9	0	0	9	98	23	53	174
1975-1976	11	7	7	25	—	—	—	—
1977-1978	8	10	3	21	—	—	—	—
1979-1980	11	10	42	63	95	16	—	111
1979-1980	—	—	—	—			—	
1984	—	—	52	60	168[a]		222	390
Colorado								
1973	7	17	1	25	77	10	2	89
1975-1976	9	13	3	25	—	—	—	—
1977-1978	12	13	3	28	—	—	—	—
1979-1980	11	14	6	31	78	7	—	85
1979-1980	—	—	—	—			—	
1984	—	—	—	25	82[a]		56	138

SOURCES: Same as Table 2.
[a] In 1984, no distinction was made between councilpersons and mayors; this figure represents city officials.

mayors in California has actually decreased; while in Colorado it has remained nearly the same. The more noteworthy addition to the mayoral ranks in Colorado was the 1984 election of Frederico Pena as mayor of Denver. In Arizona, an increase of 47.8 percent can be noted among Hispanic councilmembers, particularly in small communities. The number of Hispanic mayors has stayed the same. Political representation in local government bodies in these states does indicate greater numbers of Hispanic officeholders, but most gains have occurred in municipal offices since 1975.

Data on local officials in New Mexico and Texas are more complete and cover a greater number of years. Still, major gaps exist for school board offices and intervening years (1975-1978) for city officeholders in New Mexico. In New Mexico, the number of Hispanic county commissioners has declined since 1973, almost by 33 percent. Texas, on the other hand, shows a slight gain in numbers of Hispanic county commissioners. Almost 19 percent more Hispanics hold this position, primarily in southern and western Texas, than was the case in 1973. Overall, there has been a decline in the number of Hispanic county officials in New Mexico and a slight increase in Texas.

The number of Hispanic councilmembers and mayors in New Mexico appears to have increased slightly since 1973, while significant gains have occurred in Texas. A 44 percent increase in Hispanic councilpersons occurred in Texas between 1973 and 1980, though again, there have been subregional variations, with more gains occurring in south, west, and central Texas. For Hispanic mayors, gains have been made in both states, with more dramatic ones occurring in Texas (an 88 percent increase between 1973 and 1980). The recent reelection of Henry Cisneros as mayor of San Antonio further enhances the political visibility of Hispanic officeholders. The pattern of gains is more strongly demonstrated for Hispanics serving on local school boards, where their numbers almost doubled from 1968 to 1978 in Texas. The possible effects of the VRA on gains in the number of Hispanic local officeholders is clearly more visible in Texas than in any other southwestern state. It must be pointed out, however, that the overall gain, in light of the total number of public offices available, is still a small percentage for Hispanic officeholders. Dramatic gains have been made, but they have not been made uniformly across all the southwestern states, nor for all types of public offices.

A crude measure of changes of political representation for Hispanics is to take the two end points for the time periods examined and note percentage changes. We have made these calculations for federal, state, county, and city offices. No Hispanics were elected to the Congress from Arizona and Colorado during 1973-1984. Hispanic representation from New Mexico remained constant. In California and Texas, though, Hispanics captured three and two more seats in each state respectively; however, these gains were due more to reapportionment and gained seats for these Sunbelt states than direct effects of the VRA.

Slight gains are evident for state officeholding, except in Colorado. Again,

TABLE 5
Number of City and County Hispanic Elected Officials in New Mexico and Texas, 1973-1984

	Commissioners	Other county officials	Judges	Total county	Council-persons	Mayors	School board members	Total city
New Mexico								
1973	40	54	11	105	122	21	0	143
1975-1976	36	51	26	113	—	—	—	—
1977-1978	39	54	28	121	—	—	—	—
1979-1980	31	55	30	116	116	27	—	143
1979-1980	25	—	—	25	—	—	—	—
1981[a]	27	55	—	82				
1984	—	—	—	85	167[b]		164	331
Texas								
1973	69	65	8	142	194	25	205	424
1974	72	50	14	136	216	31	308	555
1975-1976	83	49	19	151	—	—	—	—
1976	79	52	21	152	223	40	401	—
1977-1978	75	58	10	143	—	—	—	748
1978	76	61	25	162	247	36	405	—
1979-1980	80	66	11	157	—	—	—	—
1979-1980	82	72	—	154	279	47	—	326
1984	—	—	—	152	401[b]		555	956

SOURCES: Same as Table 2.
[a]*Roster of State of New Mexico, 1981-1982.*
[b]In 1984, no distinction was made between councilpersons and mayors; this figure represents city officials.

TABLE 6
Increases in Numbers of Hispanic Elected Officials in
Southwestern States by Office, 1973-1984

State	Number of Hispanics 1973	Number of Hispanics 1984	Change in number	Percent change
Arizona				
Federal	0	0	0	0.0
State	11	12	1	9.1
County	12	17	5	41.7
City[a]	55	107	52	94.5
California				
Federal	1	3	2	200.0
State	5	7	2	40.0
County	9	63	54	600.0
City[a]	121	168	47	38.8
Colorado				
Federal	0	0	0	0.0
State	7	6	-1	-14.3
County	25	31	6	24.0
City[a]	87	82	-5	-5.7
New Mexico				
Federal	2	2	0	0.0
State	33	37	4	12.1
County	94	85	-9	-9.5
City[a]	143	167	24	16.8
Texas				
Federal	2	4	2	100.0
State	12	21	9	75.0
County	134	152	18	13.4
City[a]	219	401	182	83.1

SOURCES: Same as Table 2.
[a]Includes only councilpersons and mayors.

Texas shows the greatest increase. For Arizona, one more state legislator was present in 1980 than in 1973. In California, there were two more Hispanic state legislators in 1984, which still represents only 5.83 percent of all state legislators. Colorado represents one of the states with the greatest gain in the state legislature. Four more Hispanics have been elected, doubling the percentage of their representation in the legislature, a 100 percent increase in the number of Mexican Americans. New Mexico, which has historically been the state with the greatest percentage of Hispanic officials, experienced some decline of Hispanic legislators. There are two fewer Hispanic legislators now than in 1973, representing a 6 percent decrease. Finally, Texas showed a net gain of eleven Mexican American legislators over the eleven-year period. They almost doubled their percentage in the state legislature (from 6.6 percent to 11.6 percent). Clearly, gains, though modest, in the state legislative bodies have been the pattern for Hispanics in the Southwest. Yet, in the case of New Mexico, Hispanics seem to be trying to hold on to the political representation they experienced in the past.

Local government has been the scene of substantial change in political representation for Hispanics. Consistently, Hispanics have gained in county positions held in all of the states, except New Mexico. The more dramatic changes have occurred in California, as 600 percent more Hispanics serve in county positions than in 1973. More modest increases are evident in Colorado, Arizona, and Texas. It should be noted that California started with a lower base than any other state in 1973, thus making Hispanic gains in that state more dramatic. New Mexico actually experienced a decline of 9.5 percent during this period. Again, it should be noted that the changes reflect only offices for which information was available for the time period.

Patterns of increases of Hispanic political representation in municipal offices are more varied. Arizona shows a substantial increase (94.5 percent). Municipal officeholders in Colorado and New Mexico have remained fairly constant. California has experienced an increase of 38.8 percent since 1973. Texas, on the other hand, has registered substantial gains in Hispanic municipal officeholding, with an 83.1 percent increase since 1973. One should be reminded that school board members are not figured in the local official totals due to insufficient data. Overall, changes in Hispanic political representation in local offices does suggest modest gains in most of the southwestern states. Yet the numbers of local offices are numerous, so that the overall percentage of Hispanic elected officials remains small.

THE VRA AND HISPANIC POLITICAL REPRESENTATION

One of the anticipated and demonstrated effects of the VRA has been the increase of minority elected officials in covered jurisdictions. Studies by the U.S. Commission on Civil Rights and the Joint Center for Political Studies have recorded the gains in black officeholding in the South. The gains have been substantial in an absolute sense, though very modest in a relative sense. Our effort in this article has been to explore the changes in Hispanic political representation in the Southwest. One premise that underlies this work is that the 1975 VRA marks a major time point for pre- and post-VRA experiences for Hispanics in the Southwest. Despite the limited systematic data, longitudinal patterns are discernible.

Progress in winning more elected federal offices was virtually nonexistent until 1982. Southwestern Hispanics held seats in the Congress, including one Senate seat, prior to the VRA. In 1984, though, there were nine Hispanics in the U.S. House, up from four in 1973. A timely factor in the future of any progress in congressional representation lies with periodic redistricting. Eight new congressional districts were added to the five southwestern states after the 1980 census, so that the redrawn district lines provided the opportunity for the election of four more Hispanics in the U.S. House of Representatives in 1982. Arizona has recently redrawn congressional districts, and the new district will include a sizable proportion (25-35 percent) of Mexican American residents. A Hispanic in South Texas won another congressional seat in 1984.

Progress in state officeholding has been restricted to legislative seats. Other than the one-term governorships of Raul Castro and Jerry Apodaca in the mid-1970s and current Governor Toney Anaya of New Mexico, very few Hispanics have been elected to state executive offices. In fact, New Mexico was the only state having Hispanic executive officials in 1984. Numerically and proportionately, there have been more Hispanic legislators in the Southwest since 1975 than before, though Texas accounts for nearly all of the gains since 1975. Even so, the overall proportion of Hispanic legislators is still relatively low.

The levels of political representation in local offices suggest noticeable gains in county and municipal positions, particularly in Arizona, California, and Texas. One major exception has been Hispanic political representation in New Mexico. Hispanics in that state have experienced a decline in the number of county officeholders, with only a slight increase in elected municipal officials. One primary contributing factor has been a recomposition of the socioeconomic and ethnic mix of New Mexico's population, as well as a changing political culture. The net result finds "Hispanos" in New Mexico trying to hold on to past levels of representation rather than being able to augment their representation in elected offices.

Since our focus has centered on changes in political representation among Hispanics in the Southwest, some other factors should be mentioned briefly. They include: 1) voter registration, 2) political climate, 3) data gathering processes, 4) political organizations, and 5) naturalization. The first and last factors are very much interrelated. It has been assumed that VRA coverage would be accompanied by major increases in voter registration among Hispanics. U.S. Bureau of the Census reports indicate very low levels of voter registration among Hispanics compared to blacks and Anglos. This pattern has not changed significantly (for the entire Southwest) over the past eight years. But in 1982 and 1984, such organizations as the Southwest Voter Registration and Education Project engaged in targeted voter registration campaigns in the Southwest and other states with many Hispanic residents. The net results were an estimated 800,000 newly registered Hispanic voters. Yet significant variation in levels of voter registration does exist between states and within subregions of each state. The intervention of political or community organizations in stimulating more registrants can have a major impact. With low rates of naturalization among Mexican-origin populations, the question of facilitating gains in this area is a major concern. So far, many minority organizations have felt that naturalization is a personal decision that does not need organizational push. It would seem that many Hispanic organizations are reevaluating this position and considering such organizational involvement.

Political climate refers to the institutional and socioeconomic practices in geographic areas of the Southwest. That is, an open political process should enable minorities to seize the legislative protections of the VRA to maximize gains in access and representation. Yet areas that have traditionally been more closed and/or repressive have been resistant to change. Feelings of group pride and identity, on the other hand, can serve as catalysts for heightened political consciousness and participation.[16] Therefore, the political milieu of a given area can significantly affect Hispanic political participation. It is assumed that gains in voter registration will translate into higher turnout and more candidacies for Hispanics. All these factors could lead to more elected officials and more policy decisions responsive to Mexican American interests.

CONCLUSION

Our primary interest has been to examine the importance of the Voting Rights Act in expanding electoral representation among Mexican Americans in the Southwest. Our analysis indicates that increases in political representation have occurred, most noticeably in local officeholding, especially city councils and school boards. It appears that the expanded coverage of the VRA into the Southwest (especially with its preclearance and bilingual provisions) removed the more "blatant" barriers to electoral participation. At the same time, other factors, particularly reapportionment, have played a role in helping to increase Hispanic political representation in the Southwest, thus making it difficult to distinguish the independent effects of the various factors. Nevertheless, it would appear that VRA protections have served as vehicles for Hispanics to push for changes in electoral structures (i.e., at-large to ward) and to mobilize organizationally for voter registration. Thus the impact of the VRA appears to have been a positive one for Hispanics, in part because Hispanic organizations and leaders capitalized on the protections and legal recourses provided by the VRA.

---

[16]John A. Garcia, "Ethnic Identification and Political Consciousness: Unraveling the Effects Among Chicanos" (Paper presented at the annual meeting of the Western Political Science Association, Denver, Colorado, 1981).

A NEW REMEDY FOR AN OLD AILMENT: CUMULATIVE VOTING AS AN ALTERNATIVE TO THE SINGLE MEMBER DISTRICT IN MINORITY VOTING RIGHTS

Maurilio E. Vigil[*]

"The 1980's witnessed a plethora of federal court lawsuits initiated by ethnic minority groups challenging discriminatory voting restrictions caused by at large voting systems in electing members of legislative bodies. Blacks, Hispanics and Native Americans have been among the aggrieved groups which have sought remedies through the courts. In New Mexico, various lawsuits were filed charging discrimination in the election of municipal councils, county commissions and school boards. Traditionally, the response of the courts in such cases where legitimate cause has been found, was to direct the establishment of single-member districts in lieu of the previous at-large methods. This is consistent with similar court decisions in other states. In 1985, to forestall similar lawsuits, the New Mexico Legislature passed a law requiring single member districts in all such governing bodies in New Mexico. Most municipalities complied with the new law. One community, Alamogordo, New Mexico, refused to alter its electoral system, claiming exemption due to its "home rule" status. In a direct challenge to Alamogordo, Hispanics filed a federal court case in 1988 seeking a court mandate to establish single member districts. In a unique precedent, the federal district judge accepted a compromise agreement which instituted a unique cumulative voting scheme instead of the single member district as a remedy to Alamogordo's at-large system. The cumulative voting system established a precedent for the United States in this type of case. The present paper investigates the background and circumstances that led to the litigation, discusses the perspectives of the litigants, explains the rationale for the acceptance of the agreement and assesses the effects for Hispanics, after the first election under the new plan.

Introduction

Since the passage of the Voting Rights Act (VRA) in 1965, much progress has been achieved in extending the suffrage to minority groups in American politics. Amendments to the VRA have altered the focus to electoral systems which were construed as denying minority access to the political process. Most notable has been the concerted attack on "at-large" or "multi-member" districts in denying minority representation.

The 1975 amendments to the VRA extended the provisions to language minorities and those of 1982 made it possible for a judge to redraw districts to

---

[*] All correspondence should be sent to: Professor Maurilio E. Vigil, Dept. of History and Political Science, New Mexico Highlands University, Las Vegas, NM 87701.

give minorities minimum representation [Grant and Omdahl, 1987].

Armed with these laws, organizations like the Mexican American Legal Defense and Education Fund (MALDEF), Southwest Voter Registration and Education Project (SVREP), and Texas Rural Legal Aid (TRLA) have litigated dozens of cases on behalf of Hispanics in Texas, New Mexico and California.

The well known premise on which these lawsuits are based is that, in communities with significant minority populations, at-large or multi-member district elections, tend to reduce the possibility of success of minority candidates. A number of studies have confirmed this proposition [Karnig, 1976; Karnig and Welch, 1978 and 1982; Engstrom and McDonald 1981 and 1986]. It has, moreover, been confirmed in before and after comparisons in communities which shifted from at-large to single-member districting schemes [Cotrell and Fleischman, 1979; Davidson and Korbel, 1981; Heileg and Mundt, 1980; and Grofman, Migalski and Noviello, 1986]. Most of these studies were done on Black or Black and other minority populations. Although the number of studies focusing on Hispanics are more limited, several have confirmed the proposition that Hispanic underrepresentation is related to the multi-member district and that underrepresentation declines when a single-member district system is adopted [Davidson and Korbel, 1981 and Polinard and Wrinkle, 1988].

In the number of cases so far litigated, the courts have generally found that use of multi-member districts are in violation of the Voting Rights Act on the basis of several conditions: if the minority population has exhibited cohesive voting behavior; if voting in the community is divided along racial lines; and if the minority population is compact and contiguous enough to form one district within the existing multi-member district if it were districted.

In virtually every successful challenge to "at-large" or "multi-member district" voting, the standard remedy has been for the court to order creation of single-member districts and to monitor the districting process to prevent discrimination against minorities. In 1987, however, in a little publicized case in Alamogordo, New Mexico, a federal district judge approved a settlement which allowed a unique method of cumulative voting to be used in electing city commissioners. The new scheme was approved in lieu of the creation of single-member districts. This paper will relate the events and circumstances leading to the court case, discuss the essence of the judge's decision, and analyze the immediate effects on the electoral process in Alamogordo resulting from the unique agreement.

Apportionment and Districting in New Mexico

New Mexico's entry into the thicket of districting problems occurred somewhat casually and belatedly. Because New Mexico has been the exception to the generally low levels of Hispanic voter participation and electoral involvement of other states, most public officials were unaware that serious problems of disenfranchisement of Hispanics existed here. Even Hispanic political leaders were cavalier in their assertions and denials that most of the provisions of the Voting Rights Act did not apply to New Mexico.

Thus it came as some surprise when various lawsuits began to appear in New Mexico in the early 1980's involving challenges to multi-member districts in city councils and school boards. One of the first lawsuits occurred in Portales, New Mexico, where two Mexican Americans challenged the at-large election system for electing the eight city council members who governed the city [*Albuquerque Journal*, October 21, 1983]. A second lawsuit filed by a Mexican American in Roswell charged similar discriminations in its at-large voting system [*Albuquerque Journal*, April 11, 1985].

The seriousness of the state's minority representation problem also became dramatically apparent during the state legislative reapportionment battles in 1982. The battle began when a special session of the New Mexico Legislature meeting in January issued its state legislative reapportionment plan. The Southwest Voter Registration and Education Project filed suit on January 22, 1982 (less that a week after the governor had signed the bill), charging that the reapportionment discriminated against Hispanics and Native Americans. At least five other lawsuits, including one from the U.S. Justice Department accompanied the initial lawsuit. On April 8, a federal district court panel rescinded the reapportionment because the "votes cast" formula that had been used to apportion the legislature created House districts that violated the "one person, one vote" principle that had long been a standard in apportionment. A special session of the legislature was called in mid-June to address the sole issue of reapportionment. This time the legislature discarded the controversial "votes cast" formula in favor of absolute census figures. Although the new reapportionment plan created House districts that were more numerically equal, minorities criticized the plan as discriminatory and as expected filed suit in federal court challenging the new reapportionment. A federal court panel took two years to hear the case and eventually issued a ruling in 1984 that invalidated the reapportionment as discriminatory to minorities (Hispanics and Indians) and proceeded to reapportion the legislature itself. This new reapportionment plan eventually resulted in the election of the first Hispanic to represent Chaves County and the first Indian to represent Sandoval County in the New Mexico Legislature.

What these various lawsuits underscored was that while New Mexico had generally incorporated the Hispanic community into its state and local level politics, there were several instances primarily involving counties and municipalities in the so-called "Little Texas" region (Southeastern New Mexico) where Hispanics were being systematically excluded from the political process. It also became evident that Native Americans were similarly excluded in some counties.

In response to these various lawsuits, the New Mexico Legislature in 1985 enacted legislation requiring that members of governing bodies in municipalities having populations in excess of ten thousand, to reside in and be elected from single-member districts. It also allowed—but did not require—municipalities with populations of ten thousand or less to establish single-member districts. The law which applied to both Mayor-Council and Commission-Manager forms of government required the governing body to divide the municipality into districts of equal size after every decennial census [New Mexico Municipal League, 1985]. Similar laws were also enacted to require governing bodies in counties (county commissions) with over 13,000 populations and school boards (in districts over 10,000) to establish single-member districts [New Mexico Municipal League, 1985]. Shortly after Governor Toney Anaya signed the districting laws, an attorney for the New Mexico Risk Management Division sought dismissal of several pending lawsuits saying that the law provided "the substantive relief" sought by the plaintiffs. The plaintiffs' attorneys, however, asked the federal judge to remain in the cases to oversee the districting process [*Albuquerque Journal*, April 11, 1985].

Given such clear cut legislative mandate most municipalities began to conform to the new standards by the 1986 elections.

The Alamorgordo Case

The one notable exception to the general compliance following the passage of the New Mexico districting laws was the city of Alamogordo.

Alamogordo, located in the heart of the southestern quadrant of the State of New Mexico is a city of 24, 239 residents. Although originally a farming/ranching community, its present day economy is largely based on its close proximity to Holloman Air Force Base and the White Sands Missile Range. Of Alamogordo's population, 5, 830, or 24.1 percent are Hispanics (mainly Mexican American), and 1,283, or 5.3 percent are Black [Alamogordo:

Demographic Analysis, 1987]. Alamogordo is governed by a seven member commission who exercise both legislative and executive authority. In addition to electing one from their own ranks as "mayor," a largely ceremonial role, the commission also selects a manager who is in charge of the day-to-day administration of the city.

As it prepared for the 1986 municipal elections, the Alamogordo Commission discussed the new law and its effect on their electoral structure. Eventually, after securing legal advice the commission opted to proceed with the regular at-large election based on the assumption that as a "home rule" charter municipality, Alamogordo was not required to conform to the new state districting law.

In January, 1986, three Alamogordo voters, two Hispanics and one Black filed a lawsuit in federal district court alleging that Alamogordo's electoral arrangement for electing commissioners discriminated against minority voters [*Albuquerque Journal*, March 3, 1987]. The plaintiffs, represented by veteran civil rights Attorney Stanley Halpin of the Southwest Voter Registration and Education Project (SWVREP), sought the creation of seven single-member districts, two of which would have a majority of ethnic minority voters. After fourteen months of legal sparring, the litigants reached a compromise agreement the week before the trial was scheduled to take place on March 2, 1987.

Under the compromise agreement, Alamogordo would retain its seven member commission, each of whom serves a four year term. Four commissioners were to be elected by single- member districts in one election. In the succeeding election three commissioners would be elected "at-large," that is, all voters in the community were to vote for all three positions. In the at-large election, however, voters would now have the option of casting all three of their votes for a single candidate rather than casting three separate votes for separate candidates. The procedure known as "cumulative voting" or "plumping," originated in a few American cities in the 1800's but was most recently used in Illinois between 1970 and 1980 for election to the lower house of the Illinois Legislature. Proponents of plumping contend that it helps minority groups gain representation by concentrating their votes on their one or two candidates. Consequently, legislative bodies are thus more representative. Opponents contend that the system contributes to creating splinter parties necessitating more unstable coalition government [*American Political Dictionary*, 1985]. Dr. Richard Engstrom, a Louisiana political science professor who testified for the plaintiffs contended that if 25 percent or more of minority voters turn out and each casts three votes for one candidate, it is mathematically impossible for that candidate to lose. Thus, if the 30 percent of

Alamogordo's 24,030 people who are minorities vote for a single candidate, that candidate would be elected. In a setting where minority voters are dispersed, cumulative voting would offer more of a chance for minorities to gain representation than the single-member district method. The single-member district does not give minorities representation if they do not constitute a majority within the district.

The consent order establishing the Alamogordo voting plan was signed by U.S. District Judge Santiago Campos, who also set the first at-large election for July 21, 1987. Judge Campos also directed that a series of public meetings be held to educate voters on the use of cumulative voting. The order also prohibits amending Alamogordo's city charter as it affects elections, until 1994 by which time the method will have been fully tried. Following the announcement of the settlement one of the plaintiffs, Rev. Ernesto Hall, a Mexican-American, announced that "we're not as well trained in the way others are about politics [but] we're learning fast, we'll catch up" [*Albuquerque Journal*, March 3, 1987].

Alamogordo's First Election Under Cumulative Voting

Although Alamogordo's Mexican-American and Black voters had won a significant victory in the courts, they were not overwhelmingly aggressive about capitalizing on their victory, a function, perhaps of past disillusionment. None of the leading Mexican American politicians entered the race for commissioner. Finally, a thirty-five year old Mexican American woman, Inez Moncada, who had run for the Alamogordo school board in 1987 and lost by two votes, entered the race. Moncada resides in a section of Alamogordo known as *"Chihuahuita"* (Little Chihuahua), a 36 block neighborhood with the heaviest concentration of Mexican-Americans. The neighborhood lies within District 3 of the Alamogordo city commission and Hispanics account for about 42 percent of its 6,077 voters.

Although entering the race belatedly, Moncada plunged into the campaign vigorously. She introduced herself to the voters through a letter where she discussed the new cumulative voting scheme, her unprecedented position as a Mexican-American woman seeking election to the commission, and her position on some of the issues such as property taxes. In her second letter, Moncada included instructions on cumulative voting including a graphic design showing a voting machine with the simple message: "Moncada, Moncada, Moncada." The message aimed to suggest to voters to pull the lever three times [Tafoya, 1988]. In this at-large election Moncada found herself with some formidable opponents, including incumbent Mayor Ron Carroll, incumbent

Mayor Pro-Tempore Dorothy Watts, and five others. The results of the election, summarized in Table I were both surprising and interesting. They were surprising in that the top incumbents Carroll and Watts were both defeated. Also surprising was Moncada's support in the Heights and Buena Vista polling places which include the greatest concentration of Anglo, higher income, business and professional people. The top three vote getters were Downs, Riordan and Moncada in that order, and although their totals were quite close (within 100 votes), their margins over the remaining candidates were greater (over 400 votes).

Table 1. RESULTS OF 1987 ALAMOGORDO CITY COMMISSION ELECTION*

Candidate	Buena*** Vista	Heights***	Sacramento**	Sierra	Mid High	Absentee	Tot.
Downs	815	738	160	464	238	54	2469
Riordan	816	652	191	419	225	115	2418
Moncada	379	516	822	395	238	48	2398
Carroll	653	520	149	341	164	92	1919
Watts	222	198	141	130	71	44	806
Total	2,885	2,624	1,463	1,749	936	353	10,010

Source: Alex Tafoya, "Cumulative Voting and The 1987 Alamogordo, New Mexico Election," p. 16

* Included are only top 5 vote getters.
** Sacramento is the polling place located within District 3, with the most concentration of Mexican-American voters.
*** Greater concentration of Anglo, higher income, professional business people.

Downs with 24.6 percent was the top vote getter with 24.1 percent for Riordan and 23.9 percent for Moncada of the votes cast for the top five candidates.

The most dramatic effect of the cumulative voting effects were seen in Moncada's own polling place, Sacramento. Moncada received 56 percent of the votes cast in that polling place. The Sacramento vote alone constituted 34 percent of Moncada's total vote. Although Moncada could not have been elected without some support in other polling places, it is clear that her overwhelming victory in Sacramento was the core of her victory. The cumulative effect of the "plumping" done in the Sacramento polling place was also repeated in all other polling places thus giving Moncada an exaggerated show of support in all parts of the city. Moncada herself attributed her victory to the effective use of plumping as did Dorothy Watts one of her defeated, opponents, who commented, "They knew how to use it [plumping] and they did it very well. . . It (the voting) was strictly along racial lines" [Tafoya, 1988].

Conclusion

The experience of Alamogordo, New Mexico, clearly illustrates that cumulative voting or plumping is indeed a realistic alternative to the single-member district as a remedy for minority groups who have suffered from political exclusion resulting from the adverse effects of at-large voting. The election of the first Mexican American woman to the city commission in Alamogordo's history was accomplished because of the unique electoral method. However, it is important to note that Moncada's election also shows that the minority candidate must campaign effectively (possibly utilizing a show and tell approach) in order to educate the voters on the process. Inez Moncada was later elected as Mayor-Pro Temp by her colleagues in the Alamogordo commission, a recognition befitting her emerging stature and that of Mexican Americans in Alamogordo politics. The struggle and triumph of Mexican-Americans in Alamogordo, in court and at the voting booth, may be felt beyond New Mexico as other communities and other courts struggle with the problems of minority voting rights and participation.

References

Grant, Daniel H. and Lloyd Omdahl. 1987. *State and Local Government in America.* Boston: Allyn and Bacon,.

Brischetto, Robert and Bernard Grofman. "The Voting Rights Act and Minority Representation in Texas: Implications For Change in the Southwest." Paper presented at the Western Political Science Association, San Francisco, California, 1988.

"Attorney Seeks Dismissal of Lawsuit." *Albuquerque Journal*, April 11, 1985.

"Hispanic Sues City of Roswell Over Election." *Albuquerque Journal*, December 4, 1983.

"Lawsuit Calls Election Setup Discriminatory." *Albuquerque Journal*, October 21, 1983.

Summary of 1985 Laws Affecting Municipalities. Santa Fe, New Mexico Municipal League, 1985.

"Alamogordo Demographic Analysis." Alamogordo: Office of the City Manager.

Plano, Jack C. and Milten Greenberg. *The American Political Dictionary.* New York: Holt, Rinehart and Winston, 1985.

Tafoya, Alexander. "Cumulative Voting and the 1987 Alamogordo New Mexico Municipal

Election." Unpublished seminar paper, New Mexico Highlands University, 1988.

Voting Rights and the Constitution: The Disenfranchisement of Non-English Speaking Citizens

Sandra Guerra

In 1980, more than twenty-three million Americans spoke languages other than English in their homes.[1] Most non-English speaking Americans are native-born citizens, who have a constitutional right to vote. Yet before the enactment of the 1975 amendments to the Voting Rights Act, which require multilingual voting assistance[2] in areas with large numbers of non-English speakers,[3] people who did not understand English were effectively disenfranchised by elections held only in English.

These multilingual election provisions of the Voting Rights Act, however, do not sufficiently guarantee non-English speaking citizens' right to vote. The language of the statute, as well as its implementation, have limited the reach of this federal statutory right.[4] Some localities supplement the Voting Rights Act protection through state and local multilingual voting legislation.[5] However, political organizations in many states currently are promoting state constitutional amendments, commonly referred to as "English Language Amendments," which would designate English as the official language of those states.[6] Critics of the "English-only" movement anticipate that states will attempt to use these amendments to bar the provision of multilingual voting assistance except as required by the Voting Rights Act.[7] That the voting rights of non-English speakers are

---

1. See BUREAU OF THE CENSUS, U.S. DEP'T OF COMMERCE, STATISTICAL ABSTRACT OF THE UNITED STATES 34 (1986).
2. Throughout this Note, "voting assistance" refers to all written and oral assistance, including the provision of multilingual ballots.
3. The 1975 amendments to the Voting Rights Act of 1965, 42 U.S.C. § 1973b(f)(4) (1982), provide that, in any jurisdiction covered by the Act, "[w]henever any [jurisdiction] . . . provides any registration or voting notices, forms, instructions, assistance, or other materials or information relating to the electoral process, including ballots," it shall provide them on a multilingual basis to members of applicable language minority groups.
4. See infra note 26.
5. See infra note 30.
6. N.Y. Times, Jan. 17, 1987, at A7, col. 2. Efforts to amend the federal constitution also persist. See, e.g., Note, *The Proposed English Language Amendment: Shield or Sword?*, 3 YALE L. & POL'Y REV. 519, 519 (1985); Note, *Language Minority Voting Rights and the English Language Amendment*, 14 HASTINGS CONST. L.Q. 657 (1987).
7. The proponents of the English language amendments, spearheaded by a national group, U.S. English, are opposed to multilingual elections, whether mandated by federal or state law. See ENGLISH UNITES US (California campaign pamphlet) (on file with author); U.S. ENGLISH, FACT SHEET:

threatened by the English-only movement starkly reveals the inadequacies of the Voting Rights Act as the sole guarantor of non-English speakers' right to vote.

This Note argues that because voting is a specially protected fundamental right, the equal protection clause of the Fourteenth Amendment guarantees that absent compelling justification states may not provide voting assistance to English speakers without also providing equivalent assistance to non-English speakers. Ensuring this right fully will require a judicial determination that the Constitution requires states to provide multilingual voting assistance for non-English speakers—a position that courts have yet to adopt fully.

Section I of the Note will address the interplay between the judiciary and Congress in the development of multilingual voting rights and will expose the shortcomings of the current federal statutory scheme. Section II sets forth a constitutional argument for a right to multilingual voting assistance. Section III provides tentative policy suggestions for Congressional improvement of the Voting Rights Act multilingual election provisions.

I. The Development of Federal Protection of Non-English Speakers' Right to Vote

A. *The 1965 Voting Rights Act: Origins of Federal Protection*

The restrictive reading of constitutionally protected voting rights in the United States Supreme Court's 1959 decision in *Lassiter v. Northhampton County Board of Elections*[8] prompted Congress to enact the Voting Rights Act of 1965.[9] The far-reaching provisions of the 1965 legislation were designed to eliminate literacy tests and other discriminatory "tests and devices" that effectively disenfranchised blacks in the South.[10] Thus, the 1965 Voting Rights Act secured the right to vote for

---

BILINGUAL VOTING BALLOTS (1986) (on file with author); N.Y. Times, Feb. 22, 1987, at 23 CN 1, col. 1; *see also* Note, *"Official English": Federal Limits on Efforts to Curtail Bilingual Services in the States*, 100 HARV. L. REV. 1345, 1345-47 (1987).

8. 360 U.S. 45 (1959). In *Lassiter*, the Supreme Court upheld the use of English literacy tests as a means of qualifying voters in North Carolina, despite the fact that literacy tests effectively eliminated a large segment of the black voting constituency. The Court found that absent invidious discrimination the states could limit the franchise to literate persons "to promote intelligent use of the ballot." *Id.* at 51.

A lower federal court decision extended the logic of *Lassiter* to require literacy specifically in English. Mexican-American Federation-Washington State v. Naff, 299 F. Supp. 587 (E.D. Wash. 1969), *vacated and remanded sub nom.*, Jimenez v. Naff, 400 U.S. 986 (1971) (vacated in light of Oregon v. Mitchell, 400 U.S. 112 (1970), which upheld Voting Rights Act literacy test ban). For a criticism of Naff's misinterpretation of both *Lassiter* and the stricter post-*Lassiter* standard of review, see Note, *Constitutional Law—Voting Rights—State English Literacy Requirement Upheld*, 45 WASH. L. REV. 401 (1970).

9. Pub. L. No. 89-110, 79 Stat. 437 (codified at 42 U.S.C. §§ 1971, 1973 (1982)).

10. In 1975, Congress made the literacy test ban permanent. *See* S. REP. No. 295, 94th Cong., 1st Sess. 8, *reprinted in* 1975 U.S. CODE CONG. & ADMIN. NEWS 774 [hereinafter 1975 S. Rep.]; *see also* H.R. REP. No. 439, 89th Cong., 1st Sess. 12-13, *reprinted in* 1965 U.S. CODE CONG. & ADMIN. NEWS 2437, 2443-44.

English illiterates, a right that the Supreme Court had not been willing to require as a constitutional matter.[11]

The 1965 statute also included a provision that recognized the need for multilingual assistance for non-English speakers. It barred language discrimination at the polls for literate Spanish-speaking Puerto Rican voters who emigrate to the mainland.[12]

The Voting Rights Act, in turn, has been consistently upheld by the Supreme Court.[13] The two most important Supreme Court opinions relating to the question of non-English speaking voters are the majority opinion in *Katzenbach v. Morgan*[14] and Justice Douglas' dissent in *Cardona v. Power*.[15] Although they address the legality of imposing English literacy requirements on non-English speaking voters, these opinions also provide a strong legal rationale for the requirement of state multilingual voting assistance. The *Morgan* opinion represented a significant shift in the Court's tolerance for voting devices that exclude non-English speakers:

> We are told that New York's English literacy requirement originated in the desire to provide an incentive for non-English speaking immigrants to learn the English language and in order to assure the intelligent exercise of the franchise. Yet Congress might well have questioned, in light of the many exemptions provided, and some evidence suggesting that prejudice played a prominent role in the enactment of the requirement, whether these were actually the interests being served. Congress might have also questioned whether denial of a right deemed so precious and fundamental in our society was a necessary or appropriate means of encouraging persons to learn English, or of furthering the goal of an intelligent exercise of the franchise.[16]

Justice Douglas' dissenting opinion in *Cardona v. Power*[17] is also important as one of the few judicial pronouncements on the constitutional issues raised by voting in a multilingual society. Justice Douglas, who wrote the opinion for the Court in *Lassiter*, found that the Fourteenth Amendment prohibited discrimination among literate persons,[18] as is the

---

11. Professor Tribe predicts that literacy tests would most likely be overturned on constitutional grounds given that *Lassiter* antedates the use of strict scrutiny when fundamental rights such as voting are implicated. L. TRIBE, AMERICAN CONSTITUTIONAL LAW § 13-15, at 1093 (2d ed. 1988).
12. *See* 42 U.S.C. § 1973b(e) (1982).
13. *See* South Carolina v. Katzenbach, 383 U.S. 301 (1966) (upholding Voting Rights Act of 1965 under § 2 of the Fifteenth Amendement); Katzenbach v. Morgan, 384 U.S. 641 (1966) (upholding under § 5 of the Fourteenth Amendment provision [§ 4(e)] of the Voting Rights Act which protects Puerto Rican voters).
14. 384 U.S. 641 (1966).
15. 384 U.S. 672, 675 (1966) (Douglas, J., dissenting).
16. *Katzenbach*, 384 U.S. at 654.
17. *Cardona*, 384 U.S. at 675 (Douglas, J., dissenting).
18. *Id.*

case when English literacy tests are applied to Spanish-speaking literate persons.[19] He wrote:

> The heavier burden [of an English literacy requirement] which New York has placed on the Spanish-speaking American cannot . . . be sustained under the Equal Protection Clause of the Fourteenth Amendment. . . . [T]here is no rational basis—considering the importance of the right at stake—for denying those with equivalent qualifications except that the language is Spanish.[20]

Thus, prior to the enactment of the 1975 legislation which provides more extensive multilingual voting assistance, Congress and the Supreme Court had begun to recognize that a non-English speaker's right to vote is violated when elections are held only in English. *Morgan* and the *Cardona* dissent perceived that government action short of an absolute denial of the vote can effectively disenfranchise electors.

B. *The 1975 Amendments: A Federal Right to Multilingual Voting Assistance*

In response to overwhelming evidence of discrimination in voting directed against racial and ethnic minority non-English speakers,[21] Congress enacted the 1975 amendments to the Voting Rights Act of 1965.[22] The 1975 Amendments created a multilingual voting system that has brought about a significant increase in voter participation[23] by non-English speak-

---

19. The plaintiff in *Cardona* was a Spanish-speaking Puerto Rican voter who sought a judicial declaration that the New York English literacy requirement, as applied to her, denied her right to vote under the Federal Constitution. *Id.* at 673.
The majority opinion held that the record did not indicate whether the plaintiff was literate in Spanish. If she were, the case would be covered by § 4(e) of the Voting Rights Act of 1965 and would therefore be moot. Because the New York courts did not determine whether the federal statute applied, the Court vacated and remanded the cause of action. *Id.* at 674.
20. *Id.* at 676; *see also* Cox, *The Supreme Court, 1965 Term—Foreword: Constitutional Adjudication and the Promotion of Human Rights*, 80 HARV. L. REV. 91, 96-97 (discussing Justice Douglas' *Cardona* dissent).
21. Only language minorities that are also racial and ethnic minorities are protected by the Voting Rights Act. 42 U.S.C. § 1973aa-1a (e). The list of groups as specified by the Bureau of the Census includes the following: Japanese, Chinese, Filipino, Korean, Vietnamese, Asian-Indian, Spanish/Hispanic, American Indian, Eskimo, Aleut and Hawaiian. *See* Bureau of the Census, *Directions for Determining Coverage under Voting Rights Act, 1982*, Attachment A3 (Aug. 13, 1984) (on file with author).
22. The 1975 Amendments require certain jurisdictions to provide all voting assistance, oral and/or written, on a multilingual basis. *See* 42 U.S.C. § 1973b(f)(4). The 1975 amendments also make permanent a nationwide ban on literacy tests and other discriminatory tests or devices. The definition of "test or device" was expanded in 1975 to include English-only elections where large numbers of language minority persons live. *See* 1975 S. REP., *supra* note 10.
23. Voting should be encouraged, particularly in light of the tragically low voter turnout in this country. *See* J. COHEN & J. ROGERS, ON DEMOCRACY 32-33 (1983). On election day in 1980, the 53.2% turnout was the third lowest in American history. *Id.* at 33. Turnout rates for "off-year" congressional elections are even lower. In 1982 only 35.7 percent of the eligible electorate went to the polls. *Id.*

ers and enhanced their political influence in their communities.[24] However, the Act has proven inadequate to fully safeguard the constitutional rights of non-English speakers.

The 1975 Amendments mandate the use of multilingual ballots in areas that meet certain requirements.[25] The determinative requirement has proven to be that five percent of the eligible voters belong to a single language minority.[26] In 1980, 386 jurisdictions (most jurisdictions are counties or towns) were determined to meet the requisite five percent figure.[27] Although the Act covers a large number of jurisdictions, the use of a trigger calculated as a percentage of the voting population is problematic. Jurisdictions with millions of voters can deny multilingual voting assistance to tens of thousands of non-English speakers so long as they fall below the five percent threshold.[28]

Furthermore, the Act only protects certain racial and ethnic minorities. Given the past discrimination against these groups in voting, it is understandable that Congress especially concern itself with the protection of racial and ethnic groups. Nonetheless, all non-English speakers, regardless of race or ethnicity, are effectively disenfranchised by elections held only in English. The voting rights of all non-English speaking American citizens are infringed when the state denies voting assistance in a language they can understand.[29]

The inadequacy of the Act has led some jurisdictions with large concentrations of non-English speakers that fall outside federal statutory coverage (such as Los Angeles, San Francisco, and San Diego) to provide mul-

---

24. R. BRISCHETTO, BILINGUAL ELECTIONS AT WORK IN THE SOUTHWEST 62-177 (1982).
25. Jurisdictions may be covered under the Voting Rights Act of 1975, 42 U.S.C. § 1973b(f)(4) (1982) or Pub. L. No. 94-73, § 203(c). Under section b(f)(4), a jurisdiction is covered if over five percent of the voting-age citizens are members of a single language minority group and if the previous presidential election was conducted only in English and less than fifty percent of voting-age citizens were registered. Section 203(c) also requires that more than five percent of voting-age citizens belong to a single language minority group. Coverage is triggered under this provision if either the jurisdiction-wide or statewide illiteracy rate exceeds the national rate. *See* GENERAL ACCOUNTING OFFICE, BILINGUAL VOTING ASSISTANCE: COSTS OF AND USE DURING THE NOVEMBER 1984 GENERAL ELECTION (1986) [hereinafter GAO REPORT].
26. The Justice Department and Bureau of the Census have interpreted a 1982 amendment to the Voting Rights Act to change the methodology used to determine whether a person belongs to a language minority group. *See* Reynolds, New Coverage Determinations Under § 203 of the Voting Rights Act 27-28 (May 11, 1984) (Justice Dep't Memorandum) (on file with author). As a result of the change, over 56% of the jurisdictions that would have been covered in 1984 were not covered. K. Hall, Chairwoman, U.S. Judiciary Subcommittee on Census and Population & D. Edwards, Chairman, U.S. Judiciary Subcommittee on Civil and Constitutional Rights, Letter to the Bureau of the Census (Aug. 29, 1984) (on file with author).
27. After the methodology change in 1982, *see supra* note 26, many cities with large language minority populations were dropped from the Act's coverage. *Compare* 28 C.F.R. § 55 app. (1980) *with* Voting Rights Act Amendments of 1982, 49 Fed. Reg. 25,887 (1984).
28. For example, Los Angeles, San Francisco, and San Diego, do not meet the requisite five percent figure. These cities are so large that despite the fact that a city like Los Angeles had roughly 69,000 Spanish monolinguals in 1984, they do not total five percent of the population. *See* Reynolds, *supra* note 26, at 27. On the other hand, a city of 100,000 need have only 5,000 non-English speakers to trigger the Act.
29. *See infra* Section II.

tilingual ballots even though not required to do so under the Act. Additionally, some states have laws that supplement the requirements of the Voting Rights Act.[30] However, English-only supporters in several states are currently aiming to prohibit this local action.[31]

The 1975 Voting Rights Act amendments were a major step forward in allowing most language minorities to vote unhindered by language barriers. The current political trend, however, reveals the limitations of the Act. The voluntary provision of multilingual ballots in areas outside the reach of the Voting Rights Act is threatened by English language amendments. The extent to which non-English speakers have a constitutionally protected right to multilingual voting assistance has yet to be judicially determined. The following section develops an argument for the full vindication of non-English speakers' right to vote.

II. Multilingual Voting Assistance and the Constitutional Right to Vote

The Constitution gives the states the authority to regulate elections subject to the power of Congress to override state regulations.[32] Both state and federal regulations are required to meet constitutional standards. In articulating constitutional norms in the voting rights area, the Supreme Court has relied primarily on the equal protection clause of the Fourteenth Amendment. The Supreme Court has employed a "strict scrutiny" standard of review[33] in cases implicating fundamental rights,[34] such as the

---

30. *See, e.g.*, MASS. GEN. LAWS ANN. ch. 51, § 36 (West Supp. 1988) (providing that registration affidavits must be in Spanish for Spanish speakers); LA. REV. STAT. ANN. §18:106 (West Supp. 1988) (interpreters provided for persons who do not speak, read, or write English); N.M. STAT. ANN. ch. 1 arts. 1J-19, 2-5, 4J-15, 8-10, 10-3, 11-14, 12-12, 16-8 (West Supp. 1986) (providing for elections conducted entirely in both Spanish and English).

31. Voter-initiated referendums to declare English the official language of a state have been proposed or are being considered in 33 states, and 13 have adopted them. N.Y. Times, Aug. 2, 1987, at A32, col. 1; N.Y. Times, Feb. 22, 1987, at § 11, p. 1, col. 1.

32. Article I, section 4 of the Constitution has been interpreted by the Supreme Court to invest Congress with broad power to regulate the entire area of voting practices by the states in federal elections. *See* L. TRIBE, *supra* note 11, § 13-10, at 1084–85. When states employ voting practices that contravene Fourteenth Amendment guarantees, Congress may act in pursuance of its enforcement powers in § 5 to regulate both federal and state elections.

33. The Supreme Court applies a "strict scrutiny" standard of review to classifications that infringe rights considered "fundamental" or classifications singling out "suspect classes," which are limited to race or national-origin groups. *See* L. TRIBE, *supra* note 11, § 16-6, at 1451–54. An intermediate level of scrutiny is applied to classifications that implicate the rights of "quasi-suspect" groups, such as classifications on the basis of sex or physical disabilities. *Id.* § 16-33, at 1610–18. Classifications that do not implicate either specially protected rights or specially protected persons are granted broad deference by the courts under a third standard of review, the "rational basis" standard. *Id.* § 16-2, at 1439–43.

34. The Court has identified a number of fundamental rights in addition to the right to vote, including, for example, procreation, Skinner v. Oklahoma *ex rel.* Williamson, 316 U.S. 535, 541 (1942); rights with respect to criminal procedure, *see, e.g.*, Griffin v. Illinois, 351 U.S. 12, 17 (1956); the right to travel, Shapiro v. Thompson, 394 U.S. 618, 630 (1969).

right to vote.³⁵ The government classification will be upheld only if it is the "least restrictive means" of promoting a "compelling" state interest.³⁶

This Note argues that elections held only in English effectively deny a fundamental right of non-English speakers. A state's preference in favor of English-speaking voters is, thus, unequal treatment that should trigger strict scrutiny review.³⁷

A. *Strict Scrutiny of Fundamental Rights*

Political minorities have long used the equal protection clause to obtain judicial protection from majoritarian legislative processes that tend to discount their interests.³⁸ In scrutinizing infringements of fundamental rights, courts show less than usual deference to legislative judgments in several respects. First, courts have ruled that state action violates the equal protection clause even if it causes an effective, but not an absolute, infringement of a fundamental right.³⁹ The equal protection clause is also violated whenever state action gives preference to the exercise of the fundamental rights of some and not others, when it burdens the exercise of those rights for some but not for others, or when it penalizes some individuals who choose to exercise their constitutional rights.⁴⁰

---

35. Non-English speakers have never been considered a "suspect class" per se. Thus, their claims have not received strict scrutiny review. *See, e.g.,* Soberal-Perez v. Heckler, 717 F.2d 36, 41 (2d Cir. 1983) (rejecting plaintiff's challenge to English-only Social Security notices), *cert. denied,* 466 U.S. 929 (1984); Guadalupe Org. v. Tempe Elem. School Dist. No. 3, 587 F.2d 1022 (9th Cir. 1978) (rejecting plaintiffs' claim to a constitutional and statutory right to bilingual education). However, since the vast majority of non-English speaking persons in this country are members of racial or ethnic minorities, non-English speakers are in most cases a directly derivative group of a clearly suspect class. Hence, in cases where plaintiffs can prove an intent to discriminate against them on the basis of their race or national origin, and not simply on account of their language, the courts should apply strict scrutiny. *See supra* note 33.

More recently, courts have been more receptive to the argument that one's language and one's national origin are closely related. *See, e.g.,* Olagues v. Russoniello, 797 F.2d 1511, 1520–21 (9th Cir. 1986) (en banc) (strict scrutiny triggered where Spanish-speaking and Chinese-speaking voters targeted for voter fraud investigation), *vacated as moot,* 108 S. Ct. 52 (1987).

Should a court find that neither the fundamental rights strand nor the suspect class strand trigger strict scrutiny, the court should at the very least apply an intermediate level of scrutiny accorded "quasi-suspect classes." *See supra* note 33; *see also* Note, *supra* note 7 at 1354; Note, *Quasi-Suspect Classes and Proof of Discriminatory Intent: A New Model,* 90 YALE L.J. 912 (1981) (using language minorities as model of quasi-suspect group).

36. *See* San Antonio Indep. School Dist. v. Rodriguez, 411 U.S. 1, 16–17 (1973).

37. Recognition that restrictions on multilingual ballots implicate the fundamental right to vote, triggering the most exacting judicial scrutiny, is an essential part of any equal protection analysis on voting rights. An analysis that categorizes the provision of ballots together with other state "bilingual programs" fails to take into account the constitutionally elevated status of voting rights. *See* Note, *supra* note 7, at 1352.

38. *See* J. ELY, DEMOCRACY AND DISTRUST 135–36 (1980).

39. *See, e.g.,* Griffin v. Illinois, 351 U.S. 12, 18 (1956) ("There is no meaningful distinction between a rule which would [absolutely] deny the poor the right to defend themselves in a trial court and one which effectively denies the poor an adequate appellate review accorded to all who have money enough to pay the costs in advance."); *see also infra* notes 56–57 and accompanying text.

40. *See, e.g.,* Memorial Hosp. v. Maricopa County, 415 U.S. 250, 257–58 (1974) (state may not penalize right to travel); Garza v. Smith, 320 F. Supp. 131 (W.D. Tex. 1970) (statute allowing voting assistance only to physically handicapped gave preference to physically handicapped over illiterate voters); Smith v. Arkansas, 385 F. Supp. 703, 704–05 (E.D. Ark. 1974) (candidate write-in statute

Once a court is satisfied that a legislative action violates a fundamental right, it will apply a strict scrutiny standard of review which requires the state to show that the action is necessary to advance a legitimate compelling state interest and the means employed are the "least retrictive" ones available.

1. *Voting is Fundamental*

The Supreme Court has long recognized "the political franchise of voting" to be a "fundamental political right, because preservative of all rights."[41] While the Constitution does not explicitly protect this right,[42] the Court has repeatedly held that as a fundamental right, voting has a special place within constitutional framework.[43] Substantively, the Court's decisions have found the right to vote to encompass the right "to participate in state elections on an *equal basis* with other qualified voters whenever the State has adopted an elective process for determining who will represent any segment of the state's population. . . ."[44] Accordingly, the Court has provided judicial relief to citizens who are denied their voting rights by discriminatory devices.[45]

2. *Unequal Provision of Voting Rights*

a. *Differing Treatment*

The equal protection clause prohibits states from treating voters in like circumstances differently. Some might argue, however, that the equal protection clause does not require affirmative action by the states: that is, it prohibits discrimination but does not require states to provide special benefits.[46] However, such an argument misstates the real issue raised by Eng-

---

unconstitutional as unreasonable and unjustified burden on voting rights of illiterate voters).

41. Yick Wo v. Hopkins, 118 U.S. 356, 370 (1886); *see also* Reynolds v. Sims, 377 U.S. 533, 555 (1964). *See generally* Wall, *Equal Protection: Analyzing the Dimensions of a Fundamental Right—The Right to Vote*, 17 SANTA CLARA L. REV. 163 (1977); Note, *Voter Registration: A Restriction on the Fundamental Right to Vote*, 96 YALE L.J. 1615, 1617-28 (1987).

42. The Constitution implicitly protects the "right to vote." U.S. CONST. art. IV, § 4, cl. 1 (the republican form of government clause). The Constitution explicitly protects the right to vote free from discrimination on the basis of race, *id.* amend. XV, § 1; on the basis of sex, *id.* amend. XIX, § 1; by reason of poll taxes, *id.* amend. XXIV, § 1; or on account of age for citizens who are 18 years of age or older, *id.* amend. XXVI, § 1.

43. *See, e.g.,* Dunn v. Blumstein, 405 U.S. 330 (1972); Kramer v. Union Free School Dist., 395 U.S. 621 (1969); Williams v. Rhodes, 393 U.S. 23 (1968); Reynolds v. Sims, 377 U.S. 533 (1964); *see also* Wall, *supra* note 41, at 164-65.

44. *See* San Antonio Indep. School Dist. v. Rodriguez, 411 U.S. 1, 35 n.78 (1973) (emphasis added).

45. Dunn v. Blumstein, 405 U.S. 330 (1972) (durational residency requirements unconstitutional); Cipriano v. City of Houma, 395 U.S. 701 (1969) (striking down statute restricting vote to property-owning taxpayers); Harper v. Virginia Bd. of Elections, 383 U.S. 663 (1966) (poll taxes unconstitutional).

46. The equal protection clause reads: "No state shall . . . deny to any person within its jurisdiction the equal protection of the laws." U.S. CONST. amend. XIV, § 1. Thus, the language of the clause itself seems to call for restraint from misconduct, not for the fulfillment of any affirmative

lish-only elections. States already provide voting materials to all eligible citizens, but only in English. English-only elections reflect a positive choice that states make to extend voting opportunities only for English speakers. Thus, this Note does not ask the judiciary to require that states provide a new service or benefit; multilingual voting assistance is not a *special* benefit. While a state is not required to provide every service on an evenhanded basis, the Fourteenth Amendment demands that opportunities to exercise fundamental rights be provided on an equal basis to all eligible citizens unless there is a reason that compels an unequal distribution of rights.[47] Because the states have chosen to facilitate the right to vote for some it is incumbent on the states to facilitate that right for all.

One lower court has rested its decision on equal protection principles in a case of significance to non-English speakers. The district court in *Garza v. Smith*[48] struck down an article of the Texas Constitution that allowed voting assistance *only* to persons who had "some bodily infirmity, such as renders [them] physically unable to write or to see."[49] The court found that refusal of assistance for illiterate persons violated the equal protection clause by depriving illiterate persons of their fundamental right to vote.

b. *No Alternatives Means of Voting*

The Supreme Court's jurisprudence points to an important qualifier to the general rule that voting cases are strictly scrutinized: The Court will not find an infringement of the right to vote if there are alternative means by which the complaining voters could have exercised their voting rights.[50]

---

duties. This is the equivalent of saying that a state's failure to provide multilingual voting assistance does not constitute "state action." However, given that states do provide assistance in English, failure to provide multilingual assistance should more accurately be termed an "omission," the product of an "active" choice by the state. *Cf.* Tribe, *The Abortion Funding Conundrum: Inalienable Rights, Affirmative Duties, and the Dilemma of Dependence*, 99 HARV. L. REV. 330, 331 (1985) (failure to fund abortions for poor women while funding childbirth procedures is "active" choice by government to discourage exercise of individual right).

47. Since the distribution of social services does not implicate rights that the Supreme Court has deemed "fundamental," a state may provide these services unequally as long as there is a "rational basis" for such a distribution. *See supra* note 33 and accompanying text. Thus, cases denying affirmative benefits to non-English speakers can be distinguished. *See* Frontera v. Sindell, 522 F.2d 1215 (6th Cir. 1975) (upholding English-only civil service examination); Guerrero v. Carleson, 9 Cal. 3d 808, 512 P.2d 833, 109 Cal. Rptr. 201 (1973) (upholding English-only notices of welfare benefit reductions or terminations), *cert. denied sub nom.* Guerrero v. Swoape, 414 U.S. 1137 (1974).

48. 320 F. Supp. 131 (W.D. Tex. 1970), *vacated on other grounds and remanded*, 401 U.S. 1006, *remanded*, 450 F.2d 790 (5th Cir. 1971).

49. *Garza*, 320 F. Supp. at 132.

50. This requirement has been applied more often in cases involving the right to equal access to the courts in criminal cases by means of free transcripts or court-appointed attorneys on appeal. *See, e.g.*, Douglas v. California, 372 U.S. 353, 357 (1963) (where indigent defendant has "no recourse" but to prosecute his own appeal, state violated equal protection clause by denying court-appointed counsel); Griffin v. Illinois, 351 U.S. 12, 20 (1956) (state must provide free transcripts to indigent criminal defendants).

This qualifier indicates the judiciary's unwillingness to provide a remedy if there is a showing by the state that the remedy is unnecessary.[51]

Thus, for example, in *McDonald v. Board of Election Commissioners*,[52] the Court held that the denial of absentee ballots to unsentenced inmates of an Illinois county jail did not violate the inmates' voting rights as there was nothing in the record to show that the state had precluded them from voting. Since the state could "possibly furnish the jails with special polling booths . . . or provide guarded transportation to the polls," the Court concluded that the "right to vote" had not been infringed and applied a rational relation standard of review to determine whether plaintiffs had a "right to receive absentee ballots."[53]

The Ninth Circuit reviewed a similar claim in *Selph v. Council of Los Angeles*,[54] a case brought by physically handicapped persons to require the city of Los Angeles to modify every polling place so as to make them accessible to handicapped people. The court found that the right to vote was not implicated where handicapped voters have reasonable alternatives to voting in person.[55]

3. *Effective Disenfranchisement*

As the devices used to discriminate against particular individuals in voting have become more sophisticated, the Supreme Court has had to grant relief to voters even when they are not absolutely disenfranchised by the state's actions. In most modern cases, voters find their rights impaired by devices that have the effect of disenfranchising them, even though in the literal sense they are not barred from the polls.[56]

There is no set formula for measuring the degree of harm plaintiffs must prove to establish that a state's classification "effectively" disenfranchises them. Drawing on Supreme Court jurisprudence from other fundamental rights areas, as well as voting rights cases, the test applied is whether the classification has a "real and appreciable impact" on the exercise of the protected interest,[57] such that it unfairly burdens[58] or penal-

---

51. *See, e.g.* Britt v. North Carolina, 404 U.S. 226, 227 (1971) (defendant failed to establish need for transcript in light of court's finding that alternative devices available).
52. 394 U.S. 802 (1969).
53. *Id.* at 807, 808 n.6.
54. 390 F. Supp. 58 (C.D. Cal. 1975).
55. *Id.* at 62.
56. To the extent that Rosario v. Rockefeller, 410 U.S. 752, 757 (1973), suggests that a classification must absolutely bar voters in order to violate the Fourteenth Amendment, that case misinterprets the rest of the Court's jurisprudence regarding degrees of disenfranchisement and stands alone in suggesting that proposition.
In *Rosario*, the Court held that New York's delayed enrollment scheme that required voters to enroll in a political party eleven months prior to the election simply did not disenfranchise anyone in any way. *Id.* If newly registered voters failed to register to vote, it was because they "chose not to." *Id.* at 758. Thus, the Court declined to apply strict scrutiny review.
57. *See, e.g.*, Clements v. Fashing, 457 U.S. 957, 963 (1982); Bullock v. Carter, 405 U.S. 134, 144 (1972).
58. *See, e.g.*, Lubin v. Panish, 415 U.S. 709, 716 (1974).

izes that interest.[59] Thus, if the "pratical effect[ ]"[60] of a state's action is to appreciably impair a fundamental right for certain persons, strict scrutiny is triggered.

Courts have not required that a classification adversely impair the voting rights of *all* members of the group claiming the disadvantage. Plaintiffs need only show that the classification falls with unequal weight on them.[61] Thus, the appropriate test for judging the voting rights of non-English speakers is: Does the denial of multilingual elections have a "real and appreciable impact" on the exercise of their voting rights? In other words, does the classification have the practical effect of disenfranchising non-English speakers to a significantly greater degree than English speakers.[62]

B. *Equal Protection Claims of Non-English Speakers*

Equal protection doctrine requires that aggrieved voters show that state voting practices disenfranchise them. Thus, non-English speaking voters must show that elections conducted only in English bring about their effective disenfranchisement, thus violating their fundamental right to vote and triggering strict scrutiny. They must also show that there are no alternative means available by which they can exercise this fundamental right.[63]

In 1970, the California Supreme Court squarely faced the constitutionality of English literacy requirements as applied to non-English speakers in *Castro v. State*.[64] The court found that the English literacy requirement of the California constitution violated petitioners' right to equal protection of the law. However, the *Castro* decision did not require the state

---

59. *See, e.g.,* Memorial Hosp. v. Maricopa County, 415 U.S. 250, 257 (1974).
60. Gardner v. California, 393 U.S. 367, 371 (1969).
61. *See* Bullock v. Carter, 405 U.S. 134 (1972) (voting scheme requiring candidates to pay large filing fees to enter party primaries falls with unequal weight on voters, as well as candidates, according to their economic status).
62. The Supreme Court has made its strongest statements demanding that states respect the equality of each citizen's vote in its legislative apportionment jurisprudence. In this context, the Court has found that states could not draw legislative districts so that there were fewer voters in some districts than in others because that would give greater weight to the votes of citizens in districts of lesser population.

In the landmark apportionment case of Reynolds v. Sims, 377 U.S. 533 (1964), the Court explicitly affirmed the principle that a state's voting scheme need not *absolutely* disenfranchise a particular group to offend the Constitution. The Court in *Reynolds* states: "the right of suffrage can be denied by a debasement or dilution of the weight of a citizen's vote just as effectively as by wholly prohibiting the free exercise of the franchise." *Id.* at 555. In later apportionment cases, the Supreme Court, applying strict scrutiny, has not permitted even de minimis population variations among districts absent compelling justification. *See* Karcher v. Daggett, 462 U.S. 725, 731 (1983) (de minimis population variation in Congressional districts not allowed absent compelling state interest); Kirkpatrick v. Preisler, 394 U.S. 526, 530-31 (1969) (same); P. BREST & S. LEVINSON, PROCESSES OF CONSTITUTIONAL DECISIONMAKING: CASES AND MATERIALS 635 (1983).
63. *See supra* notes 50-55 and accompanying text.
64. 2 Cal. 3d 223, 466 P.2d 244, 85 Cal. Rptr. 20 (1970).

to provide multilingual ballots. Instead the court stated: "The provision of ballots, notices, ballot pamphlets, etc. in Spanish is not necessary either to the formation of intelligent opinions on election issues or to the implementation of those opinions through the mechanics of balloting."[65] Thus, the only relevant case law assessing constitutionally based voting rights would require non-English speakers to *prove* that they are effectively disenfranchised by English-only elections in order to obtain a judicial declaration requiring states to provide multilingual assistance.

Nearly twenty years have passed since the California court's decision in *Castro*. In that time, empirical evidence has been gathered which documents the need for multilingual voting assistance. Further, federal district courts consistently have interpreted the "right to vote" of Spanish speakers under the special 1965 provision to require bilingual ballots for Puerto Rican voters, and Congress has enacted the 1975 amendments to the Voting Rights Act to expand multilingual voting assistance.[66]

1. *Empirical Evidence of Disenfranchisement By Language Barriers*

A recent empirical study, conducted under the auspices of the Mexican-American Legal Defense and Education Fund, strongly suggests that English-only elections effectively disenfranchise non-English speakers. The comprehensive 1982 report[67] was heavily relied upon in the 1982 congressional hearings on the Voting Rights Act.[68]

Conducted in three predominantly Mexican-American communities in Los Angeles, California and Uvalde and San Antonio, Texas, the study concludes that those most likely to be affected by the discontinuance of bilingual voting services are Spanish monolinguals.[69] Seventy percent of the voting citizens who spoke only Spanish reported that they would be less likely to register and less likely to vote if oral assistance in Spanish

---

65. *Id.* at 243, 466 P.2d at 282, 85 Cal. Rptr. at 34. The court distinguished *Lassiter* since the appellant in *Lassiter* made no claim to literacy in any language or to access to news media in another language. The court held that the English proficiency provision discriminated "*among* literate citizens, disenfranchising all who are literate in languages other than English . . . ." *Id.* at 233, 466 P.2d at 250, 85 Cal. Rptr. at 26.

66. *See supra* notes 21-31 and accompanying text.

67. R. BRISCHETTO, *supra* note 24. The report uses archival data including available census, registration and election records collected for the ten previous years. *Id.* at 16; *see also id.* at 61 n.1 (citing A. EDWARDS, C. ORTIZ & D. LOPEZ, 3 BILINGUAL ELECTION SERVICES: A STATE OF THE ART REPORT (1979)); *id.* at 34 n.1 (citing Cooper & Greenfield, *Language Use and the Bilingual Community*, 53 MOD. LANGUAGE J. 166 (1969)). The report is based on secondary analysis of existing survey data, including that contained in the CENSUS BUREAU SURVEY OF INCOME AND EDUCATION (1976) and the NATIONAL CHICANO SURVEY (1979), which was conducted at the University of Michigan. *Id.* at 4.

68. *See* S. REP. NO. 417, 97th Cong., 2d Sess. 66, *reprinted in* 1982 U.S. CODE CONG. & ADMIN. NEWS 244-45.

69. R. BRISCHETTO, *supra* note 24, at 49. The following results bear out this conclusion:

were discontinued.[70] Seventy-two percent indicated they would be less likely to vote if the bilingual ballot were discontinued.[71]

2. *Judicial Acknowledgment of the Need for Multilingual Voting Assistance for Non-English Speakers*

The Voting Rights Act of 1965 includes a provision protecting Puerto Rican citizens who emigrate to the mainland from language discrimination in voting.[72] A series of cases point to this provision for support for the proposition that ballots printed only in English deny non-English speakers the right to vote. Those cases construing section 4(e) of the Voting Rights Act of 1965 consistently hold that the "right to vote" entails more than a right of equal access to ballots in English—it requires equal access to ballots in a language the voter can understand. While these cases do not directly bear on the constitutionality of English-only elections, they do support the proposition that English-only elections deny non-English speakers any meaningful opportunity to exercise their voting rights.

In enacting this special provision protecting Puerto Rican citizens, Con-

Probable Effect of Removal of Bilingual Services by Language Ability

		Percent of Citizens by Language Ability		
		English Monolingual	Bilingual	Spanish Monolingual
Likelihood of registration without Spanish help				
Less Likely		17	26	70
Makes no difference		83	72	26
Don't know		0	2	3
Total		100	100	99
P = .0000	(N)	(42)	(735)	(123)
Likelihood of voting without Spanish help				
Less likely		21	26	71
Makes no difference		76	72	25
Don't know		2	2	4
Total		99	100	100
P = .0000	(N)	(42)	(740)	(122)
Likelihood of voting without bilingual ballot				
Less likely		14	25	72
Makes no difference		83	74	26
Don't know		2	2	2
Total		99	101	100
P = .0000	(N)	(42)	(739)	(124)

Id. at 51.
70. *Id.*
71. *Id.* The study further showed that those who were most likely to be disenfranchised by the elimination of bilingual election services were the poor, the least educated, and the aged. *Id.* at 47-48.
72. *See supra* note 12 and accompanying text.

gress declared only that the states could not condition the right to vote on English proficiency; it did not specify that the states should provide multilingual ballots. Nonetheless, the courts have recognized that the right to vote includes the right to understand the vote one is casting and accordingly have required multilingual materials and assistance.

The Seventh Circuit in *Puerto Rican Organization for Political Action v. Kusper*[73] found the right to vote to include "the right to be informed as to which mark on the ballot, or lever on the voting machine, will effectuate the voter's political choice."[74]

The Pennsylvania District Court in *Arroyo v. Tucker*,[75] agreeing with the reasoning of *Kusper* and its progeny, stated that " 'the right to vote' means more than the mechanics of marking a ballot or pulling a lever."[76] Non-English speakers cannot cast an effective vote "without . . . [the] ability to comprehend the registration and election forms and the ballot itself."[77]

In short, every lower court that has interpreted the statutory right that prohibits states from conditioning the right to vote of Puerto Rican citizens on an ability to understand English,[78] has concluded that that right, by force of reason, must entail voting assistance in a language the voter understands.

C. State Interests and the Means Employed to Achieve Them

State action that infringes on fundamental rights is presumptively illegitimate.[79] Under the so-called "strict scrutiny" standard of review, a state must show that the action advances legitimate and "compelling" state objectives. The state must then show that the choice of means are best suited to the stated ends.[80]

---

73. 490 F.2d 575, 579 (7th Cir. 1973).
74. *Id.* (citing Garza v. Smith, 320 F. Supp. 131, 136 (W.D. Tex. 1970)). Similarly, in Torres v. Sachs, 381 F. Supp. 309 (S.D.N.Y. 1974), the district court held: "In order that the phrase 'the right to vote' be more than an empty platitude, a voter must be able effectively to register his or her political choice. . . ." *Id.* at 312. The court in *Torres* found that all-English elections violated not only the Voting Rights Act language provision, but the Fourteenth Amendment as well.
75. 372 F. Supp. 764 (E.D. Pa. 1974) (holding that Philadelphia's English-only election system infringed Puerto Rican voters right to vote under § 4(e) of the Voting Rights Act).
76. *Id.* at 767.
77. *Id.* Other decisions, interpreting the 1965 Act, further develop the idea that persons who do not read or write English have a right to cast an effective ballot. United States v. Louisiana, 265 F. Supp. 703, 708 (E.D. La. 1966) (statute denying illiterates voting assistance was literacy test violating the Voting Rights Act) ("We cannot impute to Congress the self-defeating notion that an illiterate has the right [to] pull the lever of a voting machine, but not the right to know for whom he pulls the lever."); United States v. Mississippi, 256 F. Supp. 344 (S.D. Miss. 1966) (defining "vote" as "any and all action necessary to make a vote effective in any . . . election . . . [including] casting a ballot").
78. *See supra* note 12 and accompanying text.
79. *See supra* notes 38-40 and accompanying text.
80. *See, e.g.,* Zablocki v. Redhail, 434 U.S. 374 (1978) (state interests were "legitimate and substantial . . . but, since the means selected . . . unnecessarily impinge on the right to marry, the statute cannot be sustained").

1. Promotion of a Unilingual Government

In justifying their position, the proponents of English-only elections point to the state's compelling interest in a unilingual government[81] and the possibility that the accommodation of non-English speakers could result in a bilingual or trilingual nation.[82] Even assuming that a state language policy is constitutional and that the voting machinery is a constitutionally permissible means by which to implement it, equal protection analysis requires that English-only elections must be the least restrictive means of creating a unilingual government. There is no proof that English-only elections encourage or promote the learning of English. Elections take place only once every year or two, thereby not directly affecting individual non-English speakers regularly enough to encourage the learning

---

81. The unfairness of state action that penalizes non-English speakers in order to promote a unilingual government lies in the fact that the de jure and de facto school segregation of language minority children in public schools has contributed to the retention of the groups' mother tongues and has hindered the acquisition of English skills. *See* Laosa, *Social Policies Toward Children of Diverse Ethnic, Racial and Language Groups in the United States*, in CHILD DEVELOPMENT RESEARCH AND SOCIAL POLICY 1 (H. Stevenson & A. Siegel eds. 1984); *see also* Hernandez v. Texas, 347 U.S. 475, 479 (1954) (noting segregation of Mexican-American children and white children in public schools); Gaston County v. United States, 395 U.S. 285, 289 (1969) (recognizing causal relationship between unequal educational opportunities and exercise of right to vote of racial minorities); *cf.* Lau v. Nichols, 414 U.S. 563 (1974) (failure to provide English language instruction to non-English speaking Chinese-American students violates Civil Rights Act of 1964). *See generally* J. FISHMAN, LANGUAGE LOYALTY IN THE UNITED STATES (1966) (discussing language retention by United States immigrant groups).

82. They consider this to be an undesirable possibility. *See* Hayakawa, *English, By Law*, N.Y. Times, Oct. 1, 1981, at A35, col. 2 ("The longer they [non-English-speaking children] are instructed in the native tongue [through bilingual education programs], the more difficult it becomes for them to learn English in their later years. ... . The use of bilingual ballots compounds the problem.") (Remark of the Honorary Chairman of U.S. English, former Senator Hayakawa); *cf.* Bikales, *Make English Official by Passing New Laws*, U.S.A. Today, Apr. 10, 1985, at 8A, col. 1 ("But things are different today, and we can no longer assume that recent arrivals will automatically follow a path leading to their uneventful insertion into U.S. society.") (Remark by G. Bikales, Executive Director of U.S. English); Fundraising letter for English First from J. Horn, Texas State Representative (1986) ("Tragically, many immigrants these days refuse to learn English!") (on file with author); *see also* Guadalupe Org. v. Tempe Elem. School Dist. No. 3, 587 F.2d 1022, 1027 (9th Cir. 1978) (citing linguistic and cultural diversity as source of weakness for nation-state).

The view that recent Mexican immigrants are not learning English as rapidly as did other prior immigrant groups has been refuted by a recent Rand Corporation study, K. MCCARTHY & R. BURCIAGA VALDEZ, CURRENT AND FUTURE EFFECTS OF MEXICAN IMMIGRATION IN CALIFORNIA (1986). The research found that persons of Mexican origin are making essentially the same progress of integration as earlier European immigrants and as the state's recent Asian immigrants. *Id.* at 54-55. The study also examined the transition of Spanish speakers to English, concluding that most of the first-generation native-born are bilingual, and more than 90% are proficient in English. Among the second-generation, more than half are monolingual English speakers. Thus, the transition to English is almost immediate. *Id.* at 60; *see also English Courses: Immigrants—a Rush to the Classrooms*, L.A. Times, Sept. 24, 1986, at 1, col. 1 (In the Los Angeles Unified School District alone, officials estimate that 40,000 adults will be turned away from English as a second language (ESL) classes in 1986.).

of English.[83] On the contrary, the direct effect on disenfranchised individuals is likely to be their further alienation from the political process.[84]

Further, the deprivation of voting rights increases the possibility that, as a group, non-English speakers who already suffer economic disadvantages because of their linguistic handicap will also suffer political disadvantages because of their lack of representation.[85] They will be less likely to receive government benefits such as social services and educational facilities which are meted out by political representatives.[86] Since the availability of such benefits is widely recognized as essential to a group's ability to assimilate, English-only elections are more likely to slow the process of assimilation, rather than to "encourage" it.[87]

2. The Costs of Multilingual Elections

A state may argue that multilingual ballots and assistance are prohibitively costly, thus justifying the provision of ballots only in English. Cost efficiency, however, has not been accepted by the judiciary as a compelling governmental interest sufficient to survive even an intermediate degree of scrutiny.[88]

Assuming arguendo that a court were to scrutinize the costs of multi-

---

83. *See* Sierra v. El Paso Indep. School Dist., 591 F. Supp. 802, 807 (W.D. Tex. 1984) (finding lingering effects of past official discrimination in form of poll tax and English-only ballots deterred Mexican-Americans from registering, voting, and otherwise participating in political process); *see also* Rome v. United States, 446 U.S. 156, 176 (1980) (addressing alienating effects of discriminatory voting practices); Graves v. Barnes, 378 F. Supp. 640 (W.D. Tex. 1974) (examining discriminatory impact of multi-member districts on Mexican-American access to political process); Karst, *Paths to Belonging: The Constitution and Cultural Identity*, 64 N.C.L. REV. 303, 332-36 (1986).
84. Karst, *supra* note 83, at 332-36.
85. Disenfranchisement of non-English speakers deprives them of a vital instrument for change through the political process and points to the need for the special judicial protection granted to "discrete and insular" minorities. *See generally supra* note 33; J. ELY, *supra* note 38.
86. Katzenbach v. Morgan, 384 U.S. 641, 652 (1966) ("Section 4(e) may be viewed as a measure to secure for the Puerto Rican community residing in New York non-discriminatory treatment by government—both in the imposition of voting qualifications and the provision or administration of governmental services, such as public schools, public housing and law enforcement."); *see also* Karst, *supra* note 83, at 334.
87. This argument assumes that the best interests of non-English speakers are served by assimilation. While both English-only supporters and opponents agree that non-English speakers are better off if they learn English, some racial and ethnic groups have in the last few decades asserted their rights to maintain their native tongues while becoming proficient in English. *See, e.g.*, Karst, *supra* note 83, at 337; Comment, *Cultural Pluralism*, 13 HARV. C.R.-C.L. L. REV. 133 (1978). Moreover, discrimination in the *choice* of language deprives a person of human dignity by distorting one's conception of identity. McDougal, Lasswell & Chen, *Freedom from Discrimination in Choice of Language and International Human Rights*, 1 S. ILL. U.L.J. 151, 151-52 (1976).
88. *See* Frontiero v. Richardson, 411 U.S. 677, 689-90 (1973) (administrative convenience does not outweigh female military persons' equal protection rights to equal treatment). In Carrington v. Rash, 380 U.S. 89, 96 (1965), the Court rejected the state's claims that denying the vote to persons in the Army promoted administrative efficiency: "States may not casually deprive a class of individuals of the vote because of some remote administrative benefit . . . ."; *see also* Shapiro v. Thompson, 394 U.S. 618, 633 (1969) ("The saving of welfare costs cannot justify an otherwise invidious classification."); Memorial Hosp. v. Maricopa County, 415 U.S. 250, 263 (1974) ("The conservation of the taxpayers' purse is simply not a sufficient state interest to sustain a durational residency requirement which, in effect, severely penalizes exercise of the right [to travel]."); Rivera v. Dunn, 329 F. Supp. 554 (D. Conn. 1971), *aff'd*, 404 U.S. 1054 (1972) (same).

lingual ballots, the relevant equal protection question to ask with respect to costs is not how much more a state would have to spend to provide multilingual assistance, but how much is already spent per voter to provide English ballots and whether the comparative costs of multilingual voting would be so excessive as to override a fundamental right.[89] The information available on costs, however, looks to the question of incremental rather than comparative costs. There is a tendency to focus only on the costs of multilingual ballots, without taking into consideration the costs of English ballots; the amount of money spent per English-speaking voter has apparently never seemed relevant.

Nevertheless, the data does suggest that the cost of multilingual ballots are only a small percentage of total election expenses. A study by the General Accounting Office reports that the additional costs incurred by 83 jurisdictions that provided bilingual ballots which had record of such costs were 7.6% of the total costs to these jurisdictions to hold the November 4, 1984 election.[90] In 259 of the jurisdictions surveyed by the General Accounting Office which provided oral assistance, no costs were incurred.[91] Thus, available data strongly suggests that the costs of providing multilingual voting assistance fall within the range of expenditures that can be compelled.[92]

Furthermore, Congress was clearly not concerned that multilingual elections were excessively costly.[93] One might assume that the use of the

---

89. Many people express an instinctive worry that a constitutional rule that requires states to provide multilingual voting assistance to *every* non-English speaker would be excessively costly and administratively burdensome in areas with only a few non-English speakers. As with most constitutional requirements, however, states would have the flexibility to develop systems for identifying voters needing the assistance and for implementing the multilingual system. Courts should nonetheless place a heavy burden on the states to accomodate every voter needing assistance unless such accommodation would be clearly unreasonable. For example, if there were only one person within a 500 mile radius that needed assistance, and no one was available in that area to interpret the ballot, assistance might not be a reasonable demand on the state.
90. GAO REPORT, *supra* note 25, at 19.
91. *Id.* at 18. Moreover, the growing use of multilingual voting assistance has caused costs to decline over time, due to "better targeting of materials, and more reliance upon translations and materials used in prior elections." S. REP. NO. 417, 97th Cong., 2d Sess. 65, *reprinted in* 1982 U.S. CODE CONG. & ADMIN. NEWS 243-44. The Senate Report also notes the dramatically decreased costs in Los Angeles from 1976 to 1980, the 1980 figure constituting only 1.9 percent of the total general election budget. *Id.*
92. *Id.* As the need for multilingual election materials has grown, the economies of scale involved in the production of these materials has fallen, thus reducing the costs to individual counties. *See* GAO REPORT, *supra* note 25, at 25. Additionally, for small counties oral voting assistance may be provided at almost no cost as most interpreters volunteer their service gratuitously. *Id.* at 18. Finally, firms in the voting materials industry are exploring the possibilities for computerized voting machines. VOTING SYSTEM STANDARDS, A REPORT TO CONGRESS ON THE DEVELOPMENT OF VOLUNTARY ENGINEERING AND PROCEDURAL PERFORMANCE STANDARDS FOR VOTING SYSTEMS (1984). Such advanced technology could dramatically reduce the costs of providing written multilingual services, making it clearly unreasonable not to provide such services.
93. The Senate Judiciary Committee strongly refuted the "excessive costs" arguments with empirical evidence and further concluded: "Even if the costs of bilingual elections were higher . . . the Committee believes that certain costs should be willingly incurred to make our most fundamental political rights a reality for all Americans." S. REP. NO. 417, 97th Cong., 2d Sess. 65, *reprinted in* 1982 U.S. CODE CONG. & ADMIN. NEWS 244.

five percent trigger was intended as a cost-minimizing device. In fact, Congress used the five percent mark to identify areas where federal statutory intrusion was most needed so as not to interfere in states' decisions on voting procedures unless the situation rose to a level where federal action was warranted.[94]

Admittedly, states cannot provide voting materials without discriminating, or drawing lines, at some point. Within a constitutional framework, the states must have discretion in the operation of voting facilities and in the printing of ballots and other materials. However, states have an overriding obligation to provide voting opportunities on an evenhanded basis to all citizens and to extend meaningful voting assistance to non-English speakers.

III. Policy Suggestions

In communities with non-English speaking groups, the logistics involved in operating the voting process may become complicated. Thus, Congress might consider changing the multilingual voting provisions of the Voting Rights Act to replace the percentage trigger with a numerical trigger and to expand coverage to all non-English speakers. For example, instead of requiring multilingual elections in areas that meet the five percent requirement, the Act should be triggered in areas with, say, 1,000 non-English speakers. In areas with fewer than 1,000 non-English speakers, the states should be required to make reasonable efforts to provide assistance, either written or oral. States might be required to inquire about the voters' needs for language assistance at registration, for instance. However, the burden of notifying election officials of one's need for assistance should probably rest with the voter where there is no large, established non-English speaking community that triggers the Act. Community ethnic leagues could serve as liasons with the state to facilitate this communication. In short, multilingual elections should involve extensive communication and cooperation between state officials and community members.

---

94. A cost minimizing rationale for the five percent trigger is mentioned nowhere in the legislative history. *See Extension of the Voting Rights Act: Hearings Before the Subcomm. on Civil and Constitutional Rights of the House Comm. on the Judiciary*, 94th Cong., 1st Sess. 84 (1975) [hereinafter *1975 House Hearings*] (statement of Rep. Jordan); *id.* at 573 (statement of Mr. Pottinger); 9111 CONG. REC. S1279 (daily ed. Apr. 7, 1975) (statement of Sen. Bayh).

Representatives Roybal and Badillo lifted the five percent trigger from lower court decisions in Arroyo v. Tucker, 372 F. Supp. 764 (E.D. Pa. 1974) and Torres v. Sachs, 381 F. Supp. 309 (S.D.N.Y. 1974). *1975 House Hearings*, *supra*, at 884, 934. These decisions required bilingual ballots and materials for all Puerto Rican voters, but required bilingual election officials only in election districts in which Puerto Rican voters constituted at least five percent of the voting population. *Arroyo*, 372 F. Supp. at 768; *Torres*, 381 F. Supp. at 313.

IV. CONCLUSION

Courts have been deeply involved in extending the franchise to marginal groups that majoritarian processes exclude. A representative democracy mandates that every adult citizen have a voice in the future of the polity.[95] If courts gave the voting rights of non-English speakers federal constitutional protection, the states and Congress could better address themselves to the vindication of those rights. Additionally, through further amendment of the Voting Rights Act, Congress can most efficiently implement federal policies that protect language minorities from disenfranchisement, eliminating the need for individual state legislation. A judicial determination that the prohibition of multilingual voting assistance violates the constitutional rights of non-English speakers would firmly establish a state or national language policy that incorporates, rather than excludes, speakers of all languages into one cohesive body politic.

---

95. Professor Karst points to two fundamental values encompassed in rights of citizenship: protection of human dignity and self-respect, and protection of avenues for participation in the decisionmaking processes of the community. Karst, *The Supreme Court, 1976 Term—Foreword: Equal Citizenship Under the Fourteenth Amendment*, 91 HARV. L. REV. 1, 23 (1977). In another piece he says that respect for rights of citizenship:
> promote[s] the freedom of individual choice about cultural identification. . . . When the promise of equal citizenship is fulfilled, the paths to belonging are opened in two directions for members of cultural minorities. As full members of the larger society, they have the option to participate to whatever degree they choose. They may also look inward, seeking solidarity within their cultural groups, without being penalized for that choice.

Karst, *supra* note 83, at 337.

An Analysis of Chicano and Anglo Electoral Patterns in School Board Elections

JOHN A. GARCIA

University of Arizona

> An increase in the number of Chicanos seeking public office focuses concern on the kind of effort Chicano candidates pursue and the response pattern of Anglo voters. For this study, examining school board elections in urban Arizona, the chief research questions are the degree of voter polarization, the sociopolitical factors affecting voters' preferences, and the distinctiveness of Anglo and Chicano bloc voting. The results have definite implications for successful electoral strategies.

The recent upsurge of interest in Chicano activities and general raising of ethnic consciousness have resulted in the an increase in number of Chicanos seeking public office. This study, examining school board elections in Tucson, Arizona, focuses on three research points: (1) the extent to which voters prefer candidates of their own racial/ethnic background; (2) the sociopolitical factors affecting these voters' preferences; and (3) the degree of voter polarization among Chicano and Anglo voters.

The school board election constitutes an important political event for a Chicano community.[1] The educational systems have been criticized for their neglect of ethnic children, for inferior facilities, for monolingual–monocultural curricula, for poor quality education, for lack of policy representation, and perhaps also because the schools affect Chicano parents daily through their children. For these reasons, the educational arena has become politicized. The outcome of this new consciousness includes school walkouts, demands for bilingual–bicultural programs, legal action, and increased electoral attempts among Chicanos to win school board seats.[2] This politicization at the Chicano community level makes relevant an investigation of the general climate of electoral competition between Anglos and Chicanos, particularly in nonpartisan elections.[3]

CHICANO/ANGLO ELECTORAL ACTIVITY: BACKGROUND PERSPECTIVE

Three key factors shed light on the electoral competition between the Anglo and Chicano communities: (1) the degree of Chicano electoral activity; (2) the impact which nonpartisan elections have had on Chicano candidate preference and turnout; (3) the interplay of nonpartisan elections on candidate preference and turnout.

Revision of paper presented at the Western Political Science Association meeting in San Francisco, California, April 1–3, 1976.

Chicano Electoral Activity

Recent literature has suggested some prevalent voter participation patterns among Chicanos. The three major findings characterizing their political participation include (1) lower rates of political participation than other population groups, (2) a continuous allegiance to the Democratic party,[4] and (3) a high level of polarization or voter preferences by Chicano voters for Chicano candidates.[5] Chicano electoral behavior also shows lower registration and turnout rates than that of Anglos and blacks.[6]

Chicano participation in elections has been diminished by structural barriers. The use of literacy tests, annual registration requirements, poll taxes, gerrymandering, and at-large elections has effected a formidable barrier for potential Chicano voters. McClesky and Nimmo observed a much lower rate of registration for Mexican–Americans than for Anglos or blacks, particularly under the poll tax system.[7] Alan Shinn's study notes no significant correlation between registration and turnout; yet in other years studies have shown a positive correlation between registration and percentage of Spanish surname population.[8]

Socioeconomic status and attitudinal dispositions toward government and its agents further impede political involvement. Such participation usually increases as individuals attain higher levels of socioeconomic status.[9] The disproportionate number of Chicanos occupying lower socioeconomic status affects participation levels negatively.[10] In addition, attitudinal dispositions of cynicism, alienation, and efficacy toward the political system have restricted participation. Studies such as Grebler, Guzman and Moore,[11] and Comer, Steinman, and Welch[12] indicate that negative feelings toward government (cynicism, alienations, and inefficacy) tend to retard motivations for actively engaging in the political process.[13]

The second major characteristic of Chicano political activity is the strong association with the Democratic party. Although this association is traditional and has affected major elections (i.e., presidential elections), Chicanos have been excluded in the decision-making processes of the party. The lack of personal involvement and absence of a strong sense of identification with the Democratic party have not encouraged political consciousness among Chicanos. On the other hand, the La Raza Unida Party, with policies closer to the reality of most Chicanos, might possibly succeed in lessening Democratic ties,[15] thus inviting more Chicanos into active political participation.

The third major characteristic of Chicano political activity relates to the polarization of voters. The rise of ethnic consciousness among Chicanos has perpetuated bloc voting and, at times, increased Anglo political activity to compensate for Chicano votes. For example, Paul Castro's first attempt for the Arizona governorship received the overwhelming majority of Chicano votes although the turnout in Chicano precincts was 22% points lower than the statewide turnout.[16] Thus Castro's defeat in 1970 can be attributed to a lower than expected turnout among Chicanos whose support of his candidacy was strong and a higher than anticipated voter turnout of those not in favor of a Mexican–American governor.

The increasing significance of ethnic identification on Chicano voter preference is confirmed by two studies. Daniel Valdes' panel analysis of Hispanic-voters' support indicated a positive correlation between identification, interest, and intent to vote for Hispanic candidates.[17] The intensity of ethnicity served as a political stimulus for following campaigns as well as turning out to vote.

Rudolph de la Garza's aggregate voting study of bicultural El Paso examined Chicano voting patterns. He noted that the percentage of votes Mexican–American candidates received was affected largely by the total number of votes cast in the Mexican–American precincts. Negative correlations existed between Mexican–American precincts and turnout.[18] Thus, the presence of voter polarization exists, yet low turnout points out the need to mobilize the Chicano community effectively.

THE IMPACT OF NONPARTISAN ELECTIONS ON CHICANO VOTING

Nonpartisan elections, elections with emphasis on local issues, are of great importance and relevance to the Chicano voter. Nonpartisan ballots have shown the second major influence on the Chicano voter as indicated by voter polarization and voting turnout patterns. In the absence of party labels for candidates, partisan cues have been replaced by ethnic ones. Pomper's study of Newark's local elections indicates that ethnic groups vote disproportionately for their fellow ethnic candidates.[19] Candidates utilize ethnic symbols and cues in their campaigns, thereby reinforcing social cleavages.[20] Similarly, a mock election of Polish voters indicated that when party labels are removed, ethnicity is a better discriminator than party identification for voters' preferences.[21] Ethnicity has become institutionalized into the political life of many American communities.

The final consideration regarding nonpartisanship relates to "class bias." Nonpartisan elections diminish lower-class and minority voter participation.[22] This results, of course, in Republicans benefiting from nonpartisan and at-large elections.[23] As local elections continue to be salient for minorities and as greater numbers of Chicano candidates seek elective office, the interplay of Chicano political participation, type of elections, and Anglo response patterns work as critical factors in affecting electoral outcomes.

Electoral activity among Chicanos, the reaction of Anglos to political involvement, and the ethnic loyalty displayed in nonpartisan elections all serve as background to this study. With this foundation in mind, we may now proceed to examine Chicano electoral activity in two school board elections in an attempt to gain insight into three questions. First, what is the extent of voters' preferences for candidates of their own racial/ethnic background? Second, what are the important sociopolitical variables that affect voter preferences and turnout? Third, are the group behavioral patterns of Chicano and Anglos voters distinct?

CHICANO ELECTORAL ACTIVITY AND SCHOOL BOARD ELECTIONS

Research Design

The setting for this study is Tucson, Arizona. The major school district in the metropolitan area is the largest in the state and reflects the major composition of the state's residents—Anglos, Chicanos, blacks, and native Americans. Competition for representation on the school board has been increasing among the Chicano community and they have had some successes in other elections such as city council, county board of supervisors, and the state legislature. In other ways, Tucson is representative of other Southwestern urban areas which are experiencing significant growth and have a sizeable minority community, particularly Chicano.

The use of aggregate data enables the researcher to focus on the political entity of county precincts, as well as the group voting patterns of Anglos and Chicanos. This study has more of an environmental[24] rather than attitudinal context regarding Chicano voting patterns. The advantage of using aggregate data is that it makes possible the analysis of trends for successive elections or larger periods of time[25] which can be important in examining the long-term affects of Chicano voting behavior. In this case, two successive school board elections were examined.

Data for this research were derived from the Pima County (Ariz.) Election Bureau, and the U.S. Bureau of the Census for Spanish surname populations.[26] Individual precincts served as the unit of analysis as election data were matched with corresponding demographic characteristics of census tracts. The selection of key Chicano and Anglo precincts was determined by the concentration of each group throughout the county precincts. Only those representative precincts in which Chicanos were the dominant residential group and where Anglos exceeded 90% of the precinct were included in the analysis.[27] The school board election years utilized in the study were 1972 and 1974.

The Chicano population of Tucson comprises 25–30% of the city's residents.[28] A total of 18 Chicano and 14 Anglo precincts was selected. A range of 43.0 to 84.7% Chicano and a range of 3 to 8.2% Spanish surname population in Anglo precincts was discovered.[29] As substantiated by special reports by the U.S. Census Bureau,[30] the socioeconomic gap between Anglo and Chicanos is reflected in the Tucson data (see Table 1). The Tucson Chicano community exhibits relatively low to medium socioeconomic characteristics compared to Anglos. The median educational level was 9.1 years (12.95 for Anglos): the median income was $7098 (10,575 Anglos); and only 7.8% Chicanos were employed in white-collar occupations (68.9% Anglos).

Politically, the Anglo precincts tend to be more competitive in party registration. Anglo precincts average 45% Democratic registration whereas Chicano precincts surpass 70% in both election years. Another noteworthy characteristic is the variation in the number of persons registered each election year. Although both groups of precincts fluctuated significantly, their directional change is different. The Anglo precincts had an average registration increase of 11.4% per precinct vs a 14.2% decrease for Chicano precincts. A final difference lies in voter turnout rates. A 14-point difference exists in the 1972 school board election, and an 8-point gap in 1974, in which Anglos have higher turnout rates.

Racial/Ethnic Background and Voter Preference

Tucson School Board elections of 1972 and 1974 were of particular significance for several reasons. Although the Board was elected at-large and on a nonpartisan basis, a 1971 Arizona law changed the time of school elections to coincide with the general elections for state and federal offices. As a result, the number of votes necessary to win office would be substantially higher than in the previous off-year elections. In addition, the impact of partisanship undoubtedly would have some affect on school board elections as coterminous elections stimulate greater interest and turnout. A final background note on Tucson school board elections is that only one person with a Spanish surname[31] had ever been elected to the school board.

The school elections of 1972 and 1974 were spotlighted by a greater concern for minority representation and minority perspectives on educational policies. The Chicano candidate in 1972 pursued a barrio-oriented campaign, as well as stressing community control of schools. Between elections recent school board decisions had increased Chicano interest in the educational arena. Two key issues surfaced in the fall of 1973 and the following year. The school district decided to close two inner city schools as part of an austerity program. The schools, predominantly Mexican–American, were the scene of intense activity by Chicano parents to reverse that decision, as well as seek greater consultation before key issues was voted. Secondly, the Association of Mexican–American Educators was working closely with the School District to develop more bilingual programs as well as dealing with the issues of equality of educa-

TABLE 1
DEMOGRAPHIC AND POLITICAL CHARACTERISTICS OF CHICANO AND ANGLO PRECINCTS[a] IN TUCSON (ARIZONA) SCHOOL DISTRICT

Characteristic	Mean for Chicano precincts ($n = 16$)	Range for Chicano precincts	Mean for Anglo precincts ($n = 14$)	Range for Anglo precincts
Party affiliation				
% Democratic registration '72	75.2	58.7–86.3	45.3	34.4–51.4
% Democratic registration '74	74.1	58.9–84.6	45.9	36–52.1
% Change in voter registration 1972–1974	−14.2	−52.7–(−1.9)	11.4	−4.7–48.2
Socioeconomic status index				
Educational attainment	9.1	6.9–11.5	12.95	12.5–13.7
Type of employment				
% White-collar occupation	7.8	6.9–11.5	68.9	46.4–79.7
% Blue-collar occupation	47.9	31.9–59.8	14.6	5.2–20.2
Income ($)	7,098	4,621–8,798	10,575	7,515–13,624
Voting turnout				
Turnout 1972	52.6	33–66	66.1	56–74
Turnout 1974	56.7	44–69	64.1	52–73

[a] A Chicano precinct is defined as one which has a minimum of 50% Spanish surnamed residents. An Anglo precinct is defined as one which has a maximum of 5% minority residents.

129

tional opportunity and proposed bussing. Shortly after the closing was delayed, a class action suit was filed by Mexican–American parents contesting the inequality of educational opportunity for Chicano children.[32] In the 1974 school board election, the availability of two seats and a large field of Anglo candidates, together with increased community awareness, provided an opportunity for a Chicano to win a seat on the school board.[33]

With this background of the Tucson school situation, an examination of voters' preferences in Anglo and Chicano precincts in the 1972 and 1974 elections reveals some distinct variations. In both elections (see Table 2) the Chicano candidates secured their largest percentage of votes in Chicano precincts. Grijalva, the unsuccessful Chicano candidate, in 1972 fared a very distant third in votes received in Anglo precincts (8.9%), yet in 1974 he was much more successful in attracting Anglo votes (23.8%), and won one of the vacant seats. Thus a winning strategy entailed a strong margin of support in barrio precincts as well as establishing sizeable inroads into Anglo voting preferences. This concentration of voter support among members of the candidate's background indicates a polarizing effect.

From this standpoint of polarization, it is interesting to note that the degree of Chicano preference for Chicano candidates (50.2%) in 1974 was more pronounced than Anglo support for Anglo candidates (a high of

TABLE 2
PERCENTAGE OF VOTES CAST FOR MAJOR CANDIDATES IN 1972 AND 1974 SCHOOL BOARD ELECTION BY ANGLO AND CHICANO PRECINCTS

Candidates	Chicano precincts		Anglo precincts	
	Mean (%)	Range	Mean (%)	Range
1972				
S. Downing	12.7	5.1–22.8	27.1	22.3–33.3
R. Grijalva	46.9	27.3–72.9	8.9	4.5–14.5
S. Tom[a]	32.9	18.4–46.3	50.2	39.2–56.9
1974[b]				
S. Downing	15.0	5.8–33.7	34.1	26.6–41.0
G. Fogel	9.2	3.6–21.6	19.1	11.2–24.2
R. Grijalva[c]	50.2	30.0–75.7	23.8	19.1–29.0
H. Hafley[a]	19.0	10.0–27.4	34.5	25.9–41.3
A. Lopez	38.8	7.2–53.8	15.0	12.3–20.3

[a] Incumbents who were reelected for another term on the School Board.
[b] In 1974, two seats were vacant for the Tucson School Board.
[c] Elected in 1974 to be only the second Spanish surname individual to serve on the Tucson School Board.

34.5%). That is, Chicanos showed a greater degree of voting support for the Chicano candidate, as opposed to their Anglo voting counterparts for the Anglo candidates. Voting polarization tends to follow clusters of voting support along racial and ethnic lines.

In order to explore further the extent of polarization of voters, each pair of candidates was examined in accordance with the Spearman rho coefficients (see Table 3). The use of Spearman ρ coefficients illustrates the degree of congruence of voters' preferences as well as direction, for each pair of candidates. Compatible pairs of candidates would have high positive correlations.

The evidence of polarization is quite pronounced in the 1972 election. One can see the strong negative correlation that exists when non-Chicano candidates are involved with a Chicano candidate (Grijalva) in the Chicano precincts (i.e., −.84 Downing−Grijalva/ −.77 Tom−Grijalva). Similarly, a negative correlation exists when Grijalva is paired with non-Chicano candidates in the Anglo precincts (−.37 Tom−Grijalva) (See Table 3).

The 1974 election produced similar results in Chicano precincts. Positive correlations exist with each pair of Anglo candidates, and equally with pairs of Chicano candidates, more so in the Chicano precincts. The degree of polarization in Anglo precincts is most pronounced among the leading Anglo candidates (Downing and incumbent Hafley = .71) and the

TABLE 3
Spearman ρ Coefficients for Pairs of School Board Candidates by Chicano and Anglo Precincts

Candidate pairs	Chicano precincts	Anglo precincts
1972		
Downing−Grijalva	−.84*	.09
Downing−Tom	.68*	−.32***
Grijalva−Tom	−.77*	−.37**
1974		
Downing−Fogel	.71*	−.01
Downing−Grijalva	−.54*	−.13
Downing−Hafley	.78**	.71*
Downing−Lopez	−.45***	−.46**
Fogel−Grijalva	−.29***	−.02
Fogel−Hafley	.55**	.05
Fogel−Lopez	−.42**	−.13
Grijalva−Hafley	−.36**	−.02
Grijalva−Lopez	.64*	.08
Hafley−Lopez	−.38**	−.57**

* Significant at the .001 level.
** Significant at the .005 level.
*** Significant at the .01 level.

two Chicanos (Grijalva and Lopez .64 in Chicano precincts). That is, correlation with all pairs of Anglo candidates did not reveal a pervasive pattern of voter polarization. Interestingly enough, an informal coalition of liberal Anglo candidate Fogel with Grijalva did not produce visible payoffs for this pair. The evidence, therefore, strongly suggests identifiable voter preference among Chicano and Anglo voters (see Table 3).

Another surprising fact is that the Chicano voter preference affected all of the Chicano candidates, while Anglo preferences affected only the leading status quo[34] Anglo candidates and Chicano contenders. Part of this pattern may be attributable to the long absence of Chicanos on the school board, as well as there being relatively few Chicano candidates over the years. Thus the absence of electoral success may have heightened Chicano preferences for all Chicano candidates.

While racial/ethnic background and voting preferences constitute an important element in understanding Chicano electoral activity, there are other factors that need to be explored. A second important consideration lies with the sociodemographic factors that underlie support for the various candidates. What, for instance, is the significance of the associations of class, ethnicity, and party affiliation with votes cast for Chicano or Anglo candidates?

Sociopolitical Variables and Chicano and Anglo Voting Preferences

In the 1972 election, several distinct patterns appeared within the Chicano precincts. Socioeconomic status[35] had positive effects with non-Chicano candidates, positive correlations of .72 and .73 (see Table 4). Most of Grijalva's support came from low socioeconomic status voters

TABLE 4
Pearsonian Coefficients between Major School Board Candidates (1972) and Sociopolitical Variables for Anglo and Chicano Precincts

Sociopolitical variables	Chicano precincts		
	Downing	Grijalva	Tom
SES	.72*	−.69**	−.73*
% Democratic/precinct	−.34	.34	−.30
% Spanish surname	−.62**	.60**	−.60*
Turnout rate	.30	−.16	.09
	Anglo precincts		
SES	−.36	−.64**	.35
% Democratic/precinct	.27	.66**	−.25
% Spanish surname	−.05	.01	−.05
Turnout rate	.12	−.76*	.51***

* Significant at the .001 level.
** Significant at the .005 level.
*** Significant at the .01 level.

(−.69). In addition, the positive effect of percent Spanish surname with votes cast for Grijalva further establishes a voter polarization pattern (.60). The pattern persists in the Anglo precincts as socioeconomic status and turnout rates are related positively with Anglo candidates (rs of .35 and .51 respectively) and partisanship (percentage Democratic/precinct) is related significantly with votes for Grijalva (.66). In the case of incumbent S. Tom, turnout is related positively and significantly (.51). In both groups of precincts, turnout is negatively related with votes for Grijalva.

The 1974 election produced even more pronounced patterns of party, socioeconomic status, and ethnicity. Socioeconomic status was clearly a factor in votes for Downing, Grijalva, and incumbent Hafley (see Table 5). Votes for the Chicano candidates and socioeconomic status were related negatively reflecting a stronger base of support from the lower socioeconomic strata of the Chicano community; yet this pattern was more pronounced for Grijalva in Chicano precincts. On the other hand Anglo candidates had positive correlations with socioeconomic status in both groups of precincts (rs = .39 and .41).

The effects of partisanship in Chicano precincts played a major role for each of the candidates. For the Chicano candidates, Democratic registration was related positively, while the opposite effect existed for Chicanos in the Anglo precincts (−.57 and −.61). The significance of partisanship

TABLE 5
Pearsonian Coefficients between Major School Board Candidates (1974) and Sociopolitical Variables for Anglo and Chicano Precincts

	Sociopolitical variables			
Candidates	SES	% Democrat/ precinct	Turnout	% Spanish surname
Chicano precincts				
S. Downing	.79**	−.79*	.54***	−.82*
G. Fogel	.18	−.78*	.18	−.66**
R. Grijalva	−.40***	.61**	−.40	.53***
H. Hafley	.42	−.59**	.42	−.59***
A. Lopez	−.08	.87*	−.08	.51***
Anglo precincts				
S. Downing	.39	−.57**	.66**	.42
G. Fogel	−.17	.23	.18	−.29
R. Grijalva	−.47***	+.33	−.30	−.05
H. Hafley	.41***	−.65**	.70*	.03
A. Lopez	−.61**	.61**	−.72*	−.15

* Significant at .001 level.
** Significant at .005 level.
*** Significant at .01 level.

was greater for Lopez than any other candidate for both groups of precincts. The impact of ethnicity acted much the same as party in Chicano precincts for Grijalva and Lopez. At the same time, negative correlations of percentage Spanish surname and Anglo candidates were significant.

The final aspect of voter preference in these precincts lies in the turnout correlations with each of the candidates. Similar to the 1972 election, turnout in 1974 was negatively associated with votes cast for Chicano candidates and positively related to votes for Anglo candidates. The pattern that emerges illustrates the distinctiveness of lower socioeconomic status support for Chicano and higher socioeconomic status for Anglo candidates, and the positive effects of ethnicity for Chicano candidates in barrio precincts. In addition, the impact of party registration is strongly related, in a positive direction, with Chicano candidates. Although lower socioeconomic voters support Chicano candidates, the interplay of class and turnout come to bear. As turnout is related to increases in socioeconomic status, the Anglo candidates' support is reflected by positive associations with turnout, but a negative association exists with Chicano candidates.

The Pervasiveness of Voter Polarization between Anglos and Chicanos

Since group preference for candidates of their own background has been established, as well as the relative importance of class, ethnicity and party affiliation, the final inquiry deals with the pervasiveness of bloc voting among Anglos and Chicanos. As Chicanos increasingly engage in political campaigns, as improvements are made in their socioeconomic status, and as salient issues are clearly defined, one might expect ethnic voting clusters to decrease. The wave of ethnic politics could be replaced by more salient factor of class, partisanship and party identification. In order to assess the persistence of ethnicity in nonpartisan elections, the use of multiple discriminant analysis was selected to test the validity of the assumption that Chicanos and Anglo voters behave as distinct groups.[36] Discriminant analysis serves to examine the selection of these groups and determine whether the individuals in the defined groups were correctly classified. Discriminant coefficients indicate which independent variables discriminate between the groups, as well as their relative contribution. Finally, this technique is useful in this study because: its multivariate capability allows for the accounting of covariation among explanatory or discriminatory variables; it can handle a large number of groupings; and the significance of each discriminant function for each variable can be evaluated separately.

The discriminant analyses of the 1972 and 1974 elections verify the distinct nature of Chicano and Anglo voting patterns. In the analyses, all of the candidates were included to examine the pervasiveness of any bloc voting. As a result, 93.3% and 100% of the cases were correctly classified in the respective elections. That is, the precincts that were identified as Chicano or Anglo precincts voted as two distinct groups. The centroids for each election also reflected the different spatial location for the two groups of precincts (see Table 6). The centroids are at opposite polar positions (1.66 for Chicanos vs −1.89 for Anglos in 1972) illustrating the distinct and polarized voting preferences for these two groups. The standard discriminant coefficient is strongest for Grijalva and in the direction of the Chicano centroid location. Incumbent Tom's candidacy was not only strong in Anglo precincts, but able to make a good showing (averaging 32.9) in the Chicano precincts.

Because Chicano and Anglo voting patterns persisted through 1974, greater credence can be given comparing this bloc voting pattern in other electoral contexts. Chicano voters do behave differently than Anglos, and

TABLE 6
Discriminant Analysis of Voting Preferences for School Board Elections 1972 and 1974 for Chicano and Anglo Precincts

Elections	Standardized discriminant coefficients	Percentage of cases correctly classified
1972		
S. Downing	−.93	93.3
R. Grijalva	1.37	
R. Hall	−.03	
A. Spaletto	−.09	
S. Tom	.30	
	Canonical correlation = .88, χ^2 = 39.0 00.0	
Centroids		
Chicano precincts	= 1.66	
Anglo precincts	= −1.89	
1974		
S. Downing	−1.43	100
G. Fogel	.45	
G. Gault	.29	
R. Grijalva	.48	
H. Hafley	.81	
E. Kahn	.13	
S. Lehrling	.75	
A. Lopez	−2.12	
R. Waite	.25	
	Canonical correlations = .93, χ^2 = 49.54 00.0	
Centroids		
Chicano precincts	= −2.41	
Anglo precincts	= 2.41	

ethnicity still serves as a salient force in candidate support. The variation of class and party influences suggest factors that may also be creating these differences. That is, even in nonpartisan elections, the effect of partisanship is significant when coterminous elections are held (i.e., state, federal, and school) particularly for Chicano voters.

Chicano and Anglo Voters: Conclusions and Implications

The examination of Chicano and Anglo voting patterns in school board elections produced several distinct patterns for these groups of voters. At the outset three research questions were posed. The issue relating to voter preference clearly revealed a distinct pattern for each set of voters. Chicano voters indicated a slightly greater degree of support for their own candidates than Anglos. Nevertheless, a discernible pattern of voters' preference was evident as each group voted for candidates of similar ethnic background.

With reference to the second question, the interplay of socioeconomic status, partisanship, and ethnicity reaffirmed the tendency toward polarization of voters, as well as the differentiated impact of each of these variables for Anglos and Chicanos. Although school board elections are nonpartisan, the spillover effect of coterminous elections has particular importance for Chicano voters. The impact of partisanship had a diminishing effect on Anglo candidate support, yet it was a significant factor for the Chicano candidates' votes. Interestingly, partisanship was more important for Lopez's voters than Grijalva's. This may suggest different lines of support for Chicano candidates within the Chicano community.[37] The data confirm this finding.

Class may also be posited as an important consideration in nonpartisan elections. Class was a significant variable for both Anglo and Chicano candidates, yet its directional impact was opposite as it correlated positively with Anglo candidates and negatively with Chicanos. As Chicano voters continued to cast their votes for Chicano candidates, the variation of turnout (and its negative relation) created problems for successful campaigns. The drop-off between registration and turnout posed concerns for leadership and mobilization where voter intensity, issue crystallization, and group consciousness should act to close the gap.

Finally, the utilization of discriminant analysis reaffirms the previous research findings of voter preferences, as the voting patterns of Chicanos and Anglos were quite distinct. Their patterns followed separate paths in the same way that each candidate had a unique impact on each group. The persistence of this group pattern suggests that ethnicity and probably different perspectives on issues and candidates are salient forces in the electoral arena. Interestingly, the political activity of Chicanos in city, county, and state races has produced a sizeable number of elected officials. Yet the evidence of polarization in a relatively open, competitive political system suggests that district composition is crucial for these electoral successes and that at-large elections perpetuate the problem of ethnic voting for Chicanos. The larger arena of electoral competition, coupled with a significant yet numerically moderate sized minority population alters the strategies, resources, and types of candidates involved in at-large elections.[38]

The implication of these findings suggests the need for further systematic investigations regarding the relationship of minority mobilization with majority group responses, as well as some longitudinal analysis of Chicano voting patterns. A salient factor in minority–majority relations is the size of the Chicano population in the respective communities. Group size can affect the extent of voter mobilization, expectancies of success, range of alternatives, extent of resources, and intensity of incentives.[39] Thus varieties of strategies may emerge that are dependent on the Chicano concentration in that community. Similarly, we might expect higher degrees of success when Chicanos are 30–40% (approximately) of the total population, as mobilization becomes easier and competition is established. The more difficult situation lies with a small ethnic population having little opportunity to mobilize or develop resources upon which to build a political base. Thus examination of Chicano political power may uncover increased minority mobilization activating increased Anglo mobilization, or the pattern may be one of oscillation with between success and failure.

The pervasiveness of polarization may be a short term phenomenon or an enduring one. Although ethnicity is a salient force, it does not explain all of the variance for turnout and voter preference for Chicano candidates. The use of survey research might explore the degree of ethnic identification, salience of specific issues, and the extent of campaign organizational contact to measure their effect on voter turnout and intensity. The pattern of increased numbers of Chicano candidates in future elections will necessitate a winning strategy that effectively mobilizes the Chicano community, restricts the field of Chicano candidates for each office, and either neutralizes Anglo voters or secures a reasonable share of Anglo votes. The style of campaigning may also play an increasingly important role here. Thus the concerns of Chicano electoral activity will continue to be a key political phenomenon in broadening our perspective on the long term impact of Chicano voting behavior.

NOTES

[1] See Carter, *Mexican-Americans in School: A History of Educational Neglect.* New York: College Entrance Examination Board; 1970. Ramirez, M. and A. Casteneda *Cultural Democracy, Bi-Cognitive Development and Education.* New York: Academic Press; 1974.

[2] Moore, J. *Mexican-Americans*, Englewood Cliffs, NJ, Prentice-Hall, pp. 76-83. Lopez y Rivas, G. *The Chicanos*. New York. Monthly Review Press, pp. 43-57.

[3] Pomper, G. "Ethnic and Group Voting in Non-Partisan Elections" *Public Opinion Quarterly* 30 (Spring, 1966), p. 97.

[4] Levy, M. and M Kramer *The Ethnic Factor*, New York: Simon & Schuster; 1973, p. 73.

[5] de la Garza, R. "Voting Patterns in Bi-Cultural El Paso—A Contextual Analysis of Mexican-American Voting Behavior" in F. Chris Garcia (ed.) *La Causa Politica*. Notre Dame, IN: Univ. of Notre Dame Press; 1974, p. 256.

[6] Shinn, A. "A Note on Voter Registration and Turnout in Texas, 1960-1970" *Journal of Politics* 33 (November, 1971), pp. 1120-1129.

[7] McClesky, C. and R. Merrill "Mexican-American Political Behavior in Texas" *Social Science Quarterly* 53 (March, 1973), pp. 785-799.

[8] See Note 6, p. 1125.

[9] Verba, S. and N. Nie *Participation in America*. New York: Harper & Row; 1972, pp. 125-137.

[10] See Note 4, p. 76.

[11] Grebler, L. et al., *The Mexican-American People*. New York: The Free Press; 1970, p. 567.

[12] Welch, S., J. Comer, and M. Steinman, "Political Participation Among Mexican-Americans: An Exploratory Examination" *Social Science Quarterly* 53 (March, 1973), pp. 799-813.

[13] Comer, J., S. Welch, and M. Steinman "Satisfaction with Government Services: Implications for Political Behavior" in T. Yarborough (ed.) *Politics 1973: Minorities in Politics*. Greenville, NC: East Carolina Univ. Publications: 1973, pp. 65-82.

[14] See Note 4, pp. 77-79.

[15] Juarez, A. "The Emergence of El Partido de la Raza Unida: California's New Chicano Party" *Aztlan: Chicano Journal of the Social Sciences* 3 (Fall, 1973), pp. 177-203.

[16] See Note 4, pp. 81-82.

[17] Valdes, D. *A Sociological Analysis and Description of the Political Role, Status and Voting Behavior of Americans with Spanish Names*. Ann Arbor, MI: University microfilms: 1964, p. 5.

[18] See Note 5, p. 259.

[19] See Note 3, pp. 79-98.

[20] See Note 3, pp. 89-90.

[21] Lorinskas, R. et al., "The Persistance of Ethnic Voting in Rural and Urban Areas" *Social Science Quarterly* 49 (March, 1969), pp. 871-899.

[22] Lee, E. C. *The Politics of Non-Partisanship*. Berkeley, CA: Univ. of California Press, 1960.

[23] See Note 3, p. 78.

[24] For such excellent discussion of ecological analysis, particularly minimizing the blanket concept of ecological fallacy see M. Dogan and S. Rokkan (eds.) *Social Ecology*. Cambridge, MA, MIT Press, 1969.

[25] Rossi, "Trends in Voting Behavior Research: 1933-1963" in E. Dreyer and W. Rosenbaum (eds.) *Political Opinions and Electoral Opinions*. Belmont, CA: Wadsworth Publishing Company; 1967, pp. 69-70.

[26] U.S. Department of Commerce-Social and Economic Statistics. *Characteristics of the Spanish Surname Population by Census Tract, for SMSA's in Arizona: 1970*. Washington D.C.: U.S. Govt. Printing Office; April 1974.

[27] The study is a longitudinal one so precinct boundary changes and changes in precinct numbers were recorded in the historical record of precincts and traced with all the precinct maps from 1959 to the present.

[28] As a result of political pressure by the Pima County Board of Supervisors, and commu-

nity groups, the Census Bureau agreed to conduct a recount particularly in the Spanish-speaking areas of the county. Sufficient evidence was produced to indicate undercounting in Chicano barrios.

[29] Two precincts were included with less than 50% population because of their proximity to dominant Chicano precincts. These areas are undergoing a rapid influx of Chicano migration as the Chicano areas are expanding.

[30] U.S. Bureau of the Census. *Persons of Spanish Origin in the United States*—March, 1975 (Current Population Reports PC-20-280) U.S. Govt. Printing Office, Washington, D.C.; 1975.

[31] In 1958 Mr. Richard Salvatierra was the first Spanish surname person elected to the Tucson School District.

[32] In 1975, a group of Mexican–American parents, Mexican–Americans for Equal Education, filed a lawsuit against the school district for discriminatory practices toward Mexican–American children and ethnic isolation. The suit included eight points that dealt with lack of bilingual programs, desegregation, staffing, curriculum, etc. Presently that suit has been enjoined by a similar NAACP suit and efforts are underway to reach an out of court settlement.

[33] Mr. Paul Grijalva was the second Spanish surname person elected to the Tucson School Board in 1974. The combination of two seats available and a substantial increase in Anglo votes aided his successful campaign. Mr. Richard Salvatierra served on the board 1954–1958.

[34] In the 1974, incumbent Hafley sought reelection and candidate S. Downing, previously unsuccessful candidate, had the whole-hearted support of the present school board majority. Thus, the conservative majority of the board endorsed these individuals and followed a recognizable pattern in candidate recruitment for board members. See H. Zeigler and M. Jennings *Governing American Schools*. N. Scuituote, MA; Duxbury Press: 1974, pp. 39–53.

[35] Utilizing demographic characteristics of precincts such as adult population, median income, educational attainment, percentage below poverty, etc., a factor analysis program was employed to tap underlying dimensions. As a result, four variables comprise the SES variable (percentage high school graduates, median income, percentage employed in white collar occupations, and degree of new residents in the precincts.) These scores were standardized and multiplied by the appropriate factor scores to give a total weighting.

[36] See M. Halbert *Multiple Discriminant Analysis for Studying Group Membership*. College Park, PA: College of Agriculture. Penn State University (Bulletin 775), February 1971.

[37] For a more intensive examination of variations of Chicano candidate support, see Garcia, J. "Chicano Voting Patterns in School Board Elections: Bloc Voting and Internal Lines of Support for Chicano Candidates" *Atisbos: Journal of Chicano Research* (Winter 1976–77). Vol. 5.

[38] See Cottrell, C. "Municipal Services Equalization and Internal Colonialism in San Antonio, Texas. Explorations in Chinatown" paper presented at Rocky Mountain Social Science Convention, April 24–26, 1975.

[39] Blalock, Hubert, *Toward a Theory of Minority-Group Relations*. Capricorn Books: New York, pp. 126–130, 136–142, 150–154.

Research Note

MINORITY POPULATION PROPORTION AND BLACK AND HISPANIC CONGRESSIONAL SUCCESS IN THE 1970s AND 1980s

BERNARD GROFMAN
University of California, Irvine
LISA HANDLEY
Election Data Services, Inc.
Washington, DC

We look at the relationship between a congressional district's black and Hispanic population proportion and the likelihood of election of black or Hispanic candidates. We show that black and Hispanic gains appear to be due to an increase in the number of districts with substantial minority population, rather than to any change in the willingness of nonminority voters to support minority candidates. In contrast to earlier work we focus on the importance of the *combined* minority (black plus Hispanic) population as a determinant of minority electoral success.

A number of court cases have looked at the question of how large the minority (black or Hispanic) population percentage needs to be in a given district in order to provide the minority group with a "realistic opportunity to elect officials of their choice" (*Kirksey v.*

Authors' Note: An earlier version of this article was prepared for the Conference on Electoral Geography, University of Southern California, April 1988. Listing of authors is alphabetical. This research was partially supported by NSF Grant 85-06376, Program in Political Science, and by a grant from the UCI Academic Senate Research Committee on Cultural Diversity. It was begun while Handley was a Visiting Lecturer at UCI. We are indebted to Susan Pursche, Wilma Laws and the staff of the Word Processing Center, School of Social Sciences, UCI, for manuscript preparation, to Cheryl Larsson for preparation of figures, and to Dorothy Gormick for bibliographic assistance.

Board of Supervisors of Hinds County, Mississippi, 554 F. 2d 139, 1977). In *Kirksey*, for Hinds County, the District Court proposed that a 65% minority percentage was needed to compensate for lower levels of black voting age population and lower levels of black registration and turnout as compared to those for whites. In cases involving minority vote dilution under the Voting Rights Act of 1965 the question has arisen as to when districts in a plan have been drawn so as to deny minorities an "equal opportunity to elect candidates of choice."[1]

The aim of this article is to examine the relationship between minority population in a district and black and Hispanic congressional success. Earlier published work has dealt exclusively with effective minority voting equality in the context of state or local legislative elections (Grofman, 1982a; Brace et al., 1988; Hedges and Carlucci, 1987) and has dealt largely or exclusively with black voting behavior. Here we look at Hispanics as well as at blacks and focus on congressional elections rather than state and local ones. Moreover, unlike earlier work, we focus on the role of *combined* minority (black plus Hispanic) population as a predictor of minority electoral successes.

We consider three specific issues. First, we examine the question of how the presence of black population in a district affects the probability of Hispanic congressional success and, conversely, how the presence of Hispanic population affects the probability of black congressional success. This is an issue likely to be of increased importance in the 1990s with the growth of the Hispanic population (especially but not exclusively in the Southwest). The geographic proximity of black and Hispanic populations means that some 1990s congressional districts will be composed of both black and Hispanic populations (albeit with one group in the plurality), and the question will arise as to whether it is possible/desirable for these groups to be combined for purpose of minority representation (See, e.g., *Lulac v. Midland Independent School District*, 812 F. 2d 1494, 1500 (5th Cir.), *vacated and aff'd on other grounds*, 829 F. 2d 546, 1987; compare Brischetto and Grofman, 1987).

Second, we compare the minority proportion needed to elect black or Hispanic congressmen in the 1970s with that needed in the

1980s. Such comparison can shed some light on whether levels of "polarized" voting have declined so as to make it easier for blacks or Hispanics to be elected in districts without an overwhelming black or Hispanic population majority.

Third, we look at the permanence of minority success, that is, once a district has elected a minority congressman is it certain or near certain that it will continue to do so?

The data we look at is readily available, and our analysis is a simple descriptive one. Nonetheless, because such straightforward tabulations have not previously been compiled, we believe that we are able to provide useful information that will be directly relevant to 1990s reapportionment decision making and voting rights litigation.[2]

BLACK CONGRESSIONAL SUCCESS

In Table 1 we identify black members of Congress as of 1986 and the proportion black in the district that elected them. It can be seen from Table 1 that only districts that are at least 65% black elected blacks to Congress in every one of the three elections from 1982 to 1986. However, if we look only at the 1986 election districts, every district above 57.2% black elected a black. Also, 94.4% (17/18) of the districts with above 46.6% black population elected a black. Moreover, even over the whole time period, in the districts with between 50% and 64% black, 50% (three of six) elected a black, albeit the Georgia 5th at 65% black did not always do so. Furthermore, only 14 of 22 blacks in Congress in 1986 were elected from majority black districts; five of ten of the districts between 40% and 50% black elected blacks, and there were three blacks elected from districts with less than 40% black population (in California's 31st, California's 8th, and Missouri's 5th). However, many (six of eight) of the nonmajority black districts that elected blacks to Congress had substantial Hispanic populations, ranging from 25.1% Hispanic to 38% Hispanic.

We believe it important to distinguish between the minority population proportion needed to create "safe seats" and those that provide minority candidates a "realistic chance of election," that is, a

TABLE 1
Percentage Black and Hispanic in Congressional Districts and Black Congressional Representation in the 1980s

District	% Black (1982)	% Hispanic (1982)	Black Elected 1982	1984	1986
Illinois 1	92.1	1.1	yes	yes	yes
New York 12	80.1	10.1	yes	yes	yes
Pennsylvania 2	80.0	1.2	yes	yes	yes
Maryland 7	73.3	<1.0	yes	yes	yes
Michigan 13	71.1	3.1	yes	yes	yes
Michigan 1	70.7	2.1	yes	yes	yes
Illinois 2	70.3	7.4	yes	yes	yes
Illinois 7	66.9	4.7	yes	yes	yes
Georgia 5	65.0	1.1	no	no	yes
Ohio 21	62.3	1.0	yes	yes	yes
Tennessee 9	57.2	<1.0	yes	yes	yes
New Jersey 10	54.8	13.8	no	no	no
Mississippi 2	53.7	1.1	no	no	yes
Missouri 1	51.5	<1.0	yes	yes	yes
New York 6	50.3	9.4	no	no	yes
New York 16	48.5	37.9	yes	yes	yes
New York 11	47.1	38.0	yes	yes	yes
California 29	46.6	32.3	yes	yes	yes
Mississippi 4	45.2	<1.0	no	no	no
Louisiana 2	44.5	3.5	no	no	no
New York 18*	43.7	51.3	no	no	no
California 28	43.0	29.6	yes	yes	yes
S. Carolina 6	40.9	1.1	no	no	no
Texas 18	40.8	31.2	yes	yes	yes
N. Carolina 2	40.1	<1.0	no	no	no
California 31	33.7	25.1	yes	yes	yes
California 8	26.5	6.5	yes	yes	yes
Indiana 1	24.2	8.2	yes	no	no
Missouri 5	22.9	2.8	yes	yes	yes

NOTE: This is a list of the 25 congressional districts with the highest percentage of black residents (these percentages reflect the district configurations as of the 98th Congress). Also included at the bottom of the list are congressional districts not included in the top 25 that have also elected black representatives.
* Elected a Hispanic member of Congress in each of these years.

probability well above 50% but still rather less than certainty. For Congress, it seems apparent that black population percentages as low as 45% can provide black candidates a *near* certain chance of election.

Of course, we must be very careful in interpreting the percentages in Table 1. A number sufficient to elect a black in an urban district with a substantial Hispanic minority (e.g., California's 29th) in fact may guarantee defeat for black candidates in a district carved out of Deep South black-belt counties when there are no Hispanics. The easiest way to summarize the results in Table 1 is to say that *black members of Congress are elected from black plurality districts in which combined black plus Hispanic population is above 50%.* More particularly, with one exception, the New Jersey 10th (where Peter Rodino, a popular liberal Democrat, had received substantial black support), every district with above 50.7% black population (or plurality black and above 56.7% combined black and Hispanic population) elected a black in 1986. With Rodino's retirement in 1988, his district then also elected a black.

Our findings are little changed when we look at the relationship between black and Hispanic population percentages in the district and the election of blacks during the decade of the 1970s (see Table 2). Comparing Table 1 and Table 2 suggests that what has changed from the 1970s to 1980s is not the degree of racial polarization in congressional voting patterns, but rather the extent to which additional districts with substantial combined minority population proportions have been created in the 1980s (compare Loewen, 1987). In 1982 there were 21 "majority-minority" congressional districts, that is, districts with a majority of black or Hispanic population) with a black plurality, compared to only 14 such districts in 1972. In 1978, 13 of these 14 majority-minority black plurality districts elected a black and only two blacks were elected from non-majority-minority congressional districts. In 1986, 20 of the 21 majority-minority black plurality districts elected a black, and again only two blacks were elected from non-majority-minority districts. The one exception as noted previously was Rodino's district—one that subsequently elected a black representative.

There is another important point that seems to hold for black congressional seats, namely, that districts above 50% black that once elect a black appear to continue to do so (table omitted, but compare Tables 1 and 2).

HISPANIC CONGRESSIONAL SUCCESS

We show in Table 3 percentage Hispanic and percentage black in the 15 congressional districts with the highest Hispanic population proportions, and we show the electoral success (or absence thereof)

TABLE 2
Percentage Black and Hispanic in Congressional Districts and Black Congressional Representation in the 1970s

District	% Black (1972)	% Hispanic (1972)	Black Elected 1972	1974	1976	1978
Illinois 1	88.9	<2.5	yes	yes	yes	yes
New York 12	77.1	13.5	yes	yes	yes	yes
Maryland 7	74.0	<2.5	yes	yes	yes	yes
Michigan 1	70.0	<2.5	yes	yes	yes	yes
Ohio 21	66.3	<2.5	yes	yes	yes	yes
Michigan 13	65.8	<2.5	yes	yes	yes	yes
Pennsylvania 2	65.0	<2.5	yes	yes	yes	yes
New York 19	58.7	17.3	yes	yes	yes	yes
Illinois 7	54.9	16.6	yes	yes	yes	yes
Missouri 1	54.3	<2.5	yes	yes	yes	yes
California 21	54.2	21.1	yes	yes	yes	yes
New Jersey 10	51.8	5.8	no	no	no	no
California 37	50.7	9.3	yes	yes	yes	yes
Tennessee 8	47.5	<2.5	no	yes	yes	yes
Mississippi 2	45.9	<2.5	no	no	no	no
Georgia 5	44.2	<2.5	yes	yes	no	no
Mississippi 4	43.1	<2.5	no	no	no	no
South Carolina 6	42.2	<2.5	no	no	no	no
New York 21	41.7	43.8	no	no	no	no
Texas 18	41.6	18.6	yes	yes	yes	yes
Mississippi 3	40.4	<2.5	no	no	no	no
North Carolina 2	40.1	<2.5	no	no	no	no
California 7	25.5	7.7	yes	yes	yes	yes

NOTE: This is a list of the 22 congressional districts with the highest percentage of black residents (these percentages reflect the district configurations as of the 93rd Congress). Also included at the bottom of the list are the congressional districts not included in the top 22 that also elected black representatives.

of Hispanic candidates in these districts (compare Welch and Hibbing, 1984). There were ten Hispanic members of Congress in 1986, 2.3% of the House, compared to a 1980 U.S. Hispanic population of 6.4% (14,590,994).

In general, except in New Mexico and California, *Hispanics are not elected to Congress in districts that are less than 63% combined minority (black plus Hispanic)*. Including California and New Mexico, it would seem that a clear Hispanic plurality and a combined minority population above 55% give a substantial likelihood, although not certainty, of Hispanic success. To achieve actual certainty, a clear Hispanic plurality and a combined minority population near 70% seem necessary.[3]

TABLE 3
Percentage Hispanic and Black in Congressional Districts and Hispanic Congressional Representation in the 1980s

District	% Hispanic (1982)	% Black (1982)	Hispanic Elected 1982	1984	1986
Texas 15	71.7	<1.0	yes	yes	yes
California 25	63.6	9.6	yes	yes	yes
Texas 20	61.7	8.8	yes	yes	yes
Texas 27	61.5	2.7	yes	yes	yes
Texas 16	60.2	3.6	no	no	no
California 30	54.2	1.1	yes	yes	yes
Texas 23	53.1	4.1	no	yes	yes
New York 18	51.3	43.7	yes	yes	yes
Florida 18	50.7	15.8	no	no	no
California 34	47.6	2.3	yes	yes	yes
New Mexico 3	39.0	<1.0	yes	yes	yes
New York 11†	38.0	47.1	no	no	no
New York 16†	37.9	48.5	no	no	no
New Mexico 1	37.4	2.3	yes	yes	yes
Arizona 2	35.5	5.6	no	no	no

NOTE: This is a list of the 15 congressional districts with the highest percentage of Hispanic residents (these percentages reflect the district configurations as of the 98th Congress). There are no Hispanic representatives other than those representing districts listed above.
† Represented by a black member of Congress.

Very similar results obtain for the Hispanic congressional representation in the decade of the 1970s (see Table 4). As with blacks, the gains in Hispanic congressional representation from the 1970s to the 1980s (from five seats held by Hispanics in 1978 to ten such seats in 1986) can more readily be attributed to a change in the number of districts with substantial Hispanic population (from four districts with above 55% combined minority population and an Hispanic plurality in 1972 to 11 such districts in 1982) than to any apparent change on the willingness of non-Hispanic voters to support Hispanic candidates.

Also, for Hispanics as for blacks, with only one (temporary) exception, once a district with significant minority population elects a minority congressman, it continues to do so (table omitted, but compare Tables 3 and 4).

TABLE 4
Percentage Hispanic and Black in Congressional Districts and Hispanic Congressional Representation in the 1970s

District	% Hispanic (1972)	% Black (1972)	Hispanic Elected			
			1972	1974	1976	1978
Texas 15	75.0	<2.5	yes	yes	yes	yes
Texas 20	59.7	10.8	yes	yes	yes	yes
Texas 16	50.2	3.3	no	no	no	no
California 30	49.5	3.9	yes	yes	yes	yes
New Mexico 1	48.9	<2.5	yes	yes	yes	yes
Texas 23	47.6	3.4	no	no	no	no
New York 21	43.8	41.7	yes	yes	yes	yes
Florida 14	41.1	15.2	no	no	no	no
California 29	39.4	<2.5	no	no	no	no
Texas 14	36.5	7.2	no	no	no	no

NOTE: This is a list of the 10 congressional districts with the highest percentage of Hispanic residents (these percentages reflect the district configurations as of the 93rd Congress). There are no Hispanic representatives other than those representing districts listed above.

CONCLUSIONS

While predicting minority electoral success in any given congressional district would require us to look carefully at minority voting-age citizen population, the potential for black-Hispanic coalitions, the degree of racially polarized voting, and levels of minority registration and turnout (cf. Brace, Grofman, Handley, and Niemi, 1988), the rules of thumb we have developed to predict black and Hispanic congressional success work quite well, especially for black representation. We have reached two basic conclusions: (1) For blacks, a clear black plurality and a combined (black plus Hispanic) minority population somewhat above 50% is sufficient to create a congressional district in which a black candidate has a virtual certainty of *eventual* black success. (2) For Hispanics (except in a few states, such as California and New Mexico, where lower numbers suffice), congressional districts with a clear Hispanic plurality and a combined minority population of above 63% are needed to offer an Hispanic candidate a realistic opportunity to be elected; while a district with 70% combined minority population creates a virtual certainty of Hispanic success (except perhaps in areas like the Texas 16th, where a very high proportion of Hispanics are noncitizens).[4]

These threshold values are so stark that there is little or nothing to be gained by multivariate analysis in attempting to account for the few outliers, especially since those are disproportionately located in only two states.

Using 1980 population figures (which underestimate this fast-growing segment of the population), Hispanic congressional representation was as of 1986 already only slightly less proportional ($2.3/6.4 = .36$) than was black congressional representation ($5.1/11.5 = .44$), and differences essentially vanish when we take into account Hispanic noncitizen/nonvoting-age population, and the fact that the smaller a voting bloc, ceteris paribus, the less likely it is to be proportionally represented (Grofman, 1982b).

NOTES

1. In *United Jewish Organizations of Williamsburg v. Carey*, 430 U.S. 144 (1977), a case brought under Section 2 of the Voting Rights Act, the 65% percentage used in *Kirksey* was offered by the U.S. Department of Justice as justification for their unwillingness to preclear under Section 5 of the Voting Rights Act a New York legislative plan that fragmented Hispanic population concentrations in Brooklyn. In *Ketchum v. Byrne*, 740 F. 2d 1528 (1984), a U.S. Court of Appeals suggested that 65% was an appropriate baseline figure in judging effective equality, absent evidence to the contrary. Moreover, a number of civil rights attorneys, notably Frank Parker of the Lawyers Committee for Civil Rights Under Law (see e.g., Parker, 1984) have argued that, without a district that is 65% or more black in population, blacks are denied the opportunity to elect a candidate of their choice.

On the other hand, there is a social science literature arguing that the 65% rule is sometimes too high and sometimes too low and must always be adjusted to reflect the particular election-specific facts about minority eligibility and participation rates (Grofman, 1982a; Hedges and Carlucci, 1987; Brace et al., 1988). Also, not all courts have given deference to the 65% figure, and officials of the Voting Rights Section of the U.S. Department of Justice deny that it is presently used by the Department as a rule of thumb.

2. Because Section 2 of the Voting Rights Act of 1965 (as amended in 1982) applies to all jurisdictions in the U.S. (Grofman, Migalski, and Noviello, 1985), legal interpretation of the 65% rule will be critical in the 1990s round of redistricting. In these disputes social science testimony will play a major role.

3. The Texas 16th has a high proportion of noncitizens. Hispanics in the Florida 18th are preponderantly Cuban rather than Mexican-American. The Cuban population is more divided in its party affiliation than is the Mexican-American population, making it hard to translate numbers into electoral success, and making a black-Cuban alliance less likely.

4. We must be careful not to apply these figures directly to nonpartisan contests, where there is no party primary with a disproportionately minority electorate.

REFERENCES

BRACE, K., B. GROFMAN, L. HANDLEY, and R. NIEMI (1988) "Minority voting equality: The sixty-five percent rule in theory and practice." Law and Policy 10 (1): 43-62.

BRISCHETTO, R. and B. GROFMAN (1987) "Election system, the Voting Rights Act, and minority representation in Texas cities." Prepared for the Annual Meeting of the American Political Science Association, Chicago, September 3-6. Revised and prepared for the Annual Meeting of the Western Political Science Association, San Francisco, March 10-12, 1988.

GROFMAN, B. (1982a) Appendix C, Report to the Special Master, *Flateau et al. v. Anderson et al.* U.S. District Court, Southern District of New York, June 7. On methodology used to insure compliance with standards of the Voting Rights Act of 1965.

GROFMAN, B. (1982b) "For single-member districts, random is not equal." Pp. 55-58 in B. Grofman, A. Lijphart, R. McKay, and H. Scarrow (eds.) Representation and Redistricting Issues. Lexington, MA: Lexington Books.

GROFMAN, B., M. MIGALSKI, and N. NOVIELLO (1985) "The totality of circumstances test in section 2 of the Voting Rights Act: A social science perspective." Law and Policy 7 (2): 209-223.

HEDGES, R. and C. P. CARLUCCI (1987). "Implementation of the Voting Rights Act: The case of New York." Western Pol. Q. 40 (1): 107-120.

LOEWEN, J. (1987). "Racial bloc voting in South Carolina." Prepared for the Annual Meeting of the American Political Science Association, Chicago, September 3-6.

PARKER, F. (1984). "Racial gerrymandering and legislative reapportionment." pp. 85-118 in C. Davidson (ed.) Minority Vote Dilution. Washington, DC: Howard Univ. Press.

WELCH, S. and J. R. HIBBING (1984). "Hispanic representation in the U.S. Congress." Social Sci. Q. 65: 328-335.

ETHNIC OFFICEHOLDERS IN LOS ANGELES COUNTY

Fernando J. Guerra
Loyola Marymount University

SSR, Volume 71, No. 2, January 1987

This inquiry into ethnic participation in Los Angeles politics examines the comparative success in gaining public office which representatives of three minority-status groups have had since 1960. Specifically, the success in winning significant political office by candidates who are Latino, Black, or Jewish has been quite different. It has been much more rapid for Jews than for Blacks, who in turn have out-paced Latinos throughout the 27-year period.

In 1960, ethnic minorities held four percent of the most significant elective positions in Los Angeles County. By 1986, the ethnic communities of Los Angeles (Latino, Black, Jewish and Asian) provided fifty-four percent of the individuals holding the most significant elective positions.[1] What developments in Los Angeles have led to this inclusion of ethnic minorities into the governing circles? By exploring some trends associated with the political inclusion of minorities in the electoral arena, it is hoped that lines of inquiry will emerge which can help explain this phenomenon.

The examination of minority representation in the electoral arena of Los Angeles County would have to take into consideration over 2,000 positions. These positions are at the federal, state and local levels. With Los Angeles County having eighty-four cities, ninety-five school districts and forty-five special districts which elect governing bodies, most of the 2,000 positions are at the local level. The electoral arena of Los Angeles County also includes numerous judicial and party positions. Of these 2,000 positions, 100 emerge as significant because of the resources they control, the number of constituents served and their use as stepping stones to higher office by individual officeholders.[2] The 100 most significant elective positions in Los Angeles County are as follows: the U.S. House of Representatives (16); the California State Senate (14); the California Assembly (30); the Supervisors (5), District Attorney, Sheriff and Assessor of Los Angeles County; the Mayor, City Attorney, Controller and Council (15) of the City of Los Angeles; the Los Angeles School Board (7); and the Los Angeles Community College Board (7). Due to reapportionment, or in one case the creation of a governing body, these significant positions have not always totalled 100: from 1960 to 1961 there were 77 positions; from 1962 to 1965, 80 positions; from 1966 to 1968, 93 positions; from 1969 to 1981, 100 positions; and from 1982 to 1986, 96 positions.

Before the decade of the sixties minorities holding a significant position were few. As throughout the nation, changes occurred in the sixties in Los Angeles County which prompted increased minority representation. As figure 1 shows, beginning in the early sixties minorities gained significant positions at an ever increasing rate. The Black community was the initial recipient of this increased representation. Blacks outdistanced Latinos and Jews to such an extent that one could label the early and mid-sixties, as it applies to gaining significant electoral positions in Los Angeles County, the Black takeoff stage. Blacks continued to gain significant positions into the late sixties and through the seventies. However, their gains were not as large during this stage as in the early sixties. It was the Jewish community which enjoyed increased representation throughout the seventies. Jewish representation in the 100 significant elective positions tripled during this stage, thus the label Jewish takeoff. By the eighties, Black representation stabilized, not gaining an additional position through the first half of the decade, Jewish gains continued but at a lesser pace and Latinos more than doubled their gains. The eighties can thus be labelled the Latino takeoff stage. Asians have not been as successful in gaining significant positions in Los Angeles County. Between 1960 and 1986 only four Asians have held a significant position. Thus, Asians have yet to experience a take off period.

What follows is an examination of the trends associated with Latinos, Blacks and Jews gaining significant elective positions in each of the three stages. Specifically, the focus is on whether the positions gained were in districts which were at least one-third minority, recently reapportioned, vacant, or previously held by a similar minority.

In discussing the trends associated with minorities gaining significant elective positions in Los Angeles County, the election of each minority to a position which he or she had not previously held will consist of a case. Since the data for this study are the candidates elected and their ethnicity, names are listed in the text. Blacks are not immediately identifiable by name, Jewish names vary in recognizability, while most Latino and Asians names are recognized as such. However, there are problems with utilizing surname to identify ethnicity. For instance, using Spanish surname would overlook Latinos such as Los Angeles Superior Court Judge Plillip M. Newman or New Mexico Congressman Bill Richardson. It could also include individuals who have Spanish surnames or Spanish sounding surnames, such as Assemblyman Frank Vicencia of Portuguese ancestry or former School Board member Tony Trias of Philippine ancestry. Further, first names are of no help since they have been Americanized by most ethnic office holders. The identification of an office holder as Latino, Black or Jewish for this study was not dependent on surname, but on the confirmation of at least three sources.

Black takeoff (1960-1967). The number of significant positions held by Latinos, Blacks and Jews would more than triple from January 1960 to December 1967. Minorities holding significant positions jumped from three in 1960 to sixteen by 1967. Over half of the thirteen positions were gained by Blacks. The net gain of eight significant positions by Blacks from one to nine, out distanced the net gain of four, form one to five, by Jews and one, from one to two, by Latinos. Although there were sixteen positions held by January 1968, twenty minorities had held a significant position at one time during this period. Three of the four minorities who left the scene between 1960 to 1967 were defeated. Thus, some minority setbacks were experienced.

Between 1960 and 1967, Latinos had a net gain of one position. However, four Latinos gained positions which they had not previously held. In 1962, Ed Roybal would vacate his Council position for Congress. In 1962, John Moreno and Phil Soto were both elected to the California Assembly. By 1967, both had been defeated. In June 1967, Julian Nava was elected to the School board.

Of the four Latinos to win a significant elective position which they had not previously held, three did so in a minority district; three in a recently reapportioned district; three won vacant positions; none had previously been held by a Latino; and two of the positions would continue to be held by Latinos at the end of the first stage.

There were six cases of individual Jews gaining positions which they previously had not held: Bielenson, Sieroty and Fenton, Assembly; Edelman and Braude, City Council; and Bielenson, State Senate. Of these six cases, five were in minority (Jewish) districts, three in recently reapportioned districts, three in a vacant position; two had previously been held by Jews; and all the positions would continue to be held by Jews at the end of the first stage.

There were eleven cases of Black individuals gaining a position which they previously had not held: Hawkins, Congress; Dymally, State Senate; Dymally, Farrell, Ralph, Greene and Brawthwaite (Burke), Assembly; Bradley, Lindsay and Mills, City Council; and Jones, School Board. Of the eleven, ten were in minority districts; ten in a recently reapportioned district; nine in a vacant position; three had previously been held by a Black; and all of the positions would continue to be held by a Black at the end of the first stage.

In examining the initial takeoff stage what generalizations can be made? Minorities who gained positions did so in minority districts which either became vacant or were recently reapportioned or both, and once a position was captured by a minority it remained in minority control. This is especially the case with Blacks, almost always the case with Jews, and somewhat less so with Latinos.

Jewish Takeoff (1968-1979). The number of significant elective positions held by Latinos, Blacks and Jews during this second stage would increase from sixteen to forty-two. Of the twenty-six positions captured by these three groups, Jews would account for seventeen or over two-thirds of the gains. While Jewish representation increased from five to twenty-two positions, Blacks continued to increase their representation from nine to fifteen positions, and Latinos only had a net gain of three additional positions by the end of this stage. This three position gain for Latinos is disappointing not only when compared to the continued Black gains and the phenomenal Jewish takeoff, but because Latinos had gained up to seven positions in the middle of this stage. Even though this stage is the longest of the three being considered, twelve years compared to eight years for the Black takeoff stage and seven years for the Latino takeoff stage, Black or Latino gains for any twelve year stretch cannot come close to matching the seventeen position gain of the Jewish community from 1968 to 1979. It would take the Black community all twenty-seven years being considered by this study to gain fifteen positions.

There were twenty-four cases of individual Jews gaining positions which they had not previously held: Waxman and Bielenson, Congress; Edelman and Ward, County Supervisor; Sieroty and Robbins, State Senate; Pines, City Attorney; Reiner, City Controller; Waxman, Berman, Rosenthal, Bane and Levine, Assembly; Wachs, Yarozlavsky, Picus and Bernson, City Council; Newman, Miller, Weintraub and Fiedler, School Board; and Richman, Bronson and Reiner, College Board. Of the twenty-four, only eight were in minority (Jewish) districts; six in recently reapportioned districts; fourteen in a vacant position; six had previously been held by a Jew; and all but one would continue to be held by a Jew at the end of the second stage.

There were twenty-one cases of individual Blacks gaining positions which they had not previously held: Bradley, Mayor of Los Angeles; Burke and Dixon, Congress; Burke, County Supervisor; Holden, Greene and Watson, State Senate; Dixon, Holoman, Tucker, Hughes, Moore and Waters, Assembly; Cunningham and Farrell, City Council; Watson, Boehler and Walters, School Board; and Washington, Moore and Archie (Hudson), College Board. Of the twenty-one, fourteen did so in minority districts; nine in recently reapportioned districts; nineteen in a vacant position; fourteen had previously been held by a Black; and all positions gained by a

Black would continue to be held by a Black at the end of the second stage.

There were seven cases of individual Latinos gaining positions which they had not previously held: Garcia and Montoya, State Senate; Garcia, Montoya, Alatorre and Torres, Assembly; and Orozco, College Board. Of the seven, six were in minority districts; three were in recently reapportioned districts; six were in a vacant position; one had previously been held by a Latino; and four would continue to be held by a Latino at the end of the second stage.

Of the fifty-two cases where a minority individual gained a position he or she had not previously held, forty-one were in a recently reapportioned district, a vacant position or both. Of the eleven cases which were neither, eight were Jewish. Of the 52 cases, twenty-eight were in minority districts. Of the twenty-four which were not, sixteen were Jewish. Thus, a new pattern begins to emerge. Though in general minorities are still dependent on recently reapportioned or vacant positions in minority districts, this is increasingly not the case for Jews. The seventies is the Jewish decade because they are not bound to minority districts which are vacant or recently reapportioned.

Latino Takeoff (1980-1986). The number of significant positions held by Latinos, Blacks and Jews in the eighties would increase by nine from forty-two to fifty-one. Of these nine, six would be gained by Latinos, three by Jews. While the positions gained by Latinos are only three more than Jews it more than doubled Latino representation from five to eleven. Of the three stages of increased minority representation, the Latino takeoff stage has produced the least number of total positions gained by the three groups and by the lead group. However, as of 1986, it is not clear whether this stage has peaked. It is likely that this stage will continue into the mid-nineties.

There were ten Latino individuals who gained positions they had not previously held: Martinez and E. Torres, Congress; A. Torres, State Senate; Martinez, Molina, Calderon and Polanco, Assembly; Alatorre, City Council; Gonzalez, School Board; and Quesada, College Board. Of the ten, nine were in minority districts; six were in recently reapportioned districts; seven were in vacant positions; and four were previously held by Latinos. Latinos also expect to win a newly created vacant council position with 69 percent Latino population in early 1987.

For Blacks the third stage of increased minority representation was less fruitful than the previous two. It began with the return of Mervyn Dymally who gained the third Black congressional position. Dymally had been defeated for reelection as Lt. Governor in 1978. There was no increase, however, because Yvonne Burke was defeated in her attempt to keep the supervisorial position to which she had been appointed. It was not a Black district. For the next five years there would be no Black gains or losses. All fifteen Black incumbents would continue to win reelection. Every position, except Mayor Bradley's and Marquerite Archie-Hudson's at large College Board position, are in a district where a Black would be expected to replace an incumbent. In October 1986, David Cunningham resigned his Council position. A Black is expected to win the position in early 1987.Thus, it appears that Black representation has peaked at fifteen.

There were fifteen Jewish individuals, who between 1980 and 1986, gained positions they had not previously held: Fiedler, Berman and Levine, Congress; Block, County Sheriff; Rosenthal, State Senate; Katz,Margolin and Friedman Assembly; Finn, City Council; Bartman, Gershman and Goldberg, School Board; Conner, College Board; and Reiner, City Attorney and County District Attorney. Of the fourteen, three were in minority districts; seven were recently reapportioned; ten were in a vacant position; and four had previously been held by a Jewish representative.

Of the twenty-six cases of Latinos, Blacks or Jews who gained a position between 1980 and 1986 they had not previously held, twenty-two were in a recently reapportioned district, a vacant position or both. Of the four which were not, two were Jews, one Latino and one Black. Of the twenty-six, fourteen were in a minority district. Of the twelve which were not, all were Jewish. Thus, minorities are still dependent on reapportionment and vacant positions in the eighties. Unlike the previous stage, this is also the case for Jews. However, while Blacks and Latinos are still dependent on minority districts, Jews continue to win in non-Jewish and non-minority districts.

As of November 1986, there were fifty-one significant positions held by Latinos, Blacks or Jews. The top position of Mayor was held by a Black, Tom Bradley. At the county level, only Jews held positions: Supervisor Ed Edelman; District Attorney Ira Reiner, and Sheriff Sherman Block. Los Angeles County's congressional delegation included four Jews: Henry Waxman, Anthony Bielenson, Howard Berman and Mel Levine (this is down one with Fiedler leaving her seat to run for the United States Senate Republican nomination). There were three Latino congressmen: Ed Roybal, Marty Martinez and Esteban Torres. There were also three Blacks: Augustus Hawkins, Julian Dixon and Mervyn Dymally. In the State Senate each of the three groups held two positions: Jews Alan Robbins and Herschel Rosenthal; Blacks Bill Greene and Diane Watson; and Latinos Joseph Montoya and Art Torres. In the Assembly there were four Blacks: Curtis Tucker, Teresa Hughes, Gwen Moore, and Maxine Waters; four Jews: Tom Bane, Richard Katz, Burt Margolin and Terry Friedman; and three Latinos: Gloria Molina, Charles Calderon and Richard Polanco. In the City Council there were five Jews: Marvin Braude, Joel Wachs, Zev Yaroslavsky, Joy Picus, Hal Bernson (this is down one with the death of Howard Finn in August 1986); three Blacks: Gilbert Lindsay, David Cunningham's replacement and Robert Farrell; and one Latino, Richard Alatorre. On the School Board there were four Jews: Roberta Weintraub, Tom Bartman, Alan Gershman and Jackie Goldberg; one Black, Rita Walters; and one Latino, Larry Gonzales. On the College Board there were three Jews: Monroe Richman, Arthur Bronson and Lindsay Conner; one Black, Marguerite Archie-Hudson; and one Latina, Leticia Quesada.

Concluding Comments. This study has examined the link between increased minority representation and changes in the formal-legal electoral arena. It is clear that increased minority representation is tied to the expanding number of minority districts, reapportionment and vacancies. This is especially the case for Latinos and Blacks. What is not clear is the extent to which increased minority representation is tied to the informal workings of the electoral arena. Any further examination of minority participation in Los Angeles electoral politics should consider the unofficial rules or strategies of winning elective positions. Other than meeting the legal requirements of age, residency and filing, an individual must meet certain informal requirements to gain a public office. This is the case for both minority and non-minority alike. These informal requirements include money, know how of campaign management techniques, endorsements and support networks.

The success of many Jewish candidates can be traced to the existence of an informal network headed by congressmen Waxman and Berman. This network of elected officials, their aides, political consultants, financial contributors and others control candidate recruitment in Jewish districts and increasingly at the city, county and even state level. Incorrectly labelled a "machine," the success of the Waxman-Berman support network is dependent on financial contributions from large donors, political action committees and other politicians, effective use of computer generated mailers, well produced media advertisement and volunteers, not patronage. Latino and Black informal electoral networks do exist in Los Angeles, but have not been as successful as the Jewish network. Further gains by Latinos and Blacks especially outside minority districts may depend on the strengthening of these networks.

These networks though they are ethnically based do not automatically support fellow ethnics. The Waxman-Berman network supported Latino Marty Martinez over Jewish Assemblyman Jack Fenton in 1980. Besides ethnic affiliation, there is a geographic and partisan base to these electoral networks. While they support rival candidates at times, they usually work in tandem. It can even be argued that the emergence of these networks and the alliances among them have strengthened the two major political parties in California. This is not usually recognized because it is occurring at the elite level while mass public opinion continues to show a decline of party support.

What does this new form of electoral politics in Los Angeles portend for the future of minority representation? Will the strengthening of Latino, Black and Asian networks lead to increased minority representation? Is there room for more than one electoral network in each minority community? How does an electoral network get started? How does it function internally? Beyond quantity, what is the quality of minority representation produced by these networks? These are all questions which need to be examined to better understand minority electoral politics in Los Angeles County. Unfortunately, they are beyond the scope of the present study and wait for future treatment.

NOTES

The findings reported here are part of a larger study prepared for presentation by Fernando J. Guerra and Dwaine Marvick at the conference, "Minorities in the Post-Industrial City," held at UCLA on 9 May 1986, under the auspices of the Institute of Social Science Research, UCLA.

1. Asians have been excluded from analysis due to their lack of success in gaining significant positions in Los Angeles County. Between 1960 and 1986, only four Asians have held significant positions: Al Song, California Assembly, 1962-66, and State Senate, 1966-1978; Paul Bannai, California Assembly, 1972-1980; Tony Trias, School Board, 1980-1983; and Michael Woo, City Council, first elected in 1985.

2. The three measures of significance, control of resources, constituents served and channel to higher office are fully elaborated in a forthcoming study.

APPENDIX. Significant Positions Held by
Minorities, Los Angeles County, 1960-1986

LATINO Public Officeholders

U.S. House of Representatives: Edward R. Roybal, January, 1963 to the present. Matthew G. "Marty" Martinez, July, 1982 to the present. Esteban "Ed" Torres, January, 1983 to the present.
State Senate: Alex P. Garcia, December, 1974 to December, 1982. Joseph B. Montoya, December, 1978 to the present. Art Torres, December, 1982 to the present.
State Assembly: John Moreno, December, 1962 to December, 1964. Philip L. Soto, December, 1962 to December, 1966. Alex P. Garcia, December, 1968 to December, 1974. Joseph B. Montoya, December, 1972 to December, 1978. Richard Alatorre, December, 1972 to December, 1985. Art Torres, December, 1974 to December, 1982. Matthew G. "Marty" Martinez, December, 1980 to July, 1982. Charles M. Calderon, December, 1982 to the present. Gloria Molina, December, 1982 to the present. Richard G. Polanco, June, 1986 to the present.
Los Angeles City Council: Edward R. Roybal, July, 1949 to December, 1962. Richard Alatorre, December, 1985 to the present.
Los Angeles Unified School District Board: Julian Nava, July, 1967 to June, 1979. Larry Gonzalez, July, 1983 to the present.
Los Angeles Community College Board of Trustees (1969): J. William Orozco, July, 1969 to June, 1979. Leticia Quezada, November, 1985 to the present.

BLACK Public Officeholders

Mayor of Los Angeles: Tom Bradley, July, 1973 to the present.
L.A. County Board of Supervisors: Yvonne Brathwaite Burke, June, 1979, to December, 1980.
U.S. House of Representatives: Augustus F. Hawkins, January, 1963 to the present. Yvonne Brathwaite Burke, January, 1973 to December, 1978. Julian F. Dixon, January, 1979 to the present. Mervyn M. Dymally, January, 1979 to the present.
State Senate: Mervyn Dymally, December, 1966 to December, 1974. Nate Holden, December, 1974 to December, 1978. Bill Greene, March, 1975 to the present. Diane Watson, December, 1978 to the present.
State Assembly: Augustus F. Hawkins, January, 1935 to December, 1962. Mervyn M. Dymally, December, 1962 to December, 1966. F. Douglas Ferrell, December, 1962 to December, 1966. Yvonne Watson Brathwaite, December, 1966 to December, 1972. Bill Greene, December, 1966 to March, 1975. Leon Ralph, December, 1966 to December, 1976. Julian C. Dixon, December, 1972 to December, 1978. Frank Holoman, December, 1972 to December, 1974. Curtis R. Tucker, December, 1974 to the present. Teresa Hughes, July, 1975 to the present. Maxine Waters, December, 1976 to the present. Gwen Moore, December, 1978 to the present.
Los Angeles City Council: Gilbert W. Lindsay, January, 1963 to the present. Billy Mills, July, 1963 to January, 1974. Tom Bradley, July, 1963 to June, 1973. David Cunningham, September, 1973 to October, 1986. Robert Farrell, June, 1974 to the present.
LAUSD Board: Rev. James Jones, July, 1965 to June, 1969. Diane Watson, July, 1975 to November, 1978. Fr. Lewis Boehler, January, 1979 to June, 1979. Rita Walters, July, 1979 to the present.
L.A. Community College Board of Trustees (1969): Kenny Washington, July, 1969 to June, 1975. Gwen Moore, July, 1975 to December, 1978. Marguerite Archie-Hudson, December, 1978 to the present.

JEWISH Public Officeholders

U.S. House of Representatives: Henry A. Waxman, January, 1975 to the present. Anthony C. Bielenson, January, 1977 to the present. Bobbi Fiedler, January, 1981 to January, 1987. Howard L. Berman, January, 1983 to the present. Mel Levine, January, 1983 to the present.
State Senate: Anthony C. Bielenson, December, 1966 to December, 1976. Alan Robbins, February, 1973 to the present. Alan Sieroty, March, 1977 to December, 1982. Herschel Rosenthal, December, 1982 to the present.
State Assembly: Anthony C. Bielenson, December, 1962 to December, 1966. Jack R. Fenton, December, 1964 to December, 1980. Alan Sieroty, December, 1966 to March, 1977. Henry A. Waxman, December, 1968 to December, 1974. Howard L. Berman, December, 1972 to December, 1982. Herschel Rosenthal, December, 1974 to December, 1982. Tom Bane,* December, 1974 to the present. Mel Levine, December, 1976 to December, 1982. Richard Katz, December, 1980 to the present. Burt Margolin, December, 1982 to the present. Terry Friedman, December, 1986 to the present.
Los Angeles City Council: Rosalind (Weiner) Wyman, July, 1953 to June, 1965. Ed Edelman, July, 1965 to December, 1974. Marvin Braude, July, 1965 to the present. Joel Wachs, July, 1971 to the present. Zev Yaroslavsky, April, 1975 to the present. Joy Picus, July, 1977 to the present. Hal Bernson, July, 1979 to the present. Howard Finn, July, 1981 to August, 1986.
Los Angeles County Board of Supervisors: Baxter Ward, December, 1972 to December, 1980. Ed Edelman, December, 1974 to the present.
Los Angeles County District Attorney: Ira Reiner, December, 1984 to the present.
Los Angeles County Sheriff: Sherman Block, December, 1982 to the present.
Los Angeles City Attorney: Burt Pines, July, 1973 to June, 1981. Ira Reiner, July, 1981 to November, 1984.
City Controller of Los Angeles: Ira Reiner, July, 1977 to June, 1981.
Los Angeles Community College Board of Trustees: Monroe Richman, July, 1971 to the present. Arthur Bronson, January, 1971 to the present. Ira Reiner, July, 1975 to June, 1977. Lindsay Conner, July, 1981 to the present.
Los Angeles Unified School District Board: Donald Newman, July, 1969 to January, 1976. Howard Miller, February, 1976 to May, 1979. Bobbi Fiedler, July, 1977 to December, 1980. Roberta Weintraub, May, 1979 to the present. Tom Bartman, February, 1980 to June, 1985, May, 1986 to the present. Alan Gershman, July, 1981 to the present. Jackie Goldberg, July, 1983 to the present.

ASIAN Public Officeholders

Los Angeles City Council: Mike Woo (Chinese), July, 1985 to the present.
Los Angeles Unified School District Board: Tony Trias (Filipino), October, 1980 to June, 1983.
State Senate: Alfred Song (Chinese), December, 1966 to December, 1978.
State Assembly: Alfred Song (Chinese), December, 1962 to December, 1966. Paul Bannai (Japanese), December, 1972 to December, 1980.

*Previously served in the Assembly but had not yet converted to Judaism.

Manuscript was received on September 17, 1986 and reviewed September 23, 1986.

Figure 1 appears on p. 94.

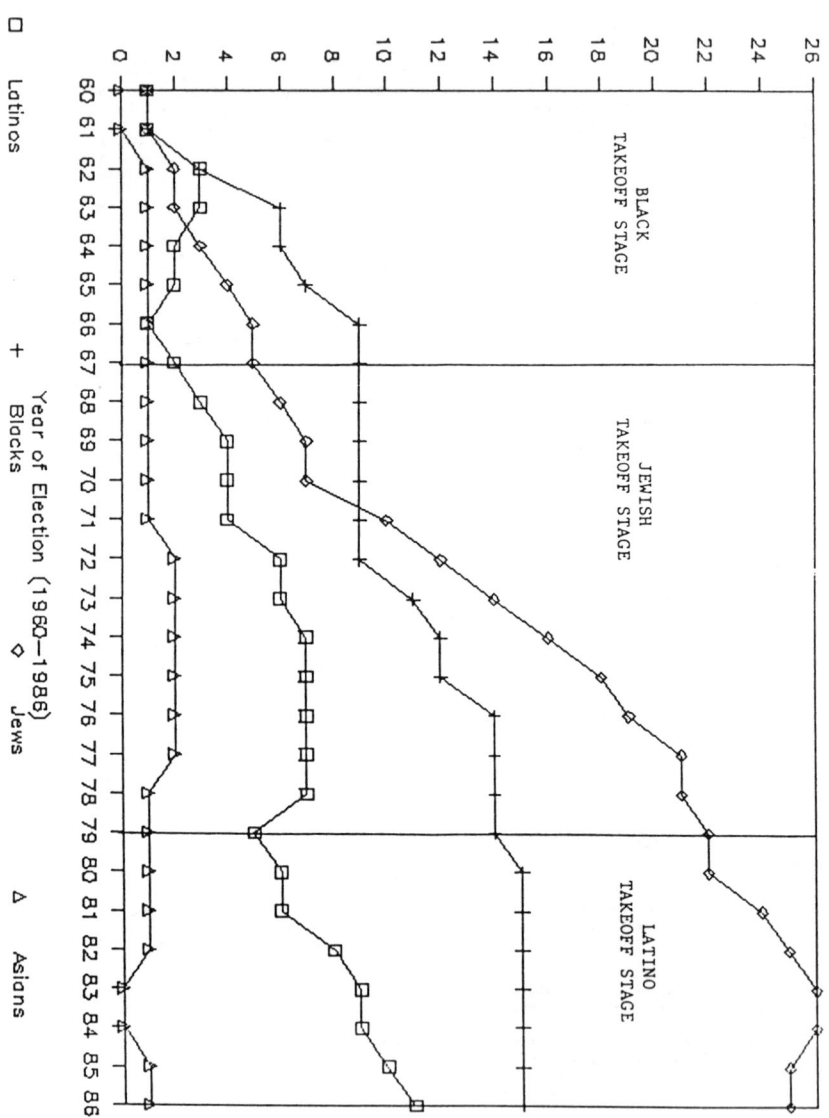

Figure 1. Significant Positions Won by Minorities in Los Angeles County, 1960 to 1986.

TOWARD AN UNDERSTANDING OF THE ROLE OF THE MASS MEDIA IN LATINO POLITICAL LIFE

Federico A. SUBERVI-VELEZ, *University of California, Santa Barbara*
Richard HERRERA, *University of California, Santa Barbara*
Michael BEGAY, *University of California, Santa Barbara*

> This essay presents an analysis of major characteristics of the Republican party's approximately six-million-dollar effort to capture, via the broadcast media, Latinos' votes for Reagan in 1984. The Democratic party's $120,000 effort on behalf of Mondale is briefly analyzed. The work is based on interviews with campaign officials, content analysis of political spot ads, and analysis of election results. An overview of the scant research that links the mass media to Latinos and politics and some guiding questions for further research on this topic are also presented.

Although many aspects of Latino political development are becoming subject to more academic research, few scholars have looked at the role the mass media play in such development. This study presents (a) an overview of the scant research that links the mass media to Latinos and politics; (b) a case study examining the media strategies used by the presidential candidates in 1984, particularly the Republicans' use of the broadcast media, in their national efforts to capture the Latino vote; and (c) some research questions for advancing the understanding of the topic of media and Latino politics. The purpose of this work is to provide some baseline information about how, in 1984, the major political parties appealed to Hispanics for their votes via the mass media. Most importantly, the study seeks to establish some foundations for guiding the research on the role of the media in the development of Latino political life in the United States.

Mass Media, Latinos, and Politics

Hispanic political life has been the subject of various recent studies (Brischetto and Velasquez, 1984; Garcia and de la Garza, 1977; Cain and Kiewiet, 1985), but the literature analyzing mass communication variables that contribute to the mobilization of Latinos during elections is scarce and difficult to find. No mention is made of the media in Garcia, de la Garza, and Torres's (1985) or Nelson's (1984) extensive compilations of research on Latino politics. Three major examinations of literature focusing specifically on Latinos and mass communication (Greenberg et al., 1983; Subervi-Velez, 1984, 1986; Valenzuela, 1985) also suggest that there is a neglect of the topic of politics. Nevertheless, the media's importance for some aspects of Hispanic political life has been recognized in at least a few writings.

According to Tan (1983), among some Mexican Americans in Lubbock, Texas, exposure to print media helps predict general public affairs knowledge and "ethnic political knowledge." De la Garza, Brischetto, and Weaver (1984) found that watching local news and reading a daily newspaper influence Latinos' political orientations among Hispanics in San Antonio and East Los Angeles. Buehler (1976) and Miyares (1980) have also affirmed the media's importance even though in their studies media exposure was analyzed only tangentially.

Although none of the above studies specify the language of the media that influence (or fail to influence) political orientations and behaviors, in context it can be assumed that they refer to English language media. By specifying the language of the media, Subervi-Velez's (1984) study of Latinos in Chicago found that exposure to Anglo print media had a significant influence on the respondents' political knowledge—but not participation—while exposure to Latino-oriented media had some positive influence on knowledge and/or participation of some Hispanics but not others. Another work, by de la Garza, Brischetto, and Vaughan (1983), further supports the importance of specifying language and content when analyzing the media's political role. The Mexican Americans they studied indicated greater reliance on English language than on Spanish language television for news.

Historically based studies also suggest an important role of media in Latino political life. Lewels (1974) described extensively how the Chicano movement's activities were connected with grassroot media channels. One of the major conclusions of his work is that on the road to significant gains in political power, Chicanos will need drastic improvements in their access and exposure to Anglo as well as Latino media channels. No other work has yet to study the media and Latino politics from such a bottom-up perspective.

On the other hand, a top-down view of the role played by the media in Latino political life is partially provided by Castro (1974), who discussed how in 1972 President Nixon and the Republicans developed a strategy to begin wooing the Chicano vote. He states that even at the highest circles of the Republican party the mass media are seen as key instruments for trying to mobilize the Latino population for the GOP's political purposes. The details of these efforts can be found scattered throughout Book 13 of the Hearings before the Select Committee on Presidential Campaign Activities of the U.S.

Role of Mass Media in Latino Political Life

Senate. Knaggs's (1986) work also provided some documentation about the Republican party's 25-year effort to woo Mexican American voters in Texas.

Evidently, the role of the mass media in Latino political life is important and merits more attention. This work now turns to the examination of the media strategies of the presidential candidates in 1984 in their national efforts to capture the Latino vote. A distinctive feature of this paper is that it may be the first to provide an extensive analysis of how emergent Hispanic political power was recognized and dealt with, via the *broadcast* media, by the Republican candidate in a presidential election.

Targeting Latino Voters via the Media: A Case Study

During the fall of 1984 a study was begun to explore the role played by the Spanish language media in that year's presidential elections. Three questions guided the research: What media-related campaign strategies were developed and implemented by the Republican and Democratic parties? What political information (e.g., news, advertisements, public service announcements, editorials) was printed or broadcast by the Spanish language media in New York, Los Angeles, Chicago, San Antonio, and Miami during the 1984 elections? And, what effects, if any, did the information and ads in the Spanish language media have on the outcome of the election? Some answers to the first question are presented below.[1] Data gathering and analysis are still in progress for answering the other two questions.[2]

Lacking previous empirical evidence to guide this area of inquiry, two contending propositions could be made about Democratic and Republican parties' strategies toward Latinos via the mass media. On the one hand, it could be hypothesized that the media efforts of the Democratic party would be greater than the Republican party's because the former would need and seek to maintain the traditionally pro–Democratic party Latino vote. On the other hand, a hypothesis could also be made that the Republican party's efforts would be greater because, aware of their limited support among Latinos, they would have to try harder in making inroads among that population. The greater efforts of the Republicans could also be due to the substantially greater size of their campaign coffers. As the data show, the Democratic

---

[1] Extensive personal interviews by Richard Herrera with key campaign strategists provided a significant part of the data presented here. Ms. Trabulsi was interviewed 13 December 1984 for information regarding the Democratic party. Mr. Sosa was interviewed 20 December 1984 for information regarding the Republican party. In addition to his insider's knowledge and views on the campaign, Mr. Sosa provided a video cassette copy of the TV spot ads aimed at the Latino population plus written transcripts in Spanish and English of those ads. Content analysis of this material was used for selected parts of the present work.

[2] The research has been made possible thanks to grants from the Funds for Improvement of Post-Secondary Education provided by the Graduate Division, University of California, Santa Barbara.

party's centralized efforts on behalf of their presidential candidate are relatively small compared to the Republican party's efforts on behalf of President Reagan. The disparity between the efforts of the two candidates to win Latino votes was reflected in both the allocation of resources (budgets) and the specific designs of the political ads. The analysis begins with a brief look at what the Democrats *did* do in 1984.

The Democrats' Strategy. Overall, the Mondale-Ferraro campaign devoted relatively few resources in their nationwide media advertising campaign to advertising targeted toward Hispanic voters. According to Ms. Trabulsi, executive vice president and media director of GSD&M advertising agency of Austin, Texas, the national headquarters spent approximately $120,000 in a nationwide effort to promote Walter Mondale to Hispanic voters. "Consultants '84," based in Washington, D.C., directed most of this effort.

Because of their substance, the national pro-Mondale ads aimed at Latinos can be classified as "argument spots" (Diamond and Bates, 1984) of two varieties. One type emphasized the position of the Democratic party on the Simpson-Mazzoli immigration bill. The second was in the form of endorsements by prominent Hispanics promoting the Democratic ticket. In Texas, promotions by San Antonio mayor Henry Cisneros and state senator Carlos Truan were used.

A major characteristic of the Democrats' efforts, however, is that their Latino-oriented ads were aired only on Spanish language radio; no Spanish or English language television ads specifically aimed at Hispanics were produced. Also, although these Spanish language ads were placed in California, Texas, New York, Chicago, and New Mexico, they were aired a maximum of only 10 days prior to the election. Whatever their messages, the Democrats left little time for them to be received and accepted by the Hispanic electorate.

Given the high cost of media campaigns, the national effort of the Democratic party on behalf of Mondale cannot be considered a serious one. There are at least three possible explanations for the apparent lack of effort: (a) financial constraints; (b) an assumption on the part of the Democrats that the Hispanic vote was a safe bet; and (c) an assumption that the limited national media efforts would be compensated by the extensive Latino-oriented media campaigns of the local Democratic party candidates. Since there are more Democratic candidates, including officeholders at the local level, than there are Republicans, the local media efforts would implicitly carry the message, and hopefully the Latino votes, for Mondale.[3]

---

[3] Analysis of this third explanation is part of the authors' current research activities. A preliminary finding shows that local Democratic candidates greatly outspent local Republican candidates in terms of spot ads aired over Spanish language radio stations in New York, San Antonio, and Los Angeles.

The Republicans' Strategy. Based on the analysis of data provided by Mr. Lionel Sosa, president of Sosa and Associates advertising agency of San Antonio, Texas, the contrasts between the Republicans and the Democrats are striking. This is illustrated in the following four sections which discuss ad production and airing, costs, language, and message theme and images.

Ad Production and Airing. The Republican presidential campaign ads aimed at the general public were produced by the "Tuesday Team," an ad hoc advertising group based in Washington, D.C. But in addition, the Reagan-Bush campaign commissioned the production of special political spot ads aimed at potential Latino voters. For this purpose, six television commercials plus four radio ads, each 30 seconds long, were produced. Sosa and Associates in San Antonio, recognized experts in Hispanic marketing, produced four of the television ads (two in English, two in Spanish). They also produced the four ads for Spanish language radio by slightly modifying the four TV ads they prepared. The other two TV ads (one in English, the other in Spanish) were produced by the "Tuesday Team."

Thus, in contrast to the Democrats, Republicans produced and aired political ads aimed at Latinos for radio *and* television and began the campaigns many weeks before election day giving Latino voters plenty of time and opportunities to listen to the pro-Reagan message. The ads were aired repeatedly in most of the major broadcasting stations in cities with Hispanic markets as large as New York and as small as Harlingen, Texas. To decide when to air the political ads, the Republicans also used the traditional market considerations, i.e., the Arbitron and Nielsen ratings which indicate the television shows most frequently watched by subpopulations, including Latinos. Thus, the pro-Reagan ads were placed to coincide with programs Hispanics tend to view most often, e.g., action shows, police shows, detective shows, etc.

Costs. In terms of resources allocated to advertising particularly aimed at Latinos, the Reagan campaign spent approximately $6 million nationwide. This represents approximately 15 percent of the total budget of approximately $40 million that the Federal Election Commission reports was spent by the Reagan-Bush reelection campaign. The distribution of this budget to capture Latino votes is also very telling: about 75 percent of the $6 million was spent on Latino-oriented English language ads on the network affiliates. In contrast, most of the remaining 25 percent of that budget was spent on Spanish language ads on Spanish language radio. Only about 10 percent was spent on Spanish language ads on Spanish language television, while no money was spent for Latino-oriented English language ads on radio. Altogether, there was an emphasis on television advertising, while radio advertising was a relatively small part of the total campaign.

Language. There are a few reasons why the Republicans spent so much of their budget on English language ads on TV to try to win Hispanic votes.

One is that the costs are much higher for Anglo television than Spanish language television or radio stations. But the new strategy stemmed from Sosa's application of "acculturation theory." Brusco (1981) explained that research conducted by Sosa and Associates established that Latinos in the United States can be divided into three main acculturation categories or "acculturation influence groups" (AIGs) classified according to linguistic, psychometric, and sociocultural indicators. Thus, she stated,

> Each AIG represents a language and culture comfort zone which corresponds in the following manner:
> AIG I: most comfortable in the Spanish language and culture, lowest degree of mainstream acculturation. [Relies primarily on Spanish media for information.]
> AIG II: comfortable in both Spanish and English language and Hispanic and mainstream culture. Represents the emerging Hispanic American who is creating a distinct cultural subgroup which is an amalgam of Hispanic and mainstream culture. [Relies on both Spanish and English media for information.]
> AIG III: most comfortable in the mainstream language and operates in a highly developed synthesis of the Hispanic and mainstream cultures. [Relies on English media for information.] (Brusco, 1981:8–9)

The number of Hispanics in AIG I, AIG II, or AIG III within any area of dominant influence (ADI) can then be ascertained using demographic data, e.g., sex, age. One of the assumptions made and presumably verified by Sosa and Associates concerns the location of the AIG categories within cities. AIG II and AIG III populations tend to live in more heterogeneous areas. AIG I populations are located in more homogeneous ones. In other words, Spanish-monolingual Hispanics tend to be located in areas densely populated by other Spanish monolinguals. That means that Latinos of AIG I are located in voting precincts with high percentages of Hispanics while Latinos of AIG II and AIG III are located in precincts with higher percentages of Anglos.

Furthermore, according to Mr. Sosa, additional research conducted by his company indicated that approximately 94 percent of high-propensity voters can be characterized as AIG II or AIG III while the remaining 6 percent are predominantly of the AIG I type. Here it should be pointed out that the judgments by Sosa and Associates are supported by research by Brischetto and de la Garza (1983, 1985), who in their surveys of Mexican Americans in San Antonio and East Los Angeles found that those with the highest electoral participation are bilingual (as opposed to Spanish monolinguals) over the age of 45. Further support also stems from the findings by de la Garza, Brischetto, and Vaughan (1983) and Subervi-Velez (1984) about the role of the Anglo mass media in Latino political orientations. Altogether, this suggests that English-speaking and bilingual Hispanics, i.e., those who reside in more integrated neighborhoods or who interact through their work or in other areas with Anglos and tune in to English language media, are the ones most

Role of Mass Media in Latino Political Life

likely to go to the polls on election day. On the other hand, those who speak predominantly Spanish, who live among other Latinos, tune in mostly to the Spanish language media, and have few if any regular contacts with Anglos, tend not to vote.

The new strategy represented quite a departure from previous national political advertising campaigns, not to mention the Democrat's strategy. Previous to this campaign, most, if not all, presidential candidate ads directed at Latinos were simply Spanish language translations (dubbed versions) of English language ads. The theoretical foundation for the old strategy is exemplified in Guernica's (1982) view that "U.S. Hispanics are most receptive to media content in the Spanish language. Spanish programming elicits an emotional response from the Hispanic audience that is missing in English language media" (p. 5).

Message Theme and Images. Based on our content analysis of the audio-visual tape provided by Mr. Sosa, the central theme of the Republican ads aimed at Latinos was that while Hispanics have traditionally been Democrats, there are reasons for them to start a new tradition by identifying with the Republican party and voting for President Reagan. A key part of this theme was the message that things were better now and would be better in the future than they were four years ago (with the Democrat administration). Thus, the ads implied that Latinos would benefit from voting for the Republican candidate—President Reagan.

The ads produced by Sosa and Associates presented this basic theme with various images. In one English language TV ad the message is delivered by a young nurse. In the other it is stated by a father figure, approximately fifty years of age; the background in this ad is a stairway wall covered with many family photographs of present and past generations. Of the Spanish language TV ads, one shows a woman approximately thirty years of age. The other ad shows a young man in an Air Force type uniform. In the transcripts we were given, the ads were respectively and appropriately labeled "Pride," "Tradition," "Mother," and "Soldier." All these characters can be easily identified with and trusted by Hispanics. Each ad shows a background of a well-kept, middle- or upper-middle-class residence with colors and styles of the furniture, lamps, decorative vases, plants, and flowers that give the impression of an all-American home. There is no distinctive decor or clothing uniquely representative of the Spanish styles or Latino culture.

Three of the four characters begin their monologues by emphasizing the traditional ties to the Democratic party. For example, the nurse states: "Four years ago, I voted for the first time the same way the family voted: Democrat all the way. 'Its our party,' Grandma said; Mom and Dad agreed." In the "father figure" ad, the man says, "Voting around this house is almost a tradition. We're Democrats. My father started it, I picked up on it; so did my kids." The soldier, for his part, indicates, "The other day I told my father that I was going to vote for the first time for President Reagan. He was surprised because the whole family has always been Democrat." Following the acknowledgment of the past tradition, two rationales for the change are stated. One is the independence of thinking. For example, the nurse says, "But this year Dad isn't saying much, and Grandma, now she's saying, 'Vote how you feel, Hija [Daughter].' [. . .] Vote my conscience, huh?" For his part the soldier states, "But I . . . I have my ideas. [. . .] Father showed me how to think on my own." The "father figure" justifies his change by saying, "But this year it doesn't feel right voting only for tradition." The other rationale is one or more of the Republican party's selling lines. For instance, the "mother type" says that she wishes the best for her children: better public schools, in a country full of pride, in a strong country. The nurse points out that "things are getting better and America is getting stronger again." The "father type" indicates that "my business is up, and my wife and daughter can shop again for those little extras." And the soldier says that with Reagan the country is stronger and that he can wear his uniform with more pride. The other common selling line by the Republicans—implicit or explicitly stated in all the ads—is that things are better now than in the past. The Spanish language radio ads were slightly modified versions of the four TV ads.

There are three additional important features about these ads that must be pointed out. First, according to Mr. Sosa, an effort was made to use "pan-Hispanic faces" and "generic Spanish" so that the ads could reach Latinos of all types, e.g., Mexican Americans, Puerto Ricans, Cubans. Thus, the spokespersons in the ads had no particular distinguishing physical features with respect to types of Hispanics. Also, other than the tan skin and "pan-Hispanic" look, the spokespersons are shown as relatively well-off or well established, not as struggling recent immigrants. Furthermore, a form of Spanish language that avoided specific dialects was used so that any Spanish-speaking Latino could relate to the characters and understand the message. Second, the spokespersons were "regular people," not Reagan, Bush (who speaks Spanish), or, with the exception of Katherine Ortega (see below), any other well-known Republican political personality as typically used in endorsement spots. Third, in the TV ads an attempt was made to present the characters as "real people" by briefly showing a caption of each spokesperson's name on the screen. This attempt was made on the radio ads by having the characters, except the soldier, begin by stating his/her name and then offering their monologue. Interestingly, however, the names in the TV ads were *different* from those in the radio ads, yet the messages were practically identical for the corresponding image spokespersons. Since we were not provided with copies of the audio tapes for the radio ads, we cannot tell if the same persons were used for producing both ads. Any appearance of real Latino people as former Democrats now turned Republican was thus only illusory.

The two other political ads, produced by the "Tuesday Team," are markedly different, having as a central theme "the American dream" but also how things were "better now than four years ago." One ad, originally produced for the general population, portrays America back at work by showing one black woman welding iron and two Anglo men each performing some industrial work; no Latino workers or faces are shown. But the message is in Spanish, stating in part that the American dream is being repaired, thanks to President Reagan. As the message comes to an end, the principal scenery is the Statue of Liberty being repaired under scaffolds. The other ad features Katherine Ortega, U.S. treasurer, speaking in English, against a backdrop of what seems to be the Republican national convention center. Its essence is the reemergence of the American dream thanks to Reagan; Ortega ends by saying, "Now that America is moving ahead, why should we ever go back?" These two ads were not modified and transmitted over Spanish language radio.

Altogether, the basic thrust of the Republican message to Latinos is not very different from the one-line basic message of the Republican party in 1980 and 1982, i.e., "Vote Republican—for a change." Thus, the political advertising spots ("polispots") proposed a conscious or subconscious thought of traditional values, combined with emotion and logic embedded in the style of the ads, in order to lead Latinos to start a new tradition of voting for a Republican presidential candidate and by extension for other Republican candidates.

Why were the themes and images of the ads produced as if Latinos were one homogeneous group? According to Mr. Sosa, there are two explanations. First, budget limitations precluded the development and production of ads for subgroups within subpopulations. Second, it was considered a myth that different types of Hispanics will not accept one central theme. What is necessary, according to Sosa, is that "an emotional nerve be touched." Additionally, the process followed by the advertisers was to "take a subconscious thought of the audience and combine it with emotion and logic." The Republican ads followed this process and developed a theme which seemingly satisfied the requirements for effective advertising. It seems to us that these explanations are not mere rationalizations for not producing more ads, since there was no indication that the Republicans would not have spent more had they felt the need.

Some Guiding Questions

The preceding discussion has shown that mass media are important factors in the development of Latino political life in the United States. The scant research and the present case study suggest that media influence may be occurring among Latinos as individuals and at institutional levels.

Regarding the present case study, the key question we would like to be able to answer is, Did Hispanic voters pay more attention to the Democratic party's Spanish language ads and keep their loyalties on election day, or did they pay more attention to the Republican party's Spanish and English language ads, abandon their traditional Democratic allegiance, and then pull the Reagan-Bush lever in 1984? Although the Republican party surely does not believe their efforts were lost, accurate answers to this question would have required meticulous longitudinal survey research linking Latinos' (a) exposure to the political ads in the Spanish and English language media to (b) their political cognitions, attitudes and behaviors. Even then, other sources of influence, such as media news information, family, peers, opinion leaders, etc., would have to be accounted for or statistically controlled before arriving at a conclusion about the effect(s) of the political ads. Unfortunately such research, to our knowledge, does not exist.

Another important question we would like to answer is, How did the 1984 Latino-oriented media strategies compare to those of previous elections? And what were the intricate decisions and decision-making processes that led to the characteristics of each party's strategies and efforts regarding the Latino voters? The answers are beyond the scope of this paper. But hopefully this study may contribute to some understanding of forthcoming congressional and presidential elections.

An additional major research area that merits immediate scrutiny is the political characteristics of the news and information available via the Spanish language media. It is true that the evidence gathered to date hardly indicates that these media directly influence Hispanics' political participation as traditionally measured. However, the effect of these media may be more indirect via their possible agenda-setting power, especially through community leaders. Anglo politicians and community leaders look at these media for cues about public opinion among the Latino population. Bilingual editorials of the Spanish language newspapers are intended for this purpose.

The importance we give to this latter research topic on Spanish language media stems from a preliminary analysis of our own data. It clearly shows that major segments of the Spanish language media are generally more partisan and conservative than their Anglo counterparts. Downing (1985) has also found more explicit ideological characteristics of such media in New York. Thus, a specific concern should be how Latino politics are shaped by the ownership patterns and content characteristics of Spanish language *daily* newspapers such as *El Diario–La Prensa* (New York), *La Opinión* (Los Angeles), *Diario Las Américas* and *El Miami Herald* (Miami), *El Mañana* (Chicago), and *Noticias del Mundo* (published in New York, Los Angeles, Chicago, and San Francisco; owned by Rev. Sun Myung Moon and his conservative Unification Church).

A similar question should be asked regarding radio and television news and information. For example, even a cursory analysis of the news and political information programs broadcast over the Cuban owned or directed radio stations in Miami will show heavy emphasis on conservative views and frequent editorialization on routine political news items. These content analyses are needed to properly contextualize studies about Latino political cognitions, attitudes, opinions and behaviors.

Finally, in addressing each of these topics, it would be valuable to know the extent to which the individual or institutional characteristics of Latino politics reflect assimilation or pluralism processes (Subervi-Velez, 1986).

In sum, research regarding if, when, and how the Hispanic *and* Anglo media influence the development of Latino political life is important and long overdue. **SSQ**

REFERENCES

Brischetto, Robert R., and Rodolfo de la Garza. 1983. *The Mexican American Electorate: Political Participation and Ideology.* Mexican American Electorate Series, Occasional Paper No. 3 (San Antonio: Southwest Voter Registration Education Project).

―――. 1985. *The Mexican American Electorate: Political Opinions and Behavior across Cultures in San Antonio.* Mexican American Electorate Series, Occasional Paper No. 5 (San Antonio: Southwest Voter Registration Education Project).

Brischetto, Robert, and Willie Velasquez. 1984. *The Hispanic Electorates* (New York: Hispanic Policy Development Project).

Brusco, Bernadette A. 1981. "Hispanic Marketing: New Applications for Old Methodologies," *Agenda,* 11 (May/June):8–9.

Buehler, Marilyn H. 1976 "Political Efficacy, Political Discontent, and Voting Turnout among Mexican-Americans in Michigan." Ph.D. dissertation, University of Notre Dame.

Cain, Bruce E., and D. Roderick Kiewiet. 1985. "Latinos and the 1984 Election: A Comparative Perspective." California Institute of Technology, Division of the Humanities. Mimeo.

Castro, Tony. 1974. *Chicano Power* (New York: Saturday Review Press).

de la Garza, Rodolfo O., and Robert R. Brischetto with D. Vaughan. 1983. *The Mexican American Electorate: Information Sources and Policy Orientations.* Mexican American Electorate Series, Occasional Paper No. 2 (San Antonio: Southwest Voter Registration Education Project).

de la Garza, Rodolfo O., Robert R. Brischetto, and Janet Weaver. 1984. *The Mexican American Electorate: An Explanation of Their Opinions and Behaviors.* Mexican American Electorate Series, Occasional Paper No. 4 (San Antonio: Southwest Voter Registration Education Project).

Diamond, Edwin, and Stephen Bates. 1984. *The Spot: The Rise of Political Advertising on Television* (Cambridge: MIT Press).

Downing, John D. H. 1985. "Spanish Language Media in Greater New York. Preliminary Survey." Hunter College, New York, Communication Department.

Garcia, F. Chris, and Rodolfo O. de la Garza. 1977. *The Chicano Political Experience: Three Perspectives* (North Scituate, Mass.: Duxbury Press).

Garcia, F. Chris, Rodolfo O. de la Garza, and Donald J. Torres. 1985. "Chapter 13, Introduction," in R. O. de la Garza et al., eds., *The Mexican American Experience,* (Austin: University of Texas Press): pp. 185–200.

Greenberg, Bradley, Michael Burgoon, Judee Burgoon, and Felipe Korzenny. 1983. *Mexican Americans and the Mass Media* (Norwood, N.J.: Ablex).

Guernica, Antonio. 1982 *Reaching the Hispanic Market Effectively* (New York: McGraw-Hill).

Knaggs, John R. 1986. *Two Party Texas: The John Tower Era, 1961–1984* (Austin, Tex.: Eakin).

Lewels, Francisco J., Jr. 1974. *The Uses of the Media by the Chicano Movement* (New York: Praeger).

Miyares, Marcelino. 1980. *Models of Political Participation of Hispanic Americans* (New York: Arno).

Nelson, Dale. 1984. "Hispanic Political Behavior: A Comparison of Chicanos, Cubans and Puerto Ricans." Fordham University, Department of Political Science. Photocopy.

Subervi-Velez, Federico A. 1984. "Hispanics, the Mass Media, and Politics: Assimilation vs. Pluralism." Ph.D. dissertation, University of Wisconsin.

———. 1986. "Ethnic Assimilation and Pluralism: The Role of the Mass Media," *Communication Research*, 13 (1):71–96.

Tan, Alex. 1983. "Media Use and Political Orientations of Ethnic Groups," *Journalism Quarterly*, 60 (1):126–32.

Valenzuela, Nicholas A. 1985. "Organizational Evolution of a Spanish-Language Television Network: An Environmental Approach." Ph.D. dissertation, Stanford University.

Vidal, David. 1980. "The Strange Case of Reverend Moon and His New Paper in New York," *Washington Journalism Review*, 4 (November):28–29.

Wirthlin, Richard, Vincent Breglio, and Richard Beal. 1981. "Campaign Chronicles," *Public Opinion*, 4 (February/March):43–49.

Casenote

Garza v. County of Los Angeles: Preservation of Minority Group Voting Strength as Justification for Deviation from One Person-One Vote Standard

Robert G. Retana†

INTRODUCTION

In *Garza v. County of Los Angeles*, a consolidation of two civil suits filed in August and September of 1988 in U.S. District Court in Los Angeles, the Los Angeles County Board of Supervisors has been charged with violating the 1965 Voting Rights Act by re-drawing its five districts in 1981 in such a way as to scatter the County's Latinos and deny them representation.[1] The suit could become one of the nation's most significant voting rights cases in terms of population affected. With 8.3 million residents, Los Angeles County is among the most populous counties in the United States.[2]

The 1965 Voting Rights Act bars any governing body from reducing the electoral participation of any minority group.[3] The suit names the

---

† Third-year student, Boalt Hall School of Law, University of California, Berkeley, B.A., 1984, Columbia University.

1. The suits are consolidated as Yolanda Garza et al., Plaintiffs, United States of America, Plaintiff, Lawrence K. Irvin, et al., Plaintiff-Intervenors v. County of Los Angeles, California, Los Angeles Board of Supervisors, et al., Defendants. Individually, the suits are United States of America v. County of Los Angeles, CV88-5435KN(EX); and Garza v. County of Los Angeles, CV88-05143KN(EX).

Final arguments for *Garza* ended April 10, 1990, closing almost three months of trial. Los Angeles Daily Journal, April 11, 1990, at 1, col. 3. As of this publication, the case was still under submission .

2. U.S. BUREAU OF THE CENSUS, COUNTY AND CITY DATA BOOK (1988). This figure represents the population of Los Angeles County for 1986.

3. The Voting Rights Act of 1965, section 1973, provides in pertinent part:

  (a) No voting qualification or prerequisite to voting or standard, practice, or procedure shall be imposed or applied by any State or political subdivision in a manner which results in a denial or abridgement of the right of any citizen of the United States to vote on account of race or color, or in contravention of the guarantees set forth in section 1973(f)(2) of this title, as provided in subsection (b) of this section.

Los Angeles County Registrar-Recorder, who oversees elections, and the five supervisors.[4] The U.S. Justice Department, the Mexican American Legal Defense and Educational Fund, and the American Civil Liberties Union filed suit to force a reapportionment before the 1990 county elections.[5] The suit contends that the all-white board split up Latino neighborhoods among three districts in violation of the federal Voting Rights Act and accused the Board of drawing its districts in such a way as to weaken the political clout of the County's 2 million Latinos.[6]

The suit indicates that the County's Latino population jumped from 1.2 million in 1970, or about 18.3 percent of the County's 7 million residents then, to over 2 million, or 27.6 percent of the County's 7.4 million residents, in 1980.[7] The Board is required to divide the population evenly when district lines are re-drawn every decade. In 1981, the Board rejected a proposal to create two inner-city districts, which would have increased the possibility that a minority member would be elected to the Board. One district would have combined a number of African Americans and Latinos, while another district would have contained a Latino majority. But the plan, which ran into fierce opposition from Board members, was turned down.[8] In the County's 138-year history, there have been no Latino supervisors and only one African American, who was appointed to the Board but who later lost an election to retain her seat.[9]

The Justice Department conducted a demographic study, which was confirmed by a study conducted by the Rose Institute of Claremont McKenna College, which demonstrated that a large, contiguous Latino population resides in the eastern and central section of the county. That population, which could have potentially elected a Latino supervisor, was divided among three supervisorial districts in the County's 1981 re-

---

(b) A violation of subsection (a) of this section is established if, based on the totality of the circumstances, it is shown that the political processes leading to nomination or election in the State or political subdivision are not equally open to participation by members of a class of citizens protected by subsection (a) of this section in that its members have less opportunity than other members of the electorate to participate in the political process and to elect representatives of their choice. The extent to which members of a protected class have been elected to office in the State or political subdivision is one circumstance which may be considered: *Provided*, That nothing in this section establishes a right to have members of a protected class elected in numbers equal to their proportion in the population.

42 U.S.C. § 1973 (as amended June 29, 1982).

4. See Los Angeles Daily Journal, Aug. 25, 1988, at 1, col. 3.
5. See Id.
6. See Los Angeles Daily Journal, Oct. 6, 1988, at 4, col. 1.
7. For statistical data see U.S. BUREAU OF THE CENSUS, 1980 CENSUS OF POPULATION, CHARACTERISTICS OF THE POPULATION 18 (1981) (vol. 1); See also Los Angeles Times, March 23, 1989, § B, at 2, col. 1.
8. Los Angeles Times, May 26, 1988, at 1, col. 2
9. Los Angeles Times, Jan. 27, 1989, § 2, at 7, col. 3.

districting plan.[10]

A redistricting plan which was proposed as a settlement to the current litigation included a majority Latino district. The proposed plan did not create a new district. It realigned the presently existing districts so that one is made up primarily of Latinos. However, in order to maintain the Latino majority within that district, it must be between 6.9% and 12% smaller than the rest of the districts within Los Angeles County.[11]

However, malapportionment may occur when districts are unequal in size because votes are then unequally weighed. The votes of those residing in smaller districts count more because fewer people are able to have the same amount of representation for their district. The United States Supreme Court has allowed some deviation from the one person-one vote standard in order to further important governmental policies. This Note argues that preservation of minority group voting strength is a policy which can justify a deviation from the equal population standard in reapportioning a county's supervisorial districts.

There are two distinct concepts which emerge in the area of reapportionment to achieve fair representation. The first is that the vote of an individual as nearly as practicable should equal that of another individual. The second concept, however, views the individual as a member of a group, with shared interests with other members of each group. Therefore, although a court reviewing a reapportionment plan is concerned with affording equal weight to the vote of each individual, certain state or local governmental policies which account for group interests will allow some deviation from strict mathematical equality.

The stringent requirements found in congressional apportionment are somewhat relaxed at a state and local level, allowing more room for implementation of innovative state policies with regard to apportionment and representation. Therefore, the policy of preserving minority group voting strength has its strongest chance of withstanding constitutional challenge in a local apportionment plan. The Supreme Court has held that deviations in population equality among districts in state legislative apportionment which are less than 10% are de minimus and do not make out a prima facie case of discrimination. However, population deviations between two districts of more than 10% must always be justified by a rational state policy. The apportionment plan must also be narrowly tailored so that the deviations involved are only those which are necessary to achieve the state's policy.

Although the Supreme Court was previously presented with the policy of preserving minority group voting strength as a justification for

---

10. Los Angeles Times, June 7, 1988, at 1, col. 1.
11. Interview with Mark Rosenbaum, General Counsel, American Civil Liberties Union Foundation of Southern California, in Los Angeles (May 7, 1990).

such deviations, it did not rule on its validity due to insufficient evidence that the plan involved was drawn to achieve that goal.[12] Therefore, in approving a deviation from the one person-one vote principle, the plan submitted must be demonstrated to deviate from equality in population only to the extent absolutely necessary to achieve the proffered governmental goal. This Note will argue that a court should allow a reapportionment plan with a majority Latino district which is smaller than other districts, as was proposed in Los Angeles County, in order to preserve that minority group's voting strength.

I.
GENERAL FRAMEWORK FOR CONGRESSIONAL APPORTIONMENT

Article 1 § 2 of the Federal Constitution has been the guiding constitutional provision in congressional apportionment. The requirement of Article 1 § 2 that congressional representatives be chosen "by the people of the Several States" mandates equal representation for equal numbers of people.[13] Although the Supreme Court has recognized that "it may not be possible to draw congressional lines with mathematical precision,"[14] it nonetheless requires that districts be apportioned to achieve population equality "as nearly as practicable."[15] This standard permits only those limited population variances which are unavoidable despite a good-faith effort to achieve precise mathematical equality, or for which justification is shown.[16] Even variances of less than one percent in congressional districts are unconstitutional if a good faith effort to achieve precise mathematical equality could have produced smaller variances.[17]

There is therefore a two-part test for determining the constitutional validity of congressional apportionment. First, the court must consider whether the population differences among the congressional districts could have been reduced or eliminated altogether by a good faith effort to draw districts of equal population. If not, the apportionment plan will be upheld. Second, if the population differences were not the result of a good faith effort to achieve population equality, each significant variance must be shown to have been necessary to achieve some legitimate goal.[18]

---

12. *See* Karcher v. Daggett, 462 U.S. 725, 743 (1983) (attempt to justify population deviations in reapportionment plan on the ground that they preserved the voting strength of minority groups was not supported by the evidence).
13. Wesberry v. Sanders, 376 U.S. 1 (1964).
14. *Id.* at 18.
15. *Id.*; *see* Karcher v. Daggett, 462 U.S. 725, 730 (1983).
16. Kirkpatrick v. Preisler, 394 U.S. 526 (1969).
17. Karcher v. Daggett, 462 U.S. 725, 731-35 (1983).
18. *Id.* at 730-31.

If the court considers the proffered goal legitimate and the variances necessary, the plan will pass constitutional muster.

II.
STANDARDS FOR STATE LEGISLATIVE REDISTRICTING

While population alone has been the sole criterion of constitutionality in congressional redistricting under Article 1 § 2, the Equal Protection Clause affords states broader lattitude in state legislative redistricting. In *Reynolds v. Sims*,[19] the Court held that some deviations from a strict equal population principle are constitutionally permissible in the two houses of a bicameral state legislature, where incident to the effectuation of a rational state policy, so long as there is no significant departure from the basic standard of equality of population among districts.

> In [*Westbury*] the Court stated that congressional representation must be based on population as nearly as is practicable. In implementing the basic constitutional principle of representative government as enunciated by the Court in *Wesberry*—equality of population among districts—some distinctions may well be made between congressional and state legislative representation. Since, almost invariably, there is a significantly larger number of seats in state legislative bodies to be distributed within a State than congressional seats, it may be feasible to use political subdivision lines to a greater extent in establishing state legislative districts than in congressional districting while still affording adequate representation to all parts of the State. To do so would be constitutionally valid, so long as the resulting apportionment was one based substantially on population and the equal-population principle was not diluted in any significant way. Somewhat more flexibility may therefore be constitutionally permissible with respect to state legislative apportionment than in congressional districting.[20]

The Court therefore held that insuring some voice to political subdivisions in at least one legislative body may, within reason, warrant some deviations from population-based representation in state legislatures.[21] The Court declined, however, to spell out any precise constitutional test for state legislative apportionment schemes, stating "Developing a body of doctrine on a case-by-case basis appears to us to provide the most satisfactory means of arriving at detailed constitutional requirements in the area of state legislative apportionment."[22]

In *Mahan v. Howell*,[23] the principal question presented for review

---

19. 377 U.S. 533 (1964).
20. *Id.* at 577-78.
21. *Id.* at 580.
22. *Id.* at 578.
23. 10 U.S. 315 (1973).

173

was whether or not the Equal Protection Clause of the Fourteenth Amendment, like Article 1 § 2, permits only the limited population variances which are unavoidable despite a good-faith effort to achieve absolute equality in the context of state legislative reapportionment. The principle that Article 1, § 2 of the Constitution permits only population variances among congressional districts which are unavoidable despite a good faith effort to achieve absolute equality, or for which justification is shown, was first expounded in *Wesberry v. Sanders*,[24] and in *Kirkpatrick v. Preisler*.[25] However, in *Mahan v. Howell*, the Supreme Court stated that although the *Wesberry, Kirkpatrick*, and *Wells* line of cases would continue to govern congressional reapportionments, the rigor of the rule of those cases was inappropriate for state reapportionment challenges under the Equal Protection Clause of the Fourteenth Amendment.[26]

The facts in *Mahan v. Howell* were that in 1971 the Virginia General Assembly had reapportioned the state for the election of state delegates and senators. The apportionment statutes were invalidated by a District Court which ruled that a 16.4% variation from the ideal district population of 46,485, where one district was overrepresented by 6.8% and another being underrepresented by 9.6%, caused the reapportionment plan to violate the one person, one vote principle.[27] Although the District Court noted that the deviations were traceable to the desire of the General Assembly to maintain the integrity of traditional county and city boundaries, and that it was impossible to draft district lines to overcome unconstitutional disparities while maintaining such integrity, it held that the State proved no governmental necessity for strictly adhering to political subdivision lines.[28] The District Court thereby substituted its own plan which had a percentage variation from the ideal district of about 10%, but which did not follow political subdivisions in many instances.[29]

The Supreme Court held that the constitutionality of Virginia's legislative redistricting was not to be judged by the more stringent standards that *Kirkpatrick* and *Wells* make applicable to congressional reapportionment, but instead by the Equal Protection test enunciated in *Reynolds v. Sims*. "Application of the 'absolute equality' test of *Kirkpatrick* and *Wells* to state legislative redistricting may impair the normal functioning of state and local governments."[30]

We reaffirm its holding [*Reynolds*] that "the Equal Protection Clause re-

---

24. 376 U.S. 1 (1964).
25. 394 U.S. at 527-528; *see also* Wells v. Rockefeller, 394 U.S. 542, 546 (1969).
26. 410 U.S. 315 (1973).
27. *Id.* at 319.
28. *Id.* at 319-320.
29. *Id.* at 323-324.
30. *Id.* at 323.

quires that a State make an honest and good faith effort to construct districts, in both houses of its legislature, as nearly of equal population as is practicable." We likewise reaffirm its conclusion that "[s]o long as the divergences from a strict population standard are based on legitimate considerations incident to the effectuation of a rational state policy, some deviations from the equal-population principle are constitutionally permissible with respect to the apportionment of seats in either or both of the two houses of a bicameral state legislature."[31]

Although the District Court had held that the State had proved no governmental necessity for strict adherence to political subdivisions lines, the Supreme Court stated that the proper equal protection test is not framed in terms of governmental necessity but instead in terms of a claim that a State may rationally consider.[32] Under this test, the Supreme Court held that the decision of the Virginia General Assembly to provide representation to subdivisions was valid when measured against the Equal Protection Clause of the Fourteenth Amendment.

> The inquiry then becomes whether it can reasonably be said that the state policy urged by Virginia to justify the divergences in the legislative reapportionment plan of the House is, indeed, furthered by the plan adopted by the legislature, and whether, if so justified, the divergences are also within tolerable limits. For a State's policy urged in justification of disparity in district population, however rational, cannot constitutionally be permitted to emasculate the goal of substantial equality.[33]

The Supreme Court stated that since the latitude afforded to states in legislative redistricting is somewhat broader than that afforded to them in congressional redistricting, "Virginia was free as a matter of federal constitutional law to construe the mandate of its Constitution more liberally in the case of legislative redistricting than in the case of congressional redistricting, and the plan adopted by the legislature indicates that it has done so."[34] The Court also held that the population disparities among the districts that have resulted from the pursuit of this plan do not exceed constitutional limits.[35] The Court declined, however, to impose a stringent mathematical standard for state legislative apportionment.

> Neither courts nor legislatures are furnished any specialized calipers that enable them to extract from the general language of the Equal Protection Clause of the Fourteenth Amendment the mathematical formula that establishes what range of percentage deviations is permissible, and what is not. The 16-odd percent maximum deviation that the District Court found to exist in the legislative plan for the reapportionment of the House

---

31. *Id.* at 324-325 (quoting *Reynolds*, 377 U.S. at 577, 579).
32. *Id.* at 325-26.
33. *Id.* at 326.
34. *Id.* at 327.
35. *Id.* at 328.

is substantially less than the percentage deviations that have been found invalid in the previous decisions of this Court. While this percentage may well approach tolerable limits, we do not believe it exceeds them. Virginia has not sacrificed substantial equality to justifiable deviations.[36]

The Supreme Court thereby concluded that the policy of maintaining the integrity of political subdivisions lines which was advanced as justification for disparities in population among districts was rational, and that the plan did in fact advance that policy. In recognizing the legitimacy of preserving political subdivisions, the court has noted their shared distinct interests and values due to occupation, social class, or racial or ethnic composition.[37] The minority representation interests of political subdivisions are similar in principle to those of racial minorities seeking equality of representation. Residents of political subdivisions share an interest in the outcome of local legislation by virtue of living in the same political unit, as do racial minority voters.

The constitutionality of a state's legislative redistricting plan is therefore not to be judged by the same stringent standards that are applicable to congressional reapportionment, but by the substantial equality standard of the Equal Protection Clause. Variations from a strict equal population principle are constitutionally permissible if based on legitimate considerations incident to a policy which a state may rationally consider, and if the reapportionment plan is narrowly tailored to achieve the goals of that policy.

III.
APPLICABILITY TO COUNTY GOVERNMENTS

In *Sailors v. Board of Education*[38] the Supreme Court decided that the "one man-one vote" rule did not apply to elections of members of a county school board where the members of the board were not chosen by popular election and were considered to have held nonlegislative offices as to which the Constitution did not require popular elections.

> Viable local governments may need many innovations, numerous combinations of old and new devices, great flexibility in municipal arrangements to meet changing urban conditions. We see nothing in the Constitution to prevent experimentation. At least as respects nonlegislative officers, a State can appoint local officials or elect them or combine the elective and appointive systems as was done here.[39]

---

36. *Id.* at 329.
37. *See* Brown v. Thompson, 462 U.S. 835, 841 n.5 (1983) (citing special economic and social needs of individual counties as justifying representation by counties); Karcher v. Daggett, 462 U.S. 725, 776 n.12 (White, J., dissenting) (criticizing one person, one vote rule for failing to allow grouping of constituencies with similar concerns).
38. 387 U.S. 105 (1967).
39. *Id.* at 110-111.

In *Dusch v. Davis*,[40] electors of five boroughs brought suit against local and state officials claiming that a consolidation plan violated *Reynolds v. Sims*.[41] An amended plan was approved by the District Court; however, the Fourth Circuit Court of Appeals reversed.[42] The Supreme Court reversed the Court of Appeals stating "In *Sailors v. Board of Education* we reserved the question whether the apportionment of municipal or county legislative agencies is governed by *Reynolds v. Sims*. But though we assume *arguendo* that it is, we reverse the Court of Appeals."[43] The Court went on to hold that the constitutional test under the Equal Protection Clause is whether there is "invidious discrimination."[44] As the Court found no such discrimination, the requirement that each of the councilpersons be a resident of the electing borough did not render the plan unconstitutional.[45] The Court approvingly quoted the District Court:

> The plan does not preserve any controlling influence of the smaller boroughs, but does indicate a desire for intelligent expression of views on subjects relating to agriculture which remains a great economic factor in the welfare of the entire population. As the plan becomes effective, if it then operates to minimize or cancel out the voting strength of racial or political elements of the voting population, it will be time enough to consider whether the system still passes constitutional muster.[46]

The decision in *Avery v. Midland County*,[47] however, settled the conflict of authority in lower federal courts regarding the applicability of the "one man-one vote" rule to county and municipal governments. In an opinion by Justice White, expressing the views of five members of the Court, it was held that the Midland County Commissioners Court was a unit of local government having general governmental powers over the county's entire geographic area, and therefore was subject to the "one man—one vote" rule, and the Constitution did not permit its members to be apportioned among single member districts of substantially unequal population.[48] The Court noted that the Equal Protection Clause does not require that the State never distinguish between citizens, only that the

---

40. 387 U.S. 112 (1967).
41. 377 U.S. 533 (1964).
42. *Dusch*, 387 U.S. at 114.
43. *Id*. (citation omitted).
44. *Id*. at 116 (citing Reynolds v. Sims, 377 U.S. at 561 (judicial focus must be upon ascertaining whether there has been any discrimination against certain of the State's citizens which constitutes an impermissible impairment of their constitutionally protected right to vote. Such a case presents questions of alleged invidious discriminations against groups or types of individuals in violation of constitutional guarantees)).
45. *Id*. at 115.
46. *Id*. at 116-117.
47. 390 U.S. 474 (1968).
48. *Id*. at 483-485.

distinctions that are made not be arbitrary or invidious.[49]

> The *Sailors* and *Dusch* cases demonstrate that the Constitution and this Court are not roadblocks in the path of innovation, experiment, and development among units of local government. We will not bar what Professor Wood has called "the emergence of a new ideology and structure of public bodies, equipped with new capacities and motivations. . . ." Our decision today is only that the Constitution imposes one ground rule for the development of arrangements of local government: a requirement that units with general governmental powers over an entire geographic area not be apportioned among single-member districts of substantially unequal population.[50]

In *Avery*, although each of the four districts in Midland County elected one commissioner, one of the districts contained about 95% of the county's population.[51] Therefore, although a county's redistricting plan may include districts with unequal populations, if the size of the variations are substantial as in *Avery*, without adequate justification they may be considered impermissible and violative of the Equal Protection Clause.

Note also that extending the application of the Equal Protection Clause to local legislatures was motivated, in part, by a desire to preserve the voting strength of minority groups from strict majoritarian rule.

> Inequitable apportionment of local governing bodies offends the Constitution even if adopted by a properly appointed legislature representing the majority of the State's citizens. The majority of a State—by constitutional provision, by referendum, or through accurately apportioned representatives—can no more place a minority in oversized districts without depriving that minority of equal protection of the laws than they can deprive the minority of the ballot altogether, or impose upon them a tax rate in excess of that to be paid by equally situated members of the majority.[52]

Therefore, where a minority group has been found to have suffered debasement of their voting strength by being divided into various districts, in none of which they constituted a majority, the preservation of that group's voting strength is arguably a rational consideration which may allow a local government some deviation from the equal population standard. An advocate for such a plan should argue that based on *Reynolds* and *Mahan*,[53] the line of cases governing congressional apportionment are inapplicable. So long as the plan is based substantially on population, variations should be justified by the Supreme Court's reason-

---

49. *Id.* at 484.
50. *Id.* at 485-486 (quoting R. Wood, 1400 GOVERNMENTS 175 (1961)).
51. *Id.* at 486.
52. *Id.* at 481 n.6.
53. *See supra* notes 19-23 and accompanying text.

ing in *Mahan, Sailors, Dusch,* and *Avery*. That is, the policy of preserving minority voting strength need not be a governmental necessity, but instead a rational state policy.

As with Affirmative Action, the fact that this plan is remedial in nature, as opposed to an unjustified preference, will make it more likely to be upheld by a court.[54] The cases show that local governments are given more latitude with regard to apportionment so long as they are within tolerable limits, and the policy is in fact furthered by the plan. Arguments regarding local flexibility and changing urban conditions should be used as well as responsiveness to local concerns, so that, as stated in *Avery*, the Constitution does not become a roadblock to innovation. If *Dusch* allowed deviation from the one person-one vote principle to permit intelligent expression of views regarding agriculture, it seems that a minority group which is now a significant percentage of the state and county's population should be able to have its views articulated as well. Similarly, providing representation to political subdivisions, as in *Mahan*, is an analogous governmental interest which has been deemed permissible. *Mahan* recognized that, notwithstanding equality of representation, there are groups with distinct interests who are entitled to representation as such. Therefore, where there is evidence of past discrimination against a minority group, a local government should be able to use its latitude in reapportionment to remedy past debasement of that group's voting strength. Even if such a justification would not be allowed under a congressional reapportionment plan, it should be argued that at a local level, under the relaxed Equal Protection test of "substantial equality," it should be permissible.

Arguments to the contrary are likely to be as follows. Some courts have held that there is no different standard for local governments than that used in congressional apportionment. If this is successfully argued, it will make it much harder to justify the necessary deviations and arguments regarding local control will be useless. For example, the California Supreme Court, in *Calderón v. City of Los Angeles*,[55] rejected the argument that based on *Avery v. Midland County*, the City of Los Angeles was not subject to the strict rule of equality with regard to local apportionment. The Court invalidated an article of the Los Angeles City Charter which provided that districts "shall not deviate in numbers of voters by more than ten percent above or below one-fifteenth of the total number of registered voters in the City of Los Angeles."[56] The State

---

54. *See, e.g.* Califano v. Webster, 430 U.S. 313 (1977) (Social Security Act provision upheld which allowed women to exclude three more lower-earning years than men because it was based on objectively-verifiable discrimination against women.)
55. 4 Cal.3d 251, 481 P.2d 489, 93 Cal. Rptr. 361 (1971).
56. *Id.* at 266, 481 P.2d at 499, 93 Cal. Rptr. at 371.

Supreme Court reviewed various U.S. Supreme Court decisions and concluded, "[t]hose decisions involved congressional districting, which is based on article 1, section 2, of the federal Constitution and for which the Court has prescribed a rule of equality 'as nearly as practicable.' "[57] The Court continued:

> By contrast, state and local apportionment is guided by the dictates of the equal protection clause; for such jurisdictions, the constitutional mandate, enunciated first in *Reynolds*, has been "substantial equality." Despite the different constitutional bases and the varying formulae, however, "it has never been apparent that the Court sees these two clauses as producing different yardsticks for districting matters."[58]

In support of this argument, the State Supreme Court cited the decision in *Kirkpatrick v. Preisler*, [59] where the United States Supreme Court invalidated population variances among Missouri congressional districts. The State Court noted that *Kirkpatrick* repeatedly cited *Swann v. Adams*,[60] which involved redistricting of the Florida State Legislature. Also, "on the same day the Court decided *Swann*, it reversed and remanded a *congressional* apportionment case" for further consideration in light of *Swann v. Adams*.[61]

The State Supreme Court in *Calderón*, therefore concluded that "the [U.S. Supreme] court clearly seems to imply that decisions concerning state legislatures are interchangeable with those involving congressional districts so far as the constitutionally required standard of mathematical uniformity is concerned."[62]

The California Supreme Court therefore rejected the argument of the City of Los Angeles that based on the language in *Avery v. Midland County*,[63] the strict rule of equality in congressional apportionment does not apply to local governmental bodies like the Los Angeles City Council. The Court noted that the passage cited in *Avery* was illustrated by citation to decisions involving representatives chosen at large such as *Dusch v. Davis*, supra, or officials who were appointed instead of

---

57. *Id.* at 267, 481 P.2d at 499-500, 93 Cal. Rptr. at 371-372 (citing Wesberry v. Sanders, 376 U.S. 1 (1964)).

58. *Id.* (citing Reynolds v. Sims, 377 U.S. 533, 579 (1964); and quoting Dixon, *The Warren Court Crusade for the Holy Grail of 'One Man-One Vote,'* THE SUPREME COURT REVIEW 219-224 (1969).)

59. 394 U.S. 526 (1969).

60. 385 U.S. 440 (1967).

61. Calderón v. City of Los Angeles, 4 Cal.3d at 267, 481 P.2d at 500, 93 Cal. Rptr. at 372. The case referred to is Duddlston v. Grills, 385 U.S. 455 (1967).

62. *Id.* at 267, 481 P.2d at 500, 93 Cal. Rptr. at 372.

63. "This Court is aware of the immense pressures facing units of local governments, and of the greatly varying problems with which they must deal. The Constitution does not require that a uniform straightjacket bind citizens in devising mechanisms of local government suitable for local needs and efficient in solving problems." Avery v. Midland County, 390 U.S. 474, 485 (1968). *See supra* notes 47-52 and accompanying text.

elected.[64] "Such cases hardly support a contention that popularly elected representatives, chosen from the individual districts, may represent significantly unequal numbers of people."[65] However, note that it was not this analysis of *Avery* alone which proved fatal to the City of Los Angeles' argument.

> While the above analysis alone might not convince us of the *per se* invalidity of the charter provision here at issue, when it is coupled with another factor, we are satisfied that the section cannot stand. That factor is the Supreme Court's frequent rejection of any mathematical formula which purports to establish an "acceptable" variance from ideal equality. Correspondingly, the court has insisted that any such deviation be justified by the governmental unit on the basis of "legitimate considerations incident to the effectuation of a rational state policy. . . ."[66]

Therefore, the fact that the Los Angeles Charter provision flatly validated variances of ten percent from the ideal per-district figure and dispensed with the legal requirement that the City justify each deviation, caused the State Supreme Court to hold that it was unconstitutional.[67] The government runs a strong risk of being held in violation of the Equal Protection Clause if it can not justify its plan with a state interest that will account for the figures involved.[68]

This second reason distinguishes *Calderón*. While the City of Los Angeles sought to legislate a generally permissible level of deviation without justification by some rational state policy, a redistricting plan should be demonstrated as narrowly tailored to deviate from absolute equality only as is necessary to implement the rational state policy of preserving minority voting strength. Unlike *Calderón*, a redistricting plan should not seek an unjustified variation or attempt to adopt a permissible level of variation within a county's districts without requiring justification.

In addition, it is not so clear that congressional, state legislative and local apportionment plans are all measured by the same yardstick. The language cited in *Avery* as well as *Mahan v. Howell*, supra, clearly indicate that congressional apportionment is measured by a more stringent standard. Until the United States Supreme Court overrules its decisions or presents a new holding to the contrary, it should be argued that these

---

64. 4 Cal.3d at 268, 481 P.2d at 500, 93 Cal. Rptr. at 372.
65. *Id.* at 268, 481 P.2d at 500. 93 Cal. Rptr. at 372.
66. *Id.* at 269, 481 P.2d at 501, 93 Cal. Rptr. at 373 (quoting Reynolds v. Sims, 377 U.S. 533, 579; *see supra* note 19 and accompanying text).
67. *Id.* at 270, 481 P.2d at 502, 93 Cal. Rptr. at 374.
68. *See, e.g.*, Regents of University of California v. Bakke, 438 U.S. 265 (1978) (affirmative action may only be used where explicit judicial, legislative or administrative findings have been made of special constitutional or statutory violations).

cases are still good law, and lower court cases to the contrary are less persuasive and even incorrect.

IV.
PERMISSIBLE DEVIATIONS

In *Abate v. Mundt*,[69] the Supreme Court held that a reapportionment plan for New York's Rockland County Board of Supervisors, which produced a total deviation of equality of 11.9%, did not violate the Equal Protection Clause. The Board of Supervisors consisted of five members, each of whom also served as the executive of one of the County's five towns.[70] Under this system of local government, the County Legislature was not separately elected; rather, its members held their County offices by virtue of their election as town supervisors.[71]

> In assessing the constitutionality of various apportionment plans, we have observed that viable local governments may need considerable flexibility in municipal arrangements if they are to meet challenging societal needs, and that a desire to preserve the integrity of political subdivisions may justify an apportionment plan which departs from numerical equality. These observations, along with the fact that local legislative bodies frequently have fewer representatives than do their state and national counterparts and that some local legislative districts may have a much smaller population than do congressional and state legislative districts, lend support to the argument that slightly greater percentage deviations may be tolerable for local government apportionment schemes. . . . Of course, this Court has never suggested that certain geographic areas or political interests are entitled to disproportionate representation. Rather, our statements have reflected the view that the particular circumstances and needs of a local community as a whole may sometimes justify departures from strict equality.[72]

Based on the long tradition of overlapping functions and dual personnel in Rockland County government, and because the plan contained no built-in bias tending to favor particular political interests or geographic areas, the Court held that the reapportionment plan did not violate the Constitution.[73]

In *Gaffney v. Cummings*,[74] the Supreme Court held that minor deviations from mathematical equality among state legislative districts are not sufficient to make a prima facie case of invidious discrimination under the Equal Protection Clause.

---

69. 403 U.S. 182 (1971).
70. *Id.* at 183.
71. *Id.*
72. *Id.* at 185 (citations omitted).
73. *Id.* at 187.
74. 412 U.S. 735, 93 S.Ct. 2321, 37 L.Ed.2d 298 (1973).

> We have repeatedly recognized that state reapportionment is the task of local legislators or of those organs of state government selected to perform it. Their work should not be invalidated under the Equal Protection Clause when only minor population variations among districts are proved. Here, the proof at trial demonstrated that the House districts under the State Apportionment Board's plan varied in population from one another by a *maximum* of only about 8% and that the average deviation from the ideal House district was only about 2%. The Senate districts had even less variations. On such a showing, we are quite sure that a prima facie case of invidious discrimination under the Fourteenth Amendment was not made out.[75]

Gaffney stands for the proposition that with respect to state legislative reapportionment, minor deviations from population equality are considered legally irrelevant. If the deviations involved in a plan such as that proposed for Los Angeles County are not in the de minimus range, they should then be argued to be permissible subject to justification by the state's interest in preserving Latino voting strength. Although the cases discussed so far deal with protecting minority interests of structural units such as political subdivisions, the values for providing such protection are the same for racial minorities. If the court recognizes that towns or counties often constitute communities with shared distinct interests and values, that concept can easily be extended to racial minorities, especially when they live in a contiguous area. Presumably minorities concentrated in a specific area of a county are close enough in economic status that their interests as a group would be compatible enough to support the analogy to a political subdivision.

In a most recent decision regarding local government deviations from the "one person-one vote" standard, the Supreme Court, in *Board of Estimate v. Morris*,[76] invalidated apportionment of New York City's Board of Estimate, which consisted of three members elected citywide and the president of each of the city's five boroughs. The structure of the Board of Estimate was held inconsistent with Equal Protection because although the boroughs have widely disparate populations, each had equal representation on the Board.[77] The Court noted that the parties had stipulated that the deviation involved was 78%, and somewhat larger with respect to budget matters when only two citywide members participate.[78]

> We note that no case of ours has indicated that a deviation of some 78% could ever be justified. At the very least, the local government seeking to support such a difference between electoral districts would bear a very difficult burden, and we are not prepared to differ with the holding of the

---

75. *Id.* at 751 (emphasis in original).
76. 489 U. S. —, 109 S.Ct. 1433 (1989).
77. *Id.* at 1436.
78. *Id.* at 1442.

courts below that this burden has not been carried. The city presents in this court nothing that was not considered below, arguing chiefly that the board, as presently structured, is essential to the successful government of a regional entity, the City of New York.[79]

The Court concluded that the City's proffered governmental interests (accomodation of "natural and political boundaries as well as local interests")[80] did not suffice to justify such a substantial departure from the one person-one vote ideal.[81]

The cases cited above by the Supreme Court in *Board of Estimate v. Morris,* regarding permissible deviations, are helpful in understanding when deviations may be considered permissible. *Brown v. Thompson,*[82] involved a deviation from population equality with an average deviation of 16% (from the ideal number of residents per representative) and a maximum percentage deviation of 89% (between the largest and the smallest number of residents per representative). The Supreme Court held that Wyoming's long standing and legitimate policy of preserving county boundaries justified the deviations.[83] In discussing deviations which are generally permissible, the Court noted:

> We have held that "minor deviations from mathematical equality among state legislative districts are insufficient to make out a prima facie case of invidious discrimination under the Fourteenth Amendment so as to require justification by the State." Our decisions have established, as a general matter, that an apportionment plan with a maximum population under 10% falls within this category of minor deviations. A plan with larger disparities in population, however, creates a prima facie case of discrimination and therefore must be justified by the State.[84]

Wyoming's constitutional requirement that each county have at least one representative in its House of Representatives justified a county with only 2,924 persons having its own representative. The ideal apportionment would have been 7,337 persons per representative.[85] The court emphasized that it was not deciding whether Wyoming's policy of adherence to county boundaries justified the deviations throughout Wyoming's districts. Rather, the issue was whether it justified "the additional deviations from population equality resulting from the provision of rep-

---

79. *Id.* at 1442 (the Court cites as examples Brown v. Thompson, 462 U.S. 835, 846-847 (1988); Conner v. Finch, 431 U.S. 407, 410-420 (1977); Chapman v. Meier, 420 U.S. 1, 21-26 (1975); Mahan v. Howell, 410 U.S. 315, 329 (1973)).
80. *Id.*
81. *Id.* at 1443.
82. 462 U.S. 835 (1983).
83. *Id.* at 847.
84. *Id.* at 842-43 (quoting *Gaffney,* 412 U.S. at 745; and citing as examples Connor v. Finch, 431 U.S. 407, 418 (1977) and White v. Register, 412 U.S. 755, 764 (1973).).
85. *Id.* at 839.

resentation to Niobrara County."[86] The court concluded that "[i]t can scarcely be denied that in terms of actual effect on appellants' voting power, it matters little whether the 63-member or 64-member House is used."[87] The court noted further that under the 63-member plan, the average deviation per representative would be 13% and the maximum deviation would be 66%. "These statistics make clear that the grant of a representative to Niobrara County is not a significant cause of the population deviations that exist in Wyoming."[88]

This case is important to a reapportionment plan which adds a representative in order to provide representation to a minority group. It demonstrates that a court can look at a particular district being challenged and evaluate its effect on the voting strength of the challenger instead of deciding whether the entire reapportionment plan and its total deviations are constitutional. It appears to be an incremental analysis of reapportionment as opposed to a blanket judgement on the entire plan. A rational state policy will, under this analysis, allow a district to be substantially unequal from other districts so long as it does not, in and of itself, create significant total deviations.

Los Angeles County's Board of Supervisors may not lend itself to this analysis in that the Board governs a set number of districts—currently five—and the proposed reapportionment plan does not include a sixth district but rather involves a realignment of the presently existing districts.[89] However, if the total deviations involved in the proposed plan are significant even without the smaller Latino district, perhaps *Brown* could be used to show that a challenger's voting strength has not been diluted significantly through the creation of a majority Latino district, and therefore the Equal Protection Clause was not violated. On the contrary, voting strength of non-Latinos was probably previously inflated due to the division of the Latino population into three separate districts. Reapportioning to create a Latino district involves not a debasement, but a realignment of political strength to be more inclusive and remedy dilution of voting strength suffered in the past by Latinos.

A. Court Ordered Plans

In *Connor v. Finch*,[90] the Supreme Court held invalid a Mississippi District Court's legislative reapportionment plan which resulted in maximum population deviations of 16.5% in the Senate districts and 19.3% in the House districts. The Court stated that a court is held to stricter

---

86. *Id.* at 846.
87. *Id..* at 847.
88. *Id..* at 847.
89. *See supra* note 11 and accompanying text.
90. 431 U.S. 407 (1977).

standards than a state legislature when departing from the *Reynolds* "as nearly of equal population as practicable" standard, and that the burden of articulating special reasons for following such a policy in the face of substantial inequalities is correspondingly higher.[91] The Court therefore held that the District Court failed "to identify any such unique features . . . as would permit judicial protection of county boundaries in the teeth of the judicial duty to achieve the goal of population equality with little more than de minimus variation."[92]

Chapman v. Meier[93] first established that a court ordered plan must achieve the goal of population equality with little more than de minimus variation. "Where important and significant state considerations rationally mandate departure from these standards, it is the reapportionment court's responsibility to articulate precisely why a plan of single-member districts with minimal population variance cannot be adopted."[94] The Court therefore held a court-ordered reapportionment plan with a 20% variance constitutionally impermissible absent significant state policies requiring its adoption.[95]

Note that both *Connor* and *Chapman* involved court ordered plans which contained multi-member districts. Therefore, a single member district plan with detailed findings by the court as to why the variations involved are necessary could be constitutionally permissible. Even if the variations in population are over 10%, under *Abate, Brown* and *Gaffney*, one could argue that the deviations are small enough to be considered permissible so long as the justification for such deviations are spelled out explicitly on the court's record. Note also that although *Kirkpatrick v. Preisler*[96] stated that there are no variances in population small enough to be considered de minimus, *Connor* and *Chapman* indicate that a court ordered plan can have slight variations in population which are de minimus. If a plan's deviations are under 10%, such deviations are arguably de minimus. If the variations are higher however, the disparity may create a prima facie case of discrimination, and therefore must be justified by a rational state policy to be permissible.

B. *Los Angeles Distinguishable Due to Large Population*

Because of the size of Los Angeles County, it may be argued that a redistricting plan for the Los Angeles Board of Supervisors is distinguishable from other reapportionment cases with permissible or de mini-

---

91. *Id.*. at 419-420.
92. *Id.*. at 420.
93. 420 U.S. 1 (1975).
94. *Id.*. at 27.
95. *Id.* at 24.
96. 394 U.S. 526 (1969).

mus deviations due to the number of people involved in even the smallest of deviations. An argument could be made that because Los Angeles County is so large, it should be easier to make populations of districts within the County highly equalized.

> For example, assume that the local governing bodies of both Los Angeles County, California, and Hamilton County, New York, are being challenged for violations of the "one man-one vote" rule. Assume also that each county's apportionment of its ten-man legislature deviates from the ideal by 10%. Although the same standard should be applied, the factor of population size may produce a different result. The population of Hamilton County is just 4,714, while Los Angeles County boasts a population of more than seven million residents. Although both cases involve local governments, the 10% deviation affects 700,000 people in Los Angeles. Unless sufficient reason is shown why the district lines could not be redrawn to correct the disparity of approximately 70,000 people among the districts without detracting from the goal of fair and effective representation, the California legislative scheme should be invalidated. However, the same percentage deviations would involve fewer than 500 Hamilton County residents. Redrawing district lines in order to pick up only fifty people might be an enormously difficult task. Therefore, if other elements of the county's districting scheme fulfill the good-faith requirements, it should pass constitutional muster.[97]

Since the above article was written, Los Angeles County has increased in population to 8.3 million residents; therefore, a 10% deviation would now affect 830,000 people.[98] In comparison, *Gaffney v. Cummings*[99] involved reapportionment of house districts which, according to the 1970 census, contained a population of 3,032,217. In *Brown v. Thompson*, Wyoming's population, based on the 1980 census, was only 469,557.[100] In contrast to this, Los Angeles has districts which contain more people than some counties or even states involved in the cases cited above. Therefore, an attempt may be made by a challenger of such a plan to distinguish a 10% or so deviation in Los Angeles County from all other reapportionment plans which the Supreme Court has held permissible due to the number of people affected.

This type of statistical argument can be easily countered. The Supreme Court has consistently held that there is no mathematical test for the validity of a given apportionment plan. It has also repeatedly stated that what is permissible or impermissible in one state is not necessarily permissible or impermissible in another. With regard to mathe-

---

97. Note, *Reapportionment—Nine Years into the "Revolution" and Still Struggling*, 70 Mich. L.Rev. 586, 611-12 (1972).
98. U.S. BUREAU OF THE CENSUS, COUNTY AND CITY DATA BOOK (1988). This figure represents the population of Los Angeles County for 1986.
99. 412 U.S. 735 (1973).
100. 462 U.S. 835, 839 (1983).

matical formulations of the rule in apportionment cases, it has warned against any attempt to state in mathematical language the constitutionally permissible range of deviations. "In our view the problem does not lend itself to any such uniform formula, and it is neither practicable nor desirable to establish rigid mathematical standards for evaluating the constitutional validity of a state legislative apportionment scheme under the Equal Protection Clause."[101] With regard to comparisons between states, the Supreme Court has said that "what is marginally permissible in one State may be unsatisfactory in another, depending on the particular circumstances of the case."[102]

Therefore, one could demonstrate that in deciding the constitutionality of a particular reapportionment plan, a court should not look to other states and compare the number of people involved in various plans for guidance. The court has always scrutinized the rationality of a state's policy for any deviations in upholding or denying the constitutionality of a state's reapportionment plan. Policy reasons for allowing any deviations are based on notions like local autonomy and responsiveness to local concerns, not on the insignificance of the number of people involved or on numerical precision. Therefore, the fact that previous reapportionment cases which would support the deviations desired in Los Angeles County involve states or counties with significantly smaller populations should not hinder their persuasiveness. A court must look to the reasoning for allowing the deviations and not the size of the populations involved.

V.
RESULTING LEGAL FRAMEWORK

A person challenging the proposed reapportionment of Los Angeles County would therefore have to allege a dilution of his or her right to vote under the "one person, one vote standard" enunciated in *Reynolds v. Sims*.[103] This interest in voter equality is a nondeference interest which, if injured, would cause the state to have to justify its actions. That is, a challenger would have to demonstrate that allowing Latinos to have a representative in a smaller district causes his or her vote to carry less weight. Being in a district where a larger number of people have the same amount of representation as the smaller Latino district on the Board of Supervisors could establish such a diminution.

The Equal Protection Clause requires uniform treatment of persons standing in the same relation to the governmental action questioned or challenged. Therefore, the government has a duty not to make invidious

---

101. Roman v. Sincock, 377 U.S. 695 (1964).
102. Reynolds v. Sims, 377 U.S. 533 (1964).
103. 377 U.S. 533 (1964).

distinctions among its citizens absent justification. The state must have a reason for making one person's vote worth more than another's in any election. As discussed above, *Reynolds, et seq,* do not require strict mathematical equality; some deviations are permissible so long as they are justified by a rational state policy.

The Supreme Court has been willing to allow much greater deviation from mathematical equality in the apportionment of state legislatures or local governmental bodies. The Court has established a de minimus category that covers minor population variations which would include all deviations of less than 10%. Such minor deviations do not make out a prima facie violation of Equal Protection and may require no justification by the state for the variations among districts.[104] Even deviations above this 10% range can be justified by legitimate state considerations. Less justification is required for state and local redistricting than in federal congressional redistricting. A congressional apportionment plan must be equalized "as nearly practicable" with each deviation justified by an interest which can be shown to be a governmental necessity. With state and local reapportionment the justification need only be one which a state may rationally consider. This rational basis test allows local governments more latitude with respect to apportionment, thereby allowing the implementation of policies which reflect local concerns and interests.

The reapportionment cases indicate that to demonstrate a rational basis the government must show that the proposed apportionment plan is narrowly tailored to meet its proffered objectives. If the plan over-regulates or is inefficient it may be held invalid. A plan which is not drawn to achieve the state's interest with precision may cause the state's legitimate interest to fail to justify the deviations involved.

Therefore, in order to successfully challenge a reapportionment plan like that proposed for Los Angeles County, it must be demonstrated that the state interest of preserving voting strength of minorities is irrational, and/or that the deviations involved are not necessary to achieve that purpose. Without access to the specifics of the numerical figures of the plan involved, it is impossible to evaluate its vulnerability due to not being narrowly tailored. However, the rationality of a state's desire to preserve the voting strength of Latinos is evaluated below.

VI.
PRESERVING VOTING STRENGTH OF MINORITIES

The Supreme Court has pretermitted the question of the legitimacy of preserving the voting strength of racial minority groups as a legislative

---

104. *See, e.g.*, White v. Regester, 412 U.S. 755 (1973).

congressional apportionment goal. In *Karcher v. Daggett*,[105] the Supreme Court held that the attempt to justify population deviations in a New Jersey reapportionment plan on the ground that they preserved the voting strength of racial minority groups was not supported by the evidence. Although the reapportionment plan was therefore held unconstitutional, it is significant that the Court did not condemn the proffered justification as inadequate in and of itself. Instead, the problem stemmed from a plan which was not narrowly tailored to achieve such a goal of preserving minority group voting strength.

> Nowhere do appellants suggest that the large population of the Fourth District was necessary to preserve minority voting strength; in fact, the deviation between the Fourth District and other districts has the effect of diluting the votes of all residents of that district, including members of racial minorities, as compared with other districts with fewer minority voters. The record is completely silent on the relationship between preserving minority voting strength and the small populations of the Third and Sixth Districts.[106]

In the dissenting opinion, Justice White, joined by Justices Burger, Powell and Rehnquist expressed the view that population deviations in the plan were statistically insignificant and had no relevant effect on relative representation.

> Our cases dealing with state legislative apportionment have taken a more sensible approach. We have recognized that certain small deviations do not, in themselves, ordinarily constitute a prima facie constitutional violation. Moreover, we have upheld plans with reasonable variances that were necessary to account for political subdivisions, to preserve the voting strength of minority groups, and to insure political fairness. . . .[107]

In *Gaffney v. Cummings*,[108] a Connecticut reapportionment plan for the state legislature, which was based on a "political fairness" principle designed to reflect the relative strength of the major political parties, was upheld by the Supreme Court.

> [W]e have not ventured far or attempted the impossible task of extirpating politics from what are the essentially political processes of the sovereign States. Even more plainly, judicial interest should be at its lowest ebb when a State purports fairly to allocate political power to the parties in accordance with their voting strength and, within quite tolerable limits, succeeds in doing so. There is no doubt that there may be other reap-

---

105. 462 U.S. 725 (1983).
106. *Id.* at 743-44.
107. 462 U.S. at 780-81 (citing Gaffney v. Cummings, 412 U.S. 735 (1973), and White v. Regester, 412 U.S. 755 (1973), for the proposition that small deviations alone do not constitute a violation; and citing Mahan v. Howell, 410 U.S. 315 (1973), and *Gaffney* as examples of reasonable variances upheld).
108. 412 U.S. 735 (1973).

portionment plans for Connecticut that would have different political consequences and that would also be constitutional. Perhaps any of appellees' plans would have fallen into this category, as would the court's had it propounded one. But neither we nor the district courts have a constitutional warrant to invalidate a state plan, otherwise within tolerable population limits, because it undertakes, not to minimize or eliminate the political strength of any group or party, but to recognize it and, through districting, provide a rough sort of proportional representation in the legislative halls of the State.[109]

Therefore, although *Gaffney* did not specifically involve racial minorities, it does demonstrate that a political compromise, which takes into account various interests of groups within a given area, may withstand constitutional challenge so long as the deviations are not so substantial as to defy justification. In *Karcher v. Daggett*, the fatal flaw of the plan was not its justification, but the fact that the deviations from population equality were not demonstrated to be directly related to the state's goal of preserving minority voting strength.

Additionally, in *United Jewish Organizations v. Carey*[110] the Supreme Court held that the use of racial criteria in districting and apportionment is permissible.

Section 5 [of the Voting Rights Act] and its authorization for racial redistricting where appropriate to avoid abridging the right to vote on account of race or color are constitutional. Contrary to petitioners' first argument, neither the Fourteenth nor the Fifteenth Amendment mandates any *per se* rule against using racial factors in districting and apportionment. Nor is petitioners' second argument valid. The permissible use of racial criteria is not confined to eliminating the effects of past discriminatory districting or apportionment.[111]

The Court therefore allowed the use of racial criteria by the State of New York in the reapportionment of its counties.

[D]istricting plans would be vulnerable under our cases if "*racial or political groups* have been fenced out of the political process and their voting strength invidiously minimized"; but that was not the case there, and no such purpose or effect may be ascribed to New York's 1974 plan. Rather, that plan can be viewed as seeking to alleviate the consequences of racial voting at the polls and to achieve a fair allocation of political power between white and nonwhite voters in Kings County.

In this respect New York's revision of certain district lines is little different in kind from the decisions by a State in which a racial minority is unable to elect representatives from multimember districts to change to single-member districting for the purpose of increasing minority representation. This change might substantially increase minority representa-

---

109. *Id.* at 754.
110. 430 U.S. 144 (1977).
111. *Id.* at 161.

tion at the expense of white voters, who previously elected all of the legislators but who with single-member districts could elect no more than their proportional share. If this intentional reduction of white voting power would be constitutionally permissible, as we think it would be, we think it also permissible for a State, employing sound districting principles such as compactness and population equality, to attempt to prevent racial minorities from being repeatedly outvoted by creating districts that will afford fair representation to the members of those racial groups who are sufficiently numerous and whose residential patterns afford the opportunity of creating districts in which they will be the majority.[112]

The language quoted above, along with the holding in *Karcher v. Daggett*, would seem to provide a strong basis for arguing that use of race is a permissible state or local governmental interest which may justify variations in district populations. The Supreme Court had two opportunities to rule against use of race in apportionment, and declined to do so. At a local level, it should be even easier to justify such a policy since local governments are given wider latitude to deviate from the one person-one vote standard. Creation of a Latino district would be for the purpose of providing fair representation to a group that has been disenfranchised for a significant portion of the County's history.

When a local government undertakes to remedy past discrimination, however, it must now apparently do so in a manner that is narrowly tailored to findings of past discrimination.[113] The Supreme Court in *Ricmond v. Croson* explained the limitations on states in redressing societal discrimination.

That Congress may identify and redress the effects of society-wide discrimination does not mean that, a fortiori, the States and their political subdivisions are free to decide that such remedies are appropriate. Section 1 of the Fourteenth Amendment is an explicit constraint on state power, and the states must undertake any remedial efforts in accordance with that provision. To hold otherwise would be to cede control over the content of the Equal Protection Clause to the 50 state legislatures and their myriad political subdivisions. The mere recitation of a benign or compensatory purpose for the use of a racial classification would essentially entitle the states to exercise the full power of Congress under § 5 of the Fourteenth Amendment and insulate any racial classification from judicial scrutiny under § 1. We believe that such a result would be contrary to the intentions of the Framers of the Fourteenth Amendment, who desired to place clear limits on the States' use of race as a criterion for legislative action, and to have the federal courts enforce those limitations.[114]

---

112. *Id.* at 167-68 (quoting *Gaffney*, 412 U.S. at 754, and adding emphasis).
113. City of Richmond v. J.A. Croson Co., 488 U.S. —, 109 S.Ct. 706, 102 L.Ed.2d at 854 (1989).
114. 109 S.Ct. at 719, 102 L.Ed.2d at 880.

The Supreme Court in *Croson* therefore held that the Fourteenth Amendment's Equal Protection Clause was violated by the City of Richmond's minority set aside program due to the absence of adequate findings of discrimination.

> While the States and their subdivisions may take remedial action when they possess evidence that their own spending practices are exacerbating a pattern of prior discrimination, they must identify that discrimination, public or private, with some specificity before they may use race-conscious relief. . . ."[I]t is essential that state and local agencies also establish the presence of discrimination in their own fact-finding processes or upon determinations made by other competent institutions."[115]

Therefore, in addition to being narrowly tailored to show that any deviations are necessary to achieve the proffered state policy, race conscious relief must also be tailored to specific findings of past discrimination within a state or local government. In *Wygant v. Jackson Board of Education*,[116] the Supreme Court held that the fact that society as a whole has discriminated against a minority group is too amorphous a basis for imposing a racially classified remedy. A factual determination must therefore be made to provide a strong basis in evidence that remedial action is necessary. In some ways, this makes it easier to argue for preserving minority voting strength within a single county district. If the evidence introduced is sufficient to show that the Latino population has suffered a history of continuous debasement of their voting strength due to gerrymandering, the race conscious relief requested may survive challenge under *Croson*. If a long history of such debasement can be demonstrated in the court's record, having one representative, after being submerged into three white majority districts for a long period of time, does not seem to be disproportionate relief. Lack of such findings, however, can be fatal to the desired apportionment plan. In *Whitcomb v. Chavis*,[117] the Supreme Court held that evidence that an African-American ghetto in Indiana had fewer resident legislators than its proportion of the county's population did not prove invidious discrimination.

Likely challengers to such a plan would include white voters who would be placed in larger districts and could allege that Latinos are receiving disproportionate representation on the County's Board of Supervisors. Other minority groups may also challenge the plan claiming that their voting rights should also be protected by the government and that they also lack adequate representation on the Board of Supervisors.

---

115. 109 S.Ct. at 887, 102 L.Ed.2d at 889 (quoting Days, *Fullilove*, 96 Yale L.J. 453, 480-81 (1987)).
116. 476 U.S. 267 (1986).
117. 403 U.S. 124 (1971).

However, it should be argued that with respect to the white voters, their voting strength is not a reduction but an *equalization* of their previously inflated voting strength. For example, in Los Angeles County, where Latinos were divided into three districts, whites arguably have disproportionate representation on the Board of Supervisors. Therefore, allowing a Latino representative would not be a result of a preference per se for Latinos, but a remedial measure which aims at equality of representation.

With respect to other minority groups, the argument would be that the governmental policy for creating a Latino district is not based on any unique feature of the Latino population other than the history of debasement of their political strength. If another group can show it has also experienced the effects of gerrymandering in Los Angeles County, it could potentially expect that the preservation of their voting strength should also be considered in such a plan.[118]

> [W]ere we asked to decide whether any given rival group—German-Americans for example—must constitutionally be accorded preferential treatment, we do have a "principled basis" . . . for deciding this question, one that is well-established in our cases: The Davis program expressly sets out four classes which receive preferred status. . . . The program clearly distinguishes whites, but one cannot reason from this a conclusion that German-Americans, as a national group, are singled out for invidious treatment. And even if the Davis program had a differential impact on German-Americans, they would have no constitutional claim unless they could prove that Davis intended invidiously to discriminate against German Americans. . . . If this could not be shown, then . . . the only question is whether it was rational for Davis to conclude that the groups it preferred had a greater claim to compensation than the groups it excluded.[119]

Therefore, although a plan is race conscious in that it specifically seeks to form a Latino district, the resulting reapportionment plan should be able to withstand challenge from rival groups so long as any impact on those other groups was not the result of the government's intent to invidiously discriminate against them. If this can not be demonstrated, the government need only demonstrate a rational basis for preferring Latinos in a reapportionment plan. If facts indicate that Latinos have experienced exclusion from the political process in a manner unlike any potential claimants, the government should be able to withstand any such challenge.

Arguments against preserving minority group voting strength as an adequate state policy will include the fact that § 2 of the Voting Rights Act, as amended June 29, 1982, specifically disclaimed the creation of a

---

118. *See, e.g.*, Regents of University of California v. Bakke, 438 U.S. 265, 358-62 (1978) (Brennan, J., concurring).

119. *Id.* at 359 n.35.

right to proportionate representation.[120] As was noted in *Thornburg v. Gingles*,[121] the disclaimer was essential to the compromise that resulted in passage of the amendment. "We know that Congress intended to allow vote dilution claims to be brought under § 2, but we also know that Congress did not intend to create a right to proportional representation for minority voters."[122]

The preservation of minority group voting strength, however, is not dependant upon the creation of such right in the Voting Rights Act. It is instead based on constitutional claims under the Equal Protection Clause. Just as political subdivisions, or long standing political structures are allowed to justify deviations from equal population standards without being specifically sanctioned by the Voting Rights Act, preserving minority voting strength can be justified through use of Supreme Court constitutional precedent. Although minorities are not guaranteed proportional representation, where they have been victims of gerrymandering, remedial relief to preserve their voting strength can be justified as a rational state policy. That is, even though Latinos are not guaranteed a right to proportional representation under the Voting Rights Act, a unit of government should be able to correct past inequalities in order to provide representation for a victimized group. Also, even if such a justification were not sufficient for congressional reapportionment purposes, it should be argued that at a local level, the policy need only be rational. With sufficient findings on the record, if the deviations are only such as are absolutely necessary to achieve the aim of preserving minority group voting strength, one could make a strong case for the local governmental policy.

VII.
RELEVANT POPULATION BASE

There appears to be conflicting authority as to the relevant population base used in composing a district for reapportionment. For instance, the California Supreme Court has held that use of registered voters may violate equal protection, while the Ninth Circuit cases state that in a cause of action based on Section 2 of the Voting Rights Act of 1965, eligible minority voter population is the relevant population base.

A. California Law

In *Calderón v. City of Los Angeles*,[123] the California Supreme Court, Sullivan, J., held that city charter provisions and ordinances passed

---
120. S. REP. No. 97-417, 97th Cong., 2d Sess. 193-94 (1982).
121. 478 U.S. 30, 84 (1986) (O'Conner, J., concurring).
122. *Id.*
123. 4 Cal.3d 251, 481 P.2d 489, 93 Cal. Rptr. 361 (1971).

thereunder as to councilmanic district apportionment, which were based on voter registration rather than on population, denied equal protection where apportionment on such basis resulted in the largest district having 70% more people than the smallest.

> The genesis of the present controversy lies in a seeming looseness in the language of the myriad United States Supreme Court decisions which have sought to interpret the "one man, one vote" principle since the issue of electoral apportionment was first held justiciable nine years ago. Over the years, the court has "used the words 'inhabitant,' 'citizen,' 'resident,' and 'voter' almost interchangeably in describing those who deserve representation, without indicating which of these bases for measuring substantial equality is most appropriate." In particular, the court has tended to treat as fungible two quite distinct concepts: first, that each district should contain equal numbers of people—a "population" standard; and second, that each voter is entitled to to have his ballot carry an equal impact—a "voter" standard.[124]

The California Supreme Court noted in *Calderón* that this dichotomy was recognized and resolved by the United States Supreme Court in *Burns v. Richardson*,[125] which involved a Hawaii apportionment plan based on registered voters. Due to a large number of military personnel based in Hawaii and the large influx of tourists, a sizeable number of people present in the state were not permanent residents and hence ineligible for state citizenship. The Supreme Court in *Burns* held that a state was free to limit its apportionment base solely to state citizens, rather than using total population figures, thereby excluding "aliens, transients, short term or temporary residents, or persons denied the right to vote for conviction of crime."[126]

The Supreme Court, however reached a different conclusion with regard to the validity of the registered voter standard:

> Such a basis depends not only upon criteria such as govern state citizenship, but also upon the extent of political activity of those eligible to register and vote. Each is thus susceptible to improper influences by which those in political power might be able to perpetuate underrepresentation of groups constitutionally entitled to participate in the electoral process, or perpetuate a "ghost of prior malapportionment."[127]

In addition, the Supreme Court observed that the number of registered voters may fluctuate in a given election based upon such factors as a peculiarly controversial election issue, an extremely popular candidate,

---

124. *Id.* at 255, 481 P.2d at 490-491, 93 Cal. Rptr. at 362-363 (footnote and citation omitted) (quoting Note, *Reapportionment*, 79 Harv. L.Rev. 1226, 1254 (1966)).
125. 384 U.S. 73 (1966).
126. *Id.* at 92.
127. *Id.* at 92-93 (footnote omitted) (quoting Buckley v. Hoff, 243 F.Supp. 873, 876 (D.C. Vt. 1965)).

or even weather conditions.[128] In light of these considerations, the Supreme Court held that the Hawaii apportionment plan satisfied the Equal Protection Clause "only because on this record it was found to have produced a distribution of legislators not substantially different from that which would have resulted from the use of a permissible population basis. "[129]

The California Supreme Court in *Calderón* therefore reasoned that use of a population standard rather than one based on registered voters "is more likely to guarantee that those who cannot or do not cast a ballot may still have some voice in government."[130]

> Thus a 17 year old, who by state law is prohibited from voting, may still have strong views on the Vietnam War which he wishes to communicate to the elected representatives from his area. Furthermore, much of a legislators time is devoted to providing services and information to his constituents, both voters and nonvoters. A district which, although large in population, has a low percentage of registered voters would, under a voter-based apportionment, have fewer representatives to provide such assistance and to listen to concerned citizens.[131]

The State Supreme Court noted that "access to elected officials is also an important means of democratic expression—and one that is not limited to those who cast ballots."[132] The Court also noted that such access is "embodied in the First Amendment's guarantee of 'the right of the people peaceably to assemble, and to petition the Government for a redress of grievances.' There is nothing in that amendment to limit its protection to registered voters."[133]

The State Court also noted that the voter based system, according to the figures presented, resulted in severe underrepresentation of districts with heavy concentrations of African-Americans and Mexican-Americans.[134] Noting that the United States Supreme Court has asserted that an otherwise acceptable apportionment plan may fail to pass constitutional muster if it operates to minimize or cancel out the voting strength of racial or political elements of the voting population,[135] the State Court held that plaintiffs and other residents of Los Angeles were denied equal protection and the plan was therefore invalid.[136]

By our holding today we should not be understood to condemn a voter-

---

128. *Id.* at 93.
129. *Id.* at 93.
130. 4 Cal.3d at 259, 481 P.2d at 493, 93 Cal. Rptr. at 365.
131. *Id.* at 259, 481 P.2d at 494, 93 Cal. Rptr. at 366 (footnote omitted).
132. *Id.* at 260, 481 P.2d at 494, 93 Cal. Rptr. at 366 (footnote omitted).
133. *Id.* at 259 n.8, 481 P.2d at 494, 93 Cal. Rptr. at 366 (citing Tinker v. Des Moines Community School District, 393 U.S. 503, 506 (1969)).
134. *Id.* at 260, 481 P.2d at 494, 93 Cal. Rptr. at 366.
135. *Id.* at 260, 481 P.2d at 495, 93 Cal. Rptr at 367.
136. *Id.* at 262, 481 P.2d at 496. 93 Cal. Rptr. at 368.

based apportionment in all circumstances and for all time. Where such a plan is shown to fairly reflect population distribution, it may withstand constitutional attack. The Supreme Court in *Burns* isolated several factors which would contribute to such a result, and we present these as guidelines for the future.[137]

The factors the State Court laid out are as follows. First of all, the court stated that voter registration is likely to show a significant correlation to population distribution if a high percentage of those eligible to vote are in fact registered. Second, reapportionment should take place frequently in order to keep up with registration changes. Third, the use of registration statistics from presidential elections as opposed to local races will ensure a high level of participation and avoid fluctuations in interest in particular local elections which will become frozen into a given apportionment scheme. Finally, introduction of a system of permanent personal registration will help ensure stability and accuracy of registration rolls, thus making them a better reflection of population distribution.[138]

Therefore, at least for purposes of any state law claims and all constitutional claims, it should be argued that the Latino district in the proposed reapportionment plan should include as many segments of that population as possible in order to produce the smallest deviation and still maintain a Latino majority within the district. Based on *Calderón* and *Burns*, it appears that undocumented workers are clearly left out of the relevant population. However, non-voting or unregistered Latinos, as well as children and non-voting age persons should be included in the population in order to enlarge the Latino population as much as possible. Any attempt to use registered voters or even those eligible to vote as the relevant population should be resisted.

B. Federal Law

In *Romero v. City of Pomona*,[139] the Court of Appeals held that for purposes of an action under Section 2 of the Voting Rights Act of 1965,[140] the relevant population is the eligible minority voter population when determining whether a minority group can constitute a voting majority of a single-member district. The Court of Appeals interpreted *Thornburg v. Gingles*[141] as using voting majorities, rather than raw population totals, as the touchstone for determining geographical compactness.

---

137. *Id.* at 264-265, 481 P.2d at 498, 93 Cal. Rptr. at 370 (footnote omitted) (citation omitted).
138. *Id.* at 265, 481 P.2d at 498, 93 Cal. Rptr. at 370.
139. 883 F.2d 1418 (9th Cir. 1989).
140. 42 U.S.C. § 1973 (as amended June 29, 1982).
141. 478 U.S. 30 (1986). *See supra* notes 121-122 and accompanying text.

Cases before and after *Thornburg* acknowledge that a Section 2 claim will fail unless the plaintiff can establish that the minority group constitutes an effective voting majority. . . . More recently our assesment of geographic compactness was based upon the number of eligible minority voters, rather than total minority population. The district court was correct in holding that eligible minority voter population, rather than total minority population, is the appropriate measure of geographic compactness.[142]

Therefore, although in state court a strong case could be made for using overall population, in federal court, eligible voters comprise the relevant population. Theoretically, one could argue that under *Erie Railroad Co. v. Tompkins*[143] state substantive law should be applied, at least to the constitutional and state claims. In a practical sense, however, it is uncertain whether this is in any way helpful to an analysis of *Garza*, since it is based significantly on federal claims under the Voting Rights Act.

VIII.
CONCLUSION

Although there is no direct, on-point authority for the proposition that preservation of a minority group's voting strength may justify deviations from the one person-one vote standard in a county's supervisorial districts, there are several factors which will support such a justification. First of all, local governments are given more latitude in reapportionment than are congressional apportioners. Therefore, a local government's policy need only be rational instead of necessary. Secondly, minor deviations from population equality standards do not necessarily make a prima facie Equal Protection case, thus a small deviation of 10% or so could be considered a de minimus or permissible deviation at the local level.

Most importantly, the Supreme Court has allowed race to be taken into account in apportionment cases. Provided that the evidence of past discrimination is sufficient to warrant remedial relief, one could make a strong case for preserving minority voter strength by creating a district which is not exactly equal to the others. Although there is no right to minority representation in proportion to their population, there is a right to equality of representation in government, and where that has been abridged through gerrymandering, a local government seeking to remedy past discrimination may rationally do so by creating a slightly smaller Latino majority district within a county in order to preserve that group's

---

142. *Romero*, 883 F.2d at 1426 (citing Gómez v. City of Watsonville, 863 F.2d 1407, 1414 (9th Cir. 1988), cert. denied, 109 S.Ct. 1534 (1989) (presence of two districts where "Hispanics would constitute a majority of the voters and would be able to elect representatives of their choice" satisfies *Thornburg*'s geographic compactness standard)).

143. 304 U.S. 64 (1938).

voting strength. An attempt should also be made to include as many segments of the Latino population as possible, resisting the use of eligible voters as the relevant population, so as to make the Latino district larger and thereby creating less deviation between districts.

Case Note Addendum

Gárza v. County of Los Angeles

Robert G. Retana†

In our last issue, volume 3, Spring 1990, we presented a case note authored by Robert G. Retana on Gárza v. County of Los Angeles. The case note analyzed the trial court opinion. As the issue went to press, Gárza was just beginning to wind itself through the appellate process. In January, 1991, Gárza came to an end. We now offer an addendum to the earlier case note on Gárza so that our readers may be brought up to date on this history-making case.

On November 2, 1990, the Ninth Circuit Court of Appeals issued its opinion in *Gárza v. County of Los Angeles*,[1] affirming in part the district court's ruling against the County of Los Angeles, and holding that the County Board of Supervisors had violated the Voting Rights Act and the Equal Protection Clause in intentionally gerrymandering districts to minimize Latino voting strength. On January 7, 1991, the United States Supreme Court denied certiorari,[2] upholding a redistricting plan designed to allow Latinos to equally participate in the election of members to the Los Angeles Board of Supervisors.

A. Background

In 1988, Latinos were joined by the United States of America in *Gárza v. County of Los Angeles*, a voting rights case which sought a redrawing of the districts for the Los Angeles County Board of Supervisors.[3] Plaintiffs alleged violation of the Voting Rights Act and the Equal Protection Clause by the County which they contended had intentionally discriminated against Latinos in drawing district lines in 1981.[4] They also alleged that the 1981 districting plan had diluted the voting strength of Latinos in Los Angeles County. Plaintiffs sought the creation of a district with a majority of Latinos for the 1990 Board of Supervisors

---

† Robert G. Retana is an associate with Heller, Ehrman, White & McAuliffe. He received his J.D. from Boalt Hall School of Law, University of California, Berkeley, 1990 and his B.A. from Columbia University, 1984.
  1. 918 F.2d 763 (9th Cir. 1990).
  2. 59 U.S.L.W. 3421, 1991 WL 793.
  3. 918 F.2d at 765.
  4. *Id.* at 766.

election.[5]

After a three-month trial, the United States District Court found intentional discrimination in the 1981 reapportionment, and deliberate dilution of the Latino vote.[6] The 1981 plan was found to be in violation of the Voting Rights Act, and the County was ordered to propose the redistricting sought by plaintiffs, which would include the creation of a district with a Latino voting majority.[7]

The district court made detailed findings regarding the history of the Los Angeles County Board of Supervisors, including the fact that the Board of Supervisors had engaged in intentional discrimination in the redistrictings that occurred in 1959, 1965 and 1971.[8] The court also found that the 1981 redistricting was calculated in part to keep the effects of the prior discriminatory reapportionments in place, and to prevent Latinos from attaining a majority in any district in the future.[9] Among the findings set forth by the district court was the following:

> The Supervisors appear to have acted primarily on the political instinct of self-preservation. The court found, however, that the Supervisors also intended what they know to be the likely result of their actions and a prerequisite to self-preservation — the continued fragmentation of the Hispanic core and the dilution of Hispanic voting strength.[10]

The County created a redistricting plan in response to the district court's order, which was rejected by the court as less than a good faith effort to remedy the existing violations.[11] Instead, the court accepted a plan which created a district where the majority of the voting age citizens are Latino.[12] The County then appealed.[13]

The County argued that based on *Thornburg v. Gingles*,[14] there can be no successful challenge to a districting system without showing that the minority group challenging that plan could have constituted a voter majority in a single member district.[15] The County argued that in 1981 it was impossible to draw a district map with equal population in each district that contained a district with a majority of Latino voters.[16]

---

5. *Id.* at 765.
6. *Id.* at 766.
7. *Id.*
8. *Id.* at 766-67.
9. *Id.* at 767-68.
10. *Id.* at 768.
11. *Id.*
12. *Id.*
13. *Id.* There was also a second appeal from a candidate for a district seat under the existing plan who sought to oppose the redistricting which would result in a new election in which other candidates could run for the seat she was seeking. *Id.* at 769.
14. 478 U.S. 30, 106 S.Ct. 2752, 92 L.Ed. 2d 25 (1986).
15. 918 F.2d at 769.
16. *Id.* at 769.

Plaintiffs argued that no such majority requirement should be imposed where there has been intentional dilution of minority voting strength.[17] The County, therefore, also challenged the sufficiency of the district court's findings regarding discriminatory intent.[18]

B. Thornburg v. Gingles

The Voting Rights Act,[19] was amended by Congress in 1982 to provide a remedy for minorities whose vote had been diluted, without requiring proof that the majority had engaged in intentional discrimination.[20] In *Thornburg v. Gingles*,[21] the Supreme Court interpreted the new amendment, and established three requirements for liability under the Voting Rights Act for claims based on discriminatory effects: (1) geographic compactness of the minority group; (2) minority political cohesion, and (3) majority block voting.[22]

The Court of Appeals in *Gárza* noted that the *Gingles* court did not consider claims that the disputed districting plan had been enacted deliberately to dilute minority voting.[23] The *Gingles* court was deciding whether multi-member districts being used had the effect of diluting minority voting, regardless of intent.[24]

> Thus, the court instituted the "possibility of majority" requirement in a case in which it was asked to invalidate a political entity's choice of a multi-member district system, and impose a system of single-member districts, and was not asked to find that the multi-member scheme had been set up with a discriminatory purpose in mind.[25]

Because the plaintiffs in *Gárza* were not alleging disparate impact from a seemingly neutral electoral scheme, but instead were claiming intentional dilution of the Latino vote, the Court of Appeals declined to impose the majority requirement desired by the County.[26]

> To impose the requirement the County urges would prevent any redress for districting which was deliberately designed to prevent minorities from electing representatives in future elections governed by that districting. This appears to us to be a result wholly contrary to Congress' intent in enacting Section 2 of the Voting Rights Act and contrary to the equal protection principles embodied in the fourteenth amendment.[27]

---

17. *Id.*
18. *Id.*
19. 42 U.S.C. § 1973.
20. 918 F.2d at 769-70.
21. 478 U.S. 30, 106 S.Ct. 2752, 92 L.Ed. 2d 25 (1986).
22. 478 U.S. at 50-51, 106 S.Ct. at 2766-67.
23. 918 F.2d at 770.
24. *Id.*
25. *Id.*
26. *Id.* at 771.
27. *Id.*

Additionally, the Court of Appeals found that the detailed findings by the district court of intentional discrimination by the County Board of Supervisors was "amply supported by the evidence in the record."[28] The Court of Appeals also found evidence of injury in the intentional splitting of the Latino vote, resulting in diminished opportunity for Latinos to participate in the political process.[29] The court concluded that the intentional discrimination violated both the Voting Rights Act and the Equal Protection Clause.[30]

C. Other Arguments

Among the various arguments rejected by the Court of Appeals was the County's assertion that the reapportionment plan approved by the district court was erroneous as a matter of law because it was based on overall population instead of the voting population.[31] In addition to relying on the intent of the framers, the Court of Appeals noted:

> There is an even more important consideration. Basing districts on voters rather than total population results in serious population inequalities across districts. Residents of the more populous districts thus have less access to their elected representatives. Those adversely affected are those who live in the districts with a greater percentage of non-voting populations, including aliens and children. Because there are more young people in the predominantly Hispanic District 1 . . . citizens of voting age, minors and others residing in the district will suffer diminishing access to government in a voter-based apportionment scheme.[32]

The court noted that a districting plan based on voting population rather than total population would "abridge the rights of aliens and minors,"[33] recognizing that aliens are entitled to equal protection.[34] This is significant in that a large segment of undocumented Latinos can now be counted in creating districts where Latinos constitute a majority of the population. When voting population is used it becomes more difficult to create a district where Latinos are a majority since many Latinos are non-citizens. Therefore, *Gárza*'s holding has great potential to permit Latinos to assert their political clout by including all segments of the population.

D. Resulting Election

As a result of the *Gárza* litigation, Los Angeles County held a spe-

---

28. *Id.*
29. *Id.*
30. *Id.*
31. *Id.* at 773.
32. *Id.* at 774-75.
33. *Id.* at 775.
34. *Id.*

cial run-off election for the newly created 1st District on January 22, 1991. City Councilwoman Gloria Molina topped the nine-candidate field; State Senator Art Torres finished second. On February 19, 1991, Gloria Molina, by receiving 55% of the vote to 45% for Art Torres, became the first Latino to serve on the Board of Supervisors in over 100 years and the first woman ever elected to the Board.[35]

---

35. *Hispanic Woman Wins Los Angeles Vote*, San Francisco Chronicle, Feb. 21, 1991, at A3, col. 1.

THE ELECTION OF HISPANICS IN CITY GOVERNMENT: AN EXAMINATION OF THE ELECTION OF FEDERICO PEÑA AS MAYOR OF DENVER

RODNEY HERO

University of Colorado

WHILE the election of ethnic and racial minorities to positions in city government has received considerable attention, there have been few analyses of the election of Hispanics (Taebel 1978; Browning, Marshall, and Tabb 1984; Henry and Munoz 1985; de la Garza 1974, 1977). The purpose of this article is to examine the election of Federico Peña, a Mexican-American, as mayor of Denver. This is important for several reasons. Available evidence indicates that the political orientation and achievements of Hispanics have been different from those of other groups, including blacks (Browning, Marshall, and Tabb 1984; Lovrich and Marenin 1976). Secondly, the Denver mayor holds a visible and powerful position. Denver has a strong mayor system. The formal powers of the Denver mayor appear stronger than those in most other cities, such as San Antonio, where Hispanic mayors have been elected and are probably greater than in most cities where minority mayors have been elected. Thus, the Denver mayor is in a favorable position to influence city policy. Finally, Denver has a relatively small Hispanic population (18-20 percent) and its overall minority population (30-35 percent Hispanic and black) is somewhat smaller than those of most other large cities with minority mayors.

How a Hispanic was elected to such a powerful position in a city with such a small minority population warrants attention. The analysis seeks to address this question as follows. First, a discussion of relevant scholarly literature is presented to provide a theoretical grounding for the subsequent analysis. The Peña campaign strategy is then discussed, followed by a consideration of the major themes of the Peña campaign and a general description of the campaign. This portion of the discussion draws upon a personal interview with one of the major Peña campaign strategists, Peña campaign materials, and a close reading of the Denver newspaper with the largest circulation, the Denver *Post*, between January and July, 1983. An analysis draws upon precinct-level voting data and demographic and related data purchased from a public agency and a private vendor. Finally, the analysis will provide a baseline from which to compare other elections involving

---

Received: September 26, 1985
First Revision Received: February 13, 1986
Second Revision Received: March 4, 1986
Accepted for Publication: March 8, 1986

NOTE: The author would like to thank Dale Rogers Marshall, Jody L. Fitzpatrick, Carlos Munoz and several anonymous reviewers for their helpful comments on previous drafts of this article. Any remaining shortcomings of the paper are, of course, mine alone.

Hispanics to consider such matters as whether such campaigns raise unique issues, whether certain types of issues receive greater or lesser attention, and to compare electoral coalitions.

THEORETICAL DISCUSSION

Research suggests that the electoral response to minority candidates is significantly influenced by such factors as the nature of the constituency in which they are running, the strategies that they pursue, and the particular circumstances of an election (Hahn, Klingman, and Pachon 1976). Scholars have identified several strategies that minority mayoral candidates have employed given different constituency contexts. Holloway (1968) describes three types of coalitions between minority (black) and white voters: the "conservative coalition," the "independent power politics" approach, and the "liberal coalition." The conservative coalition is a linkage between the minority community and powerful white business and financial interests. The independent power approach occurs when white votes are either unnecessary to secure a majority or seemingly impossible to obtain. The liberal coalition seeks to unite ethnic-racial minorities with low-income whites, labor unions, and white or Anglo liberals from the business and professional world.

A recent study found that the major factor leading to the election of blacks and Hispanics (primarily Mexican-Americans) in a group of northern California cities with small minority populations was the emergence of liberal coalitions (Browning, Marshall, and Tabb 1984). Such liberal coalitions were generally made up of ethnic-racial minorities, the poor, white liberals, particularly Democrats, and labor unions. De la Garza (1974), however, found that despite the "bi-cultural" image projected in El Paso, Texas, Anglos were reluctant to vote for Mexican-American candidates in state and local elections, particularly when the Mexican-American candidate made "ethnic" appeals (cf. Hahn, Klingman, and Pachon 1976; Vigil 1978).

Bullock and Campbell (1984) found considerable evidence of racial, as distinct from racist, voting in Atlanta municipal elections. That is, their evidence indicates that whites as well as blacks are likely to vote for persons of their own race in the absence of compelling reasons to do otherwise. Candidates' issue positions may be an important factor leading citizens to vote for candidates of another racial or ethnic background.

Previous research suggests, then, that when minority candidates run for office in a city where the minority population does not comprise a majority or near-majority of the electorate, they most frequently seek to develop a "liberal coalition," i.e., they tend to make broad-based and issue-oriented appeals and do not overly emphasize "ethnic" concerns which might entail redistributive policies (Hahn, Klingman and Pachon 1976; de la Garza 1974). Evidence also indicates that in the absence of compelling reasons, such as strong issue agreement, candidate image or personality and the like, voters will generally support candidates of their own racial-ethnic background. The implications of the foregoing will be considered relative to the Peña campaign.

THE PEÑA CAMPAIGN

Strategies

The Peña election strategy had several components, which were developed after a careful analysis of mayoral elections in the city dating back to the mid-1970s. The Peña camp perceived that recent mayoral races in Denver had had lackluster campaigns whose candidates and policies failed sufficiently to excite many voters either to turn out at all or to vote for an alternative to the incumbent mayor. Data from state and national elections suggested that many of the white voters who did not usually turn out for city elections were moderate to liberal (Rocky Mountain *News*, January 10, 1983: B6; personal interview). The Peña campaign therefore sought to generate an exciting, dynamic contest, one which would increase turnout from the common 50 to 55 percent range to 70 percent or more. This higher turnout, it was believed, would benefit Peña and upset the slim margins by which the incumbent had won in the past.

Another part of the Peña election strategy was to undertake a drive to register Hispanics and the poor, who had had the city's lowest registration rates (cf. Henry and Munoz 1985: 19,22). Peña had previously worked for the Mexican-American Legal Defense and Education Fund and the Chicano Education Project. And, as a member of the state House of Representatives, Peña had strongly and visibly supported efforts to provide more equitable funding for education, a particular concern for Mexican-Americans and blacks. Given this background of support for minority concerns, the belief was that these constituencies were naturally Peña's (personal interview). Also, it was perceived that as a result of his state legislative activities and voting record Peña had built strong ties with labor, neighborhood organizations, environmentalists, the handicapped, young professionals and the elderly. Peña's voting record as a state legislator had been given high marks by labor, environmental, women's, and elderly groups.

Campaign Themes

The Peña campaign did not emphasize his ethnic heritage (see e.g., Denver *Post*, April 26, 1983: B7; June 12, 1983). However, his obviously ethnic name and previous record as a proponent of minority concerns were important. The major campaign themes focused on issues and leadership. The emphasis on issues served several purposes. First, it helped put Peña's views on record and attract news coverage which, with relatively scarce financial resources, was deemed essential. It also helped to establish an image of Peña as a forward-looking, bold leader and diminish his image as a "one-issue," namely minority-oriented, candidate (Denver *Post*, April 26, 1983 and *passim*; cf. Hahn, Pachon, and Klingman 1976). Some campaign material may help give a sense of this issue appeal. One piece of campaign material indicated the following concerns and goals for Peña's "first 100 days" in office, should he be elected:

1. "Denver is unprepared for the future. We have not planned or prepared adequately for the city's physical, economic, or social development." Peña claimed that he would: consolidate city agencies responsible for plan-

ning and development; restore planning and staff resources; review current zoning citywide; put forth an agenda for developing the city's major undeveloped parcels parcels of land; evaluate Denver's economic base and future revenue sources through a blue ribbon panel.

2. "Denver's government lacks accountability and sound management." Peña claimed that he would: recruit qualified replacements for all cabinet positions; review all existing city leases and contracts; begin management and efficiency studies of each department; institute an open, performance-based budget process; conduct town meetings throughout the city.

3. "Denver must pursue cooperative relationships with suburban jurisdictions and the state." Peña specified a number of intergovernmental efforts he would undertake to address several intergovernmental issues facing the city, including air pollution.

Along with these and other concerns, Peña issued a number of detailed position papers dealing with various issues including airport expansion, neighborhood preservation, economic development and job creation, bringing a major league baseball team to the city, and the city's financial future.

It appears, then, that the campaign's strategy and themes were geared toward building an aggregate of electoral support or a "chowder of constituencies" (Denver *Post*, March 6, 1983: B1) most similar to what has previously been described as a "liberal coalition." It is also clear that these themes had a non-divisive, "distributive," or "developmental" politics flavor to them.

Particular Circumstances and the Campaign

Denver mayoral elections are held in odd-numbered years and thus separately from national and state elections. The elections are nonpartisan, although all the major candidates in 1983 were Democrats. The 1983 elections required a runoff because no candidate received a majority in the first general election. The candidates in the 1983 first election were the incumbent three-term mayor, the district attorney, who had previously run for mayor, two members of Governor Richard Lamm's cabinet, one of whom was black, and two other candidates, along with Federico Peña, the former two-term member of the state House of Representatives. Peña had served as the Democratic party leader during his second term.

Along with some of the issues noted above and several others, the campaign often focused on the incumbent administration's (alleged) lack of energy and leadership and its mismanagement, cronyism and the like. These allegations made the incumbent quite vulnerable and, along with related factors, made Denver "ripe for a change" (Henry and Munoz 1985: 20). In the course of the campaign Peña received a number of endorsements, most prominently from labor groups, including the American Federation of State, County, and Municipal Employees, the Denver Area Labor Federation and the local chapter of the International Brotherhood of Electrical Workers.

Other notable endorsements were an early one from a "respected Republican developer" who had "strong ties to the downtown business community" (Denver *Post*, March 3, 1983: B1) and from the Sierra Club (Denver

Post, April 21, 1983: B4). Of the city's two major newspapers, the Denver *Post* and the Rocky Mountain *News*, the former endorsed the incumbent district attorney and the latter endorsed Peña but neither endorsed the incumbent mayor. Peña was also aided by the Southwest Voter Education Project's substantial efforts to register Mexican-American voters.

Peña surprised most observers by not only making the runoff but by leading the field in the first election. Peña won 36.4 percent of the vote; the district attorney received 30.8 percent to join Peña in the runoff election. The incumbent was third, receiving only 19.1 percent of the vote and thus not making the runoff. The black candidate, who was the last to enter the race, received 7.1 percent of the vote and none of the other candidates received more than 5 percent of the vote. Peña's success was attributed to several factors: his early entrance into the race and his relentless campaigning; a very well-organized campaign, which had large numbers of volunteers; new registrants and high turnout (see Table 1); and the highly effective use of relatively limited money in his media campaign (Denver *Post*, May 18, 1983: A10-A12).

TABLE 1
REGISTRATION AND TURNOUT IN DENVER MAYORAL ELECTIONS, 1975-1983

	Registration	Turnout	% Turnout
1975 May	227,478	121,478	53.4
1975 June	227,447	116,381	51.2
1979 May	203,016	108,142	53.3
1983 May	211,235	134,189	63.5
1983 June	217,313	155,895	71.7

Few major issues were introduced in the runoff election. Peña's runoff opponent raised an argument that had been made earlier in the campaign: that Peña had little if any administrative experience. Peña responded that state legislative leadership had provided some experience. More significantly, however, Peña argued that his opponent had an overly managerial or technocratic perspective of the mayor's role. Peña contended that a mayor must be more than a manager; that person also must be "a leader, a policy maker, an advocate, a catalyst, an innovator, a promoter and a mediator." Peña's opponent also argued that as a state legislator Peña's voting record indicated that he was "soft on crime," a charge which Peña characterized as a "gross misrepresentation" of his (Peña's) voting record (Denver *Post*, May 25, 1983: A1).

Several other issues raised in the runoff can be noted. Peña's runoff opponent once suggested that Peña's "backers were mostly on the [political] left" (Denver *Post*, May 18, 1983: A15), and at other times called Peña a "liberal." Peña responded that his support was broad-based. Peña also contended that there were not strong philosophical differences between him and his opponent and that classifying "by philosophy" in a nonpartisan election was "unfortunate" and "inappropriate." Peña added that whether or not streets get paved, how airport expansion is done and how air pollution is reduced are not liberal or conservative issues (Denver *Post*, May 18, 1983: A15). Another point of contention concerned collective bargaining for city employees; Peña supported it, his opponent did not (Denver *Post*, June 14, 1983: B1).

Finally, Peña criticized his opponent for running a negative campaign. Among the points Peña raised in this regard were his opponent's misrepresentation of his (Peña's) voting record as a state legislator and his opponent's suggestion that if Peña were elected it might have effects on Denver similar to those which the election of Dennis Kucinich had had in Cleveland (Denver *Post*, June 3, 1983: A1). Moreover, Peña aides expressed annoyance that pollsters for his opponent had questioned citizens about whether they were concerned that Peña is Hispanic, about the possibility of homosexuals being appointed to city administrative positions, and other questions which his opponent later said were "inappropriate" (Denver *Post*, May 28, 1983: B1). Peña argued that, in contrast, his own campaign had been "positive and upbeat."

In the runoff, Peña received the endorsement of most of the candidates who had been defeated in the first election, including the black candidate. The defeated black candidate cited Peña's sensitivity to "affordable housing, public safety and helping the elderly" as reasons for his endorsement (Denver *Post*, May 21, 1983: A1). The defeated incumbent, whom Peña had visited on election night shortly after the results of the first election were known, did not endorse either candidate. However, the defeated incumbent's brother, himself a former governor of the state, endorsed Peña. Many observers took this to be an implicit endorsement by the defeated incumbent. Another important development during the runoff campaign was a registration drive, which was promoted by Peña supporters. During the three-day period between the first and runoff elections that registration was allowed, over 6,200 persons registered (Denver *Post*, May 20, 1983: A1 and May 25, 1983: A12) Finally, Peña received a $10 thousand contribution from a highly prominent oil billionaire (Denver *Post*, May 29, 1983: B4). This seemed significant for reasons other than the obvious financial ones. This contributor had supported the defeated incumbent mayor in past elections and his visibility and prominence in the business community probably enhanced Peña's status among supporters of the defeated incumbent and with business groups.

Peña won the runoff election by a narrow 51.4 to 48.6 percent margin. The election was notable in two respects: the election of the city's first Mexican-American mayor and a record turnout.

Analysis of Election Results

The success of Peña's campaign strategy, outlined above, is assessed by using two sources of data. First, the precinct-level election results were obtained from the City and County of Denver Election Commission.[1] Sec-

---

[1] The total number of precincts is 389; however, the number of precincts used in the analyses in Tables 3 and 4 varies from 371 to 385 due to missing data.

ond, data on precinct-level demographic characteristics, party registration, and other information were purchased from a private vendor, Voter Contact Services. Because of possible limitations in the data[2] and the well-known problem of making inferences about individual behavior from aggregate-level data, in this case precincts, certain of the data presented below should be interpreted cautiously.

Evidence concerning the Peña strategy to increase registration and turnout is presented in Tables 1 and 2.

Table 1 indicates that the 1983 elections had considerably higher levels of registration than did the 1979 election. While the number of registered voters for the 1975 election exceeded that of the 1983 election, that may partly be because Denver had a larger population in 1975; Denver's population declined over 4 percent during the 1970s. The turnout rate among registered voters for the first election in 1983 was a full 10 percentage points above that for any of the 1975 and 1979 elections. The runoff election turnout in 1983 was a record for Denver city elections.

Table 2 more specifically attempts to assess the extent to which (precinct-level) registration and turnout are correlated with the (precinct-level) vote

TABLE 2
RELATIONSHIPS (R) BETWEEN REGISTRATION AND TURNOUT AND VOTE FOR PEÑA

Registration and Turnout Variables	% for Peña First Election	% for Peña Runoff
Registration between March* and May (first election)	.252	.362
% Registration between First and Runoff Election	.706	.595
% Registration between March* and June (runoff election)	.368	.452
% Turnout - First election	-.054	-.119
% Turnout - Runoff	-.049	-.185
Average Turnout in 1981 and 1979 State Primary Elections†	-.297	-.311

* March 1983, two months prior to the first election, was taken as a "baseline" period with which to compare subsequent registration.

† These elections are examined to consider how turnout in previous elections compared with that in the 1983 city elections.

Note: The analyses presented in this and subsequent tables are all based upon precinct-level data for all the variables.

---

[2] The major data limitation is related to "reprecincting." Denver precincts are redrawn from time to time to accomodate the larger registration and turnout for state and national elections. Thus the precincts for which the electoral results were drawn, which are the "correct" precincts, and those from which the demographic and related data are drawn do not coincide exactly. However, if caution is taken in interpreting the results, the data are useful. Other evidence suggests that the statistical results produced can be used with considerable confidence. An examination by the author of the precinct maps before and after the re-precincting indicates that the affects appear minor. Also, assuming that the re-precincting is done randomly, which conversations with staff officials of the Denver Election Commission indicate is the case, the effect on the statistical output is probably minor. In any case, the potential data limitations noted here are not uncommon for analyses of municipal elections (cf. Bullock and Campbell 1984; Hahn 1969).

213

for Peña. The data concerning registration indicate that, whatever period is considered, Peña benefited from new registration. The strongest relationships are those of registration between the first and runoff election and the vote for Peña. And the increase in registration during the three-day period between the first and runoff elections were strongly positively related (.706) to the vote for Peña in the first election; i.e., registration between the elections was generally greatest where Peña had done best in the first election. Moreover, the simple correlations between percent Spanish and new registration for the several time periods noted in Table 2 are .214, .739, and .361. These data on registration would suggest, then, that increased registration was quite important to Peña's ultimate victory (cf. Henry and Munoz 1985: 26).

The data in Table 2 also show negative, albeit weak, relationships between turnout and the vote for Peña. These findings must be considered in the context of the considerable new registration and the overall higher levels of turnout. That is, while high levels of turnout at the precinct-level are not positively related to the vote for Peña, it should be remembered that the precincts that had historically turned out at the highest levels were relatively affluent and conservative areas, areas presumably not supportive of minority candidates. Thus, if these affluent areas increased their turnout, somewhat, and the minority areas increased their turnout considerably — remembering that registration in these minority and poorer areas had also increased considerably — a negative relationship between turnout and vote for Peña is less surprising, particularly when those negative relationships are weak. And data support this speculation. The simple correlations between percent new registration from the first to the runoff election with percent non-minority is −.540 (Henry and Munoz 1985: 22). It is also important to note that the (positive) relationships between registration and vote for Peña are somewhat stronger than those (negative relationships) between turnout and vote for Peña.

The simple correlations between various demographic characteristics and other variables and the vote for Peña, shown in Table 3, provide evidence of a "liberal coalition." The correlation between percent Spanish and vote for Peña is rather strong for both elections. The relationship between the vote for Peña and percent black is rather strong and positive for the runoff election, although it is weakly negative for the first election. This negative relationship is almost certainly the result of the black candidate's presence and good showing among black voters. While the relationships between Peña's vote in the runoff and percent Spanish and black are strong, they may not be as strong as one might expect. However, Henry and Munoz, using aggregate data, claim that 96 percent of Hispanics and 86 percent of blacks who actually voted in the runoff supported Peña. The reason that these aggregate numbers do not translate into stronger correlations seems to be related to differences between groups in levels of registration and turnout. Henry and Munoz's data (26,22) indicate that only about 42 percent of Latinos, as compared to 65 percent of blacks and 68 percent of whites, were registered for the runoff election. Thus, while Hispanic registration had increased substantially over precious city elections, it still lagged considerably behind that of other groups (cf. Lovrich and Marenin 1976). Similarly, while turnout among Hispanics increased over past elections, data suggest that Hispanics (and blacks) still turned out at much lower levels than did whites. As a result of lower registration and turnout, then, the strength of the relationship between percent Spanish and black and the vote for Peña is lessened.

TABLE 3
SIMPLE CORRELATION (R) OF VOTE FOR PEÑA WITH INDEPENDENT VARIABLES

Variables (Precinct Level)	% for Peña First Election	% for Peña Runoff
% Spanish (18 + yrs. old)	.654	.519
% Black (18 + yrs. old)	-.199	.537
% Non-minority (18 + yrs. old)	-.359	-.776
Median Income	-.178	-.133
Median Value of Housing	-.006	.004
% Unemployed	.456	.586
% w/ Some College	-.327	-.468
% Democratic Registration	.363	.743

The simple correlation between vote for Peña and percent non-minority is negative for both elections and is particularly strong in the runoff election. However, Henry and Munoz's aggregate analysis found that Peña received about 42 percent of the white vote in the runoff. In this instance, the especially high registration and turnout among whites generally may exaggerate the strength of the negative relationships. These and subsequent data indicate considerable "racial" voting. Despite the general lack of explicit emphasis in his campaign on ethnic concerns, Peña's name and record, along with several endorsements, brought him strong minority group support. There is also considerable evidence of racial voting among non-minorities which, as will be noted momentarily, was modified by several factors.

The negative relationship with "percent with some college" and the rather strong relationship with "percent unemployed" provides further evidence that Peña fared relatively well among the less educated and lower status economic groups. While Denver elections are nonpartisan and all the major candidates in both elections were Democrats, it is clear that Peña did much better in Democratic areas of the city than the Republican ones (cf. Browning, Marshall, and Tabb 1984). This pattern, particularly notable in the runoff election, is important because Democrats comprise about 15 percent more of Denver's registered voters than do Republicans.

Some further, although tentative, evidence of the liberal coalition is the weak relationships between two measures of income, median income and median value of housing, and the vote for Peña. In previous elections, analyses by Peña campaign strategists suggested, the affluent had voted for relatively conservative candidates, most often the defeated incumbent mayor. That the relationship of these measures of income were not strongly related to the Peña vote would seem to suggest some success in gaining the support of professionals and the like. The findings in Table 3 are generally consistent with those of Browning, Marshall and Tabb. (The possible influence of the labor element of the liberal coalition could not be examined for lack of appropriate measures.)

Further multivariate analysis, such as regression analysis, might be desirable. However, substantial intercorrelation among several of the independent variables makes the utility of such an analysis questionable. Instead, several partial correlation analyses were undertaken; these are shown in Table 4 (cf. Hahn, Klingman, and Pachon 1976).

TABLE 4
PARTIAL CORRELATIONS ANALYSES OF VOTE FOR PEÑA- RUNOFF
WITH INDEPENDENT VARIABLES

A. Percent for Peña - Runoff with Ethnic-Racial Background Controlling for Socioeconomic Variables and Party Affiliation

	Ethni-Racial Background		
Controlling for	% Spanish	% Black	% Non-minority
(None)	.519	.537	-.776
Median Income	.502	.551	-.775
Median Value of Housing	.534	.541	-.794
% w/ Some College	.336	.498	-.714
% Unemployed	.237	.497	-.644
% Democratic Registration	.182	.213	-.432

B. Percent for Peña - Runoff with Socioeconomic Variables and Party Affiliation Controlling for Ethnic-Racial Background

	Controlling for			
Socioeconomic and Party Variables	(None)	% Spanish	% Black	% Non-minority
Median Income	-.133	-.028	-.196	-.023
Median Value of Housing	.004	.150	.001	.225
% w/ Some College	-.468	-.209	-.403	.090
% Unemployed	.586	.404	.557	.163
% Democratic Registration	.743	.645	.634	.283

Controlling for median income and value of housing has rather little impact on the already weak simple relationship between vote for Peña and ethnic background. However, when education (percent with some college), percent unemployed, and party affiliation are controlled, the simple relationships are affected considerably. When education is controlled, the positive relationships of vote for Peña with percent Spanish and black, particularly the former, are diminished. This would suggest some lack of cohesion among Hispanics related to education levels (cf. Hahn, Klingman, and Pachon 1976). Similarly, as shown in Part B of the Table, when percent Spanish is controlled, a weak negative relationship between vote for Peña and the education measure remains. A similar although stronger relationship results when percent black is controlled, while controlling for percent non-minority makes the initial negative relationship disappear and become very weakly positive. That controlling for education has rather strong impacts in not surprising given that the simple relationships between percent with some college and percent Spanish, black, and non-minority are −.612, −.246, and .642, respectively. These interrelationships make interpretation difficult but the data do indicate that those minority voters who did not support Peña were probably those with higher levels of education while among whites, education has a negligible or slightly positive affect overall on the vote for Peña.

Unemployment is related to the vote for Peña in ways somewhat similar to education. Controlling for unemployment lessens the positive relationship between vote for Peña and percent Spanish and black while controlling for this variable lessens the negative relationship with percent non-minority. Relatedly, Part B indicates that controlling for percent Spanish weakens the relationship between percent unemployed and vote for Peña slightly, while controlling for percent black affects that relationship almost not at all. Controlling for percent non-minority considerably weakens the relationship between vote for Peña and percent unemployed, from .586 to .163 (cf. Hahn, Klingman, and Pachon 1976). Again, it should be noted that the simple relationships between percent unemployed and percent Spanish, black, and non-minority are .623, .262, and −.623, respectively.

Finally, the impact of Democratic party affiliation is similar to, but stronger than, that for education and percent unemployed. When this variable is controlled, the relationship of minority status (Spanish or black) to vote for Peña declines rather dramatically and that for non-minority becomes somewhat less negative. Similarly, the relationship between vote for Peña and Democratic registration drops substantially, from .743 to .283 when percent non-minority is controlled (cf. Browning, Marshall, and Tabb 1984). However, controlling for percent Spanish and black has relatively little impact on the simple relationships. Once again, the high correlations among the independent variables probably account for substantial changes that occur. The simple relationships between percent Democratic registration and percent Spanish, black, and non-minority are .562, .567, and −.831.

CONCLUSION

The description of the Peña campaign suggested that it sought to increase participation, especially among certain groups, and to develop something similar to a liberal coalition. The statistical evidence indicates the success of the campaign in generating increased registration, turnout and support among both minorities, especially Hispanics, and white liberals. The appeals to gain white liberal support stressed better management generally and better managed growth in particular. Peña was also apparently able to present a positive, dynamic image. With respect to minority voters, Peña's name and record along with his stated concern for "affordable housing" and other social issues were apparently quite important. This aggregate of support also indicates considerable racial voting, apparently modified by various factors such as issues and party affiliation. The term "aggregate of support" is used because the Peña campaign seemed to offer a "little something" for the several major groups whose support it sought, without directly confronting the question of whether these various goals might conflict.

Despite the overall indications of much "racial voting" (Bullock and Campbell 1984), there is some rather weak evidence that more educated Hispanics and blacks supported Peña less strongly than did the less educated ethnic minorities. Among whites, the impact of higher levels of education had either negligible or slightly positive impacts on the vote for Peña (cf. Hahn, Klingman, and Pachon 1976; de la Garza 1974). The tendency of racial voting was also modified by party affiliation and employment status. Economic status, as indicated by two measures of income, was weakly related to the vote for Peña, either directly or indirectly. Also, the coalition among Hispanics and blacks found here also has been found in some (Browning, Marshall, and Tabb 1984) but not all (Hahn, Klingman, and Pachon 1976) the previous research.

While these findings should be interpreted cautiously, they do indicate that the campaign appeals and electoral coalitions of minority candidates are quite important and may differ according to different constituency contexts and other factors (cf. Hahn, Klingman, and Pachon 1976; de la Garza 1974). The data also suggest that the response of minority groups to different candidates may differ within groups, often due to socioeconomic variables, between groups, and between groups of the same ethnic background in different cities (cf. Hahn, Klingman and Pachon 1976; Browning, Marshall and Tabb 1984; Henry and Munoz 1985).

The implications of these findings are unclear, but brief speculation can be offered. Hispanics and blacks strongly supported Peña and were crucial to his election. However, due to their relatively small proportion of Denver's population, lower levels of registration (for Hispanics), and low levels of turnout (for both minority groups), whites provided the major portion of the vote or Peña. Thus, despite the election of a Hispanic mayor it would appear difficult to alter substantive policy in ways which previous research suggests would be preferable to Denver's minorities (Lovrich 1974). This is due to the apparent constraints placed upon Peña by his electoral coalition, constraints that are probably even greater when actual issues of governance must be confronted (Stone 1980). Notably, Peña's top administrative appointees to date have been white (cf. Henry and Munoz 1985: 23). Beyond the likely symbolic importance and perhaps a different tone in city administration, and despite the considerable formal powers of the Denver mayor, it is unclear what the real impacts of Peña's election for minority groups will be. Further judgment on this probably should be withheld until a full term of office has been completed.

Further research is needed before the election and governing issues confronted by Hispanic candidates are better understood. That research should be sensitive to differences within and between ethnic-racial groups as well as to regional and historical factors. Until such research is undertaken, it will remain uncertain whether the election of Federico Peña is similar to or different than the election of Hispanics in other cities and offices, how Hispanics differ from other minority groups in terms of the electoral coalitions that they are able to construct, and the implications of these matters for successful governance. Despite impressive previous research, numerous significant questions such as these remain to be answered.

REFERENCES

Browning, Rufus P., Dale Rogers Marshall, and David H. Tabb. 1984. *Protest Is Not Enough — The Struggle of Blacks and Hispanics for Equality in Urban Politics*. Berkeley: University of California Press.

Bullock, Charles S. III, and Bruce A. Campbell. 1984. "Racist or Racial Voting in the 1981 Atlanta Municipal Elections," *Urban Affairs Quarterly* 20 (December): 149-64.

de la Garza, Rudolph. 1974 "Voting Patterns in 'Bi-Cultural El Paso' — A Contextual Analysis of Chicano Voting Behavior." *Aztlan* 5 (Spring-Fall): 235-60.

———. 1977. "Mexican-American Voters: A Responsible Electorate." In Frank L. Baird, ed., *Mexican Americans: Political Power, Influence, or Resources*, pp. 63-76. Lubbock: Texas Tech Press.

Garcia, F. Chris, and Rudolph O. de la Garza. 1977. *The Chicano Political Experience: Three Perspectives*. North Scituate, MA: Duxbury.

Hahn, Harlan. 1969. "Ethos and Social Class Referenda in Canadian Cities." *Polity* 2 (December): 295-315.

Hahn, Harlan, David Klingman, and Harry Pachon. 1976. "Cleavages, Coalitions, and the Black Candidate: The Los Angeles Mayoralty Elections of 1969 and 1973." *Western Political Quarterly* 55 (December): 507-20.

Holloway, Harry. 1968. "Negro Political Strategy: Coalition or Independent Power Politics?" *Social Science Quarterly* 49 (December): 534-47.

Henry, Charles P., and Carlos Munoz. 1985. "Under the Rainbow: Black and Latino Support for Minority Mayors." Paper presented at the Annual Meeting of the American Political Association, August 29-September 1, New Orleans, Louisiana.

Lovrich, Nicholas. 1974. "Differing Priorities in an Urban Electorate: Service Preference Among Anglo, Black and Mexican American Voters." *Social Science Quarterly* 55 (December): 704-17.

——— and Otwin Marenin. 1976. "A Comparison of Black and Mexican American Voters in Denver: Assertive versus Acquiescent Political Orientations and Voting Behavior in an Urban Electorate." *Western Political Quarterly* 29 (June): 284-94.

Stone, Clarence. 1980. "Systemic Power in Community Decision Making: A Restatement of Stratification Theory." *American Political Science Review* 74: 978-90.

Taebel, Delbert. 1978. "Minority Representation on City Councils: The Impact of Structure on Blacks and Hispanics." *Social Science Quarterly* 59 (June): 142-52.

Vigil, Maurilio. 1978. "Jerry Apodaca and the 1974 Gubernatorial Election in New Mexico." *Aztlan* 9 (Spring, Summer, Fall): 133-50.

Wolfinger, Raymond. 1974. *The Politics of Progress*. Englewood Cliffs, NJ: Prentice-Hall.

A GENDER GAP AMONG HISPANICS?
A COMPARISON WITH BLACKS AND ANGLOS

Susan Welch, *University of Nebraska, Lincoln*
and
Lee Sigelman, *George Washington University*

The term "gender gap" is widely used to refer to differences between men and women in political preferences, party affiliation, vote choice, and other political attitudes. Considerable, though not entirely consistent, evidence indicates that in the United States women are more likely than men to identify as Democrats, to vote for Democratic candidates, and to take more liberal positions on various issues (see, e.g., Frankovic 1982; Matlack 1987; Shapiro and Mahajan 1986). The gender gap appears to be widest on issues relating to the use of force, somewhat narrower on the compassion issues, such as treatment of the poor, the elderly, and the infirm, and narrowest on "women's issues," such as abortion and equal rights.

Virtually without exception, analyses of the gender gap have focused on political differences between men and women in general, with little or no attention given to male-female differentiation within particular subpopulations. One might wonder, for example, whether such differentiation is largely a white, middle-class phenomenon, and whether men and women who are members of racial and ethnic minority groups are more likely to share particular views associated with their group. Findings recently reported by Welch and Sigelman (1989) suggest as much, for they uncovered few differences between black men and women on a variety of issue attitudes, ideological and partisan identification, and voting; black men and women appear to have more in common politically than white men and women do.

Received: October 17, 1990
Revision Received: February 2, 1991
Accepted for Publication: February 28, 1991
Note: Is the gender gap largely a white, middle-class phenomenon? This analysis, based on data from six election day exit polls conducted in 1980, 1984, and 1988, tests for differences between Hispanic American men and women in ideological and partisan identification and in vote choice. Analysis reveals that Hispanic women are more liberal and more pro-Democratic than Hispanic men, but the magnitude of these differences varies considerably. Moreover, male/female differences are essentially equal among Hispanic, Black and Anglo Americans.

To our knowledge, no parallel examination has yet been undertaken of the gender gap among Hispanics, nor have the few existing analyses of Hispanic political attitudes explicitly considered the possible existence of a gender gap. This paper attempts to improve our understanding of both Hispanic political attitudes and gender differences in political attitudes by exploring whether Hispanic man and women are divided by differences in political viewpoints that parallel those often documented in the broader American public. Our analysis was based on six election-day "exit polls" conducted by media combines in 1980, 1984, and 1988. Although the focus is on Hispanics, we compared the gender gap among Hispanics to that found among blacks and non-Hispanic whites ("Anglos"), hoping thereby to shed new light on the extent of the gender gap in major U.S. ethnic subpopulations.[1]

THE GENDER GAP AND HISPANIC POLITICAL ATTITUDES

In several previous analyses, gender has not even been considered as a factor underlying Hispanic political attitudes and behavior (see e.g., Cain, Kiewiet, and Uhlaner 1990; Ebeling, King, and Gregg 1988; Miller, Pollinard and Wrinkle 1984). However, a few studies have examined gender as one of several determinants of partisanship or political opinions among Hispanics.[2] According to Brischetto (1987), there were no differences in partisanship or presidential vote choice between Mexican American men and women in Texas in 1984, and de la Garza, Wrinkle, and Polinard (1988) found that gender helped explain opinion differences on only one of six immigration-related issues they probed in a survey of Mexican Americans in two Texas counties. On the other hand, in a survey of California Hispanics, Cain and Kiewiet (1985) observed that women were more likely than men to favor gun registration and a nuclear freeze and were slightly, but not significantly, less likely to support Reaganomics. There were no

---

[1] When we discuss differences among Hispanics, blacks, and Anglos, we must use the expressions race and ethnicity, because "Hispanic" does not constitute a race. Some Hispanics are black; most white. In the surveys upon which our analysis is based, respondents were typically asked to choose the single category that best described them, from a list that included the terms "white," "black," and "Hispanic." Thus, within the limited context of this paper the three terms are mutually exclusive.

[2] There have also been studies in which gender is considered as a predictor of the decision to vote or to engage in other forms of political participation (see e.g., Falcon 1988; Garcia and Arce 1988; Mitofsky and Frankovic 1987; Uhlaner, Cain, and Kiewcit 1989).

differences between men and women in their attitudes toward abortion or bottle deposit legislation. Women were also more likely to be political independents and less likely to be Republicans than were men. Analyzing survey responses from Mexican Americans in East Los Angeles and San Antonio, Brischetto and de la Garza (1983) also reported that Hispanic women were less likely than their male counterparts to be Republicans, less likely to think favorably of Republicans, and more likely to have positive conceptions of Democrats.

It appears, then, that if there is a gender gap among Hispanics, it runs in the same direction as in the public at large — toward greater pro-Democratic and liberal sympathies among Hispanic women than men. But the existing evidence is fragmentary at best, since, among other things, it is based on surveys conducted in a single locale or a small set of locales. In light of the enormous diversity within the Hispanic population, such geographic restrictions impose obvious limits on the generalizability of the findings just reviewed. The contradictory and inconclusive nature of previous findings raised the question of whether we should expect to find a gender gap among Hispanics nationwide and, if so, whether we should expect it to be as large as the one often observed in the broader American population.

On the one hand, there was considerable reason for expecting the gender gap to be minimal among Hispanics. Hispanic families are larger than black or Anglo families, and fertility rates are higher (Bean, Stephen, and Opitz 1985; but see Darabi and Ortiz 1987). Sex roles in Hispanic cultures are often described as traditional, with women tending the home, children, and family while men serve as the major economic resource (Fitzpatrick 1971; Grebler, Moore, and Guzman 1970). One would not expect women fulfilling traditional roles to be intensely involved in politics or to formulate and defend independent political positions in opposition to those of their spouses.

On the other hand, much evidence suggests that Hispanic women do not really fit their traditional sterotype. For one thing, almost as many Hispanic as Anglo women (53 percent versus 57 percent) are in the workforce (U.S. Department of Labor 1989). Hispanic women increasingly enter the workforce as their educational levels and English proficiency increase. Workforce participation is especially likely among native-born women (Cooney and Ortiz 1983).[3] And along with work-

---

[3] Mexican-origin women are as likely as Anglo and black women to return to the work force within two years of childbirth (Ortiz and Fennelly 1988).

ing outside the home come changes in traditional norms (Ybarra 1982; Zavella 1988; Zinn 1980). Sex role attitudes are least traditional and labor force participation rates highest in second- and third-generation Hispanic populations, which we might expect to find voting most frequently and expressing political opinions most vigorously (Bean et al. 1985; Cain et al. 1990). Indeed, Hsipanic women vote at as high a rate as male Hispanics (Brischetto and de la Garza 1983). Overall, then, there might be a gender gap among Hispanics, but because the mix of Hispanic respondents in a diverse national sample would include some first-generation as well as later-generation respondents, we would expect it to be somewhat less pronounced than among Anglos. Thus, we tested the hypotheses that:

(1) Hispanic women are more liberal and more pro-Democratic than Hispanic men.
(2) The gender gap is narrower among the Hispanics than among Anglos but wider than among blacks.

DATA AND METHODS

We tested these hypotheses with data from the 1980 and 1988 CBS News/New York Times; 1984 and 1988 ABC News; 1984 NBC News; and 1988 NBC News/Wall Street Journal presidential election day surveys of voters departing the polling place.[4] These exit polls enabled us to generalize beyond a particular city or state. Our analyses included Hispanics, blacks, and Anglos, excluding Asians and others. The exit polls, with between 6,600 and 14,000 respondents meeting this racial-ethnic criterion, were national in scope, and all but one contained 220 to 301 respondents of Hispanic origin. The exception was the 1988 ABC poll, with 633 Hispanic respondents. The number of black respondents ranged from 600 to 1250.[5]

By far the greatest advantage of the exit polls lay in their sheer size, since no national random sample with fewer than several thousand respondents will include enough Hispanics to permit reliable generalizations. However, the exit polls also had shortcomings. They

---

[4] We obtained these data sets from the Inter-University Consortium for Political and Social Research (University of Michigan), the Roper Center (University of Connecticut), and the Louis Harris Center (University of North Carolina). Neither the original collectors nor the distributors of these data are responsible for our analyses and interpretations.

[5] See the bottom of Table 2 for precise information concerning the size of each racial-ethnic group sample.

excluded non-voters, a sizable proportion of any group but especially of Hispanics. Their questionnaires were too short to permit in-depth probing of attitudes and opinions. Even with their huge samples, they did not reach enough Hispanics to permit disaggregation according to country or area of ancestry, so we were unable to compare Mexican Americans, Cuban Americans, and Puerto Ricans. Since they employed cluster sampling, focusing on a relatively few randomly chosen precincts, and since only a few predominantly Hispanic precincts were likely to be sampled, different polls may have given quite different weights to the various Hispanic ethnic and national subgroups. This would naturally lead to diverse results (see Balz 1987; Page 1987). We tried to overcome this problem by searching for consistent patterns across six different surveys rather than relying on a single, possibly idiosyncratic, survey.

Variables

The endogenous variables in the analysis were self-declared political ideology, party identification, and presidential vote choice. In the ABC and CBS polls, political ideology was measured on a three-point scale running from low scores for conservative through medium scores for moderate to high scores for liberal, and in the NBC polls on a five-point scale differentiating between "very" and "somewhat" conservative or liberal. Similarly, party identification was measured in the ABC and CBS polls on a three-point scale including Republicans (low), Independents (medium), and Democrats (high). In the NBC polls, a five-point scale included strong Republicans, weak Republicans, independents, weak Democrats, and strong Democrats. Presidential vote choice was coded 0 for a Republican vote and 1 for a Democratic one. Respondents voting for other candidates were excluded from the analysis.

The primary exogenous variable was gender, coded 0 = male and 1 = female in the multivariate analyses. We examined the independent impact of gender by controlling for several other factors. While additional variables could conceivably have been included, these demographic and partisan factors predicted vote choice quite well, as we will see.

Age, coded in the exit polls in either five or six ordered categories, has been shown to be associated with greater conservatism in the population at large, but does not have a distinctive impact on partisan choice except that the very young are less likely than their elders to be attached to either party. Among Hispanics, older voters are more likely to be Democratic (Brischetto 1987).

Education and income have also emerged as significant predictors of ideology, partisanship, and vote choice in the general public (see, e.g., Abramson, Aldrich and Rohde 1989; ch. 5). Wealthier people tend to be more conservative and pro-Republican, and the same trends are evident for people with more formal education, at least up to the post-graduate level. Among Hispanics, too, prior research indicates that higher income and to some extent higher education are associated with increased probabilities of Republican identification and electoral support (Brischetto 1987; Cain et al. 1990). Education was measured here in four to six grade level categories, and income in five to seven, depending on the exact items used in a particular survey.

Between 60 and 80 percent of Hispanics are Roman Catholics, compared to less than one Anglo in three. However, many Hispanics belong to various evangelical Protestant sects. A few claim other religious affiliations or no religion at all. While we know of no research examining political differences between Catholic and other Hispanics, we do know that, in general, Catholics have been more pro-Democratic than Protestants, and that, even though this loyalty has waned somewhat, Catholics still are more likely to vote Democratic than Protestants are (Abramson et al. 1989: 24–25). We therefore expect the general link between Catholicism and Democratic allegiance to hold among Hispanics as well. As religious indicators, we also included dummy variables for those unaffiliated with any religion, and those affiliated with a religion other than Protestant or Catholic.

Born-again Christians have some distinctive political attitudes in the population as a whole. Generally, they are more likely to hold conservative attitudes, especially on social issues, and to vote Republican (Wald 1987; ch. 7). We expected these same patterns to hold among Hispanic born-again Christians.[6]

Analysis

We first examined the simple differences in self-described political ideology, party identification, and presidential vote choice between men and women of the three racial-ethnic groups. Then we looked

---

[6] The wording of the survey items tapping "born-again" status varied somewhat, but all were simple "yes-no" check-offs. Thus members of any Christian religion, including Roman Catholic could be considered "born- again."

more closely at these differences, taking into account the impacts of the control variables just described. The variables were linked in a structural model, the elements of which were as follows. Each of a set of exogenous variables (gender, age, education, income, and the religion variable) was assumed to have direct effects on the three endogenous variables (ideology, party identification, and presidential vote choice). We also assumed that the exogenous variables would affect vote choice, the ultimate endogenous variable, indirectly through their impacts on ideology and party identification, which in turn would directly affect vote choice. Because party identification and ideology were seen as affected by the same exogenous factors, the model provided that they would have correlated error terms. No causal link was assumed between party identification and ideology, since we did not view political ideology as causalty prior to party identification, or vice versa. The model was estimated via weighted least squares in LISREL 7, enabling us to fit a structural model in which observed variables were measured at the ordinal level (see Joreskog and Sorbom 1989: ch. 7) and to test for the impact of gender across the three racial-ethnic groups. The analysis was replicated for each of the six separate data sets.

FINDINGS

Initial Comparisons

Table 1 shows the gap between male and female Anglos, Hispanics, and blacks in self-described ideology, partisanship, and vote choice. The numbers in the table convey the liberal or pro-Democratic sympathies of women in a particular racial-ethnic group, relative to those of men in the same group. These numbers were the results of a three-step calculation. (1) For a given group, the proportion of women calling themselves conservatives or Republicans or saying they voted for the Republican candidate was subtracted from the percentage calling themselves liberals or Democrats or saying they voted for the Democratic candidate. (2) The same calculations were carried out for men. (3) The men's score was subtracted from the women's. Thus, a positive difference would indicate a higher proportion of women than men identifying as liberals or Democrats or voting Democratic. This procedure yielded a more complete picture than simply comparing the percentage of men and women who chose the liberal or Democratic option, and was much simpler than trying to compare each of the three or five options separately.

TABLE 1
Gender Differences in Political Ideology, Party Identification and Vote Choice Among Hispanics, Blacks, and Anglos

Group	CBS 1980	ABC 1984	NBC 1984	ABC 1988	CBS 1988	NBC 1988	Mean
A. Political Ideology							
Hispanics	9	5	11	2	18	-4	6.8
Blacks	-8	8	4	7	12	9	5.3
Anglos	9	14	15	17	11	14	13.3
B. Party Identification							
Hispanics	1	29	7	16	13	2	11.3
Blacks	11	15	7	13	11	8	6.8
Anglos	7	9	9	12	12	10	9.8
C. Presidential Vote Choice							
Hispanics	5	16	9	4	8	2	6.0
Blacks	6	9	1	7	7	1	5.2
Anglos	8	8	10	8	8	7	8.2

Note: As explained in the text, a positive score indicates that women were more liberal or Democratic than men.

Table 1 indicates that in all three groups, women were consistently more liberal and Democratic than men, though not always by a great margin. Among both Hispanics and blacks, five of the six comparisons of ideology and all twelve comparisons of party identification and vote choice produced positive differences. Among Anglos, all 18 of the differences were positive, indicating that in every comparison, women were more liberal or Democratic than men.

Although the pattern of signs was nearly identical across the three groups, the size of the gender differences varied from group to group. The gender gap was least pronounced among blacks, with mean differences ranging only from 5.2 for vote choice to 6.8 for party identification. Of course, blacks have long been overwhelmingly allegiant to the Democratic party, so there was little room for gender differences in partisanship to emerge among blacks. However, the gap was equally small for ideology. For ideology and vote choice, the gap was widest for Anglos, with mean gender differences ranging from 8.2 to 13.3. By contrast, the gender gap in partisan identification was largest (11 percent) for Hispanics.

These initial comparisons, then, generally supported both of our hypotheses. There did appear to be a gender gap among Hispanics, and the size of the Hispanic gender gap did appear to be intermediate between the relatively large one for Anglos and the relatively small one for blacks.

Testing the Model

To enhance our confidence that the gender differences just described were not artifacts of other factors, such as male-female differences in education or religious beliefs, we had to move from a bivariate to a multivariate mode of analysis. The results of the multivariate analysis are shown in Table 2.

TABLE 2
MODELING POLITICAL IDEOLOGY, PARTY IDENTIFICATION, AND PRESIDENTIAL VOTE CHOICE, 1980-1988

Predictor	CBS 1980	ABC 1984	NBC 1984	ABC 1988	CBS 1988	NBC 1988
A. Political Ideology							
Gender	-.11	.01	.09	-.01	.13	.02
	-.02	.07	.03	.05	.11*	.00
Age	.05	-.15	.02	.08	-.07	.06
	-.01	.10	.05	.03	.01	-.01
	-.06	-.07	-.06*	-.02*	-.02	-.01
Education	.12	.22*	.10	.15*	.06	.00
	.15*	.18*	.04	.07	.09	.04
	.03	.08*	-.01	.05*	.04*	.09*
Income	-.22*	-.21	.03	-.19*	.01	-.15
	.02	-.15	.03	.02	-.03	-.06
	-.09*	-.14*	-.11*	-.13*	-.06*	-.10*
Catholic	.16	-.03	.01	.09	.08	.13
	-.01	-.06	.05	-.04	-.01	-.04
	.08*	.07*	.12*	.08*	.04*	.11*
Other religion	.10	.01	.03	.10	.04	.04
	-.04	-.00	-.03	-.04	-.05	-.09
	.15*	.11*	.10*	.10*	.09*	.12*
No religion	.18	.07	.08	.13	.15	.22*
	.04	.06	.05	-.04	.03	-.05
	.11*	.14*	.06*	.16*	.13*	.07*

TABLE 2 (Continued)

Born-again	-.02	-.02			-.05	-.07
	-.08*	-.13*		-.10*	.00	
	-.12*	-.16*		-.21*	-.19*	
R^2	.08	.10	.03	.05	.05	.06
	.04	.06	.01	.02	.02	.01
	.07	.10	.04	.12	.07	.04

B. Party Identification

Gender	.06	.18*	-.08	.08	.10	.03
	.06	.11	.07	.14*	.10*	.07
	.03*	.06*	.06*	.08*	.07*	.06*
Age	.13	-.04	.13	.10	.17	.20*
	-.02	-.10	.12	-.01	.15*	.14*
	-.01	.05*	.05*	.08*	.07*	.08*
Education	-.07	-.01	.11	-.11	-.16	.08
	-.07	-.04	.12	-.05	.06	.12
	-.09*	-.00	.01	-.04*	-.02	.03
Income	-.19	-.38*	-.23	-.16	-.09	-.15
	-.03	-.14	-.15	-.11	-.19*	-.10
	-.10	-.14*	-.13*	-.14*	-.16*	-.13*
Catholic	.44*	.08	.12	.31	.05	.26
	-.09*	-.00	-.01	-.07	-.03	-.12*
	.18*	.16*	.13*	.15*	.11*	.15*
Other religion	.06	-.20	-.11	.06	.06	.13
	.08	.19*	.21*	.10	.12	.10
	.18*	.09*	.09*	.07*	.10*	.12*
No religion	.14	-.06	-.14	.19	.03	.04
	-.07	.01	-.06	.02	.05	-.04
	.07*	.08*	.04*	.12*	.09*	.05*
Born-again	.23*	.29*		.02	-.08	
	.06	-.04		-.01	-.08	
	-.00	-.07*		-.13*	-.12*	
R^2	.24	.29	.13	.13	.11	.09
	.05	.12	.10	.07	.08	.06
	.07	.06	.04	.09	.07	.05

C. Presidential Vote Choice — Direct Effects

Gender	.08	.07	.16	-.03	-.02	.01
	.09	.11	-.08	.05	.05	-.03
	.06*	.04*	.07*	.02	.03	.02
Age	-.10	.08	.05	-.09	-.09	-.09
	.14*	.02	.06	-.11	-.05	-.06
	-.03	.06*	.03	.01	.03	.01

TABLE 2 (Continued)

Education	-.07	.01	.00	-.02	-.16	-.00
	-.03	-.11	.14	-.01	-.06	-.14
	.05*	.07*	.10*	.05*	.07*	.06*
Income	-.04	.01	-.10	.04	.04	.03
	-.11	-.01	-.08	-.07	-.09	.03
	-.10*	-.09*	-.08*	-.05*-	.06*	-.05
Catholic	.14	.08	.06	-.01	.14	.14
	-.05	-.09	.04	-.10	-.03	.00
	-.02	-.02	.02	.02	.02	.04
Other religion	.02	.17	.11	-.08	.04	.07
	.15*	.02	.11	.07	.05	.00
	-.01	.04	.04	.02	.03	.03
No religion	.17	.15	.10	.05	.13	.03
	.05	-.15	.08	.01	.02	-.00
	.03	.05*	.04	.05*	.06*	.04*
Born-again	.06	-.01		-.03	.02	
	.05	-.05		-.06	-.09	
Political ideology	.06	.32*	.10	.30	.18	.06
	.35*	.39*	.00	.27*	.21*	.10
	.21*	.32*	.22*	.33*	.28*	.26*
Party identification	.66*	.58*	.82*	.70*	.73*	.87*
	.65*	.59*	.74*	.66*	.68*	.72*
	.60*	.59*	.72*	.60*	.62*	.69*
R^2	.59	.58	.77	.80	.72	.82
	.74	.62	.60	.77	.65	.55
	.53	.70	.74	.78	.70	.75

D. Presidential Vote Choice—Total Effects

Gender	.11	.18	.10	.02	.08	.04
	.12	.20	-.02	.15	.14	.02
	.09	.11	.13	.11	.09	.08
Age	-.01	.01	.16	.01	.02	.08
	-.15	-.00	.14	-.11	.05	.04
	-.05	.07	.05	.06	.06	.05
Education	-.11	.07	.10	-.05	-.26	.07
	-.02	-.07	.22	-.02	-.00	-.06
	-.00	.10	.11	.04	.07	.10
Income	-.17	-.28	-.29	-.13	-.02	-.11
	-.12	-.15	-.19	-.14	-.23	-.05
	-.17	-.22	-.20	-.18	-.17	-.17
Catholic	.44	.12	.16	.24	.19	.37
	-.11	-.11	.03	-.16	-.05	-.08
	.11	.10	.14	.13	.10	.17

231

TABLE 2 (Continued)

Other religion	.06	.06	.02	-.04	.09	.19
	.19	.13	.27	.12	.13	.07
	.13	.13	.12	.09	.12	.14
No religion	.27	.14	-.00	.22	.18	.08
	.02	-.12	.04	.01	.06	-.03
	.10	.15	.08	.17	.15	.10
Born-again	.21	.16		-.03	-.05	
	.06	-.12		-.10	-.14	
	-.04	-.16		-.22	-.19	
Political ideology	.06	.32	.10	.30	.18	.06
	.35	.39	.00	.27	.21	.10
	.21	.32	.22	.33	.28	.26
Party identification	.66	.58	.82	.70	.73	.87
	.65	.59	.74	.66	.68	.72
	.60	.59	.72	.60	.62	.69
E. Summary Statistics for the Model						
Number of cases	255	238	255	641	361	301
	1922	604	733	1301	1121	730
	8456	6696	7320	13788	8138	7211
Total R^2	.38	.42	.32	.26	.29	.22
	.33	.27	.16	.27	.19	.11
	.14	.19	.12	.19	.16	.10
"Constrained" model						
Chi^2	15.7	5.9	7.0	17.6	3.2	5.8
df	6	6	6	6	6	6
p	.015	.436	.317	.007	.786	.452

The first row of entries for each predictor is the coefficient for Hispanics; second, for blacks; and third, for Anglos. *t-ratio > 1.96.

The model did well at predicting vote choice within each group, with R^2 ranging between .58 and .82 for Hispanics, .55 and .77 for blacks, and .53 and .78 for whites. It did considerably less well at predicting self-described political ideology and partisan identification, as we expected of a model containing only a few demographic variables as predictors. Only for partisan identification for Hispanics did the mean R^2 across the six surveys exceed .10.

For the most part, the predictors in the model performed as expected within each racial-ethnic group. For example, higher income was associated with conservatism (though the effects were weak and inconsistent for blacks), with greater Republican sympathies, and, in terms of total effects, with higher rates of Republican voting. Anglo and Hispanic Catholics, other non-Protestants, and those with no religious affiliation were more liberal and pro-Democratic than their Protestant cohorts; among blacks, though, Catholicism and belonging to other non-Protestant religions pushed in the conservative, Republican direction, albeit weakly. Conservatives and Republicans in all three groups were substantially more likely to vote Republican.

The main departure from expectations was that in all three groups, the better educated tended to be more liberal. Along the same lines, better educated Anglos tended to be more closely aligned with the Democrats, though the association between education and party identification was weak and inconsistent among Hispanics and blacks. Being "born again" had the predicted impact on Anglos and on the political ideology of blacks, but it had much less consistent effects on Hispanics and on black partisanship.

The primary variable of interest was, of course, gender. Overall, Hispanic women were clearly more liberal and more Democratic than men, even when the control variables were taken into account. But some of these impacts were small, and some inconsistencies emerged.

Looking first at political ideology, we see that in four of six equations Hispanic women were more liberal than men. Only two of the coefficients, however, were even of modest magnitude. The average coefficient was only .02, indicating a minimal overall relationship.

There were stronger and more consistent gender-based differences for party identification. Here, five of the six equations showed the expected positive sign. Only one coefficient was statistically significant (.18) for Hispanics, but because of sample size differences it was much harder for the Hispanic coefficients to attain statistical significance than it was for the same coefficients for Anglos, or even blacks. The average coefficient for Hispanics was .06, indicative of a gender gap of modest proportions, once the other variables in the model were taken into account.

The direct effect of gender on vote choice among Hispanics was again small, with coefficients averaging about .05. The total effects were almost twice as large, however, and were quite consistent across the six equations.

There was, then, evidence of a gender gap among Hispanics that withstood, to some extent, the imposition of statistical controls for age, education, income, and religion. The gap was negligible for political ideology, but more appreciable for party identification and presidential vote choice. Hispanic women were, as predicted, more likely to be Democrats than were Hispanic men, but contrary to predictions, only a little more liberal.

How did these differences stack up against the gender gap for Anglos and blacks? As with Hispanics, among blacks the gender gap in self-described political ideology was fairly weak. It was larger for party identification, with all six coefficients running in the expected direction and averaging .09. The coefficients for the direct effects of gender on vote choice were modest and not entirely consistent, but the overall effects were generally strong, with four of the six coefficients exceeding .10. So unlike the bivariate relationships, which showed the gender gap weakest among blacks, once statistical controls were instituted the gender relationships became slightly stronger for blacks than for Hispanics.

The gender gap in political ideology was larger for Anglos than it was for either Hispanics or blacks. All the ideology coefficients for Anglos were in the expected positive direction, averaging about .08, and all were statistically significant — hardly surprising, in light of the huge Anglo sample sizes. The male-female differences in party identification were somewhat more modest, though again all the coefficients ran in the expected direction, ranging from .03 to .08 and averaging about .06. The direct effects of gender on Anglos' choice of presidential candidates were consistent but fairly small, but the total effects were more substantial. Other things being equal, there was approximately a 10 percent difference, overall, between Anglo men and women in the likelihood of voting Democratic in the presidential election. The difference was similar in magnitude to those found among Hispanics and blacks.

Overall, then, gender differences were quite similar across the three groups. Many more of the Anglo coefficients were statistically significant, and the Hispanic and black coefficients were less stable across samples, but these phenomena were largely attributable to the much greater size of the Anglo samples. Generally, racial-ethnic differences in the gender gap were largest with respect to ideology, where gender appeared a little more important in explaining Anglos' attitudes than either blacks' or Hispanics'. The size of the gender gap differed little among Hispanics, blacks, and Anglos on either party identification or vote choice. Indeed, the gender gap in party identification was, contrary to our expectations, somewhat larger for blacks than for either Hispanics or Anglos. And the gender gap in vote choice was of about the same magnitude for each group (.09 among Hispanics and .10 for the other two groups).

As a more refined test of whether gender affected ideological outlook, party identification, and vote choice similarly across the three groups of voters, we fitted "constrained" models of each, the summary statistics for which are shown in the last part of Table 2. In the constrained models, the impact of gender on the three endogenous variables was held constant across the three groups in order to test the null hypothesis of no intergroup difference in the impact of gender. If the chi-square value is high and significant, it indicates that the gender effect varies across the three groups; if the value is low and nonsignificant, it indicates that the gender group is close to equivalent across groups. For two of the six models a statistically significant chi-square value emerged, indicating that the fit of the constrained model was significantly poorer than that of the original, unconstrained model in which the impact of gender was free to vary among Hispanics, blacks, and Anglos. For both instances of significant chi-square values, however, the chi square-degrees of freedom ratio was well within commonly employed bounds for an acceptable fit.[7] These low values indicated, then, that the impact of gender was essentially equal in the three racial-ethnic groups. This means that we would lose virtually nothing if we neglected to take race or ethnicity into account in summarizing the effect of gender on self-described political ideology, party identification, and vote choice.

CONCLUSIONS

Findings based on surveys conducted in conjunction with the 1980, 1984, and 1988 presidential elections provided mixed support for the hypotheses advanced above. There was a gender gap among Hispanics, as predicted. It was barely perceptible in self-described political ideology, stronger in party identification, and strongest in vote choice. As we hypothesized, the gender gap was slightly weaker among Hispanics than among Anglos, but this difference was found only in political ideology. However, in contrast to our expectation, the gender gap among blacks, at least as measured here, was as large as that between

---

[7] That is, the significance of the chi square statistic in two instances largely reflected the large size of the samples. A chi square-degrees of freedom ratio of 3:1, or even 5:1, is often used as a rule of thumb for determining when a model displays an acceptable fit (see Wheaton, Muthen, Alwin, and Summers 1977).

Hispanic men and women, and, in vote choice, as large as that between Anglo men and women. The major difference among Hispanics, blacks, and Anglos was that the gender gap in ideology was stonger for Anglos than in either of the other groups. However in terms of overall performance of the model, there was little difference in the impact of gender across the three groups.

This conclusion modifies earlier findings by Welch and Sigelman (1989) concerning the lack of a gender gap among blacks. Can we reconcile the similar size of the gender gap for blacks and Hispanics reported here with this earlier finding? Part of the answer is that Welch and Sigelman focused primarily on opinions concerning policy issues, and less on political ideology and partisan choice. Their smaller samples also made it more difficult to achieve differences that were statistically significant. So methodological differences between the two studies help account for their different conclusions. Nor should we overstate the differences between this study and that one. The size of the black gender gap uncovered here was modest, and Welch and Sigelman also observed a modest gender gap in partisan and vote choice, especially in their 1982-83 data.

There are obvious limits to this analysis of the gender gap. By relying on exit polls we maximized sample size at the expense of substantive coverage. The number of variables available for analysis was limited, so we could not consistently tap a potential gender gap on issue attitudes. And we were unable to examine differences among different segments of the Hispanic community, most notably Cuban American, Puerto Ricans, and Mexican Americans.[8] Women in these three groups differ in their labor force participation, educational level, English language proficiency, and other factors that could influence political participation (Cooney and Ortiz 1983). And although the term "Hispanic" has been a convenient census category and one used by governments, journalists, and social scientists, such usage does not make it a meaningful social construct (see Tienda and Ortiz 1986). Still, it is hard to think of any large social category that is as homogeneous as analysts who rely on survey research are forced to treat it, no matter whether the category is, for example, "blacks" or "women" or "Americans of British descent" or "Jews." Thus, even though subject to these important caveats, we trust that the findings reported here will

---

[8] As Tienda and Ortiz (1986) point out, there are 20 Hispanic national origin groups spanning three continents.

improve our understanding of the political attitudes of Latinos and, moreover, will provide an expanded baseline for further research on the gender gap in different subgroups of the American population. Especially telling in this regard should be comparisons of black and Hispanic men and women on policy issues of special concern to members of these minority communities.

REFERENCES

Abramson, Paul, John Aldrich, and David Rohde. 1989. *Continuity and Change in the 1988 Elections*. Washington, DC: Congressional Quarterly Press.

Balz, Dan. 1987. "Polling the Latino Community." In Rodolfo de la Garza, ed., *Ignored Voices: Public Opinion Polls and the Latino Community*, pp. 32–41. Austin, TX: CMAS, University of Texas.

Bean, Frank, Elizabeth H. Stephen, and Wolfgang Opitz. 1985. "The Mexican Origin Population in the United States: A Demographic Overview." In Rodolfo de la Garza, Frank D. Bean, Charles M. Bonjean, Ricardo Romo, and Rodolofo Alvarez, eds., *The Mexican American Experience: An Interdisciplinary Anthology*, pp. 79–90. Austin, TX: University of Texas Press.

Brischetto, Robert. 1987. "The 1984 Election Exit Polls." In Rodolfo de la Garza, ed., *Ignored Voices: Public Opinion Polls and the Latino Community*, pp. 76–94. Austin, TX: CMAS, University of Texas.

Brischetto, Robert, and Rodolfo de la Garza. 1983. *The Mexican American Electorate: Political Participation and Ideology*. Austin, TX: Center for Mexican American Studies and Southwest Voter Research and Education Project.

Cain, Bruce, and D. Roderick Kiewiet. 1985. "Ethnicity and Electoral Choice: Mexican American Voting Behavior in the California 30th Congressional District." In Rodolfo de la Garza, Frank D. Bean, Charles M. Bonjean, Ricardo Romo, and Rodolfo Alvarez, eds., *The Mexican American Experience: An Interdisciplinary Anthology*. Austin, TX: University of Texas Press.

Cain, Bruce, D. Roderick Kiewiet, and Carole Uhlaner. 1990. "Race, Ideology, and Economics Shape Immigrant Party Preferences." *Public Affairs Report*, Berkeley: University of California, May, pp. 8–9.

Cooney, Rosemary Santana, and Vilma Ortiz. 1983. "Nativity, National Origin, and Hispanic Female Participation in the Labor Force." *Social Science Quarterly* 64 (September): 510–23.

Darabi, Katherine, and Vilma Ortiz. 1987. "Childbearing among Young Latino Women in the United States." *American Journal of Public Health* 77 (January): 25–28.

de la Garza, Rodolfo, Robert D. Wrinkle, and Jerry L. Polinard. 1988. "Ethnicity and Policy: The Mexican American Perspective." In F. Chris Garcia, ed., *Latinos and the Political System*, pp. 426–40. Notre Dame, IN: University of Notre Dame Press.

Ebeling, Jon, Michael King, and Jim Gregg. 1988. "Political Participation in California." Unpublished study conducted for the California State Senate Office of Research. Chico, CA: California State University at Chico.

Falcon, Angelo. 1988. "Black and Latino Politics in New York City: Race and Ethnicity in a Changing Urban Context." In F. Chris Garcia, ed., *Latinos and the Political System*, pp. 171-94. Notre Dame, IN: University of Notre Dame Press.

Fitzpatrick, Joseph. 1971. *Puerto Rican Americans: The Meaning of Migration.* Englewood Cliffs, NJ: Prentice-Hall.

Frankovic, Kathleen. 1982. "Sex and Politics—New Alignments and Old Issues." *PS* 3 (Summer): 439-48.

Garcia, John A., and Carlos H. Arce. 1988. "Political Orientations and Behaviors of Chicanos: Trying to Make Sense Out of Attitudes and Participation." In F. Chris Garcia, ed., *Latinos and the Political System*, pp. 125-51. Notre Dame, IN: University of Notre Dame Press.

Grebler, Leo, Joan Moore, and Ralph Guzman. 1970. *The Mexican American People.* New York: Free Press.

Joreskog, Karl G., and Dag Sorbom. 1989. *LISREL 7: A Guide to the Program and Applications*, 2d ed. Chicago: SPSS.

Matlack, Carol. 1987. "Women at the Polls." *National Journal*, December 19, 3208-15.

Miller, Lawrence, Jerry Polinard, and Robert Wrinkle. 1984. "Attitudes toward Undocumented Workers: The Mexican-American Perspective." *Social Science Quarterly* 65 (June): 481-94.

Mitofsky, Warren, and Kathleen Frankovic. 1987. "Exit Polls and the Latino Voter." In Rodolfo de la Garza, ed., *Ignored Voices: Public Opinion Polls and the Latino Community*, pp. 118-33. Austin, TX: CMAS, University of Texas.

Ortiz, Vilma, and Katherine Fennelly. 1988. "Early Childbearing and Employment among Young Mexican Origin, Black, and White Women." *Social Science Quarterly* 69 (December): 987-95.

Page, Benjamin. 1987. "Why Polls Matter and Why Latinos are Ignored." In Rodolfo de la Garza, ed., *Ignored Voices: Public Opinion Polls and the Latino Community*, pp. 32-41. Austin, TX: CMAS, University of Texas.

Shapiro, Robert, and Harpreet Mahajan. 1986. "Gender Differences in Policy Preferences." *Public Opinion Quarterly* 50: 42-61.

Tienda, Marta, and Vilma Ortiz. 1986. "Hispanicity and the 1980 Census." *Social Science Quarterly* 67 (March): 3-20.

Uhlaner, Carole, Bruce Cain, and D. Roderick Kiewiet. 1989. "Political Participation of Ethnic Minorities in the 1980s." *Political Behavior* 11 (September): 195-232.

U.S. Department of Labor, Women's Bureau. 1989. *Facts on Working Women: Women of Hispanic Origin in the Labor Force.* No 89-1. Washington, DC, August.

Wald, Kenneth D. 1987. *Religion & Politics in the United States.* New York: St. Martin's Press.

Welch, Susan, and Lee Sigelman. 1989. "A Black Gender Gap?" *Social Science Quarterly* 70 (March): 120-33.

Wheaton, Blair, Bengt Muthen, Duane Alwin, and Gene Summers. 1977. "Assessing Reliability and Stability in Panel Models." In David Heise, ed., *Sociological Methodology 1977*. San Francisco: Jossey Bass.

Ybarra, Leonarda. 1982. "When Wives Work: The Impact on the Chicano Family." *Journal of Marriage and the Family* 44 (1): 169-78.

Zavella, Patricia. 1988. *Women's Work and Chicano Families*. Ithaca, NY: Cornell University Press.

Zinn, Maxine Baca. 1980. "Employment and Education of Mexican American Women." *Harvard Law Review* 50 (1): 47-62.

A LONGITUDINAL EXAMINATION OF POLITICAL PARTICIPATION RATES OF MEXICAN AMERICAN FEMALES

Susan A. MACMANUS, *Cleveland State University*
Charles S. BULLOCK III, *The University of Georgia*
Barbara P. GROTHE, *Cleveland State University*

> This study examines changes between 1974 and 1984 in the registration and turnout rates of Mexican American females in a small West Texas county. It also compares their participation rates to those of their male counterparts. Political participation rates of Mexican American females increased significantly over the decade and now exceed those of Mexican American males. Age, education, and women's role as agents of social change may explain the changes.

A common perception is that Mexican American females have the lowest political participation rates of any ethnic or gender group. This perception holds despite little substantiating empirical evidence comparing the registration and turnout rates of Mexican American females with Mexican American males or Anglos.[1]

Participation Theories

Numerous propositions suggest why participation rates of Mexican American women might lag behind women of other races/ethnicities and males of their own ethnicity.[2] An interactive model is most commonly cited. Mexican

---

[1] A number of factors explain the paucity of data. First, no states regularly report registration by ethnicity. Second, the focus on language minorities did not sharpen until after passage of the 1975 Amendment to the Voting Rights Act of 1965. Consequently, there are very few data on change in Mexican American registration and turnout rates over time, and none breaking these down by gender. Registration rates are defined as the percentage of the voting population who are registered. In many studies registration rates are actually registration levels (percentage of total registered voters who are of Spanish origin.)

[2] The term Mexican American is used to describe persons of Spanish origin. The overwhelming majority of Texas residents of Latin American extraction are from Mexico. Public opinion surveys have consistently shown that a high proportion of persons of Mexican origin in the Southwest label themselves Mexican Americans, although some prefer Chicano, Mexicano, Latino, or Mexican (cf. Garcia, 1981; MacManus and Cassel, 1982).

American women have been described as "twice" or "three times" a minority by a number of scholars. Melville (1980:2) stated they are "twice a minority": Mexican American women, as Mexican American, are a minority in their relationship to the Anglo American society in that they do not possess an equitable share of political and economic resources. Furthermore they possess a minority status in relation to their own brothers and husbands due to cultural norms, reinforced by Roman Catholic traditions. It is the cultural/religious dimension which distinguishes the plight of Mexican American females from black women who also suffer from racism and sexism. Mirandé and Enríquez (1979) saw "the oppression of the Chicana as threefold . . . as an ethnic minority, as a woman, and through internal oppression within her own culture" (p. 130).

Oppression as an Ethnic Minority. The lower socioeconomic status of Mexican American women relative to others (as measured by education, income, and employment) has historically depressed their propensity to participate in political organizations, register to vote, or seek elective office (Shepro, 1980). The importance of education and employment in transmitting participatory skills, particularly to language minorities, has also been documented (cf. Lamare, 1974). Shepro (1980) noted that the inability to read and write English creates an additional barrier for approximately 30 percent of the Chicanas over 25 years of age.

Within-Ethnicity Oppression. The notion that Mexican American women are passive and subordinate is widely cited. As noted by Barragán (1980), "Within her Hispanic minority group, she has been relegated traditionally to a subordinate position because of the dual system of right and responsibilities within the Hispanic culture. . . . The male . . . assumes the dominating role in relationships with the Hispanic woman, particularly in matters outside the home, such as *politics,* education, and employment" (p. 391, emphasis added).

Yet another theory of within-ethnicity oppression perceives the plight of women slightly more optimistically, but still as restricted. Baca Zinn (1975) noted that because "the Chicano movement calls for change not only in conditions which are externally imposed by the dominant society, but also in Chicano behavior . . . Chicanas often find themselves in the ambiguous position of consciously striving to alter traditional subordinate roles while at the same time having to defend Chicano cultural conditions" (p. 21). Mason (1980) concurred with this assessment, noting that "the Chicano movement is concerned to preserve some aspects of tradition in an attempt to create new social forms—including sex roles—within the context of traditional institutions" (p. 102).

The traditional restrictive view of the status of Mexican American women has recently been attacked as a myth (Mirandé and Enríquez, 1979; Shepro,

241

1980). Shepro (1980) criticized the literature for defining the Mexican American female "as a passive, male-dominated creature: at worst the absolute subject of the male master; and at best the reflection of the male's definition of her, the protection of his ego, and/or his prendedor" (p. 125). She maintained that the literature has ignored the Mexican American woman's history as a revolutionary woman and an active agent of social change.

The key role that females play as agents of change and upward mobility within the family is well recognized (Garcia, 1971; Howell-Martinez, 1982). Banfield (1974) too noted that "the lower-class mother . . . but not the father . . . is often very much concerned about the children's welfare. . . . As a rule, it is on the mother, or mother substitute, that efforts to improve the home environment should concentrate" (p. 255). The high priority that Mexican American mothers have increasingly put on education for their children (Romo, 1984) may produce greater political participatory rates of Mexican American females, especially in school board elections (Garcia, 1979).

Unfortunately, there have been virtually no empirical examinations of voter registration or turnout rates of Mexican American females, only of Mexican Americans as a whole. Even the classic works on women and politics have failed to contrast levels of participation by race and ethnicity (cf. Lansing, 1974, and Sapiro, 1983). This lacuna exists because data on registration and turnout rates broken down by ethnicity and gender are extremely difficult to generate, especially across time.

The Study

This research note examines change in the registration and turnout rates of Mexican American females between 1974 and 1984 in one West Texas county. While the generalizability of the results is limited, the longitudinal data here are a first effort to assess trends in participation, controlling for ethnicity and gender. If lower rates of participation among Mexican American women are indeed now a myth, then such a study may record a narrowing in the gaps between participation rates of Mexican American females and other groups (cf. Orum et al., 1974, and Howell-Martinez, 1982). We hypothesize that the participation rates of Mexican American females, while previously lower than those of Mexican American males, have narrowed over time. We also expect that Mexican American participation will now more closely approximate that of Anglos.

The setting is Sutton County in West Texas, with a 1970 population of 3,175 (55 percent Mexican American) and a 1980 population of 5,130 (40 percent Mexican American).[3] Registration and turnout rate data for 1974 are based on

---

[3] The Anglo population grew at a more rapid pace between 1970 and 1980 due to the oil boom. Sutton County's economy is largely dominated by the petrochemical industry, which has supplanted ranching. Unfortunately, we do not have data on the proportion of Sutton County Mexican

a 10 percent sample of the voter registration lists, from which we determined gender and ethnicity with turnout figures based on the general election participation.[4] Turnout data for 1984 came from a full enumeration of voters in the school board election. The ethnicity of the registrants and voters was determined through a long, tedious process.[5] Voting age population figures (the base in calculating the registration rate) were extracted from the *U.S. Census of the Population.*

The Findings

Changes in Registration Rates. Between 1974 and 1984, the registration rate of Mexican American females in Sutton County more than doubled, 29 percent to 62 percent (+114 percent). (See Table 1.) Even more significantly, their participation relative to Mexican American males increased drastically. In 1974 female participation rates were barely half that of males (29 versus 49 percent), but by 1984 Mexican American female registration votes *exceeded* those of their male counterparts (62 versus 57 percent), a finding contrary to our hypothesis. A comparison of these 1984 figures with Anglos (67 percent for Anglo females; 64 percent for Anglo males) shows that Mexican American registration rates now closely resemble Anglo rates, a phenomenon also reported by Wrinkle and Miller (1984).[6]

Changes in Turnout Rates. The sharp increase in female Mexican American registration rates was also reflected in changes in turnout. (See Table 1.) In 1974 only 12 percent of those eligible actually voted; by 1984 the figure had more than tripled to 51 percent (+325 percent).[7] Likewise, whereas their turnout rates lagged behind Mexican American men in 1974 (12 versus 19 percent), they exceed the males by 1984 (51 versus 44 percent). The 1984 sexual difference is slightly larger than the 4.3 point difference reported by Page (1982:2) based on national-level data from the Census Bureau's Current Population Reports series. Combining our data with Page's, a trend emerges.

Americans who are not citizens. Based on changes in the proportion foreign-born between 1970 and 1980 (12.6 to 15.5 percent), we assume that the percentage has increased, which makes increases in participation rates even more dramatic.

[4] The 10 percent sample, while not optimal, at least offers us a pre-1975 estimate of Mexican American registration and turnout rates by gender. The registration books for 1974 were brought out of storage by the county clerk for our brief inspection. We did not have the time or resources to make copies of these documents, which would have permitted use of the universe of registrants and voters.

[5] Three individuals independently went through the list of registrants and voters and identified each person's ethnicity and gender. One of these individuals was a longtime Sutton County school board employee.

[6] Similar data for 1983 show the same pattern.

[7] The patterns for the 1974 general election presented here are similar to those for the 1972 general election and the primaries in those two years.

TABLE 1

Mexican American Registration and Turnout Rates by Gender, Sutton County, Texas, 1974 and 1984 Elections

	1974		1984		Percent Change	
	Males	Females	Males	Females	Males	Females
Registration rate (%)	49*	29	57*	62	16	114
Turnout rate (%)	19	12	44	51	132	325

Sources: Figures for 1974 are based on a 10 percent sample of voter registration cards from sign-in sheets. Figures for 1984 are based on the universe of actual voters from sign-in sheets; the number of registered voters is from the Texas Secretary of State.

Notes: The registration rate is calculated by dividing the number of registered voters by the number of persons of voting age. The 1974 number of persons of voting age is based on the 1970 U.S. Census data for number of persons 18 years of age and older. The 1984 number of persons of voting age is based on the 1980 U.S. Census data for number of persons 19 years of age and older. The turnout rate is calculated by dividing the number of actual voters by the number of registered voters.

*Significant difference ($p < .05$) for males and females on this variable, using z test for proportion.

In 1974, turnout of Mexican American females was 7 points lower than that of Mexican American males; in 1976, the disparity was reduced to 1 point; by 1980 Mexican American females' turnout exceeded the turnout of their male counterparts by 4 points and this difference grew to 7 points in 1984. The increased registration and turnout observed for Mexican American females helps account for their impressive gains in the ranks of elected officials (Pachon, 1985). By 1984, 15 percent of the Hispanic elected officials were women, up sharply from the 1970s when the National Association of Latino Elected and Appointed Officials (NALEO) began collecting such data. In turn, their gains may have further stimulated this group's participation.

Discussion

There are several explanations for the increase in the political participation rates of Mexican American females in this Texas county over a single decade. The most obvious is socioeconomic, namely improvement in the educational level of Hispanic females (Barragán, 1980). As shown in Table 2, the percentage of Mexican American females who graduated from high school increased from 18.6 percent (1970) to 22.6 percent (1980). (The national average was 23.1 percent.) In contrast, the graduation rate of Mexican American males changed very little, decreasing from 16.8 to 16.2 percent. As previous research has shown, education is the single most important factor in turnout (Wolfinger and Rosenstone, 1980:17). The more ethnic groups are assimilated into mainstream American society, the more their political participation rates reflect those of mainstream groups (cf. Welch, 1977, and Nelson, 1979).

TABLE 2

Socioeconomic Status by Ethnicity and Gender, Sutton County, Texas, 1970 and 1980

	1970				1980			
	Mexican Americans		Non-Mexican Americans		Mexican Americans		Non-Mexican Americans	
	Males	Females	Males	Females	Males	Females	Males	Females
Percent high school graduates	16.8	18.6	57.1	68.5	16.2	22.6	81.6	79.3
Population size	876	879	645	775	1,022	1,049	1,542	1,517
Percent aged 15–34	25.7	25.6	21.1	26.2	36.4	40.2	20.2	21.6

SOURCES: Figures for 1970 are calculated from U.S. Bureau of the Census, *Census of Population, 1970*, vol. 1, *Characteristics of the Population*, pt. 45 (Texas). Figures for 1980 are calculated from U.S. Bureau of the Census, *Census of Population, 1980*, *Characteristics of the Population, General Social and Economic Characteristics and Summary Characteristics for Governmental Units*, pt. 45 (Texas).

Another socioeconomic explanation emphasizes age. Hispanic women are proportionately younger than Hispanic men, with the gap increasing between 1970 and 1980. (See Table 2.) As noted by de la Garza and Brischetto (1983), younger Mexican Americans (the fastest growing cohort of the Hispanic population) face fewer discriminatory obstacles, are better educated, have higher-status jobs and higher incomes, and are less likely to be language-bound (monolingual) than the older generations. As a consequence, younger Mexican Americans (more women than men) are more likely to be politically involved than their ancestors. The higher participation rates of young Mexican American women may also be related to their role as agents of social change, particularly in light of the large number of children born to this cohort and the consequent determination of these women to expand and protect educational opportunities for their offspring.

Another plausible explanation is more culturally based. Mexican American women in their role as "revolutionaries" have chosen the mainstream avenue (traditional political participation) as opposed to more radical paths (Shepro, 1980). The choice of the mainstream route has allowed them to alter their traditional sex roles and at the same time to promote the Mexican American culture, the primary concern of Baca Zinn (1975) which was stated earlier in this article. Also as noted by Ambrecht and Pachon (1974) and Nelson (1979), increased ethnic political consciousness tightens communal bonds and this stimulates the group's participation in spite of low socioeconomic status.

It is possible that the greater turnout of Mexican American females that we observed in school board elections may be related to their role as agents of social change and does not extend to other types of offices. As noted, heavy interest in school politics is related to their desire to protect and enhance opportunities for upward social mobility for the next generation of children as well as for themselves through continuing education programs (Mirandé and Enríquez, 1979). However, since Page (1982) found turnout of Mexican American females to be greater than their male counterparts' turnout in the 1980 presidential election, the fact that we are studying a school board election may have no more than a marginal effect.

In summary, a number of theories might explain the sharp increase in the political participation rates of Mexican American females in Sutton County, Texas, between 1974 and 1984. Unfortunately, we do not have the data necessary to determine which theory is correct or the degree to which the theories are mutually exclusive. Such determinations should be the focus of future research as more political participation data broken down by ethnicity and gender become available. Meanwhile, in light of the parity Mexican American females have achieved with their male counterparts, educators and the media should refrain from strong statements which perpetuate the stereotypical image of Mexican American females as the least participatory politically of all racial, ethnic, and gender groups. SSQ

REFERENCES

Ambrecht, Biliana C. S., and Harry P. Pachon. 1974. "Ethnic Mobilization in a Mexican-American Community: An Exploratory Study of East Los Angeles, 1965–1972," *Western Political Quarterly*, 27 (September):500–519.

Baca Zinn, Maxine. 1975. "Political Familism: Toward Sex Role Equality in Chicano Families," *Aztlan*, 6:13–26.

Banfield, Edward C. 1974. *The Un-heavenly City Revisited* (Boston: Little, Brown).

Barragán, Polly Baca. 1980. "The Lack of Political Involvement of Hispanic Women as It Relates to Their Educational Background and Occupational Opportunities," in National Institute of Education, *Conference on the Educational and Occupational Needs of Hispanic Women* (Washington, D.C.: NIE, September): pp. 39–46.

de la Garza, Rodolfo O., and Robert R. Brischetto. 1983. *The Mexican American Electorate: A Demographic Profile*. Occasional Paper No. 1 (San Antonio: Southwest Voter Registration Drive and the Center for Mexican American Studies).

García, F. Chris. 1971. *Political Socialization of Chicano Children* (New York: Free Press).

Garcia, John A. 1979. "An Analysis of Chicano and Anglo Electoral Patterns in School Board Elections," *Ethnicity*, 6 (June):168–83.

———. 1981. "Yo Soy Mexicano . . . : Self-Identity and Sociodemographic Correlates," *Social Science Quarterly*, 62 (March):88–98.

Howell-Martinez, Vicky. 1982. "The Influence of Gender Roles on Political Socialization: An Experimental Study of Mexican-American Children," *Women & Politics*, 2 (Fall):33–46.

Lamare, J. W. 1974. "Language, Environment, and the Political Socialization of Mexican-American Children," in R. Niemi, ed., *The Politics of Future Citizens* (San Francisco: Jossey-Bass): pp. 63–82.

Lansing, Marjorie. 1974. "The American Woman: Voter and Activist," in Jane S. Jacquette, ed., *Women in Politics* (New York: Wiley): pp. 5–24.

MacManus, Susan A., and Carol A. Cassel. 1982. "Mexican Americans in City Politics: Participation, Representation, and Policy Preferences," *Urban Interest*, 4 (Spring):57–69.

Mason, Terry. 1980. "Symbolic Strategies for Change: A Discussion of the Chicana Women's Movement," in Margarita B. Melville, ed., *Twice a Minority* (St. Louis: C. V. Mosby): pp. 95–107.

Melville, Margarita B., ed. 1980. *Twice a Minority: Mexican American Women*. (St. Louis: C. V. Mosby).

Mirandé, Alfredo, and Evangelina Enríquez. 1979. *La Chicana: The Mexican American Woman* (Chicago: University of Chicago Press). (Especially chap. 5 [Work, Education] and chap. 7 [Feminism].)

Nelson, Dale C. 1979. "Ethnicity and Socioeconomic Status as Sources of Participation: The Case for Ethnic Political Culture," *American Political Science Review*, 73 (December):1024–38.

Orum, Anthony, Roberta Cohen, Sheri Grassmuck, and Amy Orum. 1974. "Sex, Socialization, and Politics," *American Sociological Review*, 39 (April):197–209.

Pachon, Harry. 1985. Quoted in Kathryn Baker, "Texas Elected More Hispanics in 1984 Than Any Other State," *Houston Chronicle*, 29 September.

Page, Elizabeth I. 1982. "The Voting Behavior of Mexican Americans: Turnout." Paper presented at the annual meeting of the Southwest Political Science Association, San Antonio, Texas, 17–20 March.

Romo, Harriet. 1984. "The Mexican Origin Population's Differing Perceptions of Their Children's Schooling," *Social Science Quarterly*, 65 (June):635-50.

Sapiro, Virginia. 1983. *The Political Integration of Women: Roles, Socialization, and Politics* (Chicago: University of Illinois Press).

Shepro, Theresa Aragón. 1980. "Impediments to Hispanic Women Organizing," in National Institute of Education, *Conference on the Educational and Occupational Needs of Hispanic Women* (Washington, D.C.: NIE, September): pp. 117-37.

Welch, Susan. 1977. "Women as Political Animals? A Test of Some Explanations for Male-Female Political Participation Differences," *American Journal of Political Science*, 21 (November):711-30.

Wolfinger, Raymond E., and Steven J. Rosenstone. 1980. *Who Votes?* (New Haven: Yale University Press).

Wrinkle, Robert D., and Lawrence W. Miller. 1984. "A Note on Mexican American Voter Registration and Turnout," *Social Science Quarterly*, 65 (June):308-14.

A COMPARISON OF BLACK AND MEXICAN AMERICAN VOTERS IN DENVER: ASSERTIVE VERSUS ACQUIESCENT POLITICAL ORIENTATIONS AND VOTING BEHAVIOR IN AN URBAN ELECTORATE

NICHOLAS P. LOVRICH, JR., *De Pauw University*
and
OTWIN MARENIN, *Ahmadu Bello University*

POLITICAL action is a response to a situation — to its reality and to its perception. The two need not coincide. Action is based as much on subjective image as objective reality. Lack of information, error in judgment, ideology, and false consciousness are all terms commonly used to characterize this potential incongruence between objective and subjective realities.[1]

Blacks and Mexican Americans, America's two most numerous minorities, pose a case in point of the salience of the subjective dimension mediating between objective conditions and political behavior. Blacks and Mexican Americans, to a considerable degree, exist in a similar, objectively depressed situation when contrasted with the Anglo majority.[2] Further, both groups have a number of active organizations and self-designated leaders that labor to improve the condition of their people;[3] both groups have similarly enjoyed the benefit of geographical concentration of population which creates the potential for electoral power in the American political system;[4] and both groups have suffered the pains of discrimination by the dominant Anglo majority.[5]

In spite of this similarity of condition, however, blacks and Mexican Americans have reacted, through the 1960s and early 1970s in particular, very differently to their shared conditions. Levy and Kramer point out, for example, in their analysis of electoral power among American ethnic groups, that "electoral inroads are coming with great frequency and blacks, North and South, believe that black

---

[1] A most sensitive discussion of this potential incongruence, and its meaning for political behavior, can be found in Murray Edelman, *The Symbolic Uses of Politics* (Chicago: University of Illinois Press, 1964), in particular Chapter 2, "Symbols and Political Quiescence," pp. 22–43.

[2] Leo Grebler, Joan W. Moore, and Ralph C. Guzman, "Ghettos and Barrios," in Clifford Snyder, ed., *Viewpoints: Red and Yellow, Black and Brown* (Minneapolis: Winston Press, 1972), pp. 81–96.

[3] For an interesting collection of essays describing the exploits and viewpoints of Mexican American leaders such as Cesar Chavez, Reies Lopez Tijerina, Corky Gonzales, and José Angel Gutierrez see: Tony Castro, *Chicano Power* (New York: Dutton, 1974), pp. 79–184. For an extensive summary of black political mobilization through the late 1960s see: *Congressional Quarterly, Revolution in Civil Rights*, 3rd Ed. (Washington, D.C.: Congressional Quarterly Service, 1967). For an interesting collection of essays reflecting the viewpoints and activities of black leaders such as Stokley Carmichael, Malcolm X, Eldridge Cleaver, James Farmer, Julian Bond, and Martin Luther King, Jr., see: Douglas A. Hughes, ed., *From a Black Perspective: Contemporary Black Essays* (New York: Holt, Rinehart & Winston, 1970).

[4] The U.S. black population is concentrated in the South and in the major cities of the Northeast and Midwest (according to the 1970 census 23 percent of the people living in America's central cities are black: Source, Mark R. Levy and Michael S. Kramer, *The Ethnic Factor: How America's Minorities Decide Elections* [New York: Simon & Schuster, 1972], p. 68) while the Mexican American population is concentrated mainly in California and the Southwest. On the distribution of Mexican Americans see: Bureau of the Census, U.S. Department of Commerce, *Subject Reports: Persons of Spanish Surname* (Washington, D.C.: U.S. G.P.O., 1973).

[5] Alphonso Pinkney, "Prejudice Toward Mexican and Negro Americans: A Comparison," in John H. Burma, ed., *Mexican-Americans in the United States* (Cambridge: Schenkman Pub. Co., 1970), pp. 73–80.

power is theirs for the taking. The political fact is clear: black Americans are finally using the electoral process as the way to equality in the United States."[6] In marked contrast to this assertive image of black political action they describe the Mexican American community in these terms: "On balance, Chicano voters seem to lack the political acuity which marks the Southern black voter. Years of political neglect have made the Chicano voter apathetic.... The Chicano vote of the Southwest has a long way to go before it can claim to be a powerful, informed and influential voting bloc."[7]

This characterization of the Mexican American community is at some variance with the image of political assertiveness suggested by numerous recent studies which describe Chicanos as "an awakened minority,"[8] an emergent political power,[9] or in the process of expressing the "beginnings of bronze power."[10] The aparent contradictory images may both be valid, however. There is no doubt that the Mexican American community is engaged in a process of change and reorientation as claimed by the scholars listed above,[11] but *as a voting bloc* the "Chicano power" portrayed above is not evident. Levy and Kramer point out, for instance, that despite all of the public attention focused upon Mexican American political concerns in recent years the rate of political participation among Mexican Americans has steadily *declined* since the high mark of 1960.[12]

This study seeks to investigate the contrasting political behavior of black and Mexican American voters in the setting of local politics in Denver, Colorado. It seeks to explain the differing character of political activity in terms of the differing subjective interpretations of similar objective social realities which the two ethnic communities entertain. The study makes use of voting results, a recent attitude survey, and selected supporting studies of Denver politics to develop this explanation.

Minority Representation on the Denver City Council: Black and Chicano Stakes in a Local Election

Prior to the municipal elections of 1971 the Denver City Council and the Denver Election Commission labored to design a plan for the redistricting of the City Council electorate which would give a better degree of representation to Denver's substantial minority population. According to the 1970 Census more than a quarter of Denver's population is of minority ethnicity: Mexican Americans constitute 17 percent of the city's population, while blacks make up some 9 percent.[13]

In an attempt to provide for enhancement of political representation for the city's minority communities a redistricting reform was devised which involved

---

[6] *The Ethnic Factor*, p. 72.
[7] Ibid., p. 85.
[8] Manuel P. Servin, ed., *An Awakened Minority: The Mexican Americans*, 2nd ed. (Beverly Hills: Glencoe Press, 1970).
[9] Tony Castro, *Chicano Power: The Emergence of Mexican America* (New York: Dutton & Co., 1974).
[10] Renato Rosaldo et al., *Chicano: The Beginnings of Bronze Power* (New York: William Morrow & Co., 1974) [abridged ed.]. See also Parker Frisbie, "Militancy Among Mexican American High School Students," *Social Science Quarterly* 53 (March 1973): 865–83 and Joseph L. Love, "La Raza: Mexican Americans in Rebellion," *Society* 6 (February 1969): 1–7.
[11] One example is the capture of local government by a well-organized and politically efficacious La Raza Unida party movement in Crystal City, Texas. See: John Staples Shockley, *Chicano Revolt in a Texas Town* (South Bend: University of Notre Dame Press, 1974).
[12] *The Ethnic Factor*, p. 22.
[13] Bureau of the Census, U.S. Department of Commerce, *Census Tracts: Denver, Colorado SMSA* (Washington, D.C.: U.S. G.P.O., 1972).

eleven councilmanic districts — two of which were to contain the greatest concentrations of black neighborhoods, and two of which were to contain the greatest concentrations of Mexican American areas. Table 1 reports the estimated ethnic composition of these four "minority" council districts.[14]

TABLE 1: ESTIMATED ETHNIC COMPOSITION OF
DENVER CITY COUNCIL DISTRICTS 3, 9, 8 AND 11

	ANGLOS		SPANISH SURNAME		BLACKS	
	#	%	#	%	#	%
District 3	26,115	58	18,505	41	608	01
District 9	23,226	48	24,807	51	672	01
District 8	15,233	36	10,617	25	16,755	39
District 11	18,619	41	3,858	09	22,654	50

The General Municipal Election of May 1971 produced some results not anticipated by the city reformers. In the black districts both minority candidates won by large majorities (Councilmen Caldwell and Roberts, in districts 8 and 11, respectively). However, in the Mexican American districts the presence of a large field of minority candidates caused a division of the Mexican American vote, hence necessitating a run-off election in both districts 3 and 9. The results of the general election are reported in Table 2. The division of the vote between Anglo and Mexican American candidates was very nearly even in district 3, and in district 9 the votes cast for Mexican American candidates exceeded those of the Anglos by

TABLE 2: GENERAL ELECTION VOTE DISTRIBUTION
IN THE HEAVILY MINORITY COUNCIL DISTRICTS

District 3		District 9	
Richard "Dick" Farrow	1,284	Daniel P. Campbell	1,168
Joe Clarence Medina	930	Eugene "Geno" Di Manna	2,840
J. Ivan Rosenberg	2,639	Daniel R. Esquibel	151
Melvin Salgo	297	Peter E. Garcia	1,807
Sam Sandos	1,569	David Hermosillo	198
Ed Vigil	1,004	Arcadio "Arch" Prado	190
	7,723	Paul Sandoval	1,473
		John M. Zapien	934
			8,761

Anglo Candidates
3,923 — 51%

Mexican American Candidates
3,800 — 49%

Anglo Candidates
4,008 — 46%

Mexican American Candidates
4,753 — 54%

District 8		District 11	
Elvin Caldwell	5,417	Claude E. Archie	1,787
Lewis C. Rhone	1,529	William "Bill" Roberts	6,526
	6,946		8,313

[14] Data taken from Denver Regional Council of Governments, *Profile of the Denver Region, 1960–1970* (Denver, DRCOG, 1973), Table 2A. The existence of these "ethnic" districts became an issue before the 1975 election period. The Councilmen from the two Mexican American districts are especially supportive of plans to redistrict council boundaries in a manner which would reduce the proportion of Mexican American voters in their districts. Mexican American residents of Denver's Westside have protested these plans as veiled attempts to "disenfranchise" them. See: Suzanne Weiss, "Two Redistricting Plans are Rejected," *Rocky Mountain News*, December 24, 1974, and Norm Udevitz, "Council Backs Off on District Shifts," *Denver Post*, December 31, 1974.

a margin of 8 percent. The run-off election of June involved the pairing of an Anglo and a Mexican American candidate in both districts. The results of those elections (reported in Table 3) again proved highly surprising. The *Anglo* candidates won both elections!

The end result, then, of the minority political representation plan was to gain the election of two black City Councilmen to represent the 9 percent of the city's population which is black, but to have no Mexican American City Councilmen to represent the 17 percent of the city's population which is Mexican American.

TABLE 3: RUN-OFF MUNICIPAL ELECTION VOTE DISTRIBUTION IN DISTRICTS 3 AND 9

District 3			District 9		
J. Ivan Rosenberg	3,875	54%	Eugene "Geno" Di Manna	4,339	51%
Sam Sandos	3,339	46%	Peter E. Garcia	4,104	49%
	7,214			8,443	

EXPLANATIONS OF UNEXPECTED RESULTS: REGISTRATION AND TURNOUT

One dimension of the problem of the failure of Mexican American candidates to win their elections stems from the lower rates of registration and turnout typical of their districts. Whereas the average registration of Anglo districts is 18,946[15] voters, the average for the Mexican American districts is 13,177. This fact could mean that though these districts contain sizable potential Mexican American electorates, a significant portion of those electorates may remain ineligible for participation. Furthermore, the possibility exists that within each district there may exist a differential between the rate of registration of minority and Anglo precincts.

In order to test these and other aspects of electoral behavior in these two districts, five predominantly Anglo and five predominantly Mexican American precincts were chosen for comparison from districts 3 and 9 (Table 4 matches census tracts with precinct boundaries as closely as possible to estimate ethnicity distributions within the selected precincts). In both districts the five Anglo precincts contain significantly more voters than the five corresponding minority precincts (3,946 to 3,436), indicating that the same differential of registration may be operating within as well as across districts. This conclusion must be a guarded one, for precincts do vary somewhat in size, but attempts were made to select precincts of the same size in the original matching of minority and Anglo precincts.

Somewhat strong conclusions can be drawn from the turnout data from these precincts. In district 3 the differential in turnout between the five Anglo and five Mexican American precincts is 19 percent, and in district 9 it is 3 percent for the general election, and 14 percent and 4 percent, respectively, for the run-off. The turnout differential is large in both elections in district 3, indicating that the narrow vote in that district might well have been reversed had groups interested in the election of Mexican American candidates done a more thorough job of registering and turning out their "natural" electorate. In district 9, however, the registration-turnout argument is not really a satisfactory explanation of the vote. Given the large concentration of Mexican Americans in that district (approximately 51 percent of the population), and the small differential of voting turnout, it appears that additional explanatory factors must be investigated.

An investigation of the vote distribution in the general and run-off elections in the five selected Anglo and Mexican American precincts in districts 3 and 9

TABLE 4: ESTIMATED ETHNIC COMPOSITION OF THE
SELECTED ANGLO AND MEXICAN AMERICAN PRECINCTS

DISTRICT 3

	Mexican American Precincts 711, 712, 208, 217 and 218		Anglo Precincts 313, 315, 319, 320 and 322	
Census Tracts	8.00	7.02	9.02	9.03
% Spanish Surname	71%	53%	26%	29%

DISTRICT 9

	Mexican American Precincts 608, 612, 710, 713 and 717		Anglo Precincts 605, 606, 611, 613 and 610	
Census Tracts	11.01	19.00	2.01	4.01
% Spanish Surname	62%	79%	16%	34%

reveals that the Mexican American vote was far from a solid "ethnic bloc."[16] In district 3 the Anglo candidate was able to average 45 percent of the vote in the five selected Mexican American precincts in the general election, while simultaneously winning an average of 56 percent of the vote in the five selected Anglo precincts. The pattern is similar for district 9: the Anglo candidate averaged a significant 35 percent of the vote in his five selected Mexican American precincts, and he scored an average of 61 percent of the vote in his Anglo precincts. For both candidates it was necessary to win a significant portion of the Mexican American vote in order to win election to office. This they were able to accomplish, at least as judged from these selected precincts in their districts.[17]

The important question now becomes, "Why didn't more Mexican American voters support the Mexican American candidate in a pairing of Anglo and Mexican American politicians?" An insight into the answer to this question may be gained from an analysis of the responses given by 150 Spanish-surname voters (voters defined as individuals who were recorded in precinct books as having voted in the 1971 city election) selected from the ten Mexican American precincts under study here to a series of attitude items administered by the Denver Urban Observatory.[18] One of the items on the Urban Observatory survey of particular relevance was the following: "Do you agree or disagree with the statement that any Mexican American City Councilman would be better for this district than an Anglo Councilman?" Only a narrow majority (51 percent) of the 150 Mexican American voters interviewed agreed with this statement. From this finding it might well be concluded that in addition to being Mexican American, an "ethnic" candidate must also have

---

[15] Figures on registration and calculations of turnout for the May 1971 municipal election are based upon tabulated actual vote (recorded at the Denver Election Commission) divided by the registered vote as of the Commission's final audit of April 28, 1971.

[16] In contrast, see the following study of bloc voting by blacks: Joyce Gelb, "Black Power in Electoral Politics: A Case Study and Comparative Analysis," Polity 6 (Summer 1974): 500–527.

[17] The authors are aware of the possible "ecological fallacy" which plagues attempts to explain individual group behavior through the observation of mixed aggregate units. The conclusions drawn here are meant as suggestive rather than conclusive statements. See: W. S. Robinson, "Ecological Correlations and the Behavior of Individuals," American Sociological Review 15 (June 1950): 351–57 and John L. Hammond, Jr., "Two Sources of Error in Ecological Correlations," American Sociological Review 38 (December 1973): 764–77.

[18] The Denver Urban Observatory survey included total ethnic matching of interviewers and respondents. On this question of interviewer ethnicity effects see: Donald M. Freeman, "A Note on Interviewing Mexican-Americans," Social Science Quarterly 49 (March 1969): 909–18 and James Ledvinka, "The Intrusion of Race: Black Responses to the White Observer," Social Science Quarterly 52 (March 1972), 907–20. For a full account of the Denver Urban Observatory survey see: Nicholas P. Lovrich, Jr., and G. Thomas Taylor, Majority-Minority Citizen Voter Attitudes in Denver (Denver: Denver Urban Observatory, 1973).

some broad issue appeal beyond ethnicity to win election to office among his or her own people.

The Denver Urban Observatory study also included an analysis of 500 Anglo voters from 100 percent white neighborhoods, and 150 black voters residing in ten high-concentration black precincts in the two black districts mentioned previously. A comparison of the responses of the black and Mexican American voters interviewed will help us understand the unexpected electoral behavior of the Mexican American voter.

BLACK AND MEXICAN AMERICAN VOTERS: UNIFIED AND ASSERTIVE VERSUS DIVIDED AND ACQUIESCENT POLITICAL ORIENTATIONS

A discussion of attitudes and identifications among black and Mexican American voters must be prefaced by a description of the socioeconomic condition of life for Denver's majority and minority populations. Table 5 reports the SES characteristics for the Anglo, black and Mexican American voters interviewed. The data of Table 5 indicate that Denver is similar to many other cities in the U.S. in that black and Chicano citizens occupy the lower reaches of all three class ladders, with blacks almost equidistant to the white majority and the Mexican American minority. The Mexican Americans interviewed were considerably poorer, more

TABLE 5: DEMOGRAPHIC CHARACTERISTICS OF VOTER SAMPLE AND DENVER SMSA

Family Income	DENVER VOTER SAMPLE Under $6,000	$6,000-8,999	$9,000+	N.A.
(150) Mexican Americans	46% (69)	16% (24)	21% (31)	17% (26)
(150) Blacks	14 (21)	15 (22)	36 (53)	36 (54)
(500) Anglos	12 (61)	8 (38)	70 (347)	11 (54)

Occupation	Blue Collar	White Collar	No Answer	
Mexican Americans	57% (85)	14% (23)	28% (42)	
Blacks	51 (76)	37 (56)	12 (18)	
Anglos	32 (159)	64 (317)	5 (24)	

Education	8 Grades or Less	Some or All High School	Some College or More	N.A.
Mexican Americans	51% (76)	44% (66)	6% (8)	0% (0)
Blacks	13 (19)	46 (69)	38 (58)	3 (4)
Anglos	7 (35)	40 (199)	52 (263)	1 (3)

Family Income	DENVER SMSA* Under $6,000	$6,000-8,999	$9,000+
Mexican Americans in Tracts with 400 Spanish Surname	31%	27%	42%
Blacks in Tracts with 400 Negroes	38	23	39
Total SMSA	19	19	62

Occupation	Blue Collar	White Collar	
Mexican Americans	62%	38%	
Blacks	61	39	
All SMSA	21	79	

Education	8 Grades or Less	Some or All High School	Some College or More
Mexican Americans	36%	50%	14%
Blacks	22	58	21
All SMSA	17	51	33

* Data calculated from *Census Tracts: Denver, Colorado SMSA*, Tables P-1, P-2, P-5, P-6, P-7, and P-8.

heavily working class, and less well educated than even the disadvantaged blacks of Denver.

A review of these statistics might reasonably lead one to anticipate a similarity of orientations toward certain sociopolitical questions: one might assume that the poor and oppressed have a strong incentive to band together for their common interests and hence would display a marked desire for unity within the ethnic subgroup; one might assume that the disadvantaged ethnic communities would display a strong degree of dissatisfaction with the educational, occupational, and class-stratified housing systems which have relegated them to below average conditions; one might assume that these two ethnic communities might share at least a moderate interest in political affairs and seek membership in community associations; and finally one might well assume that the disadvantaged could view the use of violence for the betterment of community conditions with some acceptance.[19] Tables 6 and 7 report findings from the Denver Urban Observatory survey on each of thees questions.

In each case under consideration the black voters interviewed expressed a more "rational"[20] or ideologically expected subjective evaluation of social and political life. On the question of unity of identification it can be seen from the data presented in Table 6 that there is a much greater degree of agreement on self-appellation among black voters than among Mexican American citizens. Whereas the black voters interviewed indicated strong agreement on two terms — 52 percent expressed a preference for BLACK, and 29 percent selected Negro — the Mexican American voters interviewed had no such consensus. Among Mexican American voters many distinct terms appear to have some frequency of use — Chicano, Mexican, Mexican American, Hispano, Spanish and Spanish American all have numerous adherents.[21] No one or two terms enjoy predominance; the term of greatest current public attention — Chicano — was particularly weak in its appeal to the voters interviewed.

On the question of satisfaction with the educational, occupational, and housing conditions of their ethnic group blacks are again more reflective of the expected orientations of disadvantaged people than are the Mexican Americans. Despite the objective facts that blacks have fared much better in the educational and occupational systems of Denver than have Mexican Americans, the black voters interviewed indicated a more critical subjective evaluation of their condition than the Mexican Americans surveyed.

On the question of political interest and community involvement it is once more clear that the black voters interviewed were much more reflective of an "awakened" minority than were the Mexican Americans. Blacks are more likely to report having paid attention to governmental affairs, more likely to report one or more associational memberships, and much more likely to report a "liberal" ideological self-identification. Interestingly, fully 41 percent of the Mexican American voters interviewed refused to apply any of the ideological self-identificational terms (left wing, liberal, conservative, right wing, other [including moderate]) offered.

Finally, on the matter of the possible use of violence for the demonstration of need for remedial action the black voters interviewed were far more willing to believe in the efficacy of violent tactics than the more highly disadvantaged

---

[19] Robert M. Fogelson, *Violence as Protest: A Study of Riots in the Ghetto* (Garden City: Anchor, 1971).

[20] Robert L. Harris, Jr. "Study of Minority Response to Oppression: Importance of the Minority's Ideology," *Journal of Human Relations* 20 (3rd Quarter 1972): 317–25.

[21] Armando Gutierrez and Herbert Hirsch, "The Militant Challenge to the American Ethos: 'Chicanos' and 'Mexican Americans,'" *Social Science Quarterly* 53 (March 1973): 830–45.

Black and Mexican Voters in Denver 291

TABLE 6: ETHNIC SELF-IDENTIFICATION FOR BLACK AND MEXICAN AMERICAN VOTERS

Which of the following terms — Mexican American, Chicano, Hispano or Mexican — would you normally use?			Which of the following terms — Black, Afro-American, Negro or Colored — would you normally use?		
Label	#	%	Label	#	%
Chicano	15	10	Black	78	52
Mexican	32	21	Afro-American	9	6
Mexican American	23	15	Negro	44	29
Hispano	18	12	Colored	11	7
Spanish American	21	14	Other*	8	5
Spanish	20	13		150	
Other*	21	14			
	150				

* American, don't know, don't use labels, some or all of them, can't say, etc.

TABLE 7: BLACK AND MEXICAN AMERICAN ORIENTATIONS TOWARD SOCIAL, ECONOMIC AND POLITICAL QUESTIONS

Here is a list of areas in which some people say blacks and Mexican Americans are not treated fairly. Do you think they are treated unfairly, the same as Anglos, or that things are actually in their favor?

In Housing	Favorably		Same		Unfairly		No Answer	
Mexican Americans	4%	(6)	36%	(54)	49%	(74)	11%	(16)
Blacks	10	(15)	7	(10)	76	(114)	7	(11)
In Jobs								
Mexican Americans	4	(6)	37	(56)	51	(77)	7	(11)
Blacks	7	(10)	9	(13)	80	(120)	5	(7)
In Schools								
Mexican Americans	4	(6)	46	(69)	35	(53)	15	(22)
Blacks	7	(10)	11	(16)	74	(111)	9	(13)

Some people seem to follow what's going on in government and public affairs most of the time, whether there's an election going on or not. Others aren't that interested. Would you say that you follow what's going on in the government and public affairs most of the time, some of the time, only now and then, or hardly at all?

	Most of the Time		Sometimes		Now and Then		Hardly Ever		N.A.	
Mexican Amer.	42%	(63)	29%	(43)	21%	(31)	7%	(11)	1%	(2)
Blacks	52	(78)	37	(56)	7	(11)	3	(4)	1	(1)

How would you characterize yourself politically — as Left Wing, Liberal, Conservative, Right Wing, or other?

	Left Wing		Liberal		Conservative		Right Wing		Other		N.A.	
Mexican Amer.	1%	(2)	25%	(37)	31%	(46)	1%	(2)	1%	(1)	41%	(62)
Blacks	1	(1)	42	(53)	28	(42)	4	(6)	5	(7)	21	(31)

Do you belong to any organizations — that is, groups like the PTA, or civic groups, clubs, unions, church groups, veteran organizations and the like?

	None		One		Two or Three		Three+		N.A.	
Mexican Amer.	65%	(97)	23%	(55)	10%	(15)	3%	(3)	0%	(0)
Blacks	34	(51)	27	(44)	23	(35)	4	(6)	9	(14)

Do you agree or disagree with the statement of some people that violence is sometimes necessary to overcome the conditions that exist in the ghetto/barrio [appropriate term read to black and Mexican American respondents]?

	Agree		Disagree		N.A.	
Mexican Americans	27%	(41)	66%	(99)	7%	(10)
Blacks	52	(78)	39	(59)	9	(13)

257

Mexican Americans. On the question of violence, as with all of the other areas discussed, the Mexican American voters of Denver express considerably more moderate, conservative (or even "colonial")[22] attitudes than do the blacks surveyed. Though their socioeconomic standing might suggest the rationality of unified political action of a critical orientation, the subjective evaluation of conditions which Mexican American voters make does not provide the basis of community support which such political action would require.

MEXICAN AMERICAN AND BLACK VOTERS: POLITICAL CONSCIOUSNESS AND POLITICAL ACTION

Let us return to the subject of the 1971 local election in Denver. From the foregoing analysis it should be possible to suggest that an underlying explanation for the failure of the two Mexican American candidates in their effort to use the ethnic vote as a path to public office may well reside in the fact that that vote is not very solid. The fact that the Anglo candidates could gather significant proportions of the vote in minority precincts may reflect the fact that Mexican American voters in the two city council districts under study did not conceive of the election in terms of a unified, ethnically cohesive political force seeking to capture political power. Armand B. Rendon's claim that "the Chicano community is undergoing one of the most rapid changes of any people of America," and that now Mexican Americans are prepared "to assert that identity and unity of purpose which would clearly manifest their peoplehood"[23] is as much hope and aspiration as it is reality. There are very important changes occuring within the Mexican community,[24] certainly, but they have as yet not penetrated the political consciousness of all Mexican Americans, and certainly not that of local voters in Denver.

CONCLUSIONS: GENERALIZATION OF FINDINGS

A very important question arises at this point, i.e., what does this study of minority voters in Denver tell us about comparative Mexican American and black political behavior generally? Are Mexican Americans, as Levy and Kramer have argued, far less politically mobilized than are blacks; or, to the contrary, are Mexican Americans now to be viewed as an "awakened" minority? This Denver study appears to provide some partial support for the former view.

Furthermore, the findings presented here coincide with those of another recent analysis of comparative Mexican American and black political behavior.[25] Antunes and Gaitz, drawing upon the findings of Orum[26] and Olsen[27] which show that when social class is controlled black social and political participation general-

---

[22] Joan W. Moore, "Colonialism: The Case of the Mexican American," *Social Problems* 17 (Spring 1970), reprinted in Livie Isauro Duran and H. Russell Bernard, eds., *Introduction to Chicano Studies* (New York: Macmillan, 1973), pp. 363-72, presents a critical analysis of the application of the colonial concept to the study of Mexican Americans in the U.S.

[23] Armand B. Rendon, *Chicano Manifesto* (New York: Macmillan, 1971), p. 280.

[24] Biliana C. S. Ambrecht and Harry P. Pachon present evidence from a panel survey, for example, of growth of political consciousness among Mexican Americans in East Los Angeles in the period 1965-1972. See their: "Ethnic Political Mobilization in a Mexican American Community: An Exploratory Study of East Los Angeles 1965-72," *Western Political Quarterly* 27 (September 1974): 500-519.

[25] George Antunes and Charles M. Gaitz, "Ethnicity and Participation: A Study of Mexican Americans, Blacks, and Whites," *American Journal of Sociology* 80 (March 1975): 1192-11.

[26] Anthony Orum, "A Reappraisal of the Social and Political Participation of Negroes," *American Journal of Sociology* 72 (July 1966): 32-46.

[27] Marvin Olsen, "Social and Political Participation of Blacks," *American Sociological Review* 35 (August 1970): 682-97.

ly exceeds that of whites, find in their analysis of data from Houston that: "Among Mexican Americans, however, participation is generally lower than that of whites. With social class controlled, participation rates among Mexican Americans exceed or equal those of whites for only four of the eleven variables."[28]

It seems fair to conclude that the full political awakening of the Mexican American has not yet arrived. However, it would be extremely misleading to overlook the obvious advances in political mobilization that have been made in Los Angeles,[29] in Crystal City by La Raza Unida,[30] in the San Joaquin and Coachella valleys under the banner of the UFW AFL-CIO,[31] in New Mexico,[32] and elsewhere. It is apparent that Mexican American political mobilization is best characterized as a growing, but highly variegated political phenomenon. There is great variation in the degree of Mexican American political activation, with some communities (e.g., Denver) yet to develop ethnic cohesion and political consciousness, and others (e.g., East Los Angeles) much further along the way to the effective expression of concentrated political power.

The greatest danger in this particular case is that of *over*-generalization. Conditions obtaining in Denver, though instructive to the general question of comparative black and Mexican American political behavior, are not necessarily relevant to the analysis of political conditions in other areas. An observation which is relevant, however, is that of the importance of the subjective perception of reality made by political actors. The perception of objective local conditions — i.e., degree of prejudice, extent of opportunity, quality of services, and the like — varies across ethnic minority groups, and also within minority groups across geographical areas. The danger for the political activist seeking to further the interest of Mexican American political power is to assume that events in East Los Angeles and Crystal City reflect the norm of Mexican American political consciousness elsewhere. What the Chicano activist may see as the rational orientation of his people toward their depressed condition, his people may take to be inappropriate to their subjective evaluation of their particular reality. This competition between assertive and acquiescent reactions to adversity on the part of minority people is a familiar one; Dudley Randall has written of the black struggle in the past:

> "It seems to me," said Booker T.,
> "That all you folks have missed the boat
> Who shout about the right to vote,
> And spend vain days and sleepless nights
> In uproar over civil rights.
> Just keep your mouths shut, do not grouse,
> But work, and save, and buy a house."
>
> "I don't agree," said W.E.B.
> "For what can property avail
> If dignity and justice fail?
> Unless you help to make the laws,
> They'll steal your house with trumped-up clause.

---

[28] Antunes and Gaitz, "Ethnicitiy and Participation," p. 1208.

[29] Antonio Camejo, "Lessons of the Los Angeles Chicano Protest," in Duran and Bernard, *Chicano Studies*, pp. 510–19.

[30] José Angel Gutierrez, "Mexicanos Need to Control Their Own Destinies," in Servin, *An Awakened Minority*, pp. 208–15.

[31] Peter Matthiesen, *Sal Si Puedes: Cesar Chavez and the New American Revolution* (New York: Random House, 1970).

[32] Richard Gardner, *Grito! Reies Tijerina and the New Mexico Land Grant War of 1967* (Indianapolis: Bobbs-Merrill, 1970).

> A rope's as tight, a fire as hot
> No matter how much cash you've got.
> Speak soft, and try your little plan,
> But as for me, I'll be a man."[33]

At present, many Mexican American voters in Denver and elsewhere may be more attentive to views such as those of Booker T. Washington than to those defended by W. E. B. Dubois. In the future, however, if the Mexican American community is to develop the kind of political power which blacks and other ethnic groups have, capable and dedicated leaders will have to develop among Mexican Americans the critical and informed orientations which underlie such political power. In this regard it is important to note that among the prerequisites for the effective development of this political consciousness is the correct determination of existing subjective orientations and political identifications. It is in the service of this goal that this analysis is presented.

---

[33] From Dudley Randall's poem, "Booker T. and W.E.B.," reprinted from the *Midwest Journal* (Winter 1952–53) as *Broadside No. 8*, February 1967, by the Broadside Press, Detroit, Michigan.

ETHNICITY AND ELECTORAL CHOICE: MEXICAN AMERICAN VOTING BEHAVIOR IN THE CALIFORNIA 30TH CONGRESSIONAL DISTRICT

Bruce E. CAIN, *California Institute of Technology*

D. Roderick KIEWIET, *California Institute of Technology*

> The 1982 election in California offers a unique natural experiment in ethnic and racial bloc voting. The race in the predominately Hispanic 30th Congressional District matched a well-financed Anglo Republican, John Rousselot, against an incumbent Hispanic, Marty Martinez. On the ballot with Martinez and Rousselot were the successful Republican candidates for governor and U.S. senator, George Deukmejian and Pete Wilson, and the losing Democratic candidates, Tom Bradley (who is black) and Jerry Brown. These variations in the race and ethnicity of the candidates on the ballot in 1982 were used to estimate the impact of ethnic and racial considerations in voting decisions.

The substantial growth of the Mexican American population during the last decade has created considerable interest in the Mexican American voter. Although national election surveys do not sample a sufficient number of Mexican Americans to permit adequate analysis of their attitudes and political behavior, there have been many excellent regional studies (Guzman, 1973; McCleskey and Merrill, 1973; Freeman, 1974; Levy and Kramer, 1974; Garcia and de la Garza, 1977; Baird, 1977; de la Garza and Brischetto, 1983a, 1983b; de la Garza and Weaver, 1983). Most of these surveys have focused on Texas, New Mexico, and Arizona, and many have looked at local council and gubernatorial races where Mexican Americans made their greatest gains in the seventies. However, nearly half of the Latino population in the Southwest currently resides in California, and Mexican Americans there have made great efforts to win representation in Congress. This study examines one of the congressional seats targeted by Californian Mexican Americans in 1982—the 30th Congressional District in Los Angeles County.

The race in the 30th matched a well-financed Republican, John Rousselot, against a Mexican American Democrat, Marty Martinez. Rousselot had lost his seat in the 1981 redistricting. Rather than face a neighboring Republican incumbent in an expensive and potentially bitter primary, Rousselot chose to contest the 30th. Although the 30th was 65 percent Democratic in registration (a safe Democratic seat by California standards), Rousselot had reason to believe that he might succeed. To begin with, Martinez had only narrowly won a July special election that was called when Danielson retired to take a position on the bench, and the bitter special election campaign had left a residue of ill feeling among the district's Anglo Democrats. It was reported that some resented the presumption that the 30th should become a Hispanic seat after Danielson's retirement. Martinez was also vulnerable on certain personal issues: he had been a Republican for some years before he joined the Democratic party and, as an assemblyman, it was alleged that he had received large payments from owners of an unpopular dumpsite. Finally, even though the seat was 50 percent Mexican American in population, the electorate was only 30 percent Mexican American, and Mexican American voters in that area had not traditionally voted in high numbers.

In the end, Martinez's 54 percent vote share was significantly below the 65 percent Democratic registration in the district. Hence, this race provides a good opportunity to answer several questions: (1) were Mexican American voters more likely to support Martinez than non-Mexican? (2) was there Anglo backlash? and (3) in what other ways did ethnicity affect the vote?

In this regard, the 1982 election offers a unique natural experiment in ethnic and racial bloc voting. On the ballot with Martinez and Rousselot were the successful Republican candidates for governor and U.S. senator, George Deukmejian and Pete Wilson, and the losing Democratic candidates, Tom Bradley (who is black) and Jerry Brown. These variations in the race and ethnicity of the candidates on the ballot in 1982 can be used to estimate the impact of ethnic and racial considerations in voting decisions. The data for this study were gathered in two surveys of the 30th Congressional District of California. The first was a telephone survey of 455 respondents administered during the third week of October 1982. The second was a poll of 409 voters as they left the voting booth on election day.

Evidence of Ethnic Voting

The first task is to assess the degree of ethnic and racial voting by comparing the choices among Anglo and Mexican American voters across the three races. Table 1 displays the possible combinations of choices and analyzes them by party (i.e., voter's registration) and ethnicity. The data reveal several things. First, Rousselot did succeed in winning Democratic support, including 14 percent of the Mexican American Democrats sampled. (This figure was arrived at by summing across the figures for Mexican American Democrats in the appropriate columns, i.e., columns 2, 5, 6, and 8.) Rousselot was also supported by about two-thirds of the small number of Mexican American Republicans interviewed. And, as Table 1

Ethnicity and Electoral Choice

TABLE 1

Pattern of Votes Cast for Congressman, Senator, and Governor by Party Registration and Ethnicity (major party registrants only)

Election	Voting Pattern								
Congress	Dem	Rep	Dem	Dem	Rep	Rep	Dem	Rep	
Governor	Dem	Dem	Rep	Dem	Rep	Dem	Rep	Rep	
U.S. Senate	Dem	Dem	Dem	Rep	Dem	Rep	Rep	Rep	n
Non–Mexican American Democrat	61%	10%	3%	1%	2%	4%	2%	17%	103
Mexican American Democrat	78	7	1	1	0	3	6	4	72
Non–Mexican American Republican	3	7	7	2	5	3	7	65	58
Mexican American Republican	27	0	0	0	0	0	9	64	11
Total	50	7	3	1	2	4	4	28	244

also shows, 7 percent of the Mexican American Democrats voted for Rousselot while simultaneously supporting both Bradley and Brown: in short, the only race on which they defected was the one in which a Mexican American candidate was running.

In general, though, the predominantly Democratic Mexican American voters in this district gave strong support to all Democratic candidates. Seventy-eight percent voted a straight Democratic ballot, 2 percent split their vote on the Senate and governor's races and supported Martinez, and 6 percent voted for the Republican candidates in all the major races except for Congress. The finding of high Democratic loyalty among Mexican American voters is very much consistent with previous studies (Levy and Kramer, 1974; de la Garza, 1977). While the numbers are too small to permit firm conclusions, it does appear that a higher fraction of Mexican American Republicans (36 percent) than of Anglo Republicans (19 percent) defected from their party to vote for Martinez.

In sum, Mexican American voters in this district exhibited a high degree of support for Martinez and for the other Democratic candidates. Still, the 14 percent defection rate among Mexican American Democrats in the congressional race is not trivial. Combined with evidence in our poll that large numbers of Mexican American voters were undecided until very late in the campaign, this reinforces the point made in previous studies that the support of Mexican American voters for Mexican American candidates— even of the same party as themselves—is by no means automatic, and that "bloc voting" is hardly inevitable (de la Garza, 1977; Baird, 1977).

What about the behavior of Anglo voters in this district? Previous studies found that credible, salient Mexican American candidates can cause backlash among Anglo voters (Guzman, 1973; de la Garza, 1974). The question in this case is whether redistricting the seat to favor a Mexican American candidate and the ethnic emphasis of the Martinez campaign caused bloc voting against his candidacy on the part of Anglos in his district. To begin with, the fact that 17 percent of the Anglo Democrats voted a straight Republican ticket is one of many indications that on average they were more disloyal than the Mexican American Democrats. On the other hand, the number who supported Rousselot but voted for Brown and Bradley—the clearest case of ethnic or candidate-specific backlash—was only 3 percent higher among Anglo Democrats than among Mexican American Democrats. Thus it appears that while the overall level of party disloyalty among Anglo Democrats was much higher than among Mexican American Democrats, the level of ticket splitting against Martinez specifically was not significantly higher.

It is possible, of course, to test more rigorously the proposition that Mexican American voters were more likely to support Martinez than other voters. Although the tabular data seem to suggest that this occurred, the bivariate evidence of higher Mexican American support may have been caused by random statistical error, or by the failure to control for other variables.

The model proposed is therefore a multivariate one that includes the voter's ethnicity, party, employment status, and religion. These were specified as dummy variables, which respectively took on the value of 1 if the voter was Mexican American, if the voter was registered as a Democrat, if the voter or a family member had been out of work in the past few months, and if the voter was Catholic. The dependent variable is based upon a six-cell classification of how the individual voted in the senatorial, gubernatorial, and congressional races in 1982. Although there are actually eight logically possible ways of voting in the three races, four of the categories were condensed to two because of their infrequency.

To estimate this model, we employed a multinomial logit procedure. The base category is referenced by having voted a straight Republican ticket; each alternative is thus considered relative to that base category. The data are displayed in Table 2. The results of this estimation reveal several things. First and foremost, Mexican Americans were statistically more likely to vote a straight Democratic ticket—even controlling for party, religion, and employment status—than non–Mexican Americans. Secondly, when they split their ticket, they were more likely to vote for Martinez. The effect is particularly strong for the Martinez-Wilson-Deukmejian category, the category in which the only Democrat the voter chose was Mexican American. It would appear, then, that Mexican Americans did tend to vote more frequently for Martinez even when other factors are controlled for.

Factors Influencing the Mexican American Vote in the 30th Congressional District

Having established that Mexican Americans did vote more heavily for Martinez, their support can now be analyzed more closely. In particular, it can be broken down into three components: issues, party loyalty, and candidate specific evaluations. To what extent did each of these components play a role in the decisions made by the voters of the 30th District?

TABLE 2

Multinomial Logit Analysis of Voting for Congressman in the
30th Congressional District of California

	Voting Pattern				
	Straight Democratic vs. Straight Republican	Rousselot, Brown, and Bradley vs. Straight Republican	Martinez, Brown, or Bradley vs. Straight Republican	Rousselot, Wilson, or Deukmejian vs. Straight Republican	Martinez, Wilson, and Deukmejian vs. Straight Republican
Democrat	3.29*	1.86*	2.27*	1.15*	0.71
	(0.41)	(0.55)	(0.75)	(0.57)	(0.70)
Mexican American	1.31*	0.37	1.11	0.61	1.99*
	(0.47)	(0.68)	(0.95)	(0.91)	(0.81)
Unemployed	1.21*	1.46*	−0.44	1.23*	−0.78
	(0.43)	(0.55)	(1.12)	(0.60)	(1.12)
Catholic	−0.26	−0.11	−1.85*	−2.16*	−0.49
	(0.40)	(0.56)	(0.92)	(0.87)	(0.81)
Constant	−2.11*	−2.68*	−2.84*	−1.89*	−2.59*
	(0.37)	(0.49)	(0.62)	(0.40)	(0.52)
n	147	23	11	18	11
Percent correctly predicted		66%			
Likelihood ratio index		.41			

NOTE: Cell entries are logit coefficients with *t* ratios in parentheses.

The first component is the set of issue attitudes Mexican American voters possess. While there are many potential issues on which Anglo and Mexican American could be compared, the focus will be on those that were salient in the congressional race, such as the economy, nuclear weapons, and the various initiatives. This precludes, of course, any overall judgment as to the similarity or dissimilarity of Mexican American and Anglo Democrats; it is quite likely that there are differences between the two on issues such as bilingualism, guest workers, and immigration on which we did not collect data.

To begin with, did Anglo and Mexican American voters in this district share the same perception of what the most important problems facing the country were in 1982? In the election day exit poll, voters were asked to report what they thought was the most important problem facing the nation. As before, the sample is partitioned by ethnicity and party registration. A perusal of the data reveals that all groups believed that unemployment was the most important problem facing the nation. This is not surprising, of course, given that unemployment was running at 10.1 percent in October 1982, and that the media gave the unemployment issue a great deal of coverage. Democrats were more inclined than Republicans to cite unemployment, but the margin is surprisingly small. Intraparty differences were even weaker. Mexican American Democrats mentioned unemployment more frequently than did Anglo Democrats, and they were also somewhat less likely than Anglo Democrats to mention other sorts of economic prob-

265

TABLE 3

Most Important Problem Facing the Nation (major party registrants only)

	Unemployment	Other Economic Problems	Foreign Policy	Social Problems	Miscellaneous Problems	n
Non–Mexican American Democrats	47%	24%	5%	8%	16	117
Mexican American Democrats	51	22	0	8	19	81
Non–Mexican American Republicans	42	27	0	20	11	59
Mexican American Republicans	40	27	0	13	20	15

TABLE 4

Voter Attitudes on Ballot Initiatives, Reagan's Economic Policies, and Abortion (major party registrants only)

	Favors Freeze	Favors Gun Registration	Favors Deposit	Reaganomics Has Hurt	Pro-Choice on Abortion
Non–Mexican American Democrats	54%	33%	38%	52%	68%
Mexican American Democrats	57	33	31	58	50
Non–Mexican American Republicans	39	23	37	16	50
Mexican American Republicans	23	27	33	25	66

lems (e.g., inflation, interest rates) and foreign policy, but these differences were much too small to be statistically significant. So while there were some differences, it would appear that party and ethnic factors were not strongly related to the perception of the most important problems facing the nation.

Although differences in the salience of issues were not great in November 1982, differences in issue positions were somewhat larger. There were, for instance, three initiatives on the ballot that drew particular attention in November 1982: Proposition 12, which called upon the United States and the Soviet Union to halt the manufacture of nuclear weapons; Proposition 15, which required the registration of handguns; and Proposition 11, which would have required a 5 cent returnable deposit with the purchase of cans and bottles. On two of these initiatives, party differences were much greater than the ethnic differences. Indeed, the nuclear freeze initiative provoked marked differences between Democrats and Republicans (Democrats being more in favor than Republicans), but no ethnic differences whatsoever. In fact, Mexican American Democrats and Republicans were more at odds on this issue than any other two groups. Party differences were less significant on the handgun registration issue, but no ethnic

Ethnicity and Electoral Choice 321

cleavage existed at all. Only on the bottle bill were there marked Latino-Anglo differences.

In light of the fact that the economy was acknowledged to be the most important problem in 1982, differences in opinions about economic issues are particularly meaningful. Since there was a fairly uniform pattern to the responses to these questions, it is not necessary to consider the whole battery of economic questions that were asked in both polls. Instead, we will consider a representative one that was designed to elicit a general evaluation of Reagan's economic policies, namely, whether the voter believed that Reagan's economic policies hurt the economy, helped it, or whether it was too early to tell. As one would expect, there were substantial party differences in the responses to this question; Democrats were far more likely to be critical of the President's policies than Republicans. By comparison, the intraparty differences were very small. As the figures in Table 4 indicate, Mexican American Democrats were slightly more opposed to Reagan's economic programs than Anglo Democrats, which is understandable given that a high percentage of them (43 percent) had either recently experienced unemployment themselves or had someone in their household who had been unemployed.

Finally, there is the issue of abortion. One conjecture that has received some attention in Republican circles recently is that Mexican Americans might be persuaded to vote Republican because they are more socially conservative than other Democrats. If this is true, then an issue like abortion should show substantial intraparty differences. Indeed, at first glance, this would appear to be the case. As Table 4 indicates, Anglo Democrats in this district were more likely than Mexican American Democrats to be pro-choice. However, these policy differences should be considered in light of the fact that 81 percent of the Mexican Americans in the sample were Catholic, as opposed to only 42 percent of the Anglos.

While the data indicate that party differences were more substantial than ethnic differences on issues, the proper statistical test again requires a multivariate procedure. Table 5 presents a series of logit equations predicting the respondent's position on each of the previously discussed issues as a function of various sociodemographic characteristics and party. The dependent variables are the individual's positions on the three most salient initiatives on the California ballot in 1982 (approval versus disapproval), whether the individual thinks that Reagan's economic policies have helped (versus whether they had hurt), and whether the individual thinks that abortions should never be permitted (as opposed to being pro-choice). The data come from the election day exit poll.

As is evident in Table 5, with the exception of the handgun initiative there is no strong association between being Mexican American and holding any of these policy attitudes, and in none of the instances is the association significant by conventional statistical standards. Even the abortion issue, which in the bivariate table showed a relation between ethnicity and attitude, displays no relationship in the presence of a control for religion. In short, there is no difference between Anglo and Mexican American Catholics on this issue: if the Hispanics are susceptible to the possibility of

TABLE 5

Binomial Logit Analysis of Issue Positions and Support for Ballot Initiatives

	Gun Registration	Bottle Deposits	Nuclear Freeze	Approve Reaganomics	Never Permit Abortion
Union member	−0.22	−0.28	−0.24	−0.21	−0.05
	(0.29)	(0.27)	(0.27)	(0.40)	(0.43)
Unemployed	−0.18	−0.01	0.41	−1.06*	−0.17
	(0.30)	(0.29)	(0.29)	(0.44)	(0.46)
Catholic	−0.19	0.09	0.08	−0.12	0.80*
	(0.30)	(0.28)	(0.28)	(0.42)	(0.45)
Mexican American	−0.19	0.04	−0.07	−0.06	0.01
	(0.33)	(0.32)	(0.31)	(0.49)	(0.48)
Republican	−2.22*	−1.28*	−0.99	1.85*	1.32
	(0.59)	(0.54)	(0.56)	(0.65)	(1.14)
Democrat	−1.46*	−1.07*	−0.27	−1.22*	1.21
	(0.54)	(0.49)	(0.52)	(0.64)	(1.08)
Female	0.59*	−0.01	0.53*	−0.46	0.00
	(0.28)	(0.27)	(0.27)	(0.39)	(0.42)
Constant	0.92	0.51	0.31	−0.11	−3.15
	(0.56)	(0.52)	(0.55)	(0.65)	(1.11)*
Percent correctly predicted	67%	66%	60%	57%	55%

NOTE: Cell entries are logit coefficients with *t* ratios in parentheses.

defection on this issue, so are other Catholic Democrats. By contrast, there are marked partisan differences on almost all of the issues, but especially on the economy. In sum, while there are some small ethnic differences on issues in the tabular data, these differences do not persist in the presence of control variables and are clearly less important than party and sex as explanatory variables.

Evaluations of the Candidates

While attitudes on the economy and the initiatives are one plausible explanation of the vote in the 30th, the impact of candidate evaluations is another. Was it the case that Mexican Americans, controlling for party and other demographic factors, had more favorable impressions of Martinez and less favorable impressions of Rousselot than did other voters? Once again, the proper way to examine this question is to look at a multivariate model. The dependent variable is whether the respondent had a favorable, unfavorable, or uncertain impression of Martinez or Rousselot, and the independent variables are whether the respondent is Mexican American, is unemployed, and is a Catholic and his/her position on the three initiatives examined earlier. As in the previous analysis, these were all entered as dummy variables. Results of this estimation procedure are reported in Table 6.

Looking at the Martinez equation first, it is clear that the party and ethnicity variables were the two most important determinants of candidate

TABLE 6

Multinomial Logit Analysis of Congressional Candidate Evaluations

	Favorable Impression of Martinez vs. Unfavorable	Uncertain Impression of Martinez vs. Unfavorable	Favorable Impression of Rousselot vs. Unfavorable	Uncertain Impression of Rousselot vs. Unfavorable
Democrat	0.85*	−0.00	−1.32*	−0.53
	(0.38)	(0.29)	(0.38)	(0.40)
Mexican American	1.68*	0.65	−1.02*	0.13
	(0.46)	(0.42)	(0.43)	(0.39)
Unemployed	0.41	0.35	−0.18	0.58
	(0.40)	(0.34)	(0.41)	(0.37)
Catholic	0.00	−0.04	0.17	−0.50
	(0.40)	(0.34)	(0.40)	(0.39)
Pro-freeze	0.37	0.08	−0.12	0.08
	(0.36)	(0.29)	(0.35)	(0.34)
Pro-gun registration	0.32	0.46	−0.33	0.18
	(0.36)	(0.30)	(0.35)	(0.34)
Pro-bottle deposit	0.49	0.01	−0.03	−0.55
	(0.36)	(0.29)	(0.35)	(0.34)
Constant	−1.61*	0.39	2.14*	1.40*
	(0.38)	(0.26)	(0.39)	(0.40)
Percent correctly predicted	51%		56%	
Likelihood ratio index	.13		.14	

NOTE: Cell entries are logit coefficients with *t* ratios in parentheses.

evaluations in this contest. That is to say, Democrats and Mexican Americans were more likely to have a favorable impression of Martinez. Conversely, they were much more likely to have an unfavorable impression of Rousselot. The coefficients on both these variables are significant by conventional statistical standards. Indeed, they are the only ones that are significant: all the other variables, including the initiatives, are not. Clearly, even when party biases and the attitudes that are normally associated with being a Democrat in California were held constant, being a Mexican American did influence one's perceptions of the candidates.

Mexican Americans and Party Registration

The final component of the voting decision is partisanship. Since this is such a widely studied factor, there is no need to discuss it at great length. Registering with a party is an expression of long-standing party loyalties. Party loyalties affect positions on issues, as is evident with the initiatives. Party loyalties also affect candidate evaluations, as just seen. In the latter instance, being a Mexican American had an effect on candidate evaluations independent of party. But if it is also the case that Mexican Americans are more likely to be registered Democrats, then there is yet another route by which being Mexican American affects issue attitudes, candidate evaluations, and ultimately the vote; namely, the indirect effect through party loyalty.

Does such a causal connection exist? Table 7 is a test of the relation between being Mexican American and party registration, once again following the procedure of controlling for other potential effects. The dependent variable is whether the respondent is a registered Democrat, an independent (or minor party voter), or a registered Republican (i.e., the suppressed category). The independent variables are dummies for being Mexican American, unemployed, Catholic, a union member, and female. The choices should be interpreted as the odds of being a Democrat versus a Republican (the first equation) and of being an independent versus a Republican (the second equation).

As is evident from the data, Mexican Americans were far more likely to be registered Democrats, even when their sex, employment status, union membership, and religion were controlled for. The coefficient is large and significant by conventional statistical standards. Union members, the unemployed, and Catholics were also more likely to be registered Democrats. Gender does not seem to be related in a significant manner to party registration. Mexican Americans were also more likely to be independents than Republicans, as were males in this district. However, no other variable seems to predict the independent category very well. In sum, it is clear that there is an important connection between ethnicity and party loyalty, adding yet another connection between being Mexican American and voting for Martinez.

Relating the Three Components to the Martinez Vote

Having so far identified three ways in which being Mexican American could have affected the voter's choice in the race for the 30th Congres-

TABLE 7
Multinomial Logit Analysis of Party Registration

	Democrat vs. Republican	Independent vs. Republican
Mexican American	1.78*	1.45*
	(0.42)	(0.67)
Unemployed	0.62*	−0.04
	(0.30)	(0.61)
Union member	0.54*	0.31
	(0.29)	(0.52)
Female	0.08	−1.21*
	(0.24)	(0.51)
Catholic	0.49	−0.40
	(0.29)	(0.60)
Constant	−0.20	−1.34
	(0.22)	(0.35)*
Percent correctly predicted	61%	
Likelihood ratio index	.30	

NOTE: Cell entries are logit coefficients with t ratios in parentheses.

Ethnicity and Electoral Choice

sional District, it is appropriate to ask at this point which components seemed to have been most important. The variable to be explained is the pre-election indication of how the respondent would have voted if the election had been held at the time of the poll (the week before the election). The pre-election poll is used for two reasons. First, it contains all of the data necessary to test the effects of the three components, whereas the post-election poll does not. Secondly, it allows us to look at the crucial question of why so many voters—especially Democrats and Hispanics—were undecided so late in the campaign. The dependent variable is constructed in a manner such that the first equation in Table 8 is the odds of intending to vote for Martinez versus Rousselot and the second equation is the odds of being undecided versus intending to vote for Rousselot.

The explanatory variables are by now familiar. Experimentation with the specification led to the final model displayed in Table 8. Earlier attempts included models that had different measures of economic performance as well as the three most salient initiatives. Since economic evaluations were highly related to party, union membership, and employment status, the presence of an economic performance variable added little to the equation,

TABLE 8

Multinomial Logit Analysis of Vote Choice for Congressman

	Martinez vs. Rousselot	Undecided vs. Rousselot
Democrat	2.05*	1.09*
	(0.54)	(0.39)
Mexican American	0.52	0.17
	(0.60)	(0.51)
Unemployed	0.67	0.22
	(0.52)	(0.43)
Catholic	0.06	0.28
	(0.55)	(0.44)
Favorable impression of Rousselot	−4.02*	−3.03*
	(0.67)	(0.41)
Unfavorable impression of Rousselot	1.45	0.40
	(0.83)	(0.77)
Favorable impression of Martinez	1.85*	0.23
	(0.60)	(0.55)
Unfavorable impression of Martinez	−1.64*	−0.78*
	(0.79)	(0.44)
Pro-freeze	0.46	0.14
	(0.48)	(0.38)
Pro–gun registration	0.80*	0.67
	(0.48)	(0.38)
Pro–bottle deposit	−0.05	−0.44
	(0.49)	(0.39)
Constant	−1.54*	0.93*
	(0.60)	(0.42)
Percent correctly predicted	73%	
Likelihood ratio index	.41	

NOTE: Cell entries are logit coefficients with t ratios in parentheses.

and so was dropped in the final specification. Candidate evaluations were captured by four dummy variables: a favorable impression of Martinez, an unfavorable impression of Martinez, a favorable impression of Rousselot, and an unfavorable impression of Rousselot. A Mexican American variable is included in order to capture any remaining unspecified relations between ethnicity and the vote in this race.

The results of the estimations reveal several things. First, there were no residual ethnicity effects, as indicated by the fact that the coefficient on the Mexican American effect is not significant. This can be interpreted as meaning that the model has comprehensively captured the various causal routes between ethnicity and choice with the other variables. Of the initiatives, only the pro–gun registration initiative shows any strong association with the Martinez vote. By far the most important components of the Martinez vote were party loyalty and candidate evaluations. Of these, the largest effects were having a positive evaluation of Rousselot and party. Those who had developed a favorable impression of Rousselot were much more likely to vote for him regardless of party. By comparison, having a favorable impression of Martinez had less effect in causing defections from Rousselot. The effectiveness of Rousselot's campaign and the failure of the Martinez campaign at that point to successfully counter Rousselot's attacks are evident in these estimations.

The equation predicting the odds of being undecided versus intending to vote for Rousselot is equally revealing. Once again, Democrats appear to have been more likely to be undecided, a fact observed in the cross-tabular data. There were also no residual ethnicity effects in this equation. Third, just as in vote choice equation, those who were pro–gun control were also more likely to be undecided than intending to vote for Rousselot. What is particularly striking about this equation is how unequivocally important the negative impressions of Martinez and the positive impressions of Rousselot were to the large undecided vote at the time of the pre-election poll. Again, the impact of campaign- and candidate-specific effects in this race is underscored. Clearly, the initiatives had far less to do with the fortunes of this race than did the strategies and personalities of the candidates themselves. Also, it seems evident that the "softness" observed earlier in Hispanic support for Martinez was candidate related, suggesting that a significant segment of the Mexican American voters did not automatically throw their support to Martinez, either because they felt that they did not know enough about him or did not like what they heard.

Conclusion

The Mexican American vote is a complex phenomenon with many indirect effects through intervening variables such as party, issue attitudes, and candidate evaluations. The attractiveness of the Mexican American candidate is suggested by certain patterns of ballot splitting and the strong effect of the candidate evaluation variable. It would appear that Mexican American voters were responsive to the attempt to create representation for them in the 30th. That support, however, should not be taken for granted, for Mexican American voters will condition their vote on their information and evaluation about the quality of the candidate, Mexican American or not. At the same time, there is strong evidence that ethnicity affected voting behavior in this race. In particular, being Mexican American influenced the voter's party loyalty and candidate evaluations significantly. **SSQ**

REFERENCES

Baird, Frank L. 1977. "The Search for a Constituency: Political Validation of Mexican-American Candidates in the Texas Great Plains," in F. Baird, ed., *Mexican-Americans: Political Power, Influence or Resource* (Lubbock: Texas Tech Press): pp. 77–93.

de la Garza, Rudolph O. 1974. "Voting Patterns in 'Bi-Cultural El Paso': A Contextual Analysis of Mexican-American Voting Behavior," in F. Chris Garcia, ed., *La Causa Politica: A Chicano Politics Reader* (Notre Dame: Notre Dame Press): pp. 250–66.

———. 1977. "Mexican-American Voters: A Responsible Electorate," in F. Baird, ed., *Mexican-Americans: Political Power, Influence or Resource* (Lubbock: Texas Tech Press): pp. 63–76.

de la Garza, Rudolph O., and Robert R. Brischetto. 1983a. "The Mexican-American Electorate: A Demographic Profile." Occasional Paper No. 1, Mexican-American Electorate Series, Southwest Voter Registration Drive and Center for Mexican-American Studies.

———. 1983b. "The Mexican-American Electorate: Information Sources and Policy Orientations." Occasional Paper No. 2, Mexican-American Electorate Series, Southwest Voter Registration Drive and Center for Mexican-American Studies.

de la Garza, Rudolph O., and Janet Weaver. 1983. "Mexican Americans and Anglos in San Antonio: A City Divided." Paper presented at the American Political Science Convention, 1 September.

Freeman, Donald M. 1974. "Party, Vote and the Mexican-American in South Tucson," in F. Chris Garcia, ed., *La Causa Politica: A Chicano Politics Reader* (Notre Dame: Notre Dame Press): pp. 55–66.

Garcia, F. Chris, and Rudolph O. de la Garza. 1977. *The Chicano Political Experience* (North Scituate, Mass.: Duxbury Press).

Guzman, Ralph. 1973. "The Function of Anglo-American Racism in the Political Development of Chicanos," in F. Chris Garcia, ed., *Chicano Politics: Readings* (New York: MSS Information Corporation): pp. 21–37.

Levy, Mark R., and Michael S. Kramer. 1974. "Patterns of Chicano Voting Behavior," in F. Chris Garcia, ed., *La Causa Politica: A Chicano Politics Reader* (Notre Dame: Notre Dame Press): pp. 241–49.

McCleskey, Clifton, and Bruce Merrill. 1973. "Mexican American Political Behavior in Texas," *Social Science Quarterly*, 53 (March):785–98.

Hispanics Gain Seats in the 98th Congress After Reapportionment*
Maurilio E. Vigil
New Mexico Highlands University
Las Vegas, New Mexico 87701, USA

The convening of the 98th Congress in January 1983 saw the greatest number of Hispanic congressmen ever in American history. A total of 11 Hispanics now belong to the Congressional Hispanic Caucus, the coalition of congressmen who represent Hispanic interests. Four new Hispanic congressmen (two from California, one from Texas, and one from New Mexico) were elected in 1982. This paper describes how the congressional reapportionment process, following the release of the 1980 census, resulted in additional congressional seats for these sun belt states and the electoral process and circumstances that enabled Hispanics to capture four of these seats. Hispanics are rapidly becoming a major political force in the United States and this article reflects that increasing importance in Congress following the 1982 elections.

Background: The Changing Face of Hispanic Politics
In the mid-1960's, after decades of seeming quiescence, Hispanic Americans added their voices of protest to those of black Americans and native Americans in the United States. This period witnessed many forms of activist protest, especially among Mexican Americans, including mass demonstrations, marches, picketing, boycotts, civil disobedience, and even some violent confrontations. For the first time, the so-called "forgotten Americans" publicly declared their demands for equal status as American citizens. As the decade of the 1970's passed, however, the signs of activism waned, creating the impression that the movement had fizzled. Now, in the 1980's, new evidence indicates that Hispanics have, like blacks, regrouped and begun to work through conventional styles for political change within the framework of the American political system.

The 1980's have seen a shift in emphasis from activist protest politics to the politics of the ballot box. There are several manifestations of this new mood, but the most important are increases in the number of Hispanics in the U.S. Congress, as a result of the 1982 congressional elections. Hispanics gained three new seats in Congress and consolidated another, won earlier in the year. Other manifestations of the changing face of Hispanic politics include increasing numbers of Hispanic voter registration and voter participation, more Hispanic municipal and county office holders, and Hispanic state legislators. Probably the most important victories, however, were the election of the first Hispanic as mayor of San Antonio, the nation's 10th largest city, and the election of a Hispanic as governor in New Mexico.

In 1981, Henry Cisneros was elected mayor of San Antonio, Texas, on the strength of overwhelming support from San Antonio's Mexican Americans, who make up 54 percent of the 785,000 population. In 1982, Toney Anaya became New Mexico's fourth Hispanic

---

Dr. Maurilio Vigil is a professor of political science at New Mexico Highlands University, where he has taught since 1972. He was born in Las Vegas, New Mexico, and received his Ph.D. in political science (1974) at the University of New Mexico. He is a Danforth associate and a member of Phi Kappa Phi, Pi Gamma Mu, the Western Political Science Association, and Western Social Science Association. His books include *Chicano Politics* **(1978) and** *Los Patrones: Profiles of Hispanic Political Leaders in New Mexico History* **(1980). He has contributed chapters to** *New Mexico Government* **(University of New Mexico Press, 1982) and** *The Chicanos as We See Ourselves* **(University of Arizona Press, 1979).**

governor in history and the second in modern history.¹ He also received overwhelming support from New Mexico's Mexican Americans, who make up 36.6 percent of the state's population. In both cases Hispanics provided evidence that they would support their own candidate, a condition which has been questioned by some social scientists in the past.²

Hispanics in Congress

The 1980 U.S. census of population revealed that Hispanics now comprise a total of 14,600,000 people, making them, next to blacks, the largest ethnic minority in the United States. More importantly, the new figure reflects an increase of 67 percent over the past decade, making Hispanics the fastest growing group in the United States. Already underrepresented in the United States Congress in 1970, Hispanics were even more underrepresented by the end of the decade, when there were only five of them serving in Congress, all being members of the House of Representatives. Hispanics made up 6.6 percent of the U.S. population in 1970, but comprised only 1.3 percent of the representation in the House of Representatives. The five Hispanics serving in the U.S. House in 1981 included Henry Gonzales, a Democrat who has represented a district comprising San Antonio, Texas, since 1961; E. "Kika" de la Garza, a Democrat who has represented a district from the Corpus Christi-Brownsville, Texas, region since 1964; Edward Roybal, a Democrat who has represented a district from Los Angeles, California, since 1962; Manuel Lujan, Jr., a Republican who has represented New Mexico since 1968; and Robert Garcia, a Democrat and the only Puerto Rican in the group (the others being Mexican Americans), who has represented a New York City district since 1978.³ Matthew J. "Marty" Martinez became the sixth Hispanic serving in the U.S. House in July 1982, when he was elected to serve the unexpired term (the remainder of 1982) of resigning California Congressman George Danielson. Because Congressman Martinez' seat was one affected by the reapportionment, it will be included in a later discussion. There have been no Hispanics serving in the United States Senate since 1976, when New Mexico's Joseph M. Montoya was defeated for reelection.⁴

Congressional Reapportionment After the 1980 Census

Although the number of representatives serving in the U.S. House of Representatives is not fixed by the Constitution but is established instead fy federal law, the size of the House has remained at 435 seats for the past four decades. The method used to distribute seats is as follows: every state is given, in accordance with Article I, Section 1 of the Constitution, one seat in the House. A formula based on the principle of "equal proportion" produces "priority numbers" on the basis of the state's population which yield to each state a second, third, or fourth seat and so on. The principle of "equal proportion" is an effort to conform to the Constitution and the "one person one vote" guideline established by the Supreme Court in the case of *Wesberry Versus Sanders* in 1964. Further court rulings have required that a district's population not deviate more than 1 percent from the average district population of that state.⁵ The priority numbers distribute seats until all 435 have been exhausted. Every 10 years after the decennial census, a redistribution of congressional seats is in order to compensate states which have gained population. Naturally, this is done at the expense of other states whose proportion of the population has declined.

Shortly after the 1980 census was completed, it was found that about three-fourths of the nation's 435 congressional districts had gained population. Of these, 10 districts had increases greater than 50 percent and 58 districts had increases greater than 30 percent.⁶ Accordingly, a U.S. Census Bureau report released on June 10, 1981, indicated that major congressional redistricting would be required. The 1980 census produced more grumbling than normal, however, because the states which lost seats included the industrial Midwestern and Northeastern states, while those that gained seats were concentrated in the South and Western sun-belt half of the country. Figure 1 shows the complexion of American

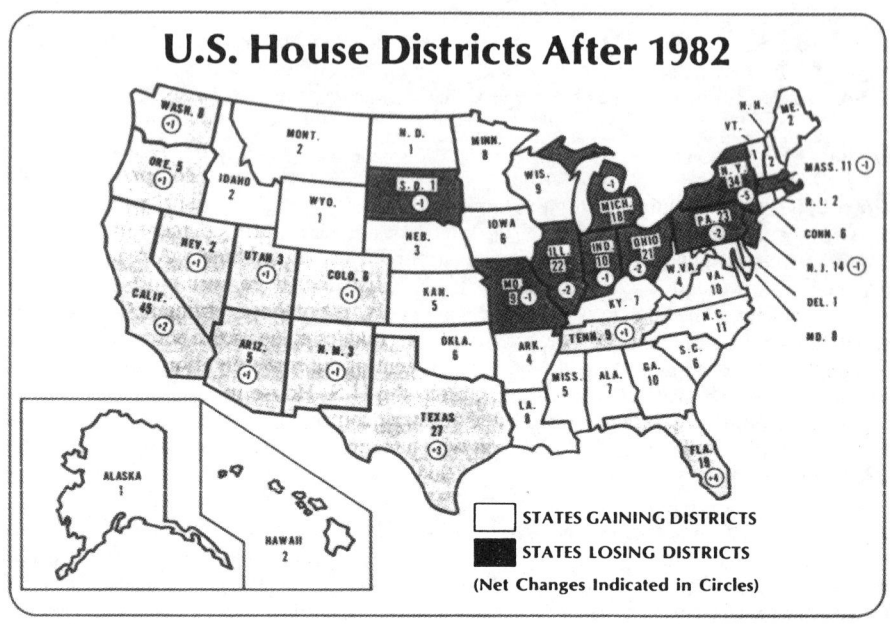

states which lost and gained seats after the 1980 census. The biggest loser was New York state, which lost five seats. Ohio, Illinois, and Pennsylvania each lost two, while Massachusetts, New Jersey, Michigan, Indiana, South Dakota, and Missouri each lost one. Florida was the biggest beneficiary, as it gained four new seats, while Texas gained three, California two, and Washington, Oregon, Nevada, Utah, Colorado, Arizona, New Mexico, and Tennessee each gained one.[7] New York, the biggest loser, filed suit in U.S. District Court challenging the census figures. Judge Henry Werker ruled that an adjustment in the congressional districts would be necessary because the Census Bureau had undercounted the population. His ruling was overturned, however, by the U.S. Court of Appeals, which said that the lower court could not order such an adjustment without considering what effect it would have on other states.

Although federal laws and court decisions have established the guidelines for congressional reapportionment, the actual determination of the composition of congressional districts is left to the states or, more specifically, to the state legislatures in most states, although some states have nonpartisan commissions which participate in the process.

The redistricting process is inherently complex because of the need to establish districts which are almost exactly equal in population size while, taking into account other demographic variables of the population, such as economics and rural or urban character. The problem is further complicated by a plethora of "political" variables which invariably emerge. The most important political influence present in the redistricting process is that of political parties. Each party traditionally sees reapportionment as a way of improving its position in Congress. The party in control of the legislature will usually have an inherent advantage in the process, while the minority party will be forced to go to court to challenge inequitable practices.

In recent years, ethnic minorities have perceived reapportionment as a way to correct traditional representational imbalances. This position was enhanced by the enactment of the 1970 Voting Rights Act which prohibited the drawing of districts that have the effect of diluting minority voting strength. In 1980, minority groups were better prepared than in 1970 to challenge congressional and state reapportionment plans that dilute their representation.

The courts, because of the provisions of the Voting Rights Act and greater vigilance by the U.S. Department of Justice, American Civil Liberties Union (ACLU), and organizations representing ethnic groups, have been more wary of state redistricting proposals, and have been inclined to favor minority groups when redistricting plans are blatant examples of efforts to dilute minority voting strength. In the case of *Washington Versus Davis*, for example, the court was concerned that "segregative policies of the political parties might deprive minority voters of the experience or benefit of political organization."[8]

The utilization of redistricting to remedy traditional underrepresentation of minorities has not been without critics. David Wells, for example, has argued that "affirmative gerrymandering," to equalize representation of specific groups, is no better than the gerrymandering which it is designed to eliminate. Says Wells: "The most effective way to prevent gerrymandering, both affirmative and negative, is not to impose arbitrary quotas; nor is it to vest special power in some judicial umpire or even in a non-partisan authority. Rather, it is to make sure that whoever draws the district's lines cannot do so in a manner calculated to bestow special advantage to any ethnic group, any political party, any partisan faction, any favored candidate or any favored geographic area. The best way is to establish firm, explicit, politically and ethnically neutral guidelines or grand rules. Such rules would eliminate a judgment as to where district boundaries shall be placed and who will be helped, and who will be hurt, which is the very essence of gerrymandering."[9]

Notwithstanding the ongoing debate on the matter, it is evident that ethnic minorities fared more favorably from the congressional redistricting process following the 1980 census. Blacks won three more seats in the House of Representatives in the 1982 election, bringing their number to 21 in the 98th Congress, which is the highest number of blacks ever. Hispanics also gained three seats, bringing their number to nine, which is also the highest number in history. The remainder of this study will be devoted to analyzing the circumstances and processes that led to such Hispanic gains in Congress.

The Reapportionment Process and Hispanics

Because the Hispanic population is most heavily concentrated in the sun-belt states where the new congressional seats were located, it was natural to expect that they might benefit. However, as the following state by state descriptions will show, the process for Hispanics was less than simple, as they had to employ sophisticated legal and political maneuvering to overcome traditional barriers.

California

In California, the 4,500,000 Hispanics who make up 19.2 percent of the population also comprise one-third of the total Hispanic population in the United States. Most of these, or 80 percent, are Mexican Americans. Despite high population numbers, Hispanics have traditionally been underrepresented in elective office. In 1982, for example, they held three State Senate and four State Assembly positions.

California qualified for two more congressional seats as a result of the 1980 census, and the resultant redistricting created two "open" districts with no incumbent congressman, and restructured several others which forced at least one incumbent congressman to relocate. A third vacancy was created when an incumbent congressman did not seek reelection. Because Hispanics were heavily concentrated in two of the above districts, they gained two of the three seats.

The redistricting process in California was specifically designed to increase Democratic Party representation in Congress, but also had the effect of helping Hispanics. In 1982, Democrats held 22 of California's U.S. House positions to 21 for Republicans, but despite population shifts to the suburbs (traditionally Republican strongholds) and already underpopulated Democratic urban districts, the state legislature, controlled by the Democrats, reapportioned the legislature in a way to enhance Democratic strength.[10]

Democratic U.S. Representative Phillip Burton, a close ally of California State Assembly Speaker Willie L. Brown, Jr., assumed the leadership role of liaison with the state legislature in congressional redistricting. Representative Burton produced the plan which was designed to secure as many as five new seats for the Democrats. The plan was structured so that at least eight incumbent Republican congressmen were placed in competition with one another. Representatives Barry Goldwater and Robert Dorman avoided an intraparty fight for their respective districts by running instead for the U.S. Senate. Representative David Dreier defeated fellow incumbent Wayne Grisham in the June primary and John M. Rousselot chose to run in a new district rather than face another incumbent, Carlos Moorhead. The Burton plan was adopted by the California legislature on September 15, 1981.

Because of its clear partisan gerrymandering nature, Republicans employed a two-pronged attack in challenging the plan, including a court suit to challenge the law and a statewide referendum asking voters to nullify it.[11] Despite their efforts, however, the plan was carried out.

A. *30th Congressional District.* California's 30th congressional district, represented by Democrat George Danielson for most of the 1970's, was changed considerably by the 1981 redistricting. The new district encompasses such suburban Los Angeles cities as El Monte, Alhambra, Monterey Park, San Gabriel, Montebello, Maywood, and Cudahy. Although once a rich agricultural area of orange, lemon, and walnut groves, the district is now heavily industrialized with major manufacturing in rocket motors, automobile parts, and electronic components.[12]

On June 8, 1982, a special election to fill the old 30th district seat vacated by Representative Danielson was held coinciding with the primary election for the new 30th seat. Matthew "Marty" Martinez, 53, a state assemblyman from Monterey Park (who was just completing his first term), was supported by the Waxman-Berman political machine and benefited from the heavy concentration of Hispanics, who make up 54 percent of the district's population. Martinez won the primary in a close race over Dennis Kazarian, who had been an aide to Representative Danielson. Martinez also won the special election with 32.4 percent of the votes over Kazarian, who received 29.1 percent, and Ralph Ramirez (a Republican), who received 15.9 percent, and two other opponents. Martinez won a special election runoff on July 13, 1982, with 51 percent of the vote over Ramirez, who received 40 percent. Martinez immediately flew to Washington and was sworn in on July 15 to serve the remaining 5.5 months of Representative Danielson's term and become the sixth voting member of the congressional Hispanic Caucus.[13] The victory gave Martinez the important advantage of incumbency in the district when he faced Republican Congressman John Rousselot, who had moved from the 26th district when the redistricting had placed him against another Republican. Martinez won the November 2 general election with 54 percent of the vote over Rousselot, who received 46 percent, a margin of 8,975 votes.

B. *34th Congressional District.* One of California's new districts, the 34th, is made up of suburban Los Angeles communities. The two largest cities in the district are located at different ends and contain about 80,000 people each. In the south is Norwalk, an older community made up of working-class people, about 40 percent of whom are Hispanics. On the other end is West Covina, a newer, still growing, and more affluent community. Also located in the district—whose population is 47 percent Hispanic—are Pico Rivera, La Puente, and South El Monte.[14]

Although the district was structured to provide a congressional base for one of several local Hispanic Democratic politicians, none entered the race. Initially, the only candidate was former three-time Congressman Jim Lloyd from West Covina, who received endorsement from the U.S. Chamber of Commerce and several Hispanic political leaders, including the mayors of Pico Rivera and La Puente. Eventually, Esteban Torres, a former White House official under Jimmy Carter and U.S. representative to UNESCO, entered the race. Although Torres's ties to East Los Angeles politicians concerned some Hispanic leaders in the suburban district who viewed his entry in the race as an attempt by the Los Angeles "Taco Mafia" to take over the 34th district, the issue soon died down when many prominent Hispanics endorsed his candidacy. Torres drew support from organized labor, national Hispanic leaders and organizations, and other national Democratic leaders. Helped by such support and a vigorous campaign, Torres defeated Lloyd and a third candidate, Fred Anderson, in the June primary.[15] Torres won convincingly in the November 2 general election, receiving 57 percent of the vote to 43 percent for Paul Jackson, his Republican opponent, a margin of 17,500 votes.

Texas

Texas, where Hispanics number 2,900,000, or 21 percent of the state population, was the only state in 1982 with more than one Hispanic congressman. Texas received three new seats as a result of the 1980 census, and the Texas state legislature adopted a new congressional district map incorporating the three new seats on August 10, 1981. In this case the plan, recommended by Republican Governor William Clements and conservative Democrat House Speaker Billy Clayton, was pushed through the legislature by a coalition of conservative Democrats and Republicans.

On August 14, a group of blacks and Hispanics filed suit in U.S. District Court claiming that the reapportionment plan discriminated against the voting rights of the two groups. Specifically, at issue was the shaping of districts in South Texas, Dallas-Fort Worth, and Houston areas. Texas is one state where election law changes must conform to guidelines established by the 1965 Voting Rights Act. Thus, the federal court deferred action on the suit, pending review by the U.S. Department of Justice.

On January 29, the Justice Department issued a ruling that the new reapportionment improperly divided the Hispanic population in two South Texas districts—the 15th and the 27th. The legislature-approved plan made the 15th district 52 percent Hispanic. The Justice Department maintained that the plan packed the 15th with Hispanics, while diluting their strength in the 27th.

When Governor Clements refused to call the legislature into special session to remedy the problem, the three-judge federal panel rearranged the two South Texas districts on February, virtually assuring that Hispanics would win both seats.[16] Since popular Hispanic Congressman E. "Kika" de la Garza was the incumbent in the 15th district, the court's redistricting plan only helped assure his reelection.

The 27th district, one of the three new Texas districts, is comprised of a strip of five counties lined up in the southeastern tip of Texas, stretching north and south along the coast of the Gulf of Mexico. At the northern tip is Corpus Christi and at the southern tip is Brownsville, the two largest cities in the district. The people of Brownsville were not too satisfied with the composition of the district as established by the court. There, residents have regarded the larger Corpus Christi as a traditional competitor for tourists and trade and worried that their interests would take second place to those of Corpus Christi. Corpus Christi is the second largest (next to Houston) Texas seaport and has large petrochemical and aluminum plants and seafood processing. Brownsville, on the other hand, is more of a Mexican-style city with a larger proportion of Hispanics. Export-import trade with Mexico is basic to the economy and it is a major agricultural producer of fruits and vegetables. Nueces (Corpus Christi) and Cameron (Brownsville) counties have traditionally been supporters of the Democratic Party and, since the new district was $2/3$ Hispanic, it was tailor-made for a Hispanic congressman.[17]

In this district, Solomon P. Ortiz, the Nueces (Corpus Christi) County sheriff, a veteran of 18 years of public officeholding in Nueces County, entered the race, and as in the past the working-class Hispanics provided the support needed for electoral victory. In the primary, Ortiz faced a crowded field of candidates which included four Hispanics. Ortiz, who got 25.6 percent of the vote, narrowly defeated former State Representative Joe Salem, a popular Lebanese jeweler who speaks Spanish and is quite popular with Hispanics, by only 653 votes. Salem got 24.8 percent of the vote. Jorge Rangel, a young Harvard-educated attorney from Corpus Christi, ran an aggressive well-financed media campaign, but ended up a distant third in the race with 18.5 percent. He was followed by State Representative Gerald Gonzales (17.3 percent) and Ruben Torres, a former state representative and chairman of the Texas Pardons and Parole Board, who got 13.8 percent.

In the run-off election, Ortiz received the endorsement of Torres, the only candidate from Cameron County, and, by thus consolidating the Hispanic vote in the district, defeated Salem by almost 6,000 votes (Ortiz 56.2 to Salem 43.8 percent).[18]

In the general election Ortiz went on to defeat the Republican nominee Jason Luby, a former mayor of Corpus Christi, in a landslide. Ortiz received 65 percent to 35 percent for Luby, a margin of 31,350 votes.

New Mexico

In New Mexico, Hispanics make up 36.6 percent of the state population, which is the largest percentage of any state. The New Mexico population increased by 28.1 percent since the 1970 census. Thus, New Mexico also qualified for a new seat in the 98th Congress.

New Mexico is the state which has maintained the most continuous Hispanic representation in the U.S. House of Representatives and the only U.S. senator. The first Hispanic U.S. senator was O. A. Larrazolo, a Republican, who was elected in 1929 to fill the unexpired term of Senator A. A. Jones, who died in office. Larrazolo, who had served as the third New Mexico governor (1919-1920), attended only the 1929 session of Congress. In 1934, Dennis Chavez, then a Democratic congressman, sought to restore Hispanic control of one of New Mexico's U.S. Senate seats, but he was defeated by Republican Senator Bronson Cutting in a close race. When Cutting was killed in a plane crash in 1935, Democratic Governor Clyde Tingley appointed Chavez to the vacancy. Chavez was reelected five times, and died in office in 1962, after serving 28 years, longer than any other person in New Mexico history. Joseph M. Montoya, then a U.S. representative, ran for Chavez' seat in 1964 and defeated Edwin L. Mechem, who had been appointed to the position. Senator Montoya served until 1976, when he was defeated by Harrison Schmitt.

When New Mexico became a state in 1912, it was entitled to only one member of the U.S. House of Representatives. The first Hispanic to serve in that position and the first Hispanic to serve as a regular voting member of Congress was Benigno "B.C." Hernandez, who served from 1915 to 1916 and from 1919 to 1920. Other Hispanics to serve in the single position were Nestor Montoya (1921-1922) and Dennis Chavez (1931-1934). New Mexico was allotted a second seat in Congress in 1942 and Antonio M. Fernandez was elected to the new seat. Fernandez served until 1956, when he died in office. He was succeeded by Joseph M. Montoya, in 1957, who served until 1962.[19] Republican Manuel Lujan, Jr., restored Hispanic parity in 1968, when he was elected to the first congressional district. Lujan, who has been reelected seven times, and is now in his 15th year in Congress, was elected from the new congressional district encompassing Bernalillo, Torrance, Guadalupe, and De Baca Counties.

Third Congressional District. Because the greatest population growth in New Mexico has been in the Albuquerque metropolitan area included in the old first congressional district, represented by Manuel Lujan, it was apparent to political demographers that one of the three new districts New Mexico was entitled to would be a metropolitan district which would serve the Albuquerque metropolitan area (Bernalillo County). Congressman Lujan, as a resident of Albuquerque, promptly announced that he would run from the metropolitan district. The only question that emerged during the reapportionment process regarding this district was which of the smaller counties near Bernalillo would be added to this central district to bring its population to approximately one third of the state population. Torrance County was proposed in the original plan, but eventually De Baca and Guadalupe Counties were also included.

The boundary lines for the remaining two districts became a matter of controversy in the legislature. Although the historical political and economic patterns of the state seemed to suggest that a northern district and a southern district were the most logical alternative, some conservative leaders in the legislature saw otherwise.

To understand the ensuing reapportionment struggle, it is necessary to profile the regional diversity of the state. New Mexico has not only been characterized by its large Hispanic and Indian populations (Indians make up 8.1 percent of the population), but also because both populations are concentrated in the northern half of the state. These groups have also been characterized by low per capita income, higher unemployment, and greater dependence on social programs—welfare and food stamps—than other groups in the state. The north has also had a large corps of skilled and unskilled labor and small farmers.

The southern half of the state, especially "Little Texas" in southeastern New Mexico, has been characterized by a greater Anglo concentration, and a more conservative orientation representative of large and medium-scale farming-ranching interests.

These traditional socioeconomic differences between the northern and southern half of the state have been reflected in political voting patterns. The north has supported liberal and moderate Democrats in national and state elections, while the south has supported conservatives and Republicans.[20]

With such clearly identifiable regional differences along ethnic, economic, and political lines, the redistricting process seemed to point to a north-south-central congressional district configuration. Predictably, however, the redistricting process was influenced by special and ideological interests.

Although Governor Bruce King had indicated in 1980 that the issue of congressional and state legislative reapportionment would be undertaken by a special session of the legislature sometime in late 1981 or early 1982 and after the final census figures were available, the first congressional redistricting bills were introduced in the 1981 session of the legislature. Although the legislature did not adopt any measure, it foreshadowed the reapportionment conflict which would emerge later. Two bills were introduced in the state House of Representatives. One bill called for the division of the state into north-south-central congressional districts. Another bill called for the division of the state into east-west-central congressional districts. This latter bill was introduced by Representative Dan Berry, a leading member of the coalition of conservative Democrats and Republicans, who controlled the House of Representatives. This Berry bill, which would have had the effect of splitting in two the heavy concentration of Hispanics in northern New Mexico, was adopted by the House voters and Election Committee and passed by the House of Representatives. The state Senate, recognizing the controversial nature of the bill and the probability that it would be challenged in court by minorities (both because of dilution of Hispanic votes and because census results were not yet complete), refused to take any action on the House-passed measure. Thus, the bill died when the legislature adjourned.

In January 1982, Governor King called the legislature into special session 10 days prior to the regular session in order to consider congressional and state legislative reapportionment. Although Governor King had earlier indicated that he would leave the matter of reapportionment to the legislature, he was clearly concerned that he might get a congressional reapportionment bill similar to the Berry plan, which had passed the House the year before. Signaling that he would probably veto such a proposal, and indicating his own preference for a plan which respected traditional regional economic, social, and political patterns, King presented his own reapportionment plan to the legislature.

The King plan was essentially a variation of the north-south-central district form, except that it divided the state almost diagonally, with boundaries for the two districts beginning near the northeast corner and running diagonally (along county lines) to the southwest corner of the state. This plan, probably more than any other proposed, recognized the regional differences in New Mexico. The Hispanic and Indian concentrations were in the proposed northwest district and the Anglo-farming-ranching conservative interests fell in the southeast district. The King plan also proposed that the central district would consist of Bernalillo County, Torrance County, and the "bedroom communities" of Corrales (in Sandoval County) and Bosque Farms (in Valencia County), since the latter were really part of the Albuquerque metropolitan area. This proposal to split counties is probably what made this plan unpopular, as the legislature seemed determined to respect county lines in reapportionment.[21]

Although at least five different plans were given serious consideration by the legislature, the basic contention was between the north-south-central district structure and the east-west-central district structure. Four of the plans were variations of the north-south-central plan, while the fifth was the Berry plan, which was reintroduced.

The debate on the measures, especially in the House of Representatives, was quite heated and bitter, with liberal Democrats condemning the Berry plan as discriminatory and a deliberate attempt to dilute Hispanic votes.[22] Representative Berry retorted, with candid irony, that Hispanics were one third of the state population and that his proposal gave them one third of the population in every district. Such reasoning, when publicly stated, would surely have been material for a court hearing on the matter if it had become necessary.

The debate on the measures reached a climax in the closing days of the special session when the Senate adopted a last-minute compromise bill prepared by Senator John Pinto (the only Indian in the Senate). The Pinto Bill, essentially a variation of the north-south-central district plan, offered a new twist in that it consolidated all the most Indian and Hispanic counties in the northern district, and it also placed Lincoln County in the northern district. Lincoln County was the home county of U.S. Congressman Joe Skeen, a Republican who had announced intentions of seeking reelection and had actively lobbied Republican state legislators to reject the Berry plan in favor of a north-south-central alternative. Alarmed at this new development, Skeen undoubtedly made known his displeasure to Republican legislators.

The House of Representatives meanwhile had adopted a slightly modified version of the Berry plan, which still retained one Hispanic county—San Miguel—in the southern district. When it became clear that neither house would accede to the other's version, a Joint House-Senate Conference Committee was created to iron out the differences in the bills. The conference committee arrived at a predictable compromise in which a trade-off of San Miguel and Lincoln Counties occurred. The Hispanic San Miguel County, along with Harding County, went to the northern district, while Lincoln County and Grant County were restored to the southern district, thus satisfying the concerns of Congressman Skeen.

The compromise version of the bill was probably as satisfactory as could be expected for Hispanics, since only one county—Guadalupe—which had traditionally been part of the Hispanic coalition, was detached in the new districting map, which sacrificed it in the central metropolitan district.

The plan could not have been more ideally tailored for Bill Richardson, a political newcomer to New Mexico, who had established his credibility as a viable congressional candidate by running a very close race against Congressman Lujan in the 1980 election. Even before the new district boundaries were arrived at, Richardson had announced that he would be a candidate. Roberto Mondragon, the popular two-term lieutenant governor, also announced his candidacy along with District Judge George Perez and Santa Fe Attorney Tom Udall, a political novice in New Mexico, who was trying to capitalize on his father

Stuart and uncle Morris Udall's name recognition.

Although a newcomer to New Mexico, Bill Richardson assumed the lead in public opinion polls and built on it with an extensive media and personal campaign. Richardson, a Hispanic by virtue of his mother's Mexican background, made his ethnicity clearly known in Spanish-language television and radio announcements. An extremely outgoing personality, Richardson devoted full-time to the campaign and for the first six months of 1982 was literally everywhere in the district. Richardson received over 60 percent of the delegate votes in the preprimary convention and top position on the ballot. Lieutenant Governor Mondragon, although the better known candidate, was hampered by lack of finances for a strong media campaign, and his duties as lieutenant governor, which prevented him from devoting more time to the campaign. The result was that Richardson received the nomination over Mondragon by 3,488 votes. Richardson received 36.3 percent, Mondragon 30.1 percent, Perez 19.2 percent, and Udall 13.7 percent of the vote.

Having won the most important Democratic primary, Richardson was able to run a more low-key campaign for the general election against the little known Republican candidate, Marjorie Bell Chambers. He won the November general election overwhelmingly, receiving 64 percent of the vote to Chambers' 36 percent, a margin of almost 38,000 votes.

Conclusion

The convening of the 98th Congress saw the greatest number of new Hispanic congressmen than ever in American history, and the greatest numbers of Hispanic members of Congress ever. A total of 11 Hispanics (counting the two nonvoting members from Puerto Rico and the Virgin Islands) now belong to the Congressional Hispanic Caucus, the coalition of congressmen who represented Hispanic interests.

Although the reapportionment process which enabled the four new Hispanics to achieve their seats in Congress was an obstacle course that presented formidable barriers, their ultimate success indicates that Hispanics have begun to move forward in the American political arena.

Assisted by significant legislation, such as the 1965 Voting Rights Act (and its revisions), the more responsive posture of the federal courts, and a more sympathetic and responsive Democratic Party, along with the growing interest, involvement, and bloc-voting by Hispanic voters, Hispanics have made impressive gains in the 98th Congress.

There is little doubt that there is room for improvement. Texas' 44th congressional district, including El Paso, with a Hispanic population of 60 percent; California's 44th congressional district, including central San Diego; Colorado's third district, including Pueblo and the San Luis Valley; and Arizona's Pima County (Tucson) district; and, of course, the greater Miami area are examples where substantial Hispanic concentrations of population might be targeted by Hispanic candidates in the future.

Ultimately, the number of Hispanics in Congress will only be as viable as the political influence they can wield individually and collectively (as the Hispanic Caucus) in pursuit of public policies favorable to Hispanics. Fortunately, the five veteran Hispanics have reached a level of seniority which yields to each substantial political influence—Representative Garza as chairman of the House Commerce Committee, Representative Lujan as the ranking Republican on the Interior Committee, Representative Gonzales as a ranking member of the Banking and Small Business Committees, and Representative Roybal as a member of the Appropriations Committee—and are among the highest ranking members of the House of Representatives. What remains is for these congressmen to act individually and collectively in pursuit of public policies that will begin to pave the way for social, economic, and political opportunities for all Hispanic Americans.

NOTES

*This paper was supported by a grant from the Institute of Research, New Mexico Highlands University.

[1] Jerry Apodaca was elected governor of New Mexico in 1974 and served from 1975 to 1978. Prior to Apodaca, Ezequiel C. de Baca, elected in 1914, served in 1915 (but died in office) and Octaviano A. Larrazolo, elected in 1916, served in 1917 and 1918.

[2] Mark Levy and Michael Cramer, "Patterns of Chicano Voting Behavior," in *La Causa Politica: A Chicano Politics Reader*, F. Garcia, editor, Notre Dame, Indiana: University of Notre Dame Press, 1974, pp. 241-249.

[3] Two other Hispanics serve as nonvoting members of Congress. They are Baltasar Corrada, who represents Puerto Rico, and Ron De Lugo, who represents the Virgin Islands.

[4] Senator Joseph M. Montoya had served in the U.S. Senate from 1964 to 1976. Before Montoya, Dennis Chavez represented New Mexico in the Senate from 1935 until his death in 1962.

[5] *Kirkpatrick Versus Preisler*, 394 U.S. 526, which says: "Equal representation for equal numbers of people is a principle designed to prevent debasement of voting power and diminution of access to elected representatives. Toleration of even small deviations detracts from these purposes."

[6] Alan Murray, "Redistricting Still Plagued by Confusion," *Congressional Quarterly Weekly Report*, January 19, 1981, pp. 69-72.

[7] *Ibid.*

[8] "Racial Dilution in Multimember Districts," *Michigan Law Review*, March 1978, p. 694.

[9] David Wells, "Affirmative Gerrymandering Compounds Districting Problems," *National Civic Review*, January 1978, p. 17.

[10] *Congressional Quarterly and Weekly Report*, May 30, 1981, pp. 941-942.

[11] Phil Duncan, "Burton Stuns GOP with California District Map," *Congressional Quarterly*, September 19, 1981, p. 1797. The court suit failed, but voters approved the Republican-sponsored referendum, which overturned the legislature's reapportionment. The legislature will have to rewrite the law.

[12] *Ibid.*, April 24, 1982, pp. 937-938.

[13] Congressional Hispanic Caucus, *ADVANCE*, August 1982, p. 1.

[14] *Congressional Quarterly*, April 24, 1982, pp. 939-940.

[15] *Ibid.*, June 12, 1982, p. 1416.

[16] Phil Duncan, "Courts at Odds Over Taxes Redistricting," *ibid.*, April 3, 1982, p. 752.

[17] *Ibid.*, p. 762.

[18] *Ibid.*, April 17, 1982, p. 885; June 12, 1982, p. 1429.

[19] For a discussion of these prominent Hispanic congressmen, see Maurilio Vigil, *Los Patrones: Profiles of Hispanic Political Leaders in New Mexico History*, Washington, D.C.: University Press of America, 1980.

[20] For a discussion of New Mexico politics and voting patterns, see Maurilio Vigil, *Chicano Politics*, Washington, D.C.: University Press of America, 1978, Chapter 7; "Jerry Apodaca and the 1974 Gubernatorial Election in New Mexico," *AZTLAN*, Volume 9, 1978, pp. 133-150.

[21] David Steinberg, "King Unveils Alternative Plan for Congressional Redistricting" *Albuquerque Journal*, January 8, 1981.

[22] Representative Raymond Sanchez, House majority floor leader and the remaining leader of the liberal Democratic Mama Lucy Faction, which controlled the House until 1978, was the most vehement critic. For more on the Mama Lucy Faction, see Maurilio Vigil, "The Mama Lucy Faction in the New Mexico Legislature: A study of Chicanos in Legislative Politics," *New Mexico Highlands University Journal*, July 1980, pp. 50-59.

Land Policy in the Spanish Southwest, 1846–1891:
A Study in Contrasts

IN CHOOSING to discuss land policy in that part of the Spanish Southwest which comprises present central and northern New Mexico and most of southern Colorado, I would appear to be using a model area of the West to demonstrate once again that the Homestead Act and principle were unworkable. In actuality the purpose is to note generally what can happen when an American land system runs into an older and highly different Spanish-Mexican one. As Howard W. Odum has observed, "Here two great culture systems have met and clashed and fused and are still in process of clashing and fusing."[1]

Americans had already experienced variants of the Spanish land system by the time they arrived in the Far Southwest—in Florida, Louisiana, Missouri, Texas, and California. But in each of these states a flood tide of American settlers overwhelmed both the land and the native peoples so that they quickly achieved Americanization by sheer numbers. In New Mexico, on the other hand, the attempt to impose American land customs was made by a minority of Americans in a predominantly Spanish-Mexican population as well as by a very casual and second-rate set of government officials. There was the further difficulty—still unique for Americans in 1846—of adjusting to the fact of subsistence agriculture on arid and irrigated lands. The ensuing compromises and peculiar results are significant not only because they comprise a peculiar chapter in American land history, but because they demonstrate the persistence of older eighteenth-century forms of American frontier land speculation and the dramatic, intimate relation which land policy can bear to the nature of government and of the economy.

To understand the unusual land situation in the area which, roughly speaking, consists of the upper Rio Grande and Arkansas River water-

---

[1] Howard W. Odum, *American Social Problems* (New York: H. Holt & Co., 1939), pp. 128–29.

sheds, one must go back to the two decades before the Mexican War and look at the whole Spanish Southwest from Texas to California. When the new Republic of Mexico assumed jurisdiction over these outer provinces, the overwhelming concern was to protect them both from the wild Indians within and the American from without. Various frontier colonization laws and schemes were put into motion. Convicts were given a chance to go to Texas or California, and aid was offered to respectable families if they would colonize. One of the results of such efforts was that during the 1820's, Moses and Stephen Austin persuaded Mexico to revive the *impresario* system—which the Spanish had tried in Missouri—in Texas. By it, foreigners declaring loyalty to Mexico would be awarded vast tracts of land in return for its successful colonization. Ironically, the first outcome of this policy was the occupation of Texas by Americans in such great numbers that Mexico lost the entire province through rebellion in 1836.

Despite this unexpected turn of events, there continued to be a lively interest in lands all along the borders of Mexico, for land speculation and fever in the Far Southwest between 1821 and 1846 was a Mexican phenomenon as well as an American one. In California, it took the form of seizing the rich and already cultivated monastery lands there in the flimsy name of "secularization." And this was followed later by a policy which granted foreigners, such as Colonel John Sutter, princely tracts and privileges resembling those given Austin in Texas.

As an older and more populated province, New Mexico had a land policy which was in some ways unique to itself. There lands had been granted by the Spanish crown, by the Mexican Congress, and by local governors. Further, the grants were to Pueblo Indians, community grants to a village, or large individual grants to influential men who agreed to defend and colonize the frontier. Finally, it should be remembered that there were differences between grants of irrigable land and grazing lands.[2]

Despite the existence of all these conditions, certain ambitious and practical businessmen and politicians in remote New Mexico also decided to capitalize on the new land policy. Taking advantage of a law which allowed local governors to make awards, a whole set of traders, frontiersmen, and local Mexican officials combined in what Harold

---

[2] Olen Leonard, *The Role of the Land Grant in the Social Organization and Social Processes of a Spanish-American Village in New Mexico* (unpublished Ph.D. dissertation, Louisiana State University [1940?]), pp. vii–ix. Frank W. Blackmar, *Spanish Institutions of the Southwest* (Baltimore, 1891), pp. 311–20.

Dunham has called the "first Santa Fe Ring" to secure vast land grants in the name of colonization, Indian defense, or the creation of buffer settlements to hold back Americans.[3] Of the 197 land grants made in New Mexico since its founding in 1598, sixty-nine were made in the nineteenth century, and twenty-three of these were made in the short period 1840–1847. In these latest grants a total of more than nine million acres was awarded.[4]

One of the first to realize these possibilities was Don José Manuel Martinez and his sons, who secured as a reward for Indian defense a grant of the beautiful Tierra Amarilla tract, which consisted of some 500,000 acres on the Chama River. Another early New Mexican *impresario* of sorts was Charles Hipolyte Trotier, Sieur de Beaubien, a Canadian-born fur trader who had settled in Taos and had acquired an interest in a Conejos Valley (Colorado) grant as early as 1832.[5] In 1835 José Tapia and seventy-five others received grants on the Mora River, and one John Scolley, described as owning "the best store" in Santa Fe, got still another. Meanwhile, the influential Baca family secured one for the region which is around Las Vegas, New Mexico.[6]

The largest operators, however, appear to have been foreign traders in the border town of Taos. There in 1841 Charles Beaubien and Ceran St. Vrain, the latter a grandson of a Frenchman who had been ruined by the frauds of the Scioto Land Company, joined the New Mexican governor himself in schemes to acquire several million acres. Also party to the deal was the governor's private secretary, Guadalupe Miranda.[7] Two years later, Luis Lee, a Missourian living in Taos, petitioned with Charles Beaubien's young son, Narcisse, for another million acres and was awarded the Sangre de Cristo grant. That same year one Gervacio Nolan is supposed to have persuaded the always amenable Governor Armijo to grant him the Valley of the Rio San

---

[3] Harold H. Dunham, *Government Handout: A Study in the Administration of the Public Lands, 1875–1891* (Ann Arbor, Mich.: Edwards Brothers, Inc., 1941), pp. 215–16, 216 n.

[4] *Annual Report of the Secretary of the Interior for 1855* (Washington, 1856), pp. 433–39. Ralph Carr, "Private Land Claims in Colorado," *The Colorado Magazine*, XXV, No. 1 (Jan. 1948), 10.

[5] Cleofas Jaramillo, *Shadows of the Past* (Santa Fe, N. Mex.: Seton Village Press, 1941), p. 13. Ralph E. Twitchell, *The Leading Facts of New Mexican History* (Cedar Rapids, Iowa: Torch Press, 1912), II, 273. Carr, "Private Land Claims," pp. 20–21.

[6] O. D. Barret, *The Mora Grant of New Mexico* (Washington, 1884), p. 13 (pamphlet in the Henry E. Huntington Library). James J. Webb, *Adventures in the Santa Fe Trade, 1844–47* (Southwest Historical Series, Glendale, Calif., 1931), p. 74 n.

[7] LeRoy R. Hafen, "Mexican Land Grants in Colorado," *The Colorado Magazine*, IV, No. 3 (May 1927), 91. Dunham, *Government Handout*, pp. 215 ff. Jim Berry Pearson, *The Maxwell Land Grant* (Norman, Okla.: Univ. of Oklahoma Press, 1961), ch. I.

Carlos near the Arkansas River. Still another vast grant was awarded to Ceran St. Vrain and Cornelio Vigil.[8] And so vague were the boundaries that the grantees were soon encroaching upon one another, upon lands granted to Pueblo Indians by the Spanish crown, and even upon wild Indian hunting grounds.[9]

Some years before American conquest, then, both natives and Americans in New Mexico—many of whom were actually of French-Canadian origin and knew of seigneurial grants there—had passed beyond furs and the Santa Fe trade to that third frontier of big business: land speculation. Since the grant was made through a governor who could play favorites, the land awards became a major political and economic issue. The competition was particularly keen in Taos, where no less than eleven grants had been made in six years.[10] There the influential Martinez family, representing native interests, fought it out with an "American Party" made up of Beaubien, Bent, Lee, Vigil and St. Vrain.[11] A friendly justice of the peace, *alcalde,* or governor, could mean the difference between a confirmed grant and a rejected one. Peace and trade with the wild Indians meant the difference between colonizing or letting the grants lie fallow and uninhabited. Thus Indian relations as well as politics became part and parcel of the history of the grants.

The land-grant saga was both interrupted and complicated by the outbreak of the Mexican War and the peaceful conquest of New Mexico by General Stephen W. Kearny in August 1846. It is interesting to find, for example, that although Kearny was ordered to keep existing officials in power and to co-operate with the leading families when he arrived in Santa Fe, he chose the American trader and landholder Charles Bent as governor, Charles Beaubien as a territorial judge, and Joab Houghton, a trader soon to be a land lawyer, as the second justice.[12]

Further, one finds that Kearny's arrangement to have New Mexicans register their land with a territorial secretary led to the wide-

---

[8] A summary account is in Carr, "Private Land Claims," pp. 10–30. See also Twitchell, *Leading Facts,* II, 451–81.

[9] David Lavender, *Bent's Fort* (Garden City, New York: Doubleday, 1954), p. 229.

[10] See tables and dates in *Annual Report of the Secretary of the Interior for 1855,* pp. 433–39.

[11] Governor Charles Bent's Letters to Manuel Alvarez, Dec. 1839 to June 1846 (microfilm in University of New Mexico Library). See especially Bent to Alvarez, Jan. 30, Feb. 19, 1841; Dec. 25, 1842; Nov. 12, 1844; March 30, 1845; March 4, April 6, 17, May 3, 1846.

[12] Twitchell, *Leading Facts,* II, 214. Ralph Bieber, ed., George R. Gibson, "Journal of a Soldier under Kearny and Doniphan, 1846–47" (Southwestern Historical Series, Glendale, Calif., 1935), p. 242.

spread rumor that this was preparatory to its confiscation by Americans.[13] This, coupled with a natural resistance to rule by outsiders, led to a December 1846 plot to wipe out the Americans. While the conspiracy failed to come off, it is significant that one of the clauses in Governor Bent's proclamation claiming that the rebellion was crushed, contained a reassurance that land titles would remain undisturbed.[14]

Nevertheless, in early January 1847, a group of rebels made up of Pueblo Indians, supporters of the Martinez family, and others struck in Taos and killed Governor Bent, Luis Lee, Narcisse Beaubien, Cornelio Vigil, and tried to get at Beaubien and St. Vrain.[15] It is too much of a coincidence that all those murdered were the largest land grantees and the most persistent aggressors of the Pueblo holdings in the province. The Taos Rebellion of 1847 has been called a failure, but it held up the land schemes of a bunch of ambitious American speculators for a generation.

After the rebellion, the land problem remained virtually suspended until 1854. That year Congress created the office of Surveyor General for Mexico and attempted to carry out the clauses of the Treaty of Guadalupe Hidalgo with regard to settlement of land claims. But this was much easier said than done, for when William Pelham, the first Surveyor General, arrived in Santa Fe he found over one thousand claims awaiting settlement. Of these, 197 involved large private grants as opposed to smaller community and Pueblo Indian grants.[16] In a comparison of California and New Mexican land problems, H. H. Bancroft has also described the difficulties Pelham faced:

> There was the same careless informality, in respect to title papers, and the same vagueness in boundaries; the [New Mexican] grants, however, were more numerous, much more complicated by transfers and subdivisions, more varied in their nature as originating from national, provincial, sectional, and local officials; and the archives were much less complete.[17]

The California holders were required to present their claims to a Federal Land Commission for confirmation. If they did not, the land was restored to the public domain. But in New Mexico Pelham was

---

[13] Donaciano Vigil, *History of New Mexico to 1851* (MS in the W. R. Ritch Collection, Box 8, Henry E. Huntington Library. Hereafter cited as HEH).

[14] Charles Bent, *Proclamation*, Santa Fe, Jan. 5, 1847 (broadside in HEH).

[15] Twitchell, *Leading Facts*, II, 233-48.

[16] William W. Morrow, *Spanish and Mexican Private Land Grants* (San Francisco, 1924; pamphlet in HEH). Herbert O. Brayer, "Pueblo Indian Land Grants in the Rio Abajo, New Mexico," Univ. of New Mexico *Bulletin* (Albuquerque, 1938), p. 20.

[17] H. H. Bancroft, *History of New Mexico and Arizona* (San Francisco, 1888), p. 643.

told that "until final action of Congress on such claims, all lands covered thereby shall be reserved from sale or other disposal by the government."[18] This was the equivalent of denying the existence of a public domain in New Mexico. At the same time, it virtually guaranteed that long legal battles climaxed by acts of Congress would characterize the history of the New Mexican land system. As various writers have observed, a paradise for lawyers and politicians had been created.

Since New Mexico was a province virtually without native lawyers, the whole land question became an exclusive concern of American attorneys, who were quick to see in it all sorts of possibilities and implications. It soon attracted the leading men of the territory. The first chief justice, Joab Houghton, was also an attorney for twelve claimants, among them Ceran St. Vrain. The first squatter delegate to Congress was in charge of at least ten land-grant clients. Later in the 1850's, future delegate and judge John S. Watts told a Congressional committee he was handling forty-three cases.[19] In the rush to clear title, Charles Beaubien and Guadalupe Miranda, two of the largest claimants, decided to take no chances and hired three lawyers, two of whom were public officials.[20]

From the very beginning it is evident that these lawyers, traders, and officials were aware of two things: first, that they were dealing with a relatively ignorant, provincial, and highly passive native population. Second, that New Mexico outside of the Santa Fe trade offered no business opportunities, had no agricultural surplus, no developed mining industry. Apart from participating in the supply of goods to the Army and Indian agencies, land speculation became the one way to acquire an estate there. Once they had fathomed the land system, they went on to use the various cloudy and contradictory Spanish and Mexican land laws to stretch their clients' holdings far beyond their original size. As Governor Lionel A. Sheldon was to remark later, the grants had taken on remarkable "India rubber" qualities.[21] Thus, almost to a man, they refused to accept an old Mexican law of 1824 which declared all grants must not be larger than eleven square leagues

---

[18] Morrow, *Spanish and Mexican Land Grants*, pp. 22–23.
[19] *John S. Watts to the Committee on Private Land Claims* (printed pamphlet, Washington, 1871), pp. 1–2. See also compiled volume, *Private Land Claims*, in the Thomas B. Catron Law Library, HEH. For names of lawyers related to each case, see *Private Land Claims*, I, 1–38.
[20] *Ibid*.
[21] William A. Keleher, *Maxwell Land Grant: A New Mexico Item* (Santa Fe, N. Mex.: Rydal Press, 1942), p. 9.

in size. Even the adoption of this law by Congress and by the Interior Department as a guide eventually had little effect in New Mexico.[22] There was the further fact that most native New Mexicans could not pay for the process of confirmation in cash and had to give the lawyers slices of land instead. The obvious result, as we shall see, was that the lawyers soon became their own best clients. Indeed, eventually over 80 per cent of the grants came to be owned by Americans.[23]

The complex and often tedious history of the hundreds of land-grant cases and their relations both to the New Mexican economy and politics might be epitomized by a brief account of the most famous and notorious of all the tracts: the Beaubien-Miranda claim, which eventually took the name of the Maxwell Land Grant. The new name arose from the fact that Beaubien's son-in-law, Lucien Bonaparte Maxwell, eventually acquired all of the grant from various heirs and settled on it to live in frontier splendor for a number of years. Lavishly hospitable to all visitors, he nevertheless managed to make money selling cattle and grain to Indian agencies and to the army. After the Civil War, however, Maxwell decided to sell the grant for a fantastic profit and price, a thing he felt he could easily do since Congress had confirmed the grant by an act of 1860.[24]

Anxious to swell his own properties to the largest possible size, Maxwell asked for a new government survey in 1869. Much to his disappointment, the government ruled that his claim as a double land grant was only twenty-two leagues, or roughly 97,000 acres.[25] But this did not stop either Maxwell or the future purchasers. In Colorado, Jerome B. Chaffee, a wealthy mine owner and future senator was interested in the purchase, as was George H. Chilcott, the former land register for Colorado. And in the background was ex-governor William Gilpin, who had been interested in the New Mexican tracts for over twenty years and who already owned vast holdings in the San Luis Valley.[26]

The importance and the extent of the interest of these Colorado land

---

[22] *Laws and Decrees of the Republic of Mexico in Relation to Colonization and Grants of Land* (New York, 1871) in HEH, reprints most of the key documents regarding land grants. See also Dunham, *Government Handout*, pp. 219–20.

[23] Herbert O. Brayer, *William Blackmore: The Spanish Land Grants of New Mexico and Colorado, 1863–1878* (Denver: Bradford-Robinson, 1949), I, 19.

[24] Keleher, *Maxwell Grant*, p. 19.

[25] Dunham, *Government Handout*, pp. 219–22.

[26] "Gilpin Interview," *Denver Daily Tribune*, May 25, 1879. Gilpin's career in land grants is covered in Brayer, *Blackmore*, I, 65–96. See also Harold H. Dunham, "Coloradoans and the Maxwell Grant," *The Colorado Magazine*, XXXII, No. 2 (April 1955).

rings becomes more obvious when it is realized that they were but one of four groups interested in Maxwell's land. In New Mexico itself a remarkably shrewd and able group of lawyers, politicians, and businessmen were also parties to the purchase. Here could be found Stephen B. Elkins, Thomas Catron, Governor William A. Pile, ex-delegate Watts, and Miguel A. Otero, the wealthy partner of Otero, Sellar and Company. And, as always, the current Surveyor General was a party to the scheme.[27] After many maneuvers the Colorado-New Mexican groups actually purchased the Maxwell grant in 1870 for $650,000. Around their acquisition the buyers created an organization called the Maxwell Land Grant and Railroad Company.[28] At the same time, Stephen Elkins, who never did things by halves, persuaded Maxwell to use part of his money to found the first regular bank in New Mexico: the First National of Santa Fe. The bank in turn was chiefly interested in handling the company's securities.[29]

The men who purchased Maxwell's grant had even larger plans than its former owners had ever envisaged. Acutely aware of the vagueness of the tract, they hired W. W. Griffin, an amenable deputy surveyor of New Mexico, to survey the grant as a two-million-acre plot, in contrast to the 97,000 acres to which Congress and the Secretary of the Interior Cox had limited it in 1869 The results of Griffin's report were filed in Washington and, without waiting for confirmation, a company agent rushed off to London to sell the grant to English purchasers for $1,350,000. Then, in a maneuver which looked suspiciously like passing the buck, the English company persuaded a fourth party, Dutch financiers in Amsterdam, to handle the mortgage. Stock was then issued up to the sum of $5,000,000.[30]

Thus far the activities of the company resembled more that of an early American land company. But with the appointment af William Jackson Palmer as president of the company it became obvious that railroad development was a major concern of the firm. At the time Palmer was superintendent of the Kansas Pacific, then building into Colorado, and he was already laying plans to build the Denver and Rio Grande.[31] What was unusual in this case was not that railroad and land speculators combined, but that they intended to build and

[27] William A. Keleher, *The Fabulous Frontier* (Santa Fe, N. Mex.: Rydal Press, 1945), p. 104n.
[28] Keleher, *Maxwell Grant*, pp. 36 ff. Pearson, *Maxwell Grant*, pp. 49–54.
[29] *Ibid.*, pp. 45–54.
[30] *Ibid.*, pp. 54–75 *passim.*
[31] Dunham, *Government Handout*, pp. 223–24.

develop with private rather than public grants, a condition which gave either the railroad or the landowners extraordinary powers with virtually no strings attached. It was also true that these grants included the famous Santa Fe trail and mountain passes which were vital to any road hoping to penetrate New Mexico.

Having acquired land, created a bank, and laid plans for a railroad, the ambitious firm still had to face up to the fact that its claims to two million acres were quite shaky. A new Interior ruling in 1871 that the grant was only 97,000 acres was countered with the opinion of a half-dozen leading lawyers, among them William G. Evarts and Judah P. Benjamin, that the enlarged grant was the valid one. Meanwhile the company continued to sell its $5,000,000 worth of stock in Europe and congratulated itself when both Jerome B. Chaffee of Colorado and Stephen B. Elkins of New Mexico were elected delegates to Congress. This was only a token of the great political power the land ring possessed in both territories.[32]

While the Maxwell Land Grant Company failed to get a favorable decision on its two-million-acre claim during the mid-seventies, it did persuade Land Commissioner James A. Williamson to establish the precedent that court decisions would henceforth determine the size and validity of a claim.[33] When a new survey was ordered, the contract was awarded to two engineering innocents, R. T. Marmon and J. T. Elkins, the latter a brother of former Delegate Elkins. After a swift and almost meaningless survey lasting only twenty-two days, they filed reports which declared that the grant was indeed nearly 2,000,000 acres in size. On May 19, 1879, a ten-year battle ended because of favorable court decisions and land office rulings. And ironic was the situation, as Dunham has noted, when the very honest reformer, Land Commissioner Williamson, was forced to issue patents of ownership for 1,714,764 acres of land.[34] By bold daring the Maxwell Company had made old Charles Beaubien's dream of empire come true.

In the realm of the remaining land grants, the methods and successes of the Maxwell Company triggered other claimants and speculators into action. At the same time the Maxwell purchase was being made, the Colorado speculators were buying the Las Animas Grant (originally called the Vigil-St. Vrain grants); the Sangre de Cristo Grant (the old Beaubien-Lee grant) was being sold to William Black-

---

[32] *Ibid.*, pp. 222–25.
[33] *Ibid.*, pp. 227–28.
[34] *Ibid.*, pp. 230–31.

more, an English investor with enormous holdings in the Southwest.[35] And by 1872, negotiations for the purchase of at least six more major grants were being carried on.[36]

In the decade from 1875 to 1885, the remaining unconfirmed grants continued to stretch impressively. When George W. Julian took over the Surveyor General's duties in the latter year, he was shocked to find that the Canada Ancha grant, which had originally been for 130 acres, ended as a claim for 375 square miles of territory. Others were even more spectacular: the Canon de Chama grant of 184,000 acres was increased by claimants and preceding surveyor generals to 472,000 acres. The Tierra Amarilla grant was by then some 932 square miles. Counting the Maxwell grant, some thirty-four claimants alone declared their holdings to be over 100,000 acres each![37] It was patent that here was the territory's largest "industry."

Naturally the lawyers of Santa Fe exacted their fees for clearing titles. Being paid in land, they themselves gradually acquired ownership of the largest grants and, as noted above, eventually laid claim to over 80 per cent of the Spanish grants.[38] Most impressive of all were the accumulated holdings of Thomas B. Catron. Never a modest man, on June 23, 1893, he listed his estate as being:

> 50,000 acres of the Mora Grant
> 80,000 acres of the Beck Grant
> ⅔ of the 78,000 acres of the Espiritu Santa Grant
> ½ of the 21,500 acres of the Tecolote Grant
> 7,600 acres of the Juana Lopez Grant
> 24,000 acres of the Piedra Lumber Grant
> 11,000 acres of the Gabaldon Grant
> 15,000 acres of the Baca Grant
> a portion of the Tierra Amarilla Grant
> 8,000 acres in patented homesteads.[39]

But not even these told the whole story. A year later the Santa Fe *New Mexican* estimated that he was interested in seventy-five grants, owned nearly 2,000,000 acres, and was part owner or attorney for 4,000,000 more.[40]

---

[35] These are described in detail in Brayer, *Blackmore*, I, especially pp. 130 ff.
[36] *Ibid.*, I, 147 ff.
[37] George W. Julian, "Land Stealing in New Mexico," *North American Review* (July 1, 1887), pp. 20–25.
[38] See note 23, above.
[39] Vioalle C. Hefferan, *Thomas B. Catron* (unpublished Master's thesis, University of New Mexico, 1940), p. 156.
[40] *Santa Fe New Mexican*, Oct. 31, 1894.

The details of the various land-grant histories have been thoroughly covered by Dunham, Herbert O. Brayer, Jim Berry Pearson, and many others, so they need not be recounted here.[41] What is of concern here is the many important consequences these land intrigues had for the political and economic makeup of New Mexico and parts of Colorado. It became obvious that to succeed in settling land questions, for example, the interested parties needed a political machine. Out of such a need grew the first American Santa Fe Ring. Although many legends surround its purpose and its membership, it was essentially a set of lawyers, territorial judges, politicians and businessmen who united to run the territory much as an oligarchy would, and proceeded to make money out of the region.[42] One of its many distinctions lay in the fact that rather than deal in some manufactured item or railroads, land was their first medium of currency.

What was also unusual about the Santa Fe Ring was that it was predominantly an American body in a territory made up largely of Spanish-Americans, and that its bosses more likely than not were also the key public officials. The Ring existed both on the territorial and local level, controlled a key newspaper, and, unlike many eastern counterparts, survived over a long period because it was realistic enough to accept under its wing any co-operative or useful official, so that every five years the personnel had changed somewhat. In a similar way the ring changed its economic interests as the economy of New Mexico slowly altered. Wrote the irate reformer, Governor Edmund G. Ross:

> From the Land Grant Ring grew others, as the opportunities for speculation and plunder were developed. Cattle Rings, Public Land Stealing Rings, Mining Rings, Treasury Rings, and rings of almost every description grew up, till the affairs of the Territory came to be run almost exclusively in the interest and for the benefit of combinations organized and headed by a few longheaded, ambitious and unscrupulous Americans . . .[43]

While it was a Republican ring, drawing heavy support from an almost unbroken line of Republican administrations in Washington, it had many Democratic adherents. Among the latter was the chairman

---

[41] Dunham, *Government Handout*. Brayer, *William Blackmore*. Pearson, *Maxwell Grant*.

[42] For a summary of the Ring's activities see H. R. Lamar, "Political Patterns in New Mexico and Utah Territories, 1850–1900," *Utah Historical Quarterly*, XXVIII, No. 4 (Oct. 1960), 371–74.

[43] Edmund G. Ross to John O'Grady, March 26, 1887 (MS letter in Edmund G. Ross Papers, Archives Division of the New Mexico State Records Center, Santa Fe).

of the New Mexico Democratic party from 1884 to 1889.[44] "A well-formed ring," wrote Governor L. B. Prince, "embraces members of both parties and the New Mexican one is remarkably well formed. They seem to fight when in reality they are pulling together."[45] Governor Ross also observed that each combination within the ring had a Republican and a Democratic lawyer "for prudential reasons, so that whichever side might come uppermost, the dominant party was represented."[46] It might also be added that Americans in New Mexico were so heavily engaged in the governing and legal business that Governor Ross estimated that one in every ten Americans there was a lawyer.

In short, a brilliant and unusual technique of exploitation, reminiscent of the Holland Land Company and of the Ohio Associates had been revived, modernized, and given the trappings both of the corporation and of the post-Civil War political ring so common to the Grant era. The Santa Fe Ring was a sophisticated combination of the eighteenth-century speculator and the nineteenth-century businessman building an edifice on a questionable Spanish land system. What is of interest here is that it permitted the American in the Southwest to control what economists call the "multiplier effect" to an extraordinary degree. To use the example of the Maxwell Grant again, its sale created a bank in Santa Fe but it remained in the hands of the ring. The capital realized by another participant, Wilson Waddingham, was used to help start the Denver and Rio Grande Railroad, whose founder was William Jackson Palmer, one of the presidents of the Maxwell Company. The Denver and Rio Grande in turn used its control of the Nolan and other grants to develop its own towns, mines, herds and the like. And from this sprang the Colorado Fuel and Iron Company. Eventually the whole of southern Colorado became the bailiwick of this company and the Denver and Rio Grande. Not content with that, Palmer dreamed of a whole area "all under one's control and with one's friends . . ." It would be made up of desirable English-type immigrants, workers made happy with schools, bath houses and libraries, and with no strikes.[47]

Yet the exclusive power to develop also meant the power to refuse

---

[44] Julian, "Land Stealing in New Mexico," pp. 28–29.
[45] Undated manuscript commentary by L. B. Prince in T. B. Catron Papers, Coronado Room, University of New Mexico Library (Albuquerque).
[46] Ross to O'Grady, March 26, 1887. Ross Papers.
[47] Herbert O. Brayer, *William Blackmore: Early Financing of the Denver and Rio Grande Railway and Ancillary Land Companies, 1871–78* (Denver: Bradford-Robinson, 1949), II, 18–19.

to develop until suitable conditions occurred. This was brought out in a report on New Mexico by her delegate in 1871:

> Of her 77,568,640 acres of land less than 8,000,000 have been surveyed, so as to be put in the way of perfecting titles. Last year only 1,114 acres were sold for cash and . . . scrip, and 3,361 acres were entered for homestead settlements . . . Less than $1,000,000 in gold, silver, and copper were taken from her mines, though some of the best are known to be within her borders.[48]

Romero also concluded that seven railroads were held up at the New Mexican borders because of confusion in land.

The question remains: what efforts were made to break the land rings and to change the nature of land policy in New Mexico? Two examples, one extralegal and one Federal, may be cited as bringing about some change.

The extralegal activity came when gold was discovered on the Maxwell Grant in 1867, and open-range ranching developed in most of eastern New Mexico as well as on the grant itself at roughly the same time. Thus, for the first time in New Mexican history a fairly large number of American citizens concentrated in various parts of the territory. Americans in Colfax County, where a major part of the Maxwell Grant was located, virtually changed its character. Both miners and ranchers coming from a public-domain heritage disliked getting licenses or permission to go about their business. What resulted was a classic company-squatter feud which went on until 1890, and perpetuated an extraordinary amount of violence and an impressive number of murders for over two decades.[49] Because of the economic involvement of many key officials in Santa Fe, efforts to bring about just settlements were both hypocritical and sporadic.[50]

Local politics became, therefore, almost purely and simply an attribute of an economic struggle between Americans with a public-domain concept of the frontier and an organization which insisted that the region, because of its Spanish-Mexican origins, was private property. While most of the squatters were not destined to win their feud with the Maxwell Company, they gave the whole problem much-

---

[48] Hon. Trinidad Romero, "Settling Private Land Claims." Speech to U. S. House of Representatives, Dec. 17, 1878 (printed pamphlet in HEH).

[49] Pearson, *Maxwell Grant*, pp. 67 ff., 88–93, 137–39; Keleher, *Maxwell Grant*, pp. 68 ff.; F. Stanley, *The Grant that Maxwell Bought* (Denver: privately printed, 1952), all cover this in great detail. For a similar feeling in Colorado see Brayer, *Blackmore*, I, 135–36, 142–44.

[50] See, for example, Keleher, *Maxwell Grant*, pp. 97–106.

Land Policy in the Southwest 511

needed publicity and pointed up the need for the final settlement of a question left unsolved for more than thirty years. Aided by an increased American immigration, the coming of railroads, and the rise of the ranching and mining industry, the old order was finally changing.

The legal, or rather Federal, fight to amend New Mexico's land system began with the election in 1884 of Grover Cleveland, who not only tried to effect land reforms in the West by appointing honest men to Interior and Land-Office posts, but tried to back his new policies in the field by choosing reformers as governors of the various territories.[51] Among these was Governor Edmund G. Ross, a former Kansas senator who had cast the deciding vote against President Johnson's impeachment in 1868. Ross was sent to New Mexico along with a new surveyor general, George W. Julian of Indiana. A former abolitionist, Civil War general, and a noted public-lands expert, Julian also was a scrupulously honest official.[52]

Ross appears to have been the first governor to come to New Mexico with the dream of making it American in culture and democratic in government. This could be achieved, he felt, with railroads, public schools, separation of church and state, the breakup of the Santa Fe Ring, and land reform.[53] Governor Ross's efforts in each of these cases make for a mock-heroic epic, but his and Julian's land proposals are particularly pertinent to the review of a hundred years of the Homestead policy.

Julian took the view that truly Draconian measures must be employed. After casting doubt on all decisions made by his predecessors in the office of Surveyor General, he announced that 90 per cent of all land entries in the territory were fraudulent.[54] While this was probably true, it also struck at every citizen of means and at the livelihood of most of the legal profession of New Mexico. Much of the intense bitterness which developed over Ross's administration, in fact, was caused by Julian's ruthless scrutiny of land records and his scathing reports to Washington.

Julian's findings led to the arrest and conviction of former Land

---

[51] Dunham, *Government Handout*, p. 180. Roy M. Robbins, *Our Landed Heritage; The Public Domain, 1776–1936* (Princeton: Princeton Univ. Press, 1942), pp. 291 ff.

[52] H. R. Lamar, "Edmund G. Ross as Governor of New Mexico Territory: A Reappraisal," *New Mexico Historical Review*, XXXVI, No. 3 (July 1961). Portions of this paper have been used throughout the present paper.

[53] *Ibid.*, pp. 181–84.

[54] Julian, "Land Stealing in New Mexico," pp. 20–25.

Register Max Frost on charges of fraudulent land entry. Julian also summarized his investigations in a blunt article for the *North American Review* in which he fiercely denounced ex-Senator Stephen Dorsey, who now operated a vast ranching enterprise in northeastern New Mexico and was a claimant to many suspect land grants.[55] Enmity to Dorsey called forth the opposition of the Maxwell Company with whom the ex-senator was allied. Then Julian in a clean sweep denounced C. H. Gildersleeve, chairman of the territorial Democratic party, as a member of the ring and as a "politician for revenue only." [56] The hornet's nest had been stirred and the effects soon began to appear. Senator Preston B. Plumb of Kansas warned Ross that letters were pouring into Washington complaining that Julian's methods had brought all business to a standstill since no one was sure of title to property.[57] In a slap at Julian and the Cleveland administration, the 1886 Democratic territorial convention unanimously adopted a resolutian to play down land frauds. The incumbent delegate, himself a dealer in a half-dozen fraudulent grants, successfully ran for re-election on such a ticket.[58]

Meanwhile, Governor Ross had placed his hopes first in the creation of a special Federal land commission such as California had used; but eventually he decided to advocate the establishment of a Court of Private Land Claims. Though one was not created until after he had left office, Ross had the pleasure of seeing his idea go into effect in 1891, the very year the General Revision Act was passed, correcting other long-standing land abuses.[59]

Ross was also active in other ways. As a free-soil Kansan he was a violent advocate of the Homestead law, and made this fact plain in hundreds of speeches. During the late 1880's this required a certain temerity, for the range-cattle industry in New Mexico was just reaching its peak and brought in some $13,000,000 a year.[60] But to Ross ranching implied a sparse population, huge landed estates—which he called a constant menace to popular government and the perpetrator of oligarchic rule. As best he could, he cracked down on ranchers who

---

[55] *Ibid.*, pp. 27–30.
[56] *Ibid.*, pp. 27–30.
[57] Preston B. Plumb to Ross, July 9, 1886. Ross Papers.
[58] Lamar, "Ross: A Reappraisal," p. 191.
[59] Ross's successor, L. B. Prince, had much to do with the creation of this court. See L. B. Prince, *A Concise History of New Mexico* (Cedar Rapids, Iowa: Torch Press, 1912), p. 207. Robbins, *Our Landed Heritage*, pp. 296–97.
[60] G. P. Hammond and T. C. Donnelly, *The Story of New Mexico: Its History and Government* (Albuquerque, N. Mex.: Univ. of New Mexico Press, 1936), p. 137.

Land Policy in the Southwest

were disobeying the law and particularly on sheriffs who were in reality the agents of cattlemen's associations.

In his first annual report to the Interior Department, Ross recommended that there be no further disposal of public lands except for homesteading purposes.[61] In subsequent reports he called the cattleman's theory of a permanent range a bad one, for cattle frontiers were by nature temporary. In a speech in 1885 he complimented the cattlemen upon their contribution to the settlement and wealth of the territory, but warned them that there must be order between them and the sheep interests. That order was needed, he said, so people would migrate to New Mexico. "People are worth more than steers . . ., for with people comes capital and the spirit of commercial adventure, development, prosperity and greatness."[62] Two years later he bluntly told a crowd at the territorial fair that the "granger was coming and coming to stay." Ross failed to make New Mexico either like free-soil Kansas or standard America, but he never gave up trying. After his term as governor, he served as secretary to the Board of Immigration and wrote articles on irrigation. And in all his actions he stressed that New Mexico was the ideal place for the small independent farmer.[63]

Meanwhile, the Federal Court of Private Land Claims began sitting in Denver and Santa Fe in 1891 and for at least a decade thereafter, and finally managed to settle land claims now some fifty years old. The Court itself left something to be desired, for the various land lobbyists managed to get friendly justices appointed to the court so that body frequently ruled in favor of the large claimants.[64] But a great stumbling bloc to the workings of a more normal American land policy had been removed.

Obviously, in a region where more than 50 per cent of the population was Spanish-American and where much of the land was already occupied and most new lands were best adapted to grazing, no great homestead or pre-emption rush occurred. Slow but basic changes were coming, however, a fact symbolized by the appearance in 1889 of a Farmers' Alliance in Colfax County and a small but vigorous Populist party in the territory soon thereafter.[65] By 1896 the influx of average

---

[61] *Report of the Governor of New Mexico . . . 1885* (Washington, 1886), pp. 7–8.
[62] *Albuquerque Morning Democrat*, Sept. 21, 1887.
[63] Lamar, "Ross: A Reappraisal," pp. 207–8.
[64] Keleher, *Maxwell Grant*, p. 9.
[65] *Springer Banner* (New Mexico), Oct. 17, Nov. 7, 1889; Jan. 23, 1890. A good account of the 1894 Populist Convention in New Mexico is in *The Western Liberal* (Lordsburg, New Mexico), Oct. 12, 1894.

American farmers, ranchers and miners had so changed things that the whole of New Mexican politics revolved around the silver issue, which split even the Santa Fe Ring for a time. One result was that for the first time in New Mexican history a reformer—Harvey Fergusson—was elected to Congress.

It would be misleading to suggest by way of a conclusion that the solution of the land-grant question made New Mexico a more or less typical American ranching, irrigated farming, and mining community. Spanish-American cultural, religious, economic and political practices still survived almost intact. The tradition of large land-owning *patrons* with almost the power of life and death over a village continued to exist.[66] Moreover, individual land-grant cases still appear in court there today.[67] It is further misleading to think that it was the peculiar land situation alone which produced the Santa Fe Ring, an economic oligarchy, or the like. Monopolies are very much a part of a frontier condition, since on-the-spot persons with capital can usually go into a multiple number of infant enterprises. What made New Mexico unique was that it was such a subsistence frontier its only medium of currency was land, and that was in the hands of a few people. Finally, the tradition of a passive, relatively illiterate electorate willing to sell its vote, obey the local *patron,* or simply to co-operate, made it easy to get away with extraordinary abuses and with an unusual concentration of power. And here again the threat to foreclose on a cloudy land title more than once determined the outcome of an election.[68] Even in a period as late as the 1920's, one finds the late Senator Cutting of New Mexico creating a successful machine out of passive Spanish-American voting blocs.

One is led to wonder if it might not have been different had the land-grant questions been solved with relative quickness as were those of California; or if the railroad had been able to come there ten years earlier; or even if the Federal Government had pursued some kind

---

[66] Olen Leonard and C. P. Loomis, "Culture of a Contemporary Rural Community, El Cerrito, New Mexico," *Rural Life Studies* (Washington: U. S. Agriculture Dept., 1941). E. E. Maes, "The World and the People of Cundiyo," *Land Policy Review* (Washington: U. S. Agriculture Dept.), March 1941. Sigurd Johansen, *Rural Social Organization in a Spanish-American Culture Area* (Albuquerque, N. Mex.: Univ. of New Mexico Press, 1948).

[67] Myra E. Jenkins, "The Baltasar Baca 'Grant': History of an Enroachment," *El Palacio*, Vol. LXVIII number (Spring 1961).

[68] Keleher, in *The Fabulous Frontier*, p. 117, remarks that when T. B. Catron died he left behind a quarter of a million dollars in outlawed and uncollectable promissory notes. "The evidence of so many outstanding loans indicated Catron's method of doing business, and furnished a key to the source of at least some of his political power and prestige."

of reconstruction policy as it did in the post-Civil War South and later in Mormon Utah. Certainly if the land system had been different the political history would have taken a different course also.

In New Mexico it appears that the United States faced, in a general way, its first imperial problem long before the acquisition of Puerto Rico and the Philippines. For there they found a different culture and people as well as a new region. Further, they found it to be a "have-not" region economically speaking, just as are many of the so-called underdeveloped areas of the world we are invading today. The difficulties even of imposing a new land policy on the Spanish Southwest met with so many hindrances it might serve as a lesson in humility for today. But most intriguing, one wonders what the region would have been like had even the rudiments of the Homestead principle been allowed to operate in New Mexico as of 1862. At least it would have ameliorated what Herbert Brayer called the process of "impoverishment, dispossession, and dislocation of population" of the native Spanish-Americans which was effected by the private land-grant speculators.[69]

HOWARD R. LAMAR, *Yale University*

[69] Brayer, *Blackmore*, I, 17. Leonard, *Role of the Land Grant*, pp. 180 ff.

SIX

Land, Water, and Ethnic Identity in Taos*

Sylvia Rodríguez

I. Introduction

Control over land and water remains the primary bone of contention in the relations among Indian, Hispano, and Anglo populations in northern New Mexico. This multifaceted set of issues has evolved out of a historical context of successive conquest, land expropriation, and sociopolitical domination by one ethnic group over another, a regional background captured by Spicer's phrase "cycles of conquest." For Hispanos alone among Mexican Americans, land remains an immediate and volatile issue rooted in everyday life. This state of affairs dates from the Treaty of Guadalupe Hidalgo, the political event that engendered the social category of *Mexican American* and signaled land expropriation for most Mexicanos outside the Hispano "homeland" region.[1] Despite the devastating land losses they suffered, Hispanos were nevertheless the only Mexicanos within the ceded territory who managed to stay on their land in significant numbers.

This essay will focus upon the contemporary case of Taos to demonstrate that essentially the same historic process of expropriation described by Knowlton, Ebright, and other land grant scholars continues today, in modified and more sophisticated form, while rural Hispanos resist their final extirpation and cling to their shrinking land base around land grant villages and their offshoot settlements.[2] During the past two decades, as Anglo in-migration and real-estate speculation have accelerated, Hispano resistance to further encroachment upon

*This essay is based upon research conducted with grants from the Wenner-Gren Foundation and the American Philosophical Society.

limited resources has intensified and become increasingly self-conscious. Evidence for this includes the emergence of popular protest against certain resort developments since 1970, and the concurrent public articulation of specific tracts of land and water as both essential to and symbolic of Hispano cultural survival. It is the central argument of this essay that the ongoing process of expropriation and its recent acceleration have, in concert with various local, regional, and macro-social factors, intensified rural Hispano resistance to further usurpation and displacement, and stimulated the crystallization of land as a symbol of Hispano cultural survival and social self-determination.

These reactions represent, I propose, strategies of ethnic boundary maintenance. They also form part of the ongoing historical process of enclavement and persistence of Hispanos as a self-identified people. The crucial element in the origin and persistence of a self-identified people is, according to Spicer, their opposition to surrounding dominant social and political forces.[3] Their proletarianization, urbanization, and variable assimilation notwithstanding, Hispanos today and at previous points in their post-American history (that is, after 1847) have in various ways expressed opposition to Anglo encroachment and domination. They continue to exhibit other features of a persistent people, including their own language, endogamy, the notion of a stable, inherited cultural tradition, a sense of shared identity, meanings, and history, and, finally, of a homeland.[4] The latter is of particular concern to the present discussion. The ways and degrees to which Hispanos have exhibited these characteristics can be seen to have fluctuated over time, with the critical events in their becoming a minority having been, of course, conquest and land expropriation, from which the population's steady proletarianization inevitably followed.[5]

While the major portion of this essay consists of historical and ethnographic narrative about Taos, the introductory and concluding sections attempt to place the descriptive material within a specific theoretical and methodological framework. The overall inquiry out of which this essay comes seeks to explore the nature of and interaction between ethnicity and stratification, under conditions of tourism development and competition for limited essential resources. The following pages present a case study of one particular manifestation of this problem. Its conceptual focus is the relationship between ethnicity and land or territory, in Taos in particular and the Rio Arriba in general. This introductory section explains the ideas which organize the historical-empirical account that will follow. The reader not especially interested in the theoretical apparatus behind the descriptive account of Taos may prefer to proceed directly to the historical and ethnographic sections, and then return to the introduction, and go on to the conclusion afterward. While theory is ultimately necessary to an understanding of Taos and is therefore included here, it may be taken up either before or after looking at the empirical situation.

Theoretical Framework

Basic to my approach is Barth's ecological model of ethnic boundary maintenance, which sees ethnic identity as reactive to intergroup contact, rather than as simply a creature of primordial isolation. In Barth's view, ethnic groups occupy ecological niches by means of their sociocultural adaptations.[6] Intergroup relations are or become competitive over access to and control of essential resources. Competition intensifies according to degree of niche "overlap," or demand for and use of the same resources within the same territory. The focus in Barth's approach is less upon the continuity of cultural tradition, and more upon the maintenance of ethnic boundaries or differentiation between groups. Boundaries, or the complex means by which ethnic difference is maintained, represent strategies for exercising claims over essential resources. Boundary maintenance through time is the essential feature of ethnic persistence, whereas specific cultural content changes more or less continuously. In a very practical sense, this perspective frees the investigator from the barren task of trying to measure or even explain cultural persistence or assimilation by means of culture trait inventories. Situational emphasis upon ethnic identity as a competitive strategy also allows for focus at the individual level, where boundaries may often be crossed at will.

To anyone acquainted with the perennial struggle over land and water in the Rio Arriba, it is readily apparent how a competitive model is applicable to interethnic—not to mention intraethnic—relations there. Indian-Hispano-Anglo relations have been determined by what can be described as chronologically successive niche overlaps by distinct populations, bearing distinct patterns of ecological adaptation and socioeconomic domination. The case of Taos will be examined here to show how this is so in one particular instance, which nevertheless is embedded in and influenced by a larger, extralocal context. Ethnographic focus will be upon the niche occupation and sociopolitical position of Hispanos via-à-vis other groups through time, with particular attention to Hispano-Anglo relations in the contemporary period. This involves looking at Taos explicitly as a changing, circumscribed situation, and, implicitly, as inseparable from an inclusive, in fact global, sociopolitical process.

Ethnic Boundaries

A bit more should be said about the concept of ethnic boundary. Anthropologists use the term to refer to the complex of rules and markers by which people identify and are identified as members of one or another ethnic group. Externally obvious ethnic markers can include language, phenotype, dress, and style, while more "subjective" ones include values, sensibilities, and manner, as well as implicit rules for identifying the ethnicity of others or of asserting one's own. Spicer offers an operational definition of ethnic boundaries as "those situations in which the sense of identity receives some kind of expression and where individuals align themselves in some manner as members of one ethnic group or another."[7] The operation of ethnic boundaries in face-to-face social interaction in Taos as elsewhere in the region is today no less important than it was 100 or 300 years ago, although to be sure the cultures "contained within" these boundaries have undergone radical transformation. Conceptual focus upon boundary maintenance rather than specific content allows us to account for the seemingly paradoxical coincidence of culture change with the persistence of ethnic difference.

Niche

The relationship between boundary and niche can also change over time, although theoretically at least, they coincide in "equilibrium."[8] The niche is both an adaptation and a

> cluster of environmental parameters which any species (or in this case ethnic group) may use . . . or overcome in order to survive. . . . The parameters of the niche, the various resource garnering abilities of the competing populations, and the carrying capacity of that portion of the environment utilized determine the relative proportions of the populations at equilibrium, and whether there can be an equilibrium.[9]

Niche theory is applicable to ethnic relations only at a local, microsocial level, and must be embedded in a larger theory of world political economy. Nevertheless it nicely captures the historical relations among Pueblo, Hispano, and Anglo populations in the Taos valley, where the three still occupy overlapping yet recognizably distinct ecological niches. The documentary record of Indian-Hispano relations is one of unending dispute over arable tracts of land in the Rio Pueblo and adjacent watersheds.[10] The political significance and intensity of this struggle were transformed by Americanization. The precise correspondences between cultural adaptation, ethnicity, and differential territory and resource control have therefore undergone profound changes during the past 400 years.

Originally of course, the Indians occupied the optimal farming, hunting, and defensible vantage point in the Taos valley, which, remarkably and through unrelenting effort, they have managed to retain. Hispanic Taos was first settled around—or radiated outward from—Taos Pueblo, in ever-widening circles as the population grew. It gradually consolidated around the central town of Don Fernando de Taos, becoming during the nineteenth century a system of fifteen interdependent but individual settlements, almost all of which encroached upon use areas claimed by the Pueblo. Today these settlements are each struggling to protect their traditionally differentiated spheres of local land and water control, as always in competition or cooperation with one another, but also against the town's urban spread, and a corresponding escalation of Anglo in-migration and ubiquitous real estate development.

The core elements in the Hispano niche have been occupation of contiguous village farmland and associated water rights ownership and management, and a numerical majority that still enables them to dominate the local political structure, which centers on town and county governments and the school system. Both Indian and Hispano attachments to a land base are rooted in their traditional subsistence economies. Attachment to a land base remains intrinsic to the ethnic self-identities of both groups, even though neither subsists any longer by agriculture, pastoralism, or hunting. The self-conscious ethnic symbolization of the subsistence base has been fueled, in the case of both Indians and Hispanos, by its progressive loss, and it represents an effort to forestall or reverse this relentless process.

Taos is of interest because it is both representative and atypical. On the one hand, it has much in common with the rest of the Rio Arriba and with the Southwest as a whole. On the other, its long-standing commercial importance has made it peculiar. Its interethnic, historic, and geographic "uniqueness," which the town markets as a tourist attraction, represents a distinctive configuration of features Taos shares with the Southwest in general. These include aridity, socioeconomic stratification along ethnic lines, and an ethnic boundary system that exhibits the characteristics identified by Spicer for the region: differential boundary awareness among dominant and subdominant groups, boundary fluidity, the reservation, and linguistic pluralism.[11] The first of these refers to the fact that the members of a dominant social stratum and ethnic group tend to be less aware of ethnic boundaries than members of a subordinated ethnic group. This has many implications for face-to-face ethnic relations, and is a major feature of Taos social life. Unidirectional boundary fluidity refers to the fact that individuals can cross ethnic boundaries, but the direction in which they assimilate tends to be "upward" along the stratification scale. The remainder of Spicer's characteristics, the reservation and linguistic pluralism, are self-explanatory. The salience of all four of these features in Taos will become clear in the narrative part of this paper.

Ethnicity and Class

Before describing Taos further, a word must be said about the relation between ethnicity and class. While interethnic competition over limited resources is a constant theme in local history, land, water, and other resource conflicts have never been exclusively interethnic matters. Conflict over resources occurs also within ethnic groups, along family and factional lines, within and between communities, and along the class lines which cross-cut community and ethnic boundaries. Indeed, instances in which class shapes or overrides ethnic interest are of particular significance in New Mexico history, as they are today. Modern examples include the regular operation of the Hispanic elite aligned with the ruling Anglo elite, or Anglo farmers and environmentalists who join in protest against resort development. That class and ethnic cleavages can both coincide and cross-cut each other is one of the complexities of the situation not adequately captured by a simple one-to-one boundary-niche model of local interethnic relations. While it is not the purpose of this essay to describe or analyze the interaction between ethnicity and class in Taos, the problem is mentioned because it is central to any kind of theoretical understanding of ethnic or race relations there or elsewhere in the Rio Arriba. I mention it also to avoid the implication that conflict over resources in the region is simply interethnic. (Nor, for that matter, do I mean to suggest that all conflict between members of different ethnic groups is necessarily over resources. Rather, I am addressing the implicitly understood ethnohistorical context of niche overlap within which intergroup relations are acted out and interpreted.) As shall be seen, the controversies described in the sections on modern Taos are as much between classes as ethnic groups.

It is therefore significant that they are commonly perceived and somewhat ambivalently regarded as interethnic conflicts, even though "on the ground," nearly everyone acknowledges the importance of class in determining peoples' choices about such matters. Beyond the most basic and obvious issue of threatened community resource domains, several other factors contribute to why the recent grassroots protests are commonly understood as ethnic conflicts and mobilizations. To begin with, the incidence of territoriality and distinct linguistic and cultural traditions tends to enhance the prospects for ethnic mobilization in any given situation. The primary ascriptive nature of ethnicity typically makes it a readier and more appealing basis than class for political mobilization in a plural or multiethnic setting.[12] Additional factors at play include the persistence of socioeconomic stratification along ethnic lines, the influence of tourism, and certain post-1960 regional and national influences. The latter two, the influences of tourism and regional and national trends or events upon local ethnic mobilization, are of particular interest to this discussion.

To recapitulate then, this paper deals with the modern symbolic identification of Hispano ethnic-cultural persistence with specific tracts of land and water in the Taos area. It pursues the obvious comparison between the emergence of Hispano ethnic land symbolism and the well-known Blue Lake case of the Taos Indians, in which the town watershed came over a period of several decades to symbolize the cultural survival of Taos Pueblo. Both Indian and Hispano ethnic land symbolizations are considered in terms of their extralocal ethnopolitical settings and significance, but my discussion will focus upon their immediate context of an evolving tourism economy.

The Significance of Taos

Taos's historic importance stems mostly from its long having been an interethnic trade center, and in this century, a focal point for tourism development and urban growth. It has also been the locus of significant interethnic violence, having served as the starting point for the Pueblo Revolt of 1680, and the site of Mexicano-Indian revolt against American occupation in 1847. Perhaps its most outstanding feature today is the effect that tourism, as the primary economic base other than federal subsidy and one molybdenum mine, exerts upon the local system of interethnic relations.

From its earliest beginnings, tourism in Taos marketed ethnicity and the natural environment, a combination that has fostered, in addition to heightened ethnic self-consciousness and the proliferation of ethnic symbolism in general, the emergence of ethnic land symbolism among Hispanos as well as Indians. Both Hispano and Indian land symbolisms link the issue of cultural survival to the preservation of a traditional land base, but they differ in other respects. Their dissimilarities are as much the result of distinctive political, economic, and legal circumstances as reflections of primordial social or cultural differences between the two groups.

Hispano ethnic land symbolism has developed within the context of continuous land loss and concomitant Anglo, federal, and apparent Indian land gain. It grows out of a very different set of legal and political conditions from those facing the Taos Indians. The American Indian "sacred land concept" originates in aboriginal animism, but today it is also a response to federal status and the reservation. The spiritual potency of Native American sacred natural areas stands in poignant contrast to actual Indian powerlessness over most reservation land and water. Pueblos differ from most reservations in that their "leagues" are held in fee simple title, and do not belong to the federal government.[13] Nevertheless, at Taos Pueblo as on other reservations, Indians are territorially segregated and directly subject to federal control, as is the administration of at least part of their land. The institutionalization of group identity, including the imposition of a colonial administrative apparatus, is more total for reservation Indians than for any other ethnic minority in this country. Yet the symbolic import of an Indian sacred land concept and the notion of Indian landownership, however ambiguously realized, are made concrete by actual geographic and associated social boundaries within Taos County. The local interpretation—or mystification—of this segregated arrangement has been for the most part unconsciously shaped by the needs and dictates of tourism.

The "Tri-Ethnic Trap" Revisited

John Bodine laid the cornerstone for the study of interethnic relations in Taos by placing the sixty-four-year legal battle for Blue Lake between Taos Pueblo and the federal government within the context of Taos's bohemian ethos of selective ethnophilia or the tri-ethnic trap.[14] The tri-ethnic trap is a situation in which Hispanos, unable to advance beyond clear-cut secondary economic status and faced with the steady and irrevocable loss of their traditional land base, must abide by a tourism-engendered Anglo glorification of Indian culture, as well as the federal protection and even restoration of Indian lands, sometimes at the expense of Hispano ownership. Conditions in Taos in the early 1980s represent a recognizable progression of what Bodine described in 1968, modified by the supercession of luxury recreational over ethnic-cultural tourism.[15] Taos has undergone two phases of tourism development in this century, the first being roughly between the two world wars, and the second extending from the 1960s to the early 1980s. The Blue Lake case preceded the first boom and lasted into the early part of the second, but its character and significance were shaped by the former. In his unpublished dissertation, Bodine showed how over a period of several decades Taos Pueblo came *publicly* and *legally* to define Blue Lake as "sacred," under the pressure of particular legal, political, social, and cultural circumstances.[16] The Blue Lake victory in 1970 enhanced a climate of already heightened ethnic self-consciousness, and served to reinforce the idea of a mystical connection between territory and indigenous population.

The most fundamental contrasts between Pueblo Indian and Hispano cases of enclavement derive from the differences in their respective political and legal positions vis-à-vis the state. Trust status has meant, among other things, that Indians cannot alienate their land and do not pay taxes on it, and that legal defense of their land, water, and other tribal claims is the responsibilty of the federal government, not infrequently in litigation against itself. Ironically, the immunities this nonetheless disastrously dependent status confers serve to preclude some of the very ways in which Hispanos have lost their land. Mexicanos were supposedly incorporated into the American state as regular citizens with full rights and privileges. The history of Mexican Americans, who have subsequently constituted the major source of cheap labor throughout the Southwest, shows otherwise. Like Mexican Americans elsewhere, Hispanos were proletarianized by means of dispossession. Because of the aridity and isolation of New Mexico, Mexicano land loss has been slower there than it was in California or Texas. In Taos their land loss has nevertheless been more or less continuous. Today the land tenure situation of Taos Pueblo appears, at least superficially, far more favorable in comparison to that of rural and semi-rural Hispanos in the area, whose farmland is being expropriated at an escalating rate by the luxury tourism real-estate boom.

The Stolen Homeland

The idea of a stolen homeland was invoked and dramatized in 1967 by Reies López Tijerina, the leader of La Alianza Federal de los Pueblos Libres, which attracted international attention to the long-buried land grant issue in New Mexico. Founded originally as La Alianza Federal de Mercedes in the early 1960s, the organization, comprised of landless Hispano poor and small ranchers and village farmers, sought to bring the matter of massive land grant loss to world attention as a violation of the Treaty of Guadalupe Hidalgo. Several years of protest activity finally culminated in the famous Tierra Amarilla courthouse raid, in which Tijerina and a score of armed Alianza followers wounded three men and kidnapped a deputy sheriff and a news reporter, setting off an intensive, five-day manhunt, and virtual military occupation of northern Rio Arriba County.[17] If the Alianza failed to restore the lost land grants, it nevertheless proclaimed Hispano existence to the outside world and inspired legal and scholarly interest in land grant history. Tijerina's contribution was to resurrect the land grant issue and link it to contemporary conditions. This galvanized Hispano-Chicano ethnopolitical awareness and changed the way in which isolated individuals would think of their personal disputes over land and water. It placed the individual problem within a larger, collective, historically defined context and gave voice to a deep, widespread, but still largely unarticulated sense of injury and outrage.

It would be difficult to measure Tijerina's impact on Hispanos in

Taos alone, where out-migration has linked rural families to the urban barrios of the Southwest, and where individual responses vary according to class, age, education, urban-rural orientation, and numerous other social factors. In Taos as elsewhere, Tijerina's impact was as much symbolic as political. Today, his enormous symbolic impact outlives his political effectiveness. Despite—or perhaps partly by means of— anomalous personal characteristics (evangelist, itinerant, Tejano), he managed to strike a chord among rural Hispanos that continues to resonate in the north even today, while their land base continues to diminish. For Chicanos in the cities, the Alianza helped to locate the homeland *mythos* of Aztlan in the geopolitical present.[18] For Hispanos in the Rio Arriba, it finally gave a name to what had happened to them as a people. Along with the California farmworkers' strike, the emergence of the Raza Unida party in Crystal City, Texas, the Crusade for Justice in Denver, and the Chicano student movement, the Tierra Amarilla courthouse raid and its aftermath became a milestone in the national process of Chicano ethnopolitical mobilization. These and instances of ethnic mobilization involving other minorities either preceded or roughly coincided with the emergence of Hispano-Chicano protest activity in Taos in the early 1970s, which at least initially took its inspiration from the spirit of the times.

Ethnic Symbolism and Tourism

The emergence of an explicit Hispano land symbolism in Taos since 1970 will be described in the final narrative sections of this paper. It will be shown to be the product of the history described in preceding sections, operating in concert with contemporary conditions, including the recent influence of extralocal Chicano ethnopolitical mobilizations. Hispano ethnic land symbolization in Taos was prefigured by the Indian example and conditioned by the type of tourism development that accompanied it. But it has been precipitated largely by the luxury tourism development generated by the ski industry. The following account will show how both Indian and Hispano cases of ethnic land symbolization have been profoundly affected by tourism, although in different ways, and at different stages of tourism development. As distinct yet comparable examples of ethnic mobilization they might seem to correspond, at first glance, to what MacCannell calls "reconstructed" and "constructed" ethnicity. The term "constructed ethnicity" refers to the self-conscious efforts of contemporary ethnopolitical activists and to "the various ethnic identities which emerged via opposition and assimilation during the colonial phase of Western history and in the new 'internal colonies.'" "Reconstructed ethnicity" on the other hand, refers to "the kinds of ethnic identities which have emerged from the pressures of tourism," it being understood that "tourism promotes the restoration, preservation, and fictional recreation of ethnic attributes."[19] In either case ethnicity is the product of a distinct pattern of colonial or post-colonial (that is asymmetrical and exploitative) intergroup relations: an explicitly political one in which the "inferior group defines itself in opposition to or the antithesis of the values of the dominant group," and a "touristic" situation in which a structurally "superior group associates itself with an inferior group" and where the latter engages in the "maintenance and preservation of ethnic forms for the entertainment of ethnically different [and structurally superior] others."[20]

Even before MacCannell and others made tourism a field of study, Bodine recognized that tourism and the art colony had deeply affected the ethnic strategy and self-image of Taos Pueblo. Certainly Taos ethnic identity is at least partly a reconstructed product in MacCannell's sense, just as the Pueblo itself has become *museumized*.[21] Yet the Pueblo's struggle to maintain its claim on the Rio Pueblo watershed and adjacent areas long antedates the advent of tourism, even though its means for doing so have now become inseparable from tourism's influence. Tourism and federal dependency became the twentieth-century political-economic context within which Taos Pueblo's ethnic boundary maintenance strategies have evolved. In a sense tourism, or a peculiar combination of ethnic-cultural tourism and federal dependency, has become a crucial component of the modern Pueblo niche. This will be elaborated upon later. The point to be made here is that both Taos Indian and Hispano ethnicity, including their respective symbolizations of land, are the products of construction as well as reconstruction, albeit in different ways. Neither represents a pure type, if such exists. They are rooted in a pre-United States history of political asymmetry and mutual niche overlap. Their respective modern characters share common elements in, yet also reflect differences between, the two groups' political, economic, and social situations.

Roadside poster in Valdez condominium dispute. Courtesy of
Sylvia Rodríguez.

The Content and Structure of This Essay

In the text that follows, Part 2, about half of the main text, is a history of Taos, divided into three sections. The first part includes a description of the area's geographical and hydrological layout, and an overview of Taos's development from 1540 to 1847. It is followed by two sections on modern history from Americanization to the present. These focus primarily upon the two phases of tourism development in this century and their distinguishable impacts on local ethnicity and ethnic relations.

The second half of the main text, or Part 3, is an ethnographic account of a grassroots protest movement against condominium development by the village of Valdez, which occurred in 1981–1982. Because it is based upon ethnographic research involving participant

The Valdez float in the Taos Fiestas. Courtesy of Sylvia Rodríguez.

observation, this section, on the Valdez "condo war," reads more vividly than what precedes it. Yet its content is fully understandable only within the context of the former, that is, when viewed against the backdrop of the past 20, 100, and indeed, 400 years. The Valdez case is the most recent and dramatic example of protest activity that has emerged in Taos since 1970. It illustrates the contemporary situation of intensifying competition over limited land and water. It reveals conflict between ethnic groups, between classes, between urban and rural orientations, and between different economic interests. The case reveals the complex ways in which all these factors overlap and interact in modern Taos, and by extension, elsewhere in the Rio Arriba. At the same time, it signals a new phase in an old, yet ongoing process—the emergence, evolution, construction, and reconstruction of Hispanos as a self-identified people. Thus these four central sections, of different lengths and styles, together ground and inform the argument explained above. All this is summarized and put into theoretical perspective once

A marcher displays the "Blood of Valdez" banner. Courtesy of Sylvia Rodríguez.

The Valdez protest march to Gilson Motor Company. Courtesy of Sylvia Rodríguez.

again in the conclusion, which is followed by recommendations for further research.

Methodology

The research upon which this essay is based involved twenty-one months of ethnographic fieldwork in Taos from 1981–1983, undertaken to investigate interethnic relations and social change since 1930. The project was designed originally to investigate the seemingly paradoxical observation that, since World War II, despite economic development and the growth of Anglo, Indian, and especially Hispano middle classes in Taos, and despite increased contact, intermarriage, and cultural commonalities among the three groups, the boundaries between them persist and appear to be maintained and protected with increasing self-consciousness, if not intensity. Drawing upon conceptual frameworks offered by Barth and by Spicer, my approach posited a correlation among

Tijerina addresses the Valdez rally.

the following: increase in demographic pressure and demand upon the limited resource of water in Taos's arid, geographically circumscribed and seemingly isolated environment; interethnic and intraethnic social diversification; and the intensification of ethnic boundaries.

The project is essentially a community study, which seeks to investigate and describe contemporary Taos while also reconstructing its recent past. Thus both ethnographic and historical (or *synchronic* and *diachronic*) methods have been used. Ethnographic methods include participant observation in multiple settings, and both extensive and intensive interviews with a broad selection of area residents. Questionnaires concerning local water quality and quantity were distributed selectively in rural areas. Participant observation has encompassed a wide range of interethnic and intraethnic (primarily Hispano) social, civil, civic, ritual, and other events, activities, and occasions, including all regular and most special local governmental meetings of all types, as well as many hours of grassroots and partisan political meetings and activities in the town and surrounding communities. Local archival research has consisted of examining the county tax rolls for settlements within the municipal district from 1931–1980, and a detailed review of Taos newspapers for the same period. The tax rolls yield data on changing landownership and comparative wealth during the past fifty years, while the newspaper review has served to guide and inform much of the interview process, and to aid in the reconstruction of recent town history. Adjunct documentary research has entailed compilation of the available physiographic, demographic, economic, and other social data on Taos, as well as a more-or-less comprehensive review of the literature on Taos, which I classify under the three general headings of scholarly, policy-oriented, and promotional, listed in order from least to most abundant.

One factor which should be mentioned is that the investigator is a native of Taos. My native bias is partly an applied one that seeks to understand Taos as thoroughly, accurately, and "objectively" as possible, in order to help change it, or at the very least to cast new light on what seems a stringently unequal and, from the standpoint of Hispano land tenure, a worsening situation. Like most members of the post-1965 generation of Chicano and other minority scholars as well as some nonminority scholars who study minorities in the United States, I do not subscribe to the assimilationist bias or alleged political detachment which previous generations of social scientists simply (and rather naively) took for granted. Only time and further study will show the extent to which my description and analysis prove accurate or useful.

The long-range goal of the project is a community study of Taos that centers upon a description and analysis of ethnic—particularly Hispano-Anglo—relations during the middle and late twentieth century. But the project represents, one hopes, only the first stage in a continuing program of research that will eventually involve cooperative interdisciplinary efforts to investigate both past and present social phenomena and conditions in Taos County, ultimately for the purpose of comparison with other counties in the state, as well as with other regions, both within and outside the Southwest. A comparative perspective and understanding of diverse systems or situations of structural inequality seems one prerequisite to knowing how to transform them into more egalitarian relations. It is within this larger conceptual framework that the present essay, on the land-water issue and its ethnic meaning in northern New Mexico, is presented.

II. The History of Taos

Geographic Overview

Taos is a collectivity of villages, consisting of an aboriginal Tiwa pueblo and approximately (depending on how you count them) fifteen Hispanic settlements which crystallized around it during the eighteenth and early nineteenth centuries. The complex is located in a shallow basin on the eastern edge of a high (approximately 7,000 feet) arid plain, at a point just before where the land rises precipitously into the Sangre de Cristo range. These mountains run north-south through Taos County, paralleling the deep cut (approximately 650 feet) of the Rio Grande gorge through the western altiplano. Water for the town (Don Fernando de Taos) and surrounding communities comes from ground water and eight mountain streams that descend via forested canyons and run through settled, irrigated valleys, and down arroyos into the gorge. These streams are, from south to north: the Rio Grande del Rancho (formed by two tributaries); Rio Chiquito; Rio Fernando; Rio Pueblo; Rio Lucero; Arroyo Seco; Rio Hondo; and San Cristobal. The settlements, scattered inside a twenty-mile radius along the upper and lower portions of each of these watersheds, include, from south to north: Llano Quemado, Ranchos, Talpa, Los Cordovas, Cordillera, Ranchitos (Lower and Upper), Don Fernando de Taos, Cañon, San Geronimo de Taos or Taos Pueblo, El Prado, Las Colonias, Arroyo Seco, Des Montes, Valdez, Arroyo Hondo, and San Cristobal. The major portion of arable, habitable land in Taos County is located inside this basin within a relatively narrow central strip or valley, bordered on the east by the mountains, and on the west by the sageland desert. Officially designated the municipal district, this area today contains roughly sixty-five percent of the county population. Taos is connected to the nearest metropolitan areas of Denver, approximately 300 miles to the north, and Albuquerque, about 150 miles to the south, by Highway 3, which runs right through the town. Highway 64 runs east-northwest through Taos, linking it to Raton and the Texas-Oklahoma Panhandle to the east, and to Tierra Amarilla and Farmington to the west. Penetrated by only these two highways and surrounded by mountains and high desert, the Taos valley creates a predominant (for many, alluring) impression of lofty geographical circumscription and isolation (see Map 12).

323

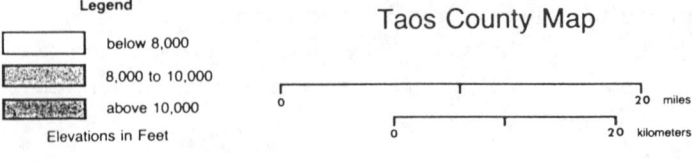

MAP 12. Taos County.

Human settlement in the Taos valley dates from about A.D. 1000–1200, although it was not until around 1350 that the present Pueblo area became the site of a major population center, following the abandonment of one to the south near Pot Creek on the Rio Grande del Rancho, which feeds the present-day Ranchos-Talpa-Llano Quemado area.[22]

1540–1847

Founded on the banks of the upper Rio Pueblo, Taos Pueblo occupies the best farming, hunting, and defensible vantage point in the valley. Its location at the base of Taos mountain gives easy access to rich mountain resources, including the river itself, as well as to fertile flatlands and meadows lying immediately west and south. The village and upland behind it afford commanding views of the entire Taos valley, and offer avenues for quick retreat into mountain canyons. The Pueblo was nearly 200 years old when Coronado's lieutenant Alvarado first saw it in 1540, and reported it to be the largest and most populous of the Indian villages he visited.[23] Northernmost of the eastern Pueblos, Taos shows signs of greater Plains culture contact[24] and reliance upon hunting than do its mostly Tewa neighbors to the south along the Rio Grande, and was undoubtedly an important point of contact between the two regions even in aboriginal times. Oñate assigned the Taos people their first mission in 1598, in the name of San Geronimo. Within another fifteen years the Pueblo had embarked upon its long career of resistance against European domination and encroachment.[25]

By the middle of the seventeenth century, Hispanic settlers were moving into the valley and occupying lands on at least two royal grants made to the south (on the Rio Grande del Rancho) and immediate west (on the Rio Lucero) of the Pueblo. Some seventy settlers and two priests were killed in the area during the Pueblo Revolt in 1680, which was planned from the kivas at Taos because of its strategic remoteness from Spanish headquarters in Santa Fe. Settlers reentered the valley with de Vargas's "bloodless reconquest," which the Taos people actively resisted until 1696. Thereafter, except for disastrous participation in the 1847 Taos revolt against American occupation, their overt resistance would assume increasingly litigious form.

The Land Grants. It was during the early to middle 1700s that

Hispanic settlers began to establish a foothold in the Taos valley. While the *casas reales* (government buildings) were housed at the Pueblo itself, the settlers lived scattered in *ranchos* (subsistence farms) around the valley. From three to five royal grants were made to individuals during this period, although only two of them were continuously occupied, after being sold by their original grantees. These included the Cristobal de la Serna, made in 1710 and revalidated in 1715, which lies south of the Pueblo and town and encompasses the Ranchos-Talpa-Llano Quemado area, and evidently corresponded to the prerevolt Duran y Chavez grant. The other was the Francisca Antonia de Gijosa grant, made in 1715. The grant lies to the west of La Serna, and contains the settlements of Los Cordovas, Cordillera, and Ranchitos. A third, on the site of the old Lucero de Godoy grant west of the Pueblo along the Rio Lucero, was issued in 1716 to Antonio Martinez of Sonora, who evidently never occupied it.[26] This grant would later contain El Prado, Las Colonias, Des Montes, and part of Arroyo Seco. Yet another, the Antoine Leroux grant, made in 1742, would overlap onto the Martinez grant, as well as onto the Pueblo league. Arroyo Seco would lie partly within this contested zone.[27] In 1730 the Pueblo filed the first of many complaints against trespassers grazing livestock along the Rio Lucero. The Spanish governor upheld the Pueblo claim and set a precedent, to be honored mainly in principle, for future decisions about this much disputed area.[28] Litigation over Hispano encroachments along the Rio Lucero has continued late into the twentieth century.

Hispano or mestizo population growth was held in check during much of the eighteenth century by generally harsh conditions, including devastating Comanche raids into the area. Despite whatever tensions persisted between them, the raiding eventually caused the settlers and Indians to pull together for purposes of mutual defense, and so while settlers maintained their fields and livestock on ranches around the valley, they lived inside the Pueblo walls, at least during the 1770s. Dominguez reported 306 non-Indian settlers living in the western portion of the heavily fortified Pueblo in 1776, while a plaza was under construciton in Las Trampas or Ranchos. The first permanently inhabited settlements seem to have been in the general Ranchos area, along the lower Rio Grande del Rancho watershed. By the 1790s the Comanche threat had subsided and various parts of the valley were being permanently resettled. In another decade the smallpox vaccination would reach the area,[29] and a population explosion was underway.

The earliest enumeration of distinct plazas for the Taos area is from 1796, the same year the town, or Don Fernando, grant was made. The account reported a non-Indian population of 774, and named six placitas, identifiable as present-day Taos, Ranchos, Upper Ranchitos, Lower Ranchitos, either Cañon or El Prado, and probably Los Cordovas.[30] The original town grant was made to sixty-three families, whose number was expanded in 1797 by two additional acts of possession.[31] The grant, including the plaza and numerous houses, overlapped onto the Pueblo league, a fact which would later result in drawn-out litigation and give the Pueblo a lingering claim over all town streets and alleys. Water from the Rio Pueblo, to which the Pueblo has first priority, would be used to irrigate lands in the town area including La Loma (now a barrio), Ranchitos, and part of Cañon. By this time, the Pueblo had begun to buy back lands north of the El Prado-Los Estiercoles area from the heirs of a Los Luceros (or Leroux) grant claimant (Sebastian Martin), whom it had first charged with trespassing nearly sixty-five years earlier. This area, part of the Lucero-Leroux-Martinez overlap, would later be known as the Tenorio tract, which the Pueblo would purchase yet again in 1818.[32]

A population explosion overtook the Taos valley around the turn of the century. Between 1794 and 1811 the non-Indian population more than doubled from 628 to 1274.[33] This resulted in the spread of existing settlements and the establishment of new ones, giving rise to Talpa and Llano Quemado in the Ranchos area, and Cordillera, above Los Cordovas to the northwest, near where six of the central valley streams drain into the Rio Grande.[34] In 1815 the Arroyo Seco, Arroyo Hondo, and San Cristobal grants were made in watersheds north of Don Fernando and the Rio Lucero, to mostly landless families from the town area. San Antonio or present-day Valdez, originally the upper placita of Arroyo Hondo, became a separate extension of that grant in 1823. The settlement of Las Colonias and Des Montes in the middle and lower Hondo-Seco drainages must also have taken place during this general period. By 1818, the Pueblo had engaged in litigation for nearly a century, and filed suit against settler-trespassers in at least Don Fernando, Ranchos, and El Prado, and had twice purchased the Tenorio tract. It would soon join with its old adversary El Prado in complaint against Arroyo Seco's upstream encroachment on the Rio Lucero, a problem that would remain volatile for many years. Population growth thus intensified the already constant pressures on the

Pueblo's league boundaries, as well as on all other arable lands and surface waters in the Taos valley. The fundamental patterns of intercommunity alliance and competition over land and water that persist today were thereby established during the early nineteenth century and, in some cases, much earlier.

Multicommunity. It was therefore during the latter eighteenth and early nineteenth centuries that Taos crystallized into a collectivity or system of differentiated, interdependent settlements, radiating outward from the Pueblo and early centers of Ranchos and Taos. This process took place more or less concurrently with the community's evolution into a lively trade and agricultural center. Some of the settlements, including most of the early six as well as La Loma, Arroyo Hondo, and San Antonio, were originally laid out as placitas. Others, like Cordillera and Des Montes, seem to have coalesced out of clusters or strings of dispersed ranchos at a point where there were no longer any vacant lands to which Taos or Ranchos or any other settlement could export their burgeoning populations. As Snow has argued for the Rio Arriba in general, the critical factor in precipitating this crystallization of distinct community boundaries was population pressure against local carrying capacity, or limited land with water.[35]

By the Mexican period, each of these settlements had become an individuated, bounded community organized around its own acequias and chapel and/or morada, and embedded in a nexus of kinship and reciprocal patterns of cooperation, exchange, and competition with its neighbors in the same or adjacent watersheds. As the components individuated, so did the whole take form. This pattern of intervillage growth and connectedness has been identified in other parts of the Rio Arriba by Van Ness who, following Reina and Aguilera, calls it a "multicommunity," with parallels in the Peten and southwestern Spain.[36] And like elsewhere in the Rio Arriba as well as other parts of highland Latin America, each village tended to acquire its own distinct character or personality. Community of origin, a person's *patria chica,* would become an important factor in defining individual social identity. Strong identification with one's community is found in Taos even today, where some settlements and their natives still have nicknames, and where old intercommunity rivalries and alliances over surface waters persevere under conditions of accelerating urbanization.

Commerce. Taos was the northern terminus of the trade route from Chihuahua and had become the site of an annual trade fair by the middle of the eighteenth century. Just as the Pueblo had been a contact point between northeastern and southern influences in pre-Hispanic times, Don Fernando soon became a kind of boom town at the edge of two frontiers. Taos was stratified by class as well as by race from its earliest frontier days. Its history as a community is largely the record of how these two forms or systems of stratification and inequality have interacted, interpenetrated, and evolved, under conditions of universal competition for land and water on the one hand, and progressive capitalist penetration and development on the other. There are different views as to when mercantile capitalism began to penetrate and transform the agro-pastoral-trade economy of the Rio Arriba. Most historians have assumed this took place during the Mexican period, after the area was opened to American trade across the Santa Fe trail. Other scholars claim the process began earlier. For example, Gutierrez has argued that it began in the 1770s, causing far-reaching social change, manifested in increasingly individualistic marriage practices and ideology and in overall transformation from a caste to a class society.[37] This might have helped to accommodate a rather swift American takeover of the local economy during the Mexican period.[38]

In any case, Taos evidently boomed during the Mexican period, when it became well-known to mountain men for its whiskey, wheat, and women, and as a rendezvous and port-of-entry. In addition to abundant wheat for sustenance and raw whiskey for inspiration, Taos supplied Mexicano labor for the construction of Bent's Fort,[39] a portent of future trends for a growing sector of landless laborers. A number of French and Anglo trapper-traders settled in Taos and married Hispanas from propertied families. Some branched out as merchants and land grant entrepreneurs, becoming recipients of such examples of Armijo's largesse as the Sangre de Cristo and Beaubien-Miranda or Maxwell grants. By American conquest these men, among them the Bents, Beaubien, St. Vrain, Lee, and Carson were well established in their roles as pillars of the new order.

After 1846 American conquest cut off Mexicano-Hispano domination by usurping the local subsistence economy and expropriating most of its land base. Hispanos were ultimately transformed from an internally stratified yet sociopolitically dominant majority into an impoverished ethnic underclass, with a small upper stratum of broker-entrepreneurs who aligned with the ruling Anglos. Overt resistance erupted shortly after occupation, when Territorial Governor Bent was scalped by a mob of Indians and Mexicanos. Too little is known about the precise nature and constituency of this uprising, except that it seems to have involved both extremes of the local social scale. It may have been partially instigated by certain elite[40] but nevertheless took its heaviest toll at the Pueblo, where resisters and others fleeing the American army were howitzered in the church. Simmons believably suggests that the revolt was motivated less by patriotism than by long-standing local frustrations and land conflicts.[41]

The Territorial Period

During the six territorial decades that followed annexation, the land situation in northern New Mexico became a whirlwind of ownership transfers, shifting boundaries, and large-scale speculation. The overall trend in ownership went from multiple communally and individually held lands to ever larger tracts concentrated in the hands of a few outside entrepreneurs. A significant proportion of these larger tracts eventually ended up under federal control. At least eighty percent of the grant land claimed by Hispano subsistence farmers in New Mexico was lost by the early 1900s, when the process of federal land adjudication was finally complete.[42] Knowlton has described the various means by which this dispossession took place, including, to name but a few, forfeiture through back taxes, credit foreclosure, lawyers' fees, outright purchase, swindle, appropriation of *ejido* (common land) into the public domain, and the arcane nature of the land claims process itself.[43] Of 650,890 acres claimed for at least twenty-six land grants in Taos County, the Court of Private Land Claims rejected 406,914.[44] Ultimately only fourteen grants in the county were confirmed by Congress and patented, beginning with the two Pueblo leagues (Taos and Picuris) and the entrepreneurial Sangre de Cristo, which lies partly in Colorado.[45] Many individually claimed nongrant holdings were also lost in one way or another, along with the entire public domain, the county's backbone mountain wilderness, containing the watersheds of every village and town. Appropriation of community common lands was probably the s ngle most devastating blow dealt the native agro-pastoral subsistence economy.[46] The only lands nonwealthy Hispanos managed to hold onto in any significant proportion were, for the most part, individual, privately owned irrigated parcels in and around the villages, in addition to some pasture and dry grazing tracts.

But the full economic repercussions of expropriation were not felt until late in the territorial period, after the ranching, timber, mining, and railraod booms which exploited the Maxwell and other nearby wilderness areas had begun to die down, and ceased providing employment. Taos maintained its reputation as the granary of New Mexico into the early 1900s. It supplied fruit and grain to Elizabethtown and other mining camps during the 1860s and 1870s, and participated in the overall increase in agricultural production that occurred in the region between 1890 and 1910, when new lands rejected by the Court of Private Land Claims became open to new settlement. A U.S. Geological Survey report from 1904–1905 tellingly conveys the tenor of this period in the following recommendation for Taos's rich timber resources:

> All of the timber can be removed by means of logging railroads built up the main streams which offer no serious engineering difficulties, or by moveable sawmills, with wagon roads constructed to haul the lumber out. This latter method is probably the more economical when the low rate of wages paid the Mexicans is taken into consideration.[47]

Gold and copper mines boomed briefly and sporadically in the upper Rio Hondo watershed at Amizette in 1893, renamed Twining in 1903. Mining enjoyed a more sustained and productive development outside the Taos valley, particularly on the Maxwell, where in addition to gold and copper, large reserves of bituminous coal were extracted.[48] Cattle ranching also centered on the Maxwell, so that Taos, which contained a higher proportion of sheep, remained just beyond the western fringe of the Colfax-San Miguel cattle ranching boom and concomitant social disruption.[49] Prior to statehood a number of outside entrepreneurs had grandiose schemes for the exploitation of Taos. These included Arthur Manby, the ill-fated Englishman who dreamed of transforming the lower Rio Hondo watershed and Antonio Martinez grant into an international health spa,[50] and Gusdorf and Laughlin, who planned large orchard projects for tracts within the Gijosa and La Serna grants, requiring elaborate water reclamation projects that never came to pass. Nor did the railroad which was to have linked Taos with St. Louis and California.[51]

Just around the time of statehood, Taos seems to have gone from a valley of golden promise to an economically stagnant backwater, awaiting touristic discovery. It seems likely that by 1910 Taos had become an established exporter of labor. The trend in agricultural employment and production has been downward ever since, and Taos became known, among other things, for its high unemployment rate. When the booms dried up and the ejido was gone, workers had to leave to make a living. At first, people were mostly seasonal migrants. Men followed the sheep camps or families followed the crops. Gradually employment became more urban, and people left for years and decades instead of months (although sheepherders were also sometimes gone for years). This meant that a significant proportion of every native generation left, for good or for many years. Little solid, longitudinal data on out-migration appear to exist for Taos.[52] Even today, many who have settled elsewhere as adults maintain family ties and come home for fiestas and funerals, and stubbornly hold onto some tiny piece of property in hope of one day returning.

In 1906, two years after the Court of Private Land Claims closed, Theodore Roosevelt proclaimed the public domain in Taos County national forest, later named for Kit Carson. This consolidated nearly half the county land mass, including the mountain wilderness containing every village watershed, under federal control and Forest Service supervision. The act curtailed all traditional Indian and Hispano uses of the wilderness. It laid the groundwork for restrictions that would be enforced with disastrous results in the 1930s on grazing, woodcutting, and other small-scale extractions rural Hispanos depended upon. It also inaugurated sixty-four years of litigation between Taos Pueblo and the Forest Service over Blue Lake, the traditional or "sacred" mountain use area containing the Pueblo-town watershed. The federal government thus became the single largest landowner and source of revenue within the county, as well as a major cause of its insufficient tax base.

This situation of federal ubiquity was underscored by the determination in 1913 that the Pueblo Indians were wards of the federal government. Prior to that, the legal status of Pueblo Indians and their lands had been ambiguous, to say the least, under all three governments—and indeed they remain so today, as Hall's essay in this volume so vividly demonstrates. Only a very simplified version of one aspect of this complex issue as it unfolded in the modern period can be offered here, with particular reference to what it meant or came to mean at a practical, local level in Taos.

During the territorial period, non-Indian settlers were favored by local courts in land-water disputes with the Pueblos, who fared similarly at the federal level, where the Indians were regarded more or less as full citizens whose land was alienable. This approach had been encouraged by an 1877 Supreme Court decision (*United States v. Joseph*) which decreed that Pueblo peoples owned complete and therefore alienable title to their lands.[53] But however confusing its legal status, de facto settler encroachment on the Pueblo league, for example in the upper and middle Rio Lucero watershed, or by downtown Taos itself, persisted as it always had. The 1913 *Sandoval* decision decreed, however, that the Pueblos be accorded trust status as tribal Indians, their lands to be administered as federal reservations. This provided the legal basis for the reclamation of alienated and encroached-upon lands. Long and bitter court battles followed or in many cases simply continued, between the Pueblo and non-Indian claimants, and most of the latter were Hispanos.

In 1922 the Bursum Bill was introduced to Congress, which proposed confirmation of all pre-1902 non-Indian titles and placement of land-water adjudication under state jurisdiction.[54] The bill was defeated with the help of a powerful Anglo lobby organized in part by artists and intellectuals who had settled around Taos and Santa Fe, including Stella Atwood, Mabel Dodge, and John Collier.[55] In 1924 the Pueblo Lands Act, also authored by Bursum as a kind of compromise, was approved. It called for immediate investigation and final settlement of all non-Indian titles to Pueblo lands and promised monetary compensation for land lost to settlers who could meet a highly restricted set of requirements. Most Taos claims were adjudicated in the 1920s and 1930s. Among the first to be considered was the town itself, including the plaza, which not surprisingly the court found irrecoverable. An oversight in the original settlement gave the Pueblo a lingering claim over all town streets and alleys. At one point in the process, which ran concurrently with the ongoing Blue Lake issue, the Pueblo was evidently misled into thinking it could exchange compensation for the town land for Blue Lake (the two were separate cases involving different branches of the federal government). Eventually Hispanos were ejected from the Tenorio tract, where in Arroyo Seco families had settled on the north side of the Rio Lucero, and also from lands in El Prado and Ranchitos. Needless to say, this caused deep resentment among many Hispanos, who saw the Indians as benefiting unjustly at Hispano expense.

Settlement of Indian claims continues into the 1980s. Among those

333

made in the 1970s, a decade inaugurated by the landmark Blue Lake victory, were recompense for the streets of Taos, return of Bear Lake or "Tract C" in the mountains, and ejection of a Hispano family from their house in El Prado. Blue Lake was resolved when President Nixon signed the bill H.R. 471, giving Taos Pueblo trust title to the lake and surrounding area. Its enormous symbolic import notwithstanding, the decision in some sense represents the administrative transfer of some 48,000 acres, containing the town watershed, from one arm of the federal octopus (Department of Agriculture) to another (Department of the Interior). As Bodine has shown, the Blue Lake case evolved under a complex and somewhat unusual set of socioeconomic and cultural circumstances. In a word, it was shaped by the course of tourism development, centered originally around the emergence of the Taos-Santa Fe art colony.

The social and economic history of Taos in the twentieth century is the history of tourism development and of the struggle of Indians and Hispanos to preserve their overlapping land bases with the political context of this essentially government-based, outsider-controlled economy. The form of capitalism that took root after the territorial period extractive booms expired would market local resources symbolically as well as literally. Indeed, it would come to rely on as literal a preservation as possible of material and cultural resources in their ostensibly "natural," "traditional," or "unspoiled" states. Such a claim necessarily constituted an elaborate if largely unconscious fiction, one that went nicely in hand with the land and Indian management agendas of the federal government, working as always in cooperation with wealthy private enterprise. This arrangement of interests and powers, themselves driven and shaped by world economic change, is at the root of Taos's and northern New Mexico's overall condition of underdevelopment. Taos since statehood has been known locally for its lack of employment opportunities. Yet to those born elsewhere, as a tourist attraction it seems far removed from the everyday struggle to survive. The unhappy marriage of these disparate views is an integral part of Taos's contemporary social reality.

Taos has undergone two tourism booms in this century. The first occurred roughly between the two world wars and centered on the marketing of Indian ethnicity, a Latin ambience, the natural environment, and art. To use V. Smith's typology, it was a blend of ethnic, cultural, and environmental tourism. The second boom began in the

1960s and continues into the early 1980s, and is essentially recreational-environmental. Between these booms were two decades of population decline and gradual modernization, punctuated by World War II and the Korean War. Each of these periods will be discussed below. This background is given in some detail in order to contextualize, and thereby make comprehensible, the Hispano ethnopolitical mobilization that emerged after 1970 and focused on issues of land and water.

The Art Colony

Tourism's earliest beginnings in New Mexico date from the latter nineteenth century, when a few health seekers, artists, and other railroad travelers began coming through the Southwest. But its real emergence in Taos coincided with the growth of the art colony, which began in earnest after Mabel Dodge arrived in 1917. Until World War I, farming and sheepherding were still important in Taos but in decline. Local commerce was firmly controlled by a number of mostly nonnative merchants with businesses in town. Santa Fe was already well on its way to becoming a health resort, and had attracted a nucleus of writers and artists much taken with the region's scenic combination of frontier wilderness and cultural exotica. A few artists had already settled in Taos, including Blumenschein and Phillips, whose broken wagon wheel incident in 1898 would become the art colony's origin myth.[56] They had been promoting the Taos Indians through their paintings for years (with the help of Fred Harvey),[57] but it was really Dodge who inaugurated the campaign to make Taos famous. She was a restless heiress from Buffalo, New York, who during World War I transferred her salon from Greenwich Village to the outskirts of Taos Pueblo. During the next two decades she invited a stream of distinguished artists and literati to Taos for the purpose of inspiring them to proclaim or interpret it, especially the Pueblo, in their works.

The development of the Taos-Santa Fe art colony is a much celebrated, still too little analyzed, psychocultural phenomenon that probably could only have occurred in a colonized region. Works by Bodine,[58] Grimes,[59] Briggs,[60] and Weigle and Fiore[61] have laid the foundation for a deeper, more comprehensive analysis that must one day be written about the relation between tourism, the art colony, and ethnic relations in New Mexico. The peculiar blend of romantic indianism and bohemian individualism that Taos and Santa Fe became famous for represents a pronounced theme in American cultural history, and perhaps bears comparison—as well as contrast—with the indianism (*indigenismo*) that emerged among Mexican artists and intellectuals during roughly the same period.[62]

The Anglo bohemian cult of indianism and creative individualism that developed in the Southwest needs to be seen in relation to the economic and social order it accompanied and mystified. The art colony took root more or less concurrently with the establishment of federal ownership of most of the county. It came to depend upon and actively lobby in favor of the policies of "preservation" and "conservation"—or de facto segregation and underdevelopment—that comprised federal programs of land and Indian management. Bodine refers to Dodge and her associates as ethnicity seekers and "cultural plunderers," while Simmons applies the softer term, "yearners," to the peculiar breed of artists, intellectuals, scholars, and dropouts who were drawn to Taos and Santa Fe, where they "in varying degrees identified with Pueblo life and affected styles of Indian dress."[63] They also spearheaded causes such as those against the Religious Crimes Code or Bursum Bill, or in favor of Pueblo ownership of Blue Lake. This enclave of culturally disaffected spiritual refugees from urban, industrial America played an important role in the development of southwestern ethnic symbolism. Members of an alien, superordinate and colonizing society, they lived like expatriates and appropriated indigenous symbols as their own in a manner that relied on and yet belied a social system of stringent ethnic-racial stratification and segregation. As Brody[64] and Briggs have shown, some of them "discovered" or "revived" and promoted Indian and Hispanic folk arts, and in the process transformed them as well. They moreover incorporated symbols from these traditions into their own works. Much of their artistic and intellectual production took its inspiration from Indian ceremonialism and from what they imagined to be the relationship between Indian culture and the natural environment. Apart from this and literary gossip about each other, their principal subject matter tended to be introspective, with the individual ego cast large against the mythic, solitary landscape.[65]

The most salient characteristic of the art produced by Taos and Santa Fe artists and writers is its almost total lack of reference to or description of the immediate social reality within which it was created. This is odd given that the art is otherwise so "regional." Rather than an arid, difficult environment governed by a pervasive system of stratified ethnic or race relations, New Mexico became an enchanted landscape populated by mystical tribes of noble savages. Insofar as Hispanos or Mexicans were included in this universe, they tended to be cast as an afflicted, somehow blameworthy source of social irritation or danger, a kind of folk who were really a class. Their culture was valued only for the quaint, "relaxed," Latin peasant ambience it lent the place, but not for any perceived intrinsic quality or beauty. As Bodine noted, only the so-called *penitente* and *santo* traditions seemed to attract the somewhat morbid fascination of these "ethnicity seekers." While the Spanish myth helped to promote the idea of New Mexico's uniqueness, the region's Hispanos were nevertheless subject to the long heritage of Anglo-American hispanophobia, anti-Mexican sentiment, and anti-Catholicism most newcomers brought with them.[66] If to the "yearner" sensibility the Indian was innocent and wise, the Hispano was ignorant but not innocent and, although poignant at times, generally troublesome. The Hispanos were seen as having subjugated the Indians and then been deservedly subjugated themselves. They partook of the corruption but not the enlightenment of European civilization, while their perceived backwardness had none of the primordial spirituality imputed to Indians. It is therefore no mere coincidence that while an Anglo lobby stepped forth to advocate the Indian land cause, none did so for the Hispano. The lineaments of this moral dichotomy between the Indian and the Mexican or "Spanish American" in the bohemian imagination were well in evidence by the end of the pre-World War II tourism boom. It would take two wars and as many decades of slow pressure to assimilate to put the finishing touches on what in 1968 Bodine would call Taos's tri-ethnic trap.

The First Tourism Boom

The twenties seem to have been a decade during which the art colony and tourism together took root as the town's economic mainstay. Workers continued to migrate out while newcomers straggled in, and the overall population continued to grow. The area got electricity in the 1920s, and by the early 1930s the Taos-Santa Fe highway was fully paved.

Tourism and the arts became fully entrenched and institutionalized in the 1930s. It was a decade when important changes took place and the modern character of the town emerged. The business-art community was fused into a civic entity when the town incorporated in 1934 and began to promote itself as a tourist attraction. This was done, for example, by inventing the "traditional" summer fiestas, replete with a well-orchestrated "historical" parade, still observed today. The figure of Kit Carson, "America's Forgotten Hero," was revived and promoted.[67] Somewhat prophetically, a group of artists and professionals formed a ski club, to promote awareness of the sport's potential in New Mexico. A hospital and a library were donated to the town by Mabel Dodge (by then Luhan) and Lucy Case Harwood respectively, and businessmen organized a volunteer fire department after a series of disastrous fires on the plaza. A few Anglos participated in local Hispano-dominated electoral politics. The first of Taos's two Anglo mayors, a well-known dentist and businessman, was elected in 1938; the second, a well-known doctor, served two terms, in 1944–1948.

A now familiar theme in Taos's interethnic politics had emerged by the 1930s, of conflict between native "progressives" who wanted modernization, and mostly upper-middle-class newcomers who wanted to preserve and enhance Taos's quaint, rustic character. Such a dispute surfaced around 1938, for example, when an artist-conservationist contingent favored gas lamps to illuminate the plaza area, while a progressive politico contingent wanted electricity. The former prevailed, temporarily.[68]

Locals who remember will jokingly comment that the Depression was not so bad in Taos, which was already long accustomed to poverty. The county population increased by twenty-eight percent during the 1930s, so far the largest increment in this century.[69] Some of this was natural growth in addition to a steady trickle of Anglo immigrants, but a significant proportion was comprised of natives who had migrated out for work and now returned. Possibly spurred by the United States movement to deport or "repatriate" Mexican nationals, people came home to get by on a combination of farming and welfare. Federal dependency and control gained significant ground in Taos during the 1930s. Hispanos continued to lose property through back taxes, while new restrictions curtailed livestock grazing in the mountains. For the first time, large amounts of federal revenue began to flow into the county, in the form of Works Progress Administration (WPA) and welfare programs. The New Deal inaugurated the federal subsidy of local politics and underwrote a wholesale transition from Republican to Democratic party domination. Sanchez's classic study *Forgotten People* captured Taos during this period, and described its still recognizable class structure:

> The social structure of Taos County embraces all levels. Wealthy, highly educated families have found in Taos an appealing environment and have established homes there. The artist group, and the writers, make up a body of people whose interest, training, and experience place them in a very favorable position. Some of the business and professional people, together with a few federal employees, join with the above groups in forming the upper stratum of Taos society. The middle social class embraces most of the school teachers, the clerks, the small shopkeepers, some of the public employees, and similar average income groups. At the lower end of the social scale are found the small farmers and laborers who constitute the bulk of the population of the county.
>
> The significance of this fairly evident demarcation of classes is appreciated when it is realized that the New Mexican of Taos County, the taoseño, constitutes over 90 per cent of the total population of the county (estimated at 14,229 for 1938) and that, as a rule, he is found in the lower social stratum, though a few are in the professions and in business. He elects the public officials. He controls the public affairs in the county and wields the political power of the county in state affairs. The leadership for this political influence of the taoseño has too often come from those of his own group who haven't the background of experience or of training or the inclination to use this influence in behalf of the people.[70]

Sanchez's study and the Carnegie-funded Taos Project it heralded took place just prior to World War II. Throughout the 1920s and 1930s the Indian land claims process continued, attended by a devoted Anglo lobby. No such lobby fought the slow process of Hispano dispossession. An important but unremarked (by the literati) land case which occurred in the immediate prewar period involved the threatened dispossession of some 250 Hispano families who had settled along the Rio Costilla on the Sangre de Cristo grant, and failed to pay back taxes. "Montana Wheat King" Thomas Campbell arranged to purchase the land from the state tax commission for the amount due and announced plans to start a large commercial sugar beet farm there. Senator Dennis Chavez loudly championed the settlers' cause and ultimately they were saved from ejection by an arrangement to repurchase their land from the government, a resolution that gave birth to the still-existent protective Rio Costilla Livestock Association.[71]

World War II and the Fifties

World War II promptly ended the town's tourism boom and flattened local morale for its duration. Taos was affected by the war early on, when the entire New Mexico National Guard minus one thousand men was drafted to defend Corregidor in the Philippines, a military disaster culminating in the Bataan Death March, and followed by nearly four years in Japanese prison camps. A substantial number of families in all three ethnic groups spent the war not knowing what had happened to these men. This experience plus the war effort in general served to pull together diverse segments of the local social structure, submerging but never dissolving the boundaries which divided them.[72] Women perforce filled more roles outside the household, and assumed additional responsibilities within it. But the greatest impact of the war was felt when the men came home, transformed, and a campaign was launched to further civilize Taos, to "clean it up" and bring it technologically and hygienically into the mid-twentieth century. Conflict emerged at the Pueblo, between conservative or traditionalist factions and progressives, often veterans, some of whom had returned with foreign wives, and who now balked at tribal proscriptions on their personal behavior or plans to modernize their homes. On such issues the bohemian element staunchly sided with the conservatives, apparently without ever doubting its own right to a public opinion.[73]

Modernization of the town was organized primarily by Anglo doctors and other professionals and businessmen who vigorously attacked Taos's high infant mortality rate and low sanitation standards. In the process Taos came to be locally identified as an unclean place, a theme that persists and crops up periodically in the newspaper.[74] A window on at least one segment of the upwardly mobile Hispano milieu is revealed in the Spanish-page editorials of the Taos newspaper during the late forties, in which rueful, often self-accusatory advice is offered. La Raza was exhorted, for example, not to indulge in the basically lower-class kinds of behavior it was stereotyped for, such as slovenliness or welfare abuse, and urged to be fastidious, reliable, and hard-working in order to advance, or not to sell one's land for so little.[75] During the late 1940s and the 1950s the town converted gradually from hand-dug wells and outhouses to indoor plumbing, and hard plaster began to replace adobe on many buildings, while new construction was increasingly of cinderblock. Many natives left to find work and commercial growth was very slow. Businessmen constantly fretted over the sluggish economy and Taos's public image. As elsewhere, the fifties in Taos were pervaded with McCarthyism, the disconcerting emergence of a rebellious adolescent subculture, and a muted pressure to assimilate into mainstream middle America, whatever that was.

In the late fifties the plaza was paved, with most town streets to follow within another decade. There were seven art galleries and two real-estate agents in the town. Overall employment in the county had decreased during the decade from an estimated 3,869 to 2,835 jobs. The most dramatic decrease was in agriculture, which had declined from 1,572 jobs in 1950 to 414 in 1960. Some employment gains were made in the services, public administration, trade, and commerce.[76] Anglo in-migration would soon pick up, and a handful of newcomers was beginning to sustain year-round businesses that did not depend largely upon native patronage. A ski resort was established in the upper Rio Hondo watershed in 1956, at the old site of Twining. It would grow steadily during the next decade.

The Sixties: The Real Estate Boom Begins

By 1960 Taos was on the threshold of rapid change. Between 1961 and 1963 five large subdivisions were made by out-of-state development corporations, covering 90 percent or 45,267 of all subdivided plats in the county. They were all located in the most arid and sparsely populated northern and western parts of the county. The largest tract, located *en la otra banda* or across the gorge, had been purchased for several thousand dollars from a single Hispano owner, who had used it for grazing. It was subdivided into over twenty thousand lots and then sold as prime residential estates to unsuspecting buyers at the World's Fair. The magnitude of the fraud came to light gradually, as thousands of disillusioned absentee landowners defaulted on their taxes. The tax rolls expanded threefold, which soon required additional personnel in the county assessor's office. Their volume and confusion continue to multiply as lots are auctioned off or transferred. In many cases the establishment of clear title is impossible, and the pattern of ownership of these lands is now so fragmented that reassembly for any single purpose, such as grazing, is seen as virtually impossible.[77]

The twenty-year population decline since World War II began to reverse itself in the 1960s, even though a steady stream of native youth continued to leave for employment, education, and before long, another war. Late in the decade Taos was hit by what is generally remembered as the Great Hippie Invasion. Over a period of about four summers, between 1968 and 1971, thousands of young, itinerant, middle-class urban (or suburban) Anglos began to arrive in Taos, in search of the same romantic utopia their bohemian predecessors had sought over a generation earlier. But unlike most tourists who had previously moved to Taos, many hippies came with dreams of going "back to the land" and living as farmers. For several years they were able to buy up parcels of irrigated land rather cheaply from Hispanos, who needed the cash and had little inkling of the transformation about to occur. After a winter or two of rustic hardship, many newcomers sold their land at a profit and moved on. Ownership turnover then escalated along with land price, and within another decade the average price of an irrigated acre had increased by as much as forty times. This meant that very few Hispanos, at least thirty percent of whom have subpoverty-level incomes,[78] could afford to buy land, and an increasing number could no longer afford to hold onto it. In concert with the subdivision flurry, this initiated Taos's contemporary real-estate boom, which by the mid-1970s was fueled primarily by the ski industry.

It is noteworthy that Hispano group violence against Anglos erupted for perhaps the first time in more than a century during the hippie period. The hippies exhibited a combination of behaviors that amused some Indians, antagonized many Hispanos, and alienated an influential segment of the Anglo population, mostly the businessmen. This rendered them vulnerable in an unprecedented manner, and some of them were openly attacked by groups of Chicano youth. The hippies were accused of being dirty, lazy, and immoral, but probably what most infuriated Hispanos about them, apart from their public displays, occasional petty thievery and land purchase, was their collection of welfare and food stamps. E. Smith attributes the demise of the hippie communes which had mushroomed around Taos to the violence, and suggests that the "flower children" who remained were forced to rationalize their preparation for self-defense.[79]

Most of the hippies who stayed in Taos gradually settled into somewhat more conventionally middle-class—or in some cases upper-middle-class or "hipoisie"—lifestyles for which they found ample margin. An important trend inaugurated during the hippie era was Anglo competition on the local unskilled labor market. Prior to around 1969, few Anglos received welfare or competed with Hispanos for the limited manual labor and service jobs in Taos. This changed with the influx of semi-transient, often college-educated youth, who today compete favorably with Hispanos in the tourism-related service and construction job markets. It has been a contributing factor in the intensification of anti-Anglo sentiment among at least some segments of the Hispano population.

The violence against hippies erupted at the same time that a new Chicano militance was emerging in the cities and universities, and it also followed the widely publicized activity of Reies Tijerina and the Alianza. Taos was not particularly known as a stronghold of Alianza membership, but Tijerina did have support there. He made it his business to visit the Pueblos, land grant villages, and hippie communes in the area, possibly operating on the assumption that anyone at odds with the "establishment" was a potential ally. The Tierra Amarilla courthouse raid took place near the beginning of the hippie period, which also happened to be the height of the Vietnam War, as well as of black and other national minority mobilizations. The intrusion of national upheaval into the local scene created conditions under which, for perhaps the first time, Taos's interethnic dynamics were openly described as racist. Taos no longer seemed isolated from the rest of America.

By the end of the sixties, the face of old Taos was changing fast. The construction industry was expanding along with the number of realtors, and many new businesses, including national franchises, had been established. Spurred by the political unease the Alianza had engendered, a new flood of federal "war on poverty" funds was flowing into the county to underwrite an increase in public employment. The ski industry, enthusiastically embraced by local businessmen as the solution to Taos's dilemma of a seasonal, feast-or-famine economic cycle, was beginning to flourish. The old Our Lady of Guadalupe church next to the plaza had burned early in the decade and been replaced by a modern, "supermarket-type" building nearby. The long-standing social influence of the parish priest and Loretto nuns in town was fading. Most of the town streets were being paved, and neon advertizing was in vogue. The county courthouse, the nerve center of local politics, was transferred from the plaza to a modern building on south Santa Fe road, a move that signaled a shift of business concentration away from a nuclear to a more dispersed or "strip" pattern. Town officials were beginning to talk about city planning and zoning. Mabel Dodge Luhan was dead, and movie star Dennis Hopper and a coterie of counterculture groupies were living in her house.

Eclipsed during the forties along with many other local issues, the Blue Lake controversy resurfaced during the fifties, gained momentum during the sixties and, as already mentioned, was finally resolved in 1970. Bodine's chronicle shows how the case was kept alive over decades by a handful of powerful Pueblo personalities who were committed to the cause, but who also used it to manipulate circumstances for their own political purposes.[80] His account reveals that the religious freedom argument became increasingly explicit through time, no doubt because it worked. This is not to say that the lake, or for that matter other locales in the Taos basin, did not have aboriginal religious significance. Rather, it points to the fact that Blue Lake came to be explicitly identified with the Taos tribe's religious freedom and continuation as a people under a particular set of legal, political, and economic circumstances. The course of the case was certainly influenced by the presence of a good many "yearners," and correspondingly, by the astute use made by prominent Pueblo individuals of their Anglo admirers' willingness to help. Not all Anglos sided with the Indians of course, and needless to say many Hispanos found the issue particularly galling in light of their own land situation, which included ejections within recent memory from Indian lands. Nevertheless, some older Hispanos did support the Pueblo and even testified in its behalf, a sympathy enhanced among the younger generation by a growing awareness that Chicanos have a common cause with other minorities. The symbolic import of the Blue Lake victory was intensified by the general social and political climate of the times, and it reinforced the already established connection in local perception not only between land, water, and physical survival, but also between land and cultural survival. This connection was dramatized for Hispanos by the Alianza, a development which itself is comprehensible only within its larger historical and sociological contexts.

Luxury Tourism and the Emergence of Protest

Events in Taos during the seventies served to deepen the sense of connection among at least some Hispanos between their continued occupation of and control over their lands, ditches, and villages, and their persistence as the people they know themselves to be, or to put it another way, as culturally and ethnically distinct from Anglos. The decade brought increased growth and development, but also an intensified—or at any rate more articulated—sense of resistance, most explicitly in the form of public protest. At the same time, cleavages were expressed between the expanding middle class of urbanized Hispano businessmen, and poorer, more rural farmers and ranchers who live in the villages and still use the ditches.

Two major protests stand out in the 1970s: the one against Indian Camp Dam, lasting from 1971 to 1976, and the other against Taos Ski Valley, a protest that emerged in 1974 and has continued into the early 1980s. Both of these cases, as well as a proliferation of similar or related ones during the early 1980s, began as disputes over water.

Indian Camp Dam. Described by both Reynolds and Nichols, the Indian Camp Dam issue involved the proposed construction of a large dam and reservoir above Talpa and Ranchos on the Rio Grande del Rancho, southeast of Taos.[81] The project allegedly was intended to boost irrigation agriculture through the formation of a conservancy district, but local opposition understood it as a government-assisted ploy to promote tourism at the expense of Hispano farmers by taxing them for what in fact would become a recreational lake. Opposition leaders included older acequia, land grant (La Serna), and community water system officers from the Ranchos-Cañon-Los Cordovas areas, some of whom had originally favored the project. In what appears to have been a first-time Hispano-Anglo alliance against big developers and "progress," these otherwise socially and politically conservative native protesters were supported by an emergent element of mostly ex-hippie environmentalists. Nichols's popular fictional account of the "Milagro Beanfield War" based on this issue both publicizes and satirizes the Hispano land plight in Taos.[82] The case dragged on for five years, but achieved at least temporary resolution when the conservancy district was annulled on a technicality.[83] The struggle against the conservancy district and dam gave birth to a still active alliance of acequias within the general *tres rios* (Rio Chiquito, Rio Grande del Rancho, Rio Fernando) area. This organization has since supported the cause of Rio Hondo acequias against developers, and has become an important participant in a larger protective organization, Acequias del Norte, which unites ditch associations from several northern counties, and which itself grew out of a water struggle near Española in the 1970s. Along with the ski valley issue that began to take shape concurrently, the Indian Camp Dam controversy marked the beginning of a new kind of protest activity in Taos. A post-1960 influence is discernible in its often ethnically mixed constituency and public, increasingly direct, style of activism.

The Ski Valley Issue. Organized protest against the ski valley emerged in 1974 when, after six years of expansion and sewage pollution of the Rio Hondo, ski valley developers sought improved access through national forest to private land where a 4,500 "pillow" resort, named Kachina Village, was planned. Taos Ski Valley is located not far below the source of the Rio Hondo, which supports Valdez nine miles downstream, Arroyo Hondo two to three miles below that, Cañoncito between them, and the western upland settlement of Des Montes. At least nineteen households on the river use its waters for domestic purposes, including drinking and cooking.[84] Roughly ninety percent of the ski area, that is, its trails and lifts, is located in Carson National Forest, on land leased from the Forest Service. Downstream residents, including Hispano farmers, ditch officers and their families, Chicano activists, and Anglo environmentalists, protested vociferously enough *en masse* at a still well-remembered public hearing to dissuade the Forest Service from improving access, at least until a bigger and better sewage treatment plant could be built. It was during the Kachina Village controversy that the image of the Rio Hondo flowing in the veins of its native downstream users was invoked and used to great effect.

During the next six years a variable, ethnically mixed committee of protesters persisted in a largely unsuccessful legalistic strategy to block formation of a Twining sanitation district, and to compel the appropriate state and federal agencies to enforce their own sanitation standards. By 1981, the Forest Service and ski valley had worked out a thirty-year master growth plan, while the Environmental Protection Agency (EPA) and the ski valley completed designs for a new, $1.5 million sewage treatment plant.

In 1982 the EPA approved the new plant without requiring a graduated hook-up policy linked to performance, and the plant was built, using private funds, in the late fall. To the downstream protesters, the failure to require a hook-up policy meant, in effect, that while the Twining district would forego federal funding, it could continue to expand to the new plant's full capacity without first demonstrating it could meet and maintain clean-water standards. After years of litigation and participation on government-sponsored citizen's advisory committees dealing with the ski valley, the protesters reached a new peak in their level of frustration. For fourteen consecutive years of violations, neither state nor federal agencies had enforced their own standards. Agency collusion with developers seemed beyond doubt.

On the day before Easter and the last weekend of the 1981–1982 ski season, about three hundred downstream residents and their supporters held an unprecedented mass demonstration at the ski valley. It was conducted as a mock funeral for the river, complete with coffin, hearse, and motorcade, in addition to religious banners and the parish priest's solicited blessing. The roughly 150-vehicle caravan departed from Arroyo Seco and wended its way slowly up Hondo Canyon, honking in unison when it reached the ski area. A second demonstration was held not long after the new plant was completed, this time the day after Christmas, at the height of the 1982–1983 season. This somewhat smaller and less elaborate but equally vocal demonstration was held despite the Forest Service's allegedly illegal refusal to grant a permit. On both occasions demonstrators picketed and leafleted skiers, and were extensively photographed by Forest Service, ski valley, and law enforcement personnel, in addition to being covered by the media. Pairs of protesters continued to leaflet skiers on weekends for the remainder of the season, while the new plant polluted heavily.

In the autumn of 1983, repeatedly postponed state and federal hearings were finally held on the matter of past violations, and the Twining Water and Sanitation District was fined $4,500 by the State District Court, payable to the Environmental Improvement Division (EID). It agreed to a $30,000 settlement out of federal court, where it might face a possible maximum fine of $1,000 per day. Out of the settlement amount, $5,000 went to the downstream acequias for "improvements," while the remainder went to the EPA.[85] It remains to be seen whether the new plant will continue to pollute, and if so, what downstream response will be.[86]

In addition to the ski valley protest against pollution, in 1982 a coalition of downstream ditch associations opposed large transfers (one for about seventeen acre-feet) of priority water rights from Arroyo Hondo to the ski valley, that were to be used for commercial purposes, including snow making. Such transfers are routinely approved by the state engineer, whose de facto policy is to consider each application in isolation, thereby ignoring their obvious cumulative impact. This impact threatens the viability and integrity of the ditch system by removing water as well as labor, and it also renders farmland forever fallow and useless for anything except residential development. This is because once the surface water rights are removed from a piece of land, it can no longer be irrigated, and the Taos area is generally too dry to allow for dryland farming. The only water such a piece of land can thereafter have legal access to must come from an underground well, and may be used for residential purposes only. Since a given ditch system must be maintained by the collective labor of its users of *parciantes,* each time a parcel loses its water rights, a proportional amount of labor and ditch fees is also lost to the system as a whole, thereby increasing the burden of maintenance upon the remaining parciantes. Each member is a link in the chain of community water use and control, and each time a member and his quota of water and labor are lost, the overall chain is weakened. This deleterious impact is maximized for those lowest on the ditch. The members of a ditch system may protest a proposed transfer, but the burden of proof of potential damage from water loss rests upon them. In other words, the applicant for the transfer is not required to prove that the transfer will not be deleterious. Moreover, the costs of filing a protest and any ensuing litigation must somehow be borne by the water users themselves.[87]

The ski valley demonstrations were part of an overall escalation of protest activity that took place in 1982, focused primarily in the Hondo watershed, but also apparent in milder form throughout much of the municipal district, where public meetings were held in almost every community to discuss the merits and dangers of rural zoning as a possible way to forestall if not prevent the steady advance of luxury housing development and its likely consumption of all remaining farmland and water.

The dozens of community meetings held in the Taos area during 1982–1983 tended to reveal that zoning was by no means an appealing or popular idea among the majority of rural Hispanos, but the one point most people could agree on was that no one wanted a condominium next door or upstream. Along with the ski valley issue, the rural zoning debate served first as a backdrop to, but then itself gained momentum from, what came to be known as the Valdez "condo war." This involved unified action by the village of Valdez against a large luxury condominium planned for the upper Valdez valley. The condo war showed how far villagers were willing to go in order to stop such a development in their midst. The case epitomizes the struggle rural Taoseños are engaged in to maintain their fragile hold on traditional uses and ownership of land and water, and it illustrates the conspiracy of structures that militates against them.

But before proceeding to the condo war and related rural zoning movement, some additional background will be given in order to elucidate more fully the conditions under which local Hispano resistance to outside encroachment has intensified.

Modern Taos

The 1970s brought a significant and locally obvious augmentation of Anglo presence and control, not simply in the economic sphere, but in most areas of public life. A corresponding self-protectiveness emerged among Hispanos with respect to those domains of their own traditional predominance, such as, for example, local politics and government, including the school system. At the same time, a handful of wealthy, upwardly mobile Hispano businessmen enhanced their niche as elite brokers within the expanding economy, and moved into higher levels of finance, such as banking.[88]

All sectors of the local economy grew during the 1970s except for agriculture, which declined from 6.4 percent to 5.4 percent of all jobs.[89] Growth was stimulated by expansion of the molybdenum mine in Questa, and by the ski industry which, in the 1979–1980 season, claimed to generate an estimated income of $11,532,000.[90] Most of the jobs generated by tourism are in trade, services, and construction, which together make up roughly 55 percent of all jobs within the county.[91] For the most part, tourism-related jobs tend to be low-paying, seasonal, and without benefits, upward mobility, or security. The best jobs to be had from the standpoint of these factors are at the "Moly" mine, the county's single largest private employer, which accounts for 11.5 percent of all jobs.[92] The other major sector is public employment or government, which includes the school system and comprises 24 percent of all jobs.[93]

Yet despite economic growth, the county still ranks in the state's bottom five in terms of unemployment, averaging 14.2 percent for the period 1970–1981.[94] The official unemployment rate in 1983 averaged 17 percent,[95] and was reported at around 20 percent early in the 1985 summer season.[96] In 1980, the average income *per capita* was $6,128, while 20 percent of all personal income came from transfer payments or some form of federal assistance.[97] Although a large proportion of Hispanos is employed in the private sector, a comparatively small, though nevertheless growing, segment occupies positions of ownership or power within it. By contrast, in the nonfederal part of the public sector, Hispanos predominate in virtually all hired positions controlled by the electorate, which they dominate by sheer numerical majority. Whereas the trend in upper and lower levels of the private sector has been toward greater integration (by virtue of expanding in-migration on the one hand, and limited upward mobility on the other), the opposite seems true in local politics and government, where in 1984 an Anglo (not to mention Indian) mayor or county commissioner seemed well beyond the realm of possiblity, and the ubiquitous Anglo school administrator of a generation ago had been replaced by a Chicano bureaucrat.[98]

It is both ironic and significant that Anglos will not infrequently complain of discriminatory treatment in the schools, or claim they cannot get a fair trial in a dispute with a Hispano.[99] While racism as an issue has surfaced as such during the past two decades, there is nevertheless a strong taboo against discussing it openly in public or ethnically mixed company, although thinly veiled allusions and pointed insinuations are often made. The long-manifest, privately acknowledged, yet almost never explicitly articulated ethnographic truth about Taos is its de facto segregation, which obtains virtually everywhere outside the everyday world of business, such that membership in one group effectively precludes full participation in the key sociocultural events of the other two. Taos in this respect is a little like the classical shamanistic cosmos of three superimposed, mutually invisible layers or worlds, where the denizens of each live mirroring but only accidentally interpenetrating lives. Exclusion of each group from intimate knowledge of or involvement in the lives of the other two is a dominant feature of Taos as an inclusive social system. For example, an event can take place which has tragic or scandalous significance among one of the ethnic groups, reverberating quickly throughout its informational and social networks, while most people in either of the other two groups barely take note. For the most part, members of each group celebrate their religious holidays, weddings, funerals, and Saturday nights in the company of their co-ethnics, class and other sociocultural subdivisions notwithstanding. Friendship is predominantly intraethnic. Yet mutual awareness among the groups is differential by virtue of differential power. Because Anglos control the media and theirs is the dominant language, events of significance to their elites receive the greatest publicity and are thus widely known. Their interpretation usually becomes the "official version." At the same time, as Spicer notes, members of a dominant group tend to be less aware of ethnic boundaries than those who are subordinated. The latter are constantly reminded of their constrained universe, while the former must seldom confront their own part in perpetuating it. This segregated, unequal reality is contradicted by the more pleasant, tourism-promotional public-relations image of Taos as a slightly zany marvel of "tri-cultural harmony" or "colorful historical pageantry." Recent demographic shifts, however, seem to have thrown Hispano-Anglo boundaries into higher relief.

Between 1970 and 1980, Anglo in-migration increased to such an extent that long-standing ethnic proportions went from 86 percent Hispano, 7 percent Anglo, and 7 percent Indian to 67 percent, 27 percent, and 7 percent, respectively, possibly the largest Anglo increment this century.[100] Moreover, by 1980 Anglos owned at least half the land in eight of the fourteen major settlement areas inside the municipal district, although they outnumbered Hispanos in only four of them, including the town, Las Colonias, San Cristobal, and Twining.[101] Las Colonias and Arroyo Seco both became predominantly Anglo-owned in the 1960s.[102] Along with Des Montes, they are located along the road to the ski valley, and together these three settlements have borne the main impact of the ski industry's secondary or associated luxury residential development. Twining, which includes the privately owned portion of Hondo Canyon above Valdez, has been mostly Anglo owned and populated since its beginnings as a mining camp in the last century.[103] By 1980, more than half the land in Twining and Las Colonias, which along with the town are the main foci of condominium development, was owned by nonnatives who live elsewhere for most of the year. All told, only 38 percent of the 1,444,480 acres of land in Taos County is privately owned.[104]

The real estate and construction boom that began in the 1960s grew during the 1970s from a number of comparatively small-scale enterprises to a multimillion dollar, increasingly luxury-oriented industry. By 1983 the real estate market supported at least eighty realtors, most of whom had lived in Taos for less than ten years. One hundred and thirty-five were reported for the county in 1985, as the boom seemed to be tapering off.[105] Their advertising in the local newspaper went from a few items in 1960 to nearly four pages in 1984. An acre of irrigated land in the Hondo watershed which sold for perhaps $600 in 1960 might sell in 1984 for as much as $22,000, while the water rights alone might bring anything from $3,000 to $6,000 per acre-foot. Most advertised adobe houses near town were going for $100,000 or more.[106]

Each of the communities around Taos has experienced and responded to the population and construction booms differently, according to its own internal composition, particular geographic locale, and relation to the town on the one hand, and to its neighbors in the same or adjacent watersheds on the other. An account of each individual village situation cannot be provided here, although each deserves its own telling. Only the broadest outline can be given.

Those communities nearest Taos are faced with whether to be absorbed by the town's relentless spread, or to resist assimilation and defend their individual autonomy, identities, and traditional boundaries. None has chosen the former alternative, and of the two inside the town's three-mile-wide extra-territorial zone, El Prado and Cañon, each has pursued a very different course in meeting the municipal mandate either to zone itself or be zoned by the town.[107] A key issue for these communities as well as for Ranchos and its neighbors is whether to maintain or construct its own independent water and sewage system, or to hook up to the town's, and thereby be incorporated into the city. The ability of these communities to maintain their autonomy is undermined by the construction of large housing or other tourism-related developments, whose promoters are eager to hook up to the town's system and other services, and whose prospective clientele has little interest in the preservation of traditional village boundaries or resource use patterns.

The town itself does not have enough water rights to accommodate more than the next twenty years of growth at most and has, for the time being, addressed its most immediate needs by purchasing 400 acre-feet of San Juan-Chama diversion water rights.[108] By law this water must be pumped from outside the Taos basin, from one or more wells, or from the Rio Grande itself. In order to qualify for federal funds to enable it to buy, locate, and pump the water into town, and also pay for its new, expanded sewage system, Taos must demonstrate and guarantee a certain level of growth. It has done this primarily by contracting with two nonlocal (but instate) housing developers who, in concert with municipal planners, have worked out designs for large housing projects to be located southeast of the town. Although these projects include graduated price ranges for their units, it is clear that not even the cheapest of these units will be affordable by most natives, except for perhaps a few young professionals or management-level employees and those of comparable strata. This is true for the vast majority of the housing being built or planned for Taos. Despite a pressing shortage of middle-to-low-cost housing, and except for single family dwellings and one or two low-cost housing projects, the new construction is being built for and by newcomers, often as second homes.

The town first zoned itself in the 1960s, although a skeletal set of regulations, never enforced, had been drawn up at the time of incorporation in 1934. During the 1970s the town came up with a more sophisticated code and additional personnel to administer it. County government has authority over subdivisions and, after the 1960s fiasco, enacted regulations for dealing with them. The county commission also has the power to zone the county, but has not done so. It therefore lacks jurisdiction over nonsubdivision construction outside the city limits and buffer zone. Such construction is approved in Santa Fe without consultation with any local body, although once approved, plans must be filed with the county clerk.

In the late 1970s public pressure induced the county commission to contract for a comprehensive planning study as prerequisite to drafting county-wide zoning regulations. The study was completed by a Santa Fe consultancy firm, and a zoning code was prepared, based largely on the one adopted by Santa Fe. A petition against the code was then widely circulated, causing the commission to kill the plan just before the election, which all three incumbents lost anyway. The new commission was loathe to take up such a despised cause, and the matter of county zoning was dropped. In the meantime ever bigger and fancier developments continued to mushroom in the vicinity of every settlement as well as in formerly unsettled areas such as the west mesa.

Once the issue of county zoning was officially dead, it began to crop up in the communities, invariably in response to some proposed and therefore imminent project that promised to consume a substantial portion of an already over-allocated and jealously guarded water supply.

Rural zoning tends to have several types of proponent in Taos: Anglo environmentalists of various stripes; mostly younger, urbanized Hispanos or Chicanos, who have lived away and returned; and a few of the older ditch and land grant officers and their families, who have been actively involved in defending the ditches since at least Indian Camp Dam. In some instances, coalitions of either the first two or all three of these categories would organize a meeting in a given community to discuss the possibility of zoning. Invariably most newcomers would favor the idea, some locals (often those with larger landholdings) would oppose it vehemently, and the usually silent majority would listen skeptically.[109] The spur to debate and in some cases to action always involved a proposed multiple-unit housing development that would consume water, discharge sewage, and serve outsiders.

This then, was the general setting in which the Valdez condo war erupted, and within which the struggle continues to unfold. This struggle involves the effort of rural and urbanizing Hispanos to preserve their community resource domains. In the autumn of 1981, and for the twenty or more months following, by far the most frequently and hotly debated public issue in town and the surrounding communities concerned the protection of increasingly scarce land and water against the onslaught of in-migration and luxury housing development.

III. *The Valdez Condo War*

Valdez

Valdez is located about twelve miles north of Don Fernando, at the mouth of Hondo or Twining canyon, nine miles below the ski valley and roughly four miles east of the church of Nuestra Señora de Dolores in upper Arroyo Hondo (see Map 13). Known originally as San Antonio, Valdez evidently acquired its present name after a postmistress in 1894.[110] It was first settled as the upper placita of Arroyo Hondo community grant in 1815, becoming a separate extension of the grant in 1823. Today the legal remnant of the grant consists of the thirty-seven-member San Antonio corporation, renamed in 1984 La Merced de Arroyo Hondo Arriba, which has pieced together and now collectively owns about 2,400 acres of nonirrigated hillside land above the Valdez valley.

Valdez is clearly bounded. It is set deep in a narrow, irrigated valley that extends for about three miles along the Rio Hondo, between Twining and the pinch of bluffs at Cañoncito, below which the Arroyo Hondo valley opens out. Valdez contains approximately 150 people living in about 50 households dispersed along the valley, with some concentration near the centrally located placita. Roughly eighty percent of the population is Hispanic, and some residents are evidently descended from original grantees. Today the placita consists of the church of San Antonio, the old schoolhouse (now a community center), a post office, and a cantina, all located in or around the original square still outlined by old houses. The valley floor is banded by strips of irrigated land, dotted with adobe houses and trailers, and divided lengthwise by the tree-lined river. Seen from above, along the rim one must descend in order to enter Valdez, the valley has a picturesque, miniature-looking beauty.

To outsiders, Valdez has a self-contained remoteness defined geographically and accentuated by its proximity to the predominantly Anglo areas of Twining and Des Montes.[111] In Taos, Valdez is known for its rural Hispanic character, its ditch that appears to run uphill (as well as one that runs right through the cantina) and its old reputation for *brujos* (witches). To neighbors it is known for its church, abundant fruit, cantina, and kin, and rights with respect to the river: upstream from (but now third priority to) Arroyo Hondo, and below the "uphill" acequia to Des Montes.[112]

Although nearest to the Swiss-style Anglo-European resort community at Taos Ski Valley, Valdez has remained the native settlement least developed by the tourism-related real estate boom that has overtaken the Hondo watershed since 1970. The deep little valley offers some prime agricultural land, but it has been less attractive than Des Montes, Arroyo Seco, or Arroyo Hondo to realtors promoting isolation, vast altiplano vistas, and luxury housing. To this sensibility Valdez has been more to be looked at than lived in, although resort and subdivision activity has nevertheless begun to eat at its peripheries. By local account, the men and some families in Valdez have long followed a pattern of seasonal out-migration for work, in sheep camps or harvesting crops. During the 1940s, 1950s, and early 1960s, Valdez's population declined, but since then the village has begun to repopulate and grow, largely with the families of young adult natives who had been working and living elsewhere. This has revitalized community life in the placita.

355

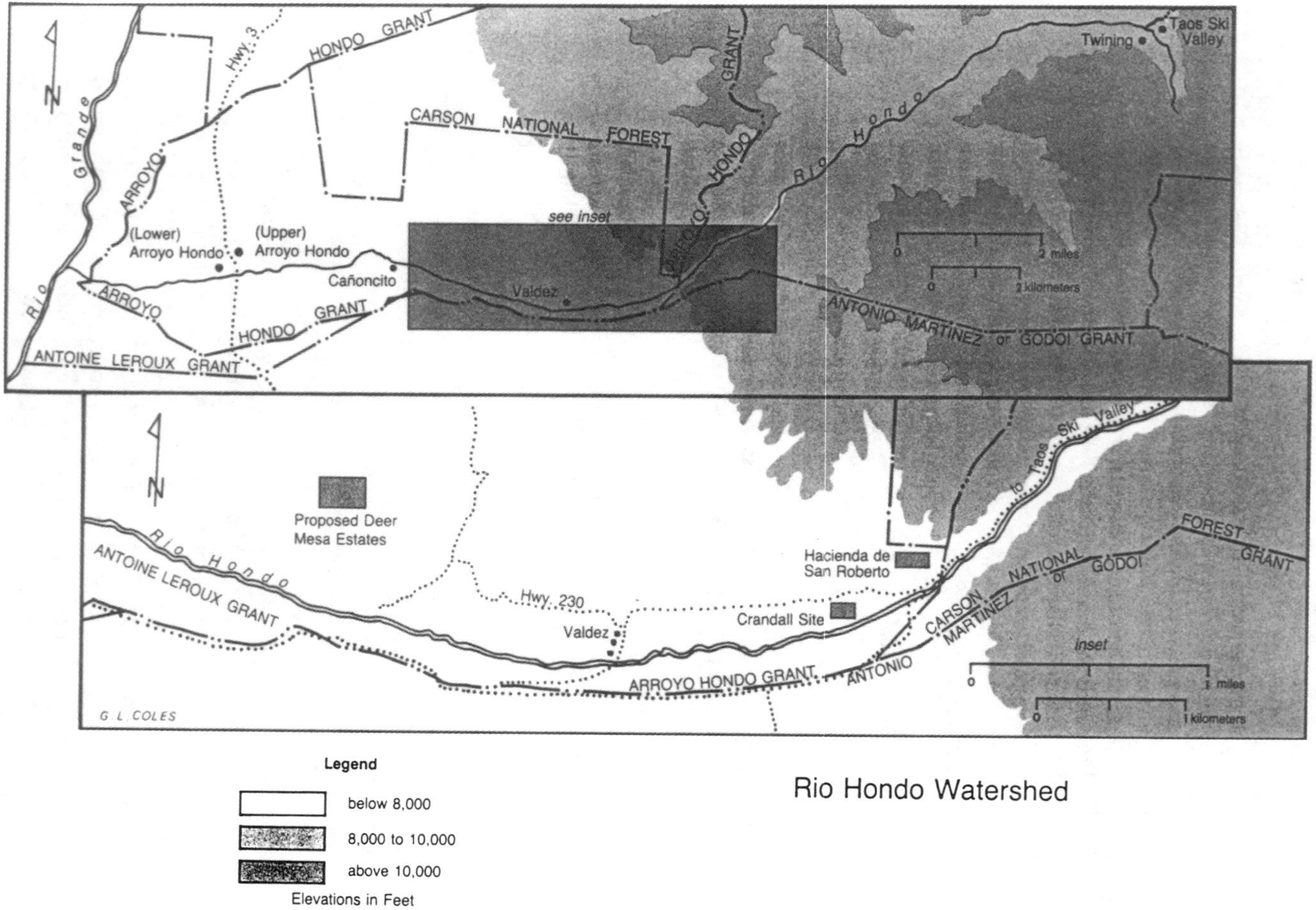

MAP 13. Rio Hondo watershed.

Today a number of Valdez men work at the mine some twenty miles away in Questa, some have jobs or businesses in town, others work at the ski valley, and a substantial proportion receive some form of federal assistance.

Anglos—including farmers, retirees, wealthy seasonal residents, hippies, and semi-tourist transients—live in or near Valdez, but none own property right on the placita. Except for the few farmer-ranchers who use the ditch system, Anglos participate little or not at all in the fundamental life of the community, which centers upon the ties of kinship and *compradrazgo* (fictive kinship) that interweave local parish, ditch, and community water organizations. Local Hispanic families participate to varying degrees and at various levels in the area's tourism-welfare-government economy, but for the most part their social interaction is with one another and takes place within the larger context of extended multicommunity ties and organizations. In Valdez, as in other villages around Taos, Spanish remains the primary language in all but intermarried or intensely upwardly mobile Hispano households, or those in which language loss has occurred through protracted out-migration.

Like other Taos area villages, Valdez both changes constantly and remains "traditional." It appears that the ability of local residents to maintain, revive, or actively defend traditional practices and resources depends in part on a certain degree of economic stability, education, and/or land tenure. The past few decades have shown that, while an overall trend toward acculturation may be taking place, the attenuation of certain forms and practices may not be permanent. Cultural revivals and innovations seem to occur right alongside apparent culture loss. Revivals are not infrequently religious in nature. Probably the most striking recent example of this is the cultural renaissance revolving around the San Francisco de Asisi parish centered in Ranchos. During the past decade, the parish has helped to initiate an annual pilgrimage for vocations to Chimayo from Amalia, undertaken the restoration of the famous church's adobe exterior by community labor, and contracted for the restoration of its two *reredos* or altar screens, one of which was rededicated in 1982 to Los Hermanos de Nuestro Padre Jesus Nazareno, or the so-called *penitente* brotherhood. Like Arroyo Hondo, Valdez sold its morada, which now sits vacant and crumbling by the roadside, owned by a nonresident outsider. The local Hermanos are still active, however, and use their various parish chapels and the Arroyo Seco morada during Lent and Holy Week and other occasions. In 1983, shortly after the condo war about to be described, Valdez revived its San Antonio mass, procession, and fiesta, which had not been conducted for at least twenty-five years. Arroyo Hondo parishioners in 1984 contracted for the 150-year anniversary reproduction of their church's reredo, the original of which is in a Colorado museum, while most of its santos and the morada are owned by a wealthy Anglo. The slow quadrupling of San Antonio Corporation acreage during the past fifty years is another indication that village residents seek not only to retain but to recover traditional boundaries.[113]

Although Valdez has borne the most direct brunt of ski valley pollution of the Rio Hondo, with the exception of one Anglo farmer married to a local Hispana, no one from there has been particularly active in the drawn-out legalistic battle to make Taos Ski Valley-Twining clean up the river. The core constituency has come mostly from Arroyo Hondo. This may be partly because Hondo is larger and more heterogeneous, and also because few people from there work at the ski valley, whereas a number from Valdez do, as maids and maintenance men. Nevertheless, the ski valley issue was the immediate context within which people in Valdez finally did protest. Protest in Valdez first emerged in the autumn of 1981, when the community succeeded in getting a sewage discharge permit denied for the Hacienda de San Roberto, a condominium then under construction just above the head of the valley. Valdez protesters persuaded the EID to deny the application to discharge sewage into the Rio Hondo by submitting nineteen affidavits which attested that nearly as many households in Valdez and Cañoncito depended on the river for all domestic uses. The construction involved the expansion of a small restaurant and lodge into a large condominium by the Sikhs, a religious-entrepreneurial sect made up of out-of-state Anglo converts and based in Española. Just after the permit was denied, the half-completed condominium went into the receivership of seven banks, all but one out-of-state.

The protest against the Hacienda was initiated by the Valdez Mutual Domestic Water Users Association (MDWUA), the organization of the users of the community well that serves about thirty households in the area of the placita. The president and secretary of the MDWUA wrote a letter to the EID requesting a public hearing on the Hacienda's sewage discharge application after a legal notice had appeared in a nonlocal newspaper—the EID having failed to publish such notice in

358

the Taos paper. After meeting with some community organizers whose prior contact with Valdez had come through ski valley protests and a rally in support of a Hispano family involved in a Rio Arriba County land grant case, the MDWUA officers decided to organize a public hearing.[114] Leaflets were circulated door-to-door in the Hondo and Valdez valleys, and a well-attended prehearing community meeting was held at the church in Valdez. The affidavits on water use were collected during this period. House-to-house contact, community strategy meetings, and careful preparation for public meetings and confrontations were to become characteristics of protest in Valdez. The community organizers later became residents of Valdez and went on to play a key facilitative role in the condo war and in the related effort to zone the valley. While the role of the organizers was critical to the success of both condominium protests in Valdez, it became obvious that the movement derived its power and legitimacy from its broad-based Hispano constituency. The precipitating factors for the protest, discussed in the previous section, were clear-cut and exerted a cumulative impact brought to bear on Valdez, the Hondo watershed, and the greater Taos area during 1982.[115]

The "Condo War"

In January 1982 a representative of the State Engineer's Office began knocking on doors in the upper Valdez valley about a mile above the placita, to ask how deep people's wells were. Residents then learned that in late November and early December, concurrently with the Hacienda protest and permit denial, Peter Crandall had applied to transfer 4.6 acre-feet of water from the San Antonio ditch to underground use in order to supply a well for a multiple-unit condominium.[116] Since no one objected to the transfer during the three-week legal notice publication period or for ten days thereafter, the request was routinely approved. The small-print legal notice in *The Taos News* mentioned tract number, the surveyor's coordinates, and the San Antonio ditch, but not the name of Valdez, and no one in the valley noticed it.

Homeowners adjacent to Crandall's nine-acre strip were quickly alarmed by the prospect of a large condominium whose well would be at least fifty feet deeper than their own wells and whose sewage would have to go into either the river or the ground-water. Their other concerns were the effect of development on traffic along the narrow winding road in the valley where children and livestock frequently play or meander, and the overall social impact so many new, wealthy, urban Anglo residents would have on the community. From the beginning, people in Valdez expressed the fear that the condo inevitably would result in the destruction of their valley and way of life. Opposition to the project was expressed as a struggle for cultural survival and community self-determination. At a community meeting held in the schoolhouse to discuss the idea of zoning in the Hondo watershed, the people of Valdez decided to send a letter of protest to the state engineer and did so on 28 January, along with a petition bearing sixty signatures. Their protest was denied some weeks later because it was "untimely." No physical tests were conducted, but the state engineer was satisfied that significant well "draw-down" would not occur.

After their protest was denied, people in Valdez joined others in the Hondo watershed in petitioning the county commission for a symbolic moratorium on major development in their area, while they undertook to zone themselves. In this, they followed the example of Llano Quemado where, faced with a proposed apartment complex that threatened an apparently dropping water table tapped by shallow, hand-dug wells, residents had successfully petitioned the new commission for a moratorium in early January. Both moratoria were said to be strictly symbolic because the county commission claimed it had no power to enforce them. The commissioners nevertheless imposed a six-month limit on the Hondo watershed moratorium, granted at a public hearing. The single dissenting voice at the hearing was that of Crandall himself, a young developer from a prominent Anglo family owning one of Taos's car dealerships. He claimed, among other things, that the sewage discharge from his condominium would be "drinking water pure."

More than a dozen public meetings on zoning were held in the Hondo watershed during the winter and spring of 1982. The immediate threat posed by Crandall's condominium moved people in Valdez to undertake the necessary steps to form a Special Zoning District (SZD), which for reasons of size and agreement they did in cooperation with Arroyo Seco and San Cristobal.[117] The widespread debate about rural zoning took its text from a rather ambiguous and scanty state statute (3-21-26 N.M.S.A. 1978), which states that residents from within an unzoned area containing a minimum of 150 households may delineate and form an independent SZD if they present a petition to the county clerk bearing the signatures of at least 51 percent of the registered voters resident within the proposed district. Once the zoning petition and zoning plat have been filed with the clerk, the county commission must set a date within sixty days for the election of a five-person zoning commission to draw up the code.

Spurred by the approach of construction season, people in Valdez managed on 4 May to vote on a broad plan and to elect a zoning commission candidate committed to that plan. The essence of their zoning plan was a code to protect customary patterns of settlement and land use and to curtail condominium and other tourism-related luxury residential and commercial development. Described as "zoning for poor people," it would place no restrictions on trailers, junk cars, livestock, and other rural and agricultural uses, including the traditional division of land among heirs. Because of its small size, Valdez was compelled to zone as part of a larger district, one that eventually came to be known as Los Tres Valles. From spring until fall, people from Valdez, Arroyo Hondo, and San Cristobal repeatedly petitioned the county commission to hasten or at least facilitate the zoning process, which in fact the commission made every effort to undermine, despite considerable public pressure and media coverage.[118]

In May, Crandall filed his condominium declaration with the county clerk, and some weeks later people in Valdez learned from it that he planned 39 units, rather than his publicly announced figure of 24 units, with options to build up to 99 over a 15-year period. On 12 July they held a meeting at the *escuelita* (schoolhouse) to discuss what they would do to stop construction, which seemed likely to begin any day. This meeting inaugurated the active phase of the protest. About fifty people attended, including adults of all ages, teenagers, and children; most were Hispanic. Some people from Arroyo Hondo and San Cristobal were also there. A majority of the tactics that would unfold during the next month were decided on at this meeting. By then people had consulted a legal services lawyer, who finally told them he was too overburdened to take the case, and realized they had at best tentative legal grounds for stopping construction. Only the sewage discharge permit, which Crandall had not yet applied for, would provide an obvious opportunity to file a legal protest, through either the EID or the EPA. A copy of a unit floor plan was passed around. It showed for each unit two fireplaces, an open shower area, a spa, and outlets for washers. Each unit was priced at $250,000. People agreed to pursue legalistic avenues as long as the effort did not incur lawyer's fees, but they also decided to apply public pressure against Crandall, as their only direct recourse.

Six basic actions were decided on at the 12 July meeting. People agreed to paint anti-condo signs and put them up around the valley; to send another letter to the state engineer and to the newspaper, pointing out that the condo was significantly larger than was stated publicly or on the water transfer application; and to give other objections to the project. They planned a float for the annual Taos fiesta "historical-hysterical parade" on 25 July, and a separate march through Taos to Gilson Motor Company, the lucrative family business established by Crandall's grandfather in the 1940s. They also decided to ask the county commission to enforce the moratorium. And people agreed to make a banner from a sheet on which community members would sign their name and age beside a stain of their own blood. The banner would be carried on a march to present to Crandall, who worked as a salesman at Gilson's, with the statement: "The blood of Valdez is on your hands." During the next three weeks, people wandered in and out of the escuelita to have their fingers pricked for signature on the banner. Customers at the cantina would be invited over to make their contribution. Interestingly, the men tended to be more squeamish about this operation than women and children. The latter were especially enthusiastic.

On the weekend after the meeting, about twenty-five adults and children met at the schoolhouse with boards and paint to make over forty signs which they then placed along the road into and through the valley. The signs read, for example:

"Pete Crandall: Give Up and Get Out"
"Pete Crandall's Condos Not Welcome in Valdez"
"Peter Crandall's Condos Are An Insult to the Community of Valdez"
"The Community is United so Don't be Misguided"
"Nuestro Pueblo No Se Vende" ["Our village is not for sale"]
"Rich People are Greedy"
"Condos Kill Raza."

And, Burma-shave fashion, "You'll Be Hated—On the Hondo—If You Buy—A Crandall Condo." Two very large signs with dripping red handprints or hearts read, "Pete Crandall: the Blood of Valdez is on Your Hands." The district attorney (D.A.) later requested the last ones be taken down for fear they "might incite to violence." The signs were featured by newspapers and television, and quickly became the talk of Taos.

The following weekend Valdez had entries in both the children's and historical parades for the Taos fiestas. In the first about ten younger Valdez children marched, wearing donated anti-condo T-shirts and carrying a sign that read, "Save Our Valley, No Condos." The entry received an honorable mention. In the other, the Valdez float featured a young Dracula hovering over an elaborately fenced-in condominium with death-heads at the windows and dollar-sign grillwork, plastered with play money, and juxtaposed on a flatbed to children and small animals seated on bales of hay, wearing their T-shirts beneath a sign that read, "The Future of Valdez." They chanted "No Condos en Valdez!" at the tops of their lungs.

The next day, people from Valdez and some neighbors asked the county commission to enforce their moratorium. The commission demurred and postponed the matter. Late the following night, the signs disappeared during a violent thunderstorm and were seen in Crandall's brother's van, before they were dropped the 650 feet or so from the Rio Grande gorge bridge. Within twenty-four hours they were amply replaced by a somewhat less varied edition of signs, featuring a number of death-head images and one sign, placed before the bridge near the placita, that read:

Commandments Against Condos:

Thou shall not build condos
Thou shall not pollute our water
Thou shall not disrespect our way of life
Thou shall not pollute our land
Thou shall not covet our land and water
Thou shall not steal what belongs to our children
Thous shall not kill our valley.

On 31 July, blessed by the parish priest, approximately eighty-five people from Valdez and other communities held a protest march from Kachina Lodge north of the plaza to Gilson Motor Company, about two miles to the south. The procession was headed by the dramatically stained "Blood of Valdez" banner, and a life-size wooden puppet with movable joints and lower jaw, that was modeled after miniature Mexican skeletons and lifted and munched a dripping red heart labeled "Valdez." People chanted and carried signs. The plan was to present Crandall with the banner. But Gilson's was closed for the occasion, and on their showcase windows were handscrawled signs which read: "To Whom it May Concern: Gilson Motor Co. has Nothing to do with Pete Crandall Building Condos in Valdez. Pete Crandall Does Not Work Here Anymore." Despite Crandall's father's disavowal of any connection with the project, Gilson's was targeted not only because Crandall worked there (having taken leave to work on his project), but also because the motor company and condominium corporation boards of directors consisted entirely of Gilson-Crandall family members, with Peter and one brother sitting on both.

Crandall's personal response to all this attention was strong. He had appeared at the cantina shortly before the meeting on 12 July, demanding to know who had written the flyer announcing the meeting, and threatening that his lawyer would attend. He harangued the Anglo owner of the photocopy store where the flyer (as well as his condominium documents) had been reproduced, and threatened her with a businessmen's boycott. He intimidated the Hispano owners of a neighborhood grocery in Des Montes near where he grew up, because they had consented to display a poster for the meeting. Two domestic employees of Crandall's parents, people from Valdez who had participated in the protest, were quietly "let go." During August Crandall avoided, then sought out, the press. He released a brief "fact sheet" on the project. He addressed the local realtor's association about it. He claimed he received telephone threats. He called a secret television press conference, which the totem-bearing protesters got wind of beforehand and partly co-opted.

The next county commission meeting was packed. Valdez's young Chicano lawyer, working pro bono, asked the commission to enact emergency interim zoning to avert a confrontation and possible violence. The D.A. was there and testified that this was "the number one issue in the county," and confirmed that both he and the sheriff knew the situation to be "explosive." He nevertheless counseled, along with the county attorney, against an emergency ordinance, for fear of incurring a "million dollar lawsuit." Crandall's paternal aunt, holding a sign, stood and announced her support for Valdez, amid applause. The volatile crowd was appeased by the promise of an afternoon meeting at which county representatives, protesters, and their lawyer supposedly would work out an agreement whereby Valdez, Arroyo Hondo, and San Cristobal would compose an interim ordinance that the county commission would pass the following week, but would not enforce, so

364

as to avoid suit. The SZD, once formed, would then file to enjoin Crandall from building. During the next week, zoners worked frantically to complete this process and held a meeting at which people from the three communities approved an expanded version of the 4 May plan already adopted by Valdez.

A day or so prior to the next scheduled commission meeting, Reies López Tijerina telephoned Valdez to express support and ask if he and some friends might attend. Zoners consented if he would not speak. This meeting, also packed beyond seating capacity with placard-bearing protesters and other interested parties, was one of those memorable occasions when all the conflicts and contradictions that seethe in Taos seem telescoped and epitomized. Crandall, dressed as usual in a three-piece suit, addressed the commission and attempted to persuade the largely hostile crowd of his native, "pre-D. H. Lawrence" pedigree, freedom from "prejudice," and beneficent intentions toward "any citizen willing to work" for his job-generating project, which would also establish a "Southwestern Institute for Human Relations," whereby he and other philosophically inclined individuals would conduct dialogue with the community. He was questioned and heckled, and finally fled the room, visibly on the verge of tears, while his mother, grandmother, brother, and brother-in-law sat frozen among the crowd. An elderly Taos Indian seated with the family, for years for employee, rose to say: "This is *our* land. The people are talking about land. *We're* the owners—what the hell are they complaining about that!" Heated speeches followed, all ignoring the attempt to raise the Hispano vs. Indian issue, and culminated in a bitter, explosive exchange between Hispana protesters and a local realtor, who had commented that surely Crandall's condos would look a lot better than the "indiscriminate shacks and trailers" scattered around the valley. Deputies were called in to restore order. The county attorney now claimed the commission had no authority to enact the interim ordinance, and they once again defused the situation by setting up another meeting, for which their attorney proposed to contact all landowners within the proposed district by registered mail. He proposed this course of action on the basis of a statute pertaining to proposed changes in established zoning regulations, but entirely unrelated to the statute for creating SZDs. The next public hearing on the proposed interim ordinance was set for 10 September, allowing for three weeks of legal publication.

Tijerina's appearance at the commission meeting heightened media attention and sent shock waves through the business and real-estate community in Taos. Outside contractors recalled recent heavy equipment vandalism in Questa and wondered just how safe the situation in Taos might be. Repeating the local truism that "only Anglos protest," town businessmen were quick to claim the protest was the work of "hippies and a few outside agitators." The perception that any ethnically mixed protest is instigated and dominated by Anglos is common and reinforced by the marked proclivity of Anglo men to monopolize public speaking, as well as by a subtle media bias. Anglo reporters have a tendency to contact Anglo members of a mixed protest. There are no Hispanic reporters on the Taos paper, and in fact all the print and television media people with whom the protesters had an opportunity to speak were Anglo.

The actual constituency of the protest is noteworthy. It included Anglos but was predominantly Hispanic, and involved farmers, miners, and service workers of both sexes and representing a broad spectrum of ages. It involved several interethnic (Anglo-Hispana) couples, including the community organizers who had joined the Hacienda protest some eight months earlier, and an enthusiastic contingent of children. This author was also an active supporter.[119] The Valdez group contained ditch, domestic water system, and land grant officers, the Democratic and Republican precinct chairmen, the postmistress, the cantina owners, and all of the church *mayordomos* (annual caretakers), as well as a range of other lifelong and recent residents, including the two Anglo subsistence farmers in the valley. Women assumed key interhousehold organizing roles. Only one prominent extended family dissented, which generated some tension. The grassroots, mixed-yet-native nature of the protest gave it legitimacy and power. Valdez's cause drew sympathy while Crandall seemed to repel people from his own. The intense level of protest activity was sustained for a period of about three months, because a number of people devoted their primary efforts to the unceasing effort to block construction. Bumper-stickers were donated, and eventually donations and fundraising activities produced some thousands of dollars of support money.

By mid-August the SZD had filed its petition and plat, so the commission was required to schedule an election, which it did belatedly and under pressure from the state attorney general who was consulted by protesters. During the following weeks, Crandall announced several starting dates, and told local realtors and television reporters that all units were presold. The turning point came when he lost his funding. A local bank had agreed to lend him $1.5 million for the first five units, but rescinded under the pressure of letters from other clients. Then his subsequent source of funding, Oklahoma-based Penn Square, collapsed. His contractors quit, and rumor had it his engineer quit, and numerous workers declined employment on the project for fear of violence. Shots were fired near Crandall's land. The electrician for the project claimed his house was shot at. Rumors were rampant about Crandall's agitated state, disintegrating domestic situation, and indiscreet public behavior.

On 18 August Valdez called for a boycott of Gilson Motor Company, and set up an eight-hour-per-day, two-person-two-hour shift picket which, after an initial attempt to thwart it by the town mayor and police chief, was maintained for sixty days, until 19 October, when protesters declared a cautious victory. At the end of August a construction trailer, double fence, locked gate, and security lights went up on the site. An all-Hispano security guard was established, increasing tension. Valdez held a well-attended benefit dance at a popular lounge in town. Two days later heavy equipment began moving earth on the land.

County commissioners failed to appear for their own public hearing on 10 September, for which presumably thousands of registered notices had been mailed out at county expense. Therewith their so-called interim ordinance which, unlike the draft zoners had given them, neither named nor described "condominium" as a prohibited use, finally died. A delegation to the attorney general in Santa Fe put pressure on the county commission to schedule an election, and one was finally held in November, when the community slate of candidates was elected, unopposed.

In late September, Valdez held a rally on land across the Rio Hondo from Crandall's site, where construction had still not begun. Some three hundred people attended and heard music and the speeches of a number of local and regionally active notables in the rural and urban Chicano movement, including Tijerina. Their recurrent themes were the connection between land, water, and cultural survival, and an appreciation of Valdez as symbolic of rural Hispano struggle against wealthy outside developers, who more than Anglos per se were seen as the "enemy." Especially reviled were the native *vendido* and *lambe,* or "sellout" and "bootlicker." The following poem was performed by Cleofes

Vigil, widely acknowledged poet laureate of *La Tierra Santa de la Sangre de Cristo*. Its text is reproduced in full and broadly translated because it expresses, in traditional form and with eloquence and passion, a mythopoetic, native version of the expropriation of La Raza in Taos:

Valles del Condado de Taos
[Valleys of Taos County]

1

Valle del Condado de Taos	Taos County valley
donde fui nacido y criado	where I was born and raised
ya se hacabo tu hermosura	your beauty is gone
que mis ojos la miraron	which my eyes beheld
Cuando tenias armonia	when you had harmony
Vecinos amigos y hermanos	neighbors friends and brothers

2

Por tu pureza retenida	For your retained pureness
de tu agua viento y campo	of your water air and land
Con sagazida de alavia	millionaires have come
an venido millionarios	with shrewd flattery
Penetrandole al celebro	penetrating to the brain
al nativo ser humano	of the native human being

3

Estrangeros avanzados	Strangers advanced
Con su grande dios dinero	With their great god money
que nomas te la enseñan	which they merely show
te arrodias ante ellos	you kneel before them
y te hechan un lazo	and they put a lasso around you
apretado hasta el hueso	tightened to the bone

4

OH hello ther mi señor	Oh hello there my lord,
Con aquella gran ansia	with that great anxiety
desea usted mi terreno	do you desire my land?
deme lo que a usted le nasca	give me what you please
que yo ahorita me muero	I will soon die
y usted necesita mi casa	and you need my house

5

Ya les damos la historia	And we gave them the history that
los que estos valles nos davan	these valleys had given us
sin mas que un cavador	with only a hoe
y una hoz en la mano	and a sickle in hand
un arado de palo	a wooden plow
y un tirito de cavallos.	and a team of horses.

6

Montaña Sangre de Cristo	Sangre de Cristo mountain
Con laderas y valles amplios	With slopes and wide valleys
Cuando llego el D. H. Lawrence	When D. H. Lawrence arrived
ya le llamavan Kit Carson	They already called it Kit Carson
donde empeso la mentira	where the lie began
la avarizia y el engaño.	the greed and deception

7

Sigio la gran epidemia	The great plague followed
de langostas desolando	of locusts desolating
la armonia que habia	the harmony that had once been
pronto la destrozaron	they destroyed it quickly
con alavia de You are my Friend	with flattery of You are my Friend
al infierno nos mandaron.	they sent us to hell

8

A nativos adiestraron	They trained natives
a lambes muy competentes	to be very competent bootlickers
a estos los an usado	they have used them
Pa que chingan a su gente	to screw their own people
Piojos resucitados	sold-out and demented
Vendidos y dementes.	resuscitated (fattened) lice.

9

Llego el fraule con papeles	The paper fraud came
al nativo de estos valles	to the native of these valleys
esto es la ley my Friend	this is the law my friend
Ya tu palabra no vale	your word doesn't matter now
si no saves alfabeto	if you don't know the alphabet
una eques X es vastante.	an "X" is enough.

369

10

Pues una vez que ya firmo	Once you have signed
ya todo es derecho	everything is legal
donde el dicho se aserto	as the saying goes
de que no hay cosa mas triste	there's nothing sadder
que un esclavo satisfecho	than a satisfied slave.

11

Antes de esta epidemia	Before this plague
Nuestros valles heran paraizo	our valleys were paradise
donde habia bendeciones	where there were blessings
Y amor para el ser humano	and love for the human being
buenos dias le de Dios	may God grant you a good day
como esta usted mi hermano.	how are you my brother.

12

Este muy grande progreso	This great progress
del estrangero tirano	of the foreign tyrant
Por amor a su dios dinero	for love of his money god
todos estamos destraidos	we are all distracted
al verdadero creador	we have forgotten
ya lo hemos olvidado	the true creator

13

Doz muy fuertes palabras	Two very strong words
escritas en dicionario	written in the dictionary
democracia y Cristiandad	democracy and Christianity
las usan para escudo	they use as a shield
Mas y mas calamidad	more and more calamity
heridas de filo agudo.	wounds from a sharp edge.

14

Con una voz consonante	With one resonant voice
es mi deseo decir	It is my desire to say
de que todo lo que aqui escrito	that Cleofes Vigil verifies
lo verifica Cleofes Vigil	everything written here
Con mi esperencia que tengo	With the experience I have
No me pueden desmentir	no one can contradict me
que solo mi Dios save	only God knows what the
que sera el Porvenir.	future will be.[120]

The picket continued and Crandall did not begin construction. His checks were said to be bouncing all over town, and his employees went unpaid. The security guard disappeared, followed by the trailer and security lights, some of which had been shot out. Crandall appeared in town with an Anglo body guard, on one occasion to harass an Anglo shopkeeper whose wife was picketing. He let go his project manager and then vacated his rented office in town. Twice he requested and then failed to show up for meetings with a few community representatives. On 19 October Valdez called a press conference in front of Gilson's to announce a cautious victory and an end of the picket but not of the boycott, until Crandall would publicly withdraw.

A few weeks later Crandall published an article, rather than a letter, in *The Taos News,* in which he announced he was leaving town for a while, that he was not bitter and "would never say quit," and cautioned against trying "to preserve Taos in amber." In late November his lawyer requested a meeting with people in Valdez, to discuss the possibility of alternative construction acceptable to the community. He acknowledged that multifamily units for seasonal occupants would not be built. He was told that perhaps one house per two acres might be acceptable. He indicated Crandall would not build the condos, and that his client simply wanted to recover his investment. On 14 February 1983, the attorney requested another meeting, and this time offered a plan for twelve condominiums. He revealed that in addition to over two dozen units, this "compromise plan" deleted the swimming pool and activity center, neither of which had been mentioned in the original condo declaration.[121] His proposal was politely rejected as insulting. On 21 April, *The Taos News* reported that Centinel Bank of Taos had initiated foreclosure proceedings for a mortgage on the land, for which Crandall and his corporation owed a total of $83,140. A "For Sale" sign was posted on the land. In late 1983 Crandall, no longer living in Taos, filed for bankruptcy. By the summer of 1985 he was back in Taos, again working at Gilson's. The bank held an auction for the land in June, but there were no bidders. However, by the end of August it had been sold to a private party, whose plans remain to be seen.

The Valdez condo war captured local and regional attention in the north, and became a popular cause among Chicano groups in Albuquerque and other urban areas. The character and outcome of the issue had a broader, albeit not universal, appeal however. It inspired hope in native peoples' ability to resist constant encroachment and displacement and stimulated interest in rural zoning. In all, during its peak period in the summer and early autumn of 1982, the controversy had been the focus of at least eight highly charged county officials' meetings, and the subject of over thirty newspaper articles, twenty-six published letters and editorials, numerous instances of television coverage, and three nonlocal radio programs. It was later named "story of the year" by *The Taos News*. The intense phase of protest activity ended with Crandall's retreat in the late autumn, although neither the sentiment of resistance nor the developmental assault it was a response to subsided.

Just as Crandall's project had surfaced immediately upon the Hacienda's demise, so did the latter revive right after Crandall's defeat, along with several other proposed projects, like the hydra which sprouts two heads for each one severed. The Hacienda reopened in the late fall with intentions to resume construction for its expansion, under the receivership of six out-of-state and one local (Centinel) bank, and under the management of the other major car dealer in Taos. The new holding corporation, named Carson, Inc., was able to obtain a septic tank and leach field sewage permit from the EID without having to publish a legal notice, and had eighteen rental units open during the 1983 and 1984 ski seasons. Not only did EID officials neglect to notify Valdez residents of the application as they had been repeatedly asked and had promised to do, but they also failed to initiate action when, during the winter of 1983, the Hacienda exceeded its 1,800 gallons-per-day discharge limit.[122] Carson, Inc. became the object of a letter campaign, and during 1983 Hacienda management met with and even attempted to buy off Valdez representatives with the offer of a cash donation to the community center.[123] Finally, in the spring of 1984, the Hacienda worked out an arrangement with the EID and Valdez whereby the condominium and its sewage treatment capacity would not expand beyond its already existing eighteen units. Also in late 1982, a wealthy Englishman with a seasonal home in Valdez planned a $40 million, 200-home "model community," named Cindercone, to be located between Valdez and Arroyo Hondo, replete with "recreational facilities and complexes for visual and performing arts, and a model farm." After several meetings with selected but decidedly recalcitrant representatives from Valdez and Hondo, this developer evidently reconsidered the wisdom of his plan and dropped it, at least for the time being. Both the Hacienda and Cindercone were the targets of another anti-condo sign campaign in the early summer of 1983, and once again Valdez children marched in the Taos fiesta parade.

During the winter and early spring of 1983, the Tres Valles Zoning

Commission composed and held a series of public meetings to discuss the new code. After due publication of legal notice, the code was officially approved and adopted by the Tres Valles Zoning Commission in June, at a public hearing held in Arroyo Hondo. Present at the hearing were the lawyer and project manager for Deer Mesa Estates, a New York-based corporation with plans to develop a ninety-one-acre subdivision in the lower Valdez valley. They objected to passage of the code, and were instructed to submit their project plans to the zoning commission for consideration. They subsequently refused to do this, preferring instead to deal exclusively with the county commission, which attempted to accommodate them. However, the commission finally was persuaded that its own treatment of the subdivision would be legally subject to Tres Valles regulations. Deer Mesa then filed suit in district court against Tres Valles on several grounds, including the claim that the SZD act is unconstitutional. This interpretation was upheld by District Judge Frank Allen, Jr., who ruled the statute unconstitutional on 9 July 1984. Tres Valles appealed the decision, and the appeal was lost in late 1985. Meanwhile, the Hacienda again went up for sale. And during the summer of 1985, the project manager for Deer Mesa left that endeavor to assume an administrative position with the EID.

Summary and Conclusions

The ability of rural zoning or, for that matter, any other tactic to help protect traditional patterns of Hispano land tenure, will be further challenged during the next months and years, along with the survival of Hispano land tenure itself. Since the middle of the last century, Hispanos in northern New Mexico and southern Colorado have faced massive and more or less continuous expropriation and displacement from their farmlands surrounding land grant villages, towns, and their offshoot settlements. Economic need has forced them from the land and out of the villages into migrant labor, towns, or cities, and into local dependency on a fragile combination of federal subsidy, outside extractive industry, and tourism. Today the forces and conditions that conspire against the ability of rural and semi-rural Hispanos to hold onto their remaining land and water around Taos appear to be multiplying and gaining momentum.

My central argument here is that this ongoing process of expropriation and its recent acceleration have, in concert with various local, regional, and macrosocial factors, intensified rural Hispano resistance to further usurpation and displacement, and stimulated the crystallization of land as a symbol of Hispano cultural survival. The articulators of this self-conscious land symbolism come mostly from living generations of Hispano-Chicano activists, artists, writers, and others, including, to name but three, Rudolfo Anaya, Cleofes Vigil, and, of course, Tijerina himself. This increasingly explicit symbolization represents not only a strategy of ethnic boundary maintenance but also a manifestation of the oppositional process. The latter concept would seem to presuppose the former, and their difference would seem to be more a matter of degree than character. What distinguishes a persistent identity system in Spicer's sense from simple ethnic identity is the oppositional process, and the self-consciousness it engenders over time.[124]

This is not to suggest, however, that the land is of only recent symbolic importance to Hispanos or that it has not long held a different meaning for them than for Anglos or, for that matter, Indians. On the contrary. The psychohistorical wellsprings of contemporary Hispano-Chicano land symbolism lie in an earlier legal, social, and cultural system of land tenure quite different from the Anglo-American system that displaced it, and in the collective trauma of massive land loss. The differences and conflicts between these two systems have been documented by various land grant scholars, including those in this volume. As Van Ness puts it:

> At the outset, the Spanish American and Anglo American forms of land tenure were in striking contrast in terms of the ways in which land units and exploitative rights to land and its resources were technically defined, distributed, and recorded in the two societies and of the economic ends to which exploitation was directed.[125]

Economic considerations serving the maximization of marketability determined the Anglo-American method of land measurement, description, recording, possession, and transfer. In the Spanish American system of land use and occupancy, however, sociopolitical and other contextual factors customarily outweighed purely commercial or profit-motivated considerations. In New Mexico, it was a system in which the use value of land, for the subsistence of the resident population, was primary, rather than its exchange value for nonresident speculators. While land could be held privately and sold, "sales were normally circumscribed by local considerations."[126] As Knowlton reports:

The village with its attached land and water rights was thought of as a single indivisible community. It was regarded as a crime against the moral order of the universe for any political authority to separate the village from its traditional land and water rights. A village community so separated was like a man who had lost an arm and a leg. The villages who have lost land or water, as most have done, regard themselves as having suffered serious moral wrongs. Even though a hundred years may have passed since a village lost its land, the village inhabitants still know the location of every acre that has been lost. The present owners and users of the land are defined as usurpers who do not have the right to use the land that once belonged to the village. There is an aching sense of injustice that will never end until the village is totally abandoned or until the land is restored to the village.[127]

Some version of this abiding resentment against Anglos smoulders deep within many if not most Hispanos in the communities around Taos, an often suppressed sentiment understandably widespread among Chicanos in general. One of the striking facts about this sense of resentment in Taos is its virtual absence from public discourse or record, which simultaneously reflects, promotes, and denies the status quo of Anglo domination. The invisible or submerged aspect of this otherwise ubiquitous ethos is further reinforced publicly by differential boundary awareness among groups or strata.

But despite the intrinsic elusiveness to outsiders of a subordinated group's ethos of resentment and resistance, the latter necessarily assumes a variety of direct, although perhaps more often symbolic, expressions. Social scientists have devised numerous techniques for measuring and, often unwittingly, influencing minority responses to conditions of oppression. A once favorite approach, today much criticized, and exemplified by Kluckhohn and Strodbeck's famous Five Cultures project, has been the "measurement" of values and attitudes as indices—and even explanations—of acculturation.[128] Following in this tradition, Eastman, et al. tested, among a sample of respondents from seven northern New Mexico counties including Taos, the hypothesis that: "Spanish-Americans are more traditional in their attitudes toward land ownership and usage than are Anglo-Americans."[129] Their summary of their findings reads as follows:

Land attitudes are strongly influenced by years of education and to a lesser extent by socioeconomic status. Residence and birthplace have an effect, because rural birth and residence seem to cause a reverse acculturation. Land ownership (past or present) also influences land attitudes. Equally important as the related variables are the several characteristics not related to land attitudes. There is no generation gap in attitudes toward land; young people have essentially the same scores as do their elders in both ethnic groups. Spanish-Americans may be acculturating, but not in their attitudes toward land. Similarly, geographical mobility—living outside the Southwest—and exposure to the mass media have little influence on land attitudes. Thus, effects associated with age are not bridging the difference between ethnic groups, nor is geographic mobility, nor exposure to the larger culture via the mass media. This leaves education as the most viable vehicle for changing land attitudes.[130]

Apart from its implicit cultural determinist framework and assimilationist bias, this approach presupposes a primordialist view of ethnic identity, or one that assumes ethnic distinctions result from geographic and social isolation and diminish in response to contact and modernization. Such a perspective fails to account for the study's actual findings, including the positive or uneven correlation between "traditional" land attitudes and several conventional measures of acculturation. Eastman's findings and other contemporary ethnic phenomena better fit Barth's more reactive view of ethnicity, which holds that ethnic distinctions are creatures and reflections of structural and institutional arrangements, and of differential patterns of use of and competition for limited resources. This view accounts for, or is at least consistent with, widely observed phenomena of ethnic resurgence, under both developing and advanced conditions of economic and political modernization.[131]

That Indians, Hispanos, and Anglos have differentially occupied, utilized, competed for, and possessed land and water around Taos constitutes the area's most overriding historical circumstance. Differential conquest, subordination, expropriation, impoverishment, and social displacement have been the hallmark of the psychohistorical experience of Indians in Taos since 1540, and of Hispanos since 1847. This experience in each case constituted a process of what I will call *minoritization*. Each case has evolved differently under different political and economic conditions, but they share several features, not simply as ethnic minorities, but also as what Spicer calls "persistent identity systems."[132]

To start with, both Indians and Hispanos have existed under two or more systems of state organization, and both groups have resisted, in different ways and at different as well as overlapping periods, pressures for economic, political, and cultural assimilation into the dominant society.[133] Within this context each has developed "well-defined symbols of identity differentiating it from other groups or the larger society."[134] Finally, each of these sets of identity symbols is "necessarily characterized by some combination of land and language elements."[135]

The case for Taos and other Pueblos as persistent peoples in Spicer's sense is obvious and easily made. Resistance to encroachment and incorporation, passive and overt, has characterized their dealings with outsiders since around 1600. The case for Hispanos in Taos and elsewhere in northern New Mexico and southern Colorado is more complex. They are, for one thing, a more "recent" people, who like other mestizos, occupy the intermediate and perhaps somewhat paradoxical position of being distinctly bounded and yet historically constituted by virtue of boundary permeability. Furthermore, the political, economic, and social incorporation of Hispanos and other Mexican Americans into the United States has been different from that of Indians, given their role as the major source of cheap labor throughout the American Southwest. Finally, less is known about the social history, cultural systems, internal community dynamics, and psychohistorical experience of Hispano and other Mexican American populations than about most southwestern Indian peoples. A great deal of ethnohistorical, ethnographic, and other social research is needed in order to illuminate the nature and dynamics of local and regional variation on the one hand, and of general socioeconomic and cultural features on the other.

It is proposed that Hispanos in Taos and northern New Mexico, like Chicanos elsewhere in the Southwest, are in the process of evolving into a self-identified, persistent people. This process has been underway for nearly four hundred years in Taos and has been tied to the preservation of a combination of land, language, and contiguous, originally kin-based village residence—that is, a core component of their traditional niche. During the late eighteenth century, Hispanos began to occupy and defend farming and grazing lands centered primarily on the lower Rio Pueblo, Rancho del Rio Grande, and lower Rio Lucero watersheds. During the course of the nineteenth century, they spread to and consolidated landownership and village boundaries within the Arroyo Seco, upper Rio Lucero, Arroyo Hondo, and San Cristobal watersheds (as well as elsewhere in the county), and then, after Americanization, suffered the loss of a large proportion of the lands they had occupied and used for generations. In this century, land has become a symbol of ethnic persistence to landless and urban Hispanos as well as to rural Hispanos who still own land. The motor of land symbolization has been its loss. A growing historical self-awareness has accompanied or followed this progressive loss, in spite of widespread institutional effort to educate against such awareness. The earlier development of ethnic land symbolization among the Taos Indians was fostered in part by a cultural climate of bohemian, selective ethnophilia, companion to a growing tourism economy. Thus the notion of a mystical connection between territory and native population was already present or "in the air" when during the modern period other influences and conditions began to precipitate the emergence of an explicit land symbolism among Hispanos. These included, on the one hand, national and regional impacts of Chicano and other ethnic group—but especially the Alianza—mobilization; and on the other, increasing demographic pressure—intensified by accelerating Anglo in-migration—upon limited local land, water, and other economic resources.

The prognosis for Hispano land tenure in Taos and its relationship to ethnic boundary maintenance is not clear. It seems to be widely assumed that rural Hispanos, like Indians, are doomed to disappear as such, but it can also be observed that ethnic boundaries have persisted and changed for four hundred years, and today show no signs of dissolving. They are sustained by the very structures of stratification, without, however, being reducible to them. Certainly one possible scenario for the future involves the complete and final expropriation of virtually all nonwealthy Hispanos within another generation. The territorial basis for Hispano ethnic differentiation would then yield to an entirely, albeit already well-entrenched, socioeconomic one. A predictable concomitant of this outcome would be continued reduction in the Hispanic proportion of the expanding population, followed by a corresponding integration and Anglo takeover of local electoral politics. Although this chain of events may or may not be inevitable, the continued increase in Anglo in-migration and takeover of local resources seems certain. The University of New Mexico Bureau of Business and Economic Research predicts a thirty-four percent population growth for Taos County in the 1980s and eighteen percent for the 1990s.[136] The response of Hispanos to these and other pressures will depend in part on local and regional economic conditions, including, for example, the commercial viability of the Moly mine, whether or not the local economy can diversify or continues to become ever more dependent upon tourism, and the impact on the Southwest in general of such factors as energy development, and Sun Belt as well as Latin American immigration.

Tourism traditionally has fostered the marketing of ethnicity as a commodity, but it otherwise affords a weak and uncertain material basis upon which to maintain a firm foothold against the onslaught of the luxury real-estate development it now spawns. While the early, ethnic-cultural phase of tourism development in Taos encouraged the preservation of Indian ethnicity along with a specific land base, the contemporary, luxury recreational type of tourism seems inimical to the preservation of a rural Hispano land base. In some sense, the Blue Lake case represents the symbolic consecration of the town watershed to the economic and cultural requirements of ethnic-cultural tourism. By contrast the ski valley-condominium issue represents the literal consecration of the Hondo watershed to the economic and material needs of luxury recreational tourism. The strategies Indians and Hispanos have pursued in trying to maintain their fragile holds over these and other "homeland" areas, including the ways in which each group has recruited Anglo support, reflect the particular opportunities and constraints imposed by their respective political and economic situations as conquered and dependent yet differentially incorporated peoples.

Those Hispanos least likely to initiate, actively participate in, or publicly support protest against tourism development are those whose entire livelihoods depend directly upon tourism. Those most likely to publicly condemn such protest are the well-off and upwardly mobile who are prospering or who hope to, from the boom. The remaining majority is by no means homogeneous with respect to source and level of income, landholdings, urban-rural orientation, ethnopolitical orientation, language use, age, or education. Diverse elements within this broad spectrum are variously subject to and critical of the economic, political, and social pressures brought to bear by local and regional power structures against ethnopolitical dissidents. While the pressure to assimilate has continued unabated for many decades, it is only comparatively recently that local Hispanos have had a broader ethos of *Chicanismo* from which to draw a renewed and expanded sense of historical identity and collective resistance to oppression. It is perhaps ironic that this influence is partly a creature of urbanization.

But while urbanization and even out-migration can be consistent with the maintenance and politicization of ethnicity, the ability of local

Hispanos to hold onto their remaining land base would seem to depend upon the creation of a solid, diversified, largely locally controlled economy. Only thus can they survive without literally losing ground, and be able to keep what they still own, and at the same time gain access to the benefits of American middle-class life, including steady, adequate employment with a possibility for advancement; adequate housing, nutrition, medical care, and post-secondary education; and a voice as well as a role in the future of their communities.

For most of this century, an official and pervasive assimilationist bias has held that the acquisition of such benefits is incompatible with the retention of a non-Anglo-Saxon ethnic or cultural identity. And indeed, the interlocking mechanisms of race, class, and ethnic stratification have made this largely the case. Upward mobility has been equated with assimilation, and ethnicity, in this case Mexicanness, with poverty, ignorance, and an intrinsic inability to advance. More recently, however, Chicano and other minority activists have explicitly challenged the justice and wisdom of such a view, while the widespread phenomena of ethnic resurgence and mobilization have caused social scientists to reconsider its accuracy. If New Mexico's and the Southwest's tourism industry has promoted the idea of cultural pluralism and flourished because of its existence, it has also gone hand-in-hand with a deeply entrenched, deeply mystified, system of structural inequality. One of the great challenges which today faces both modern and developing nations is whether and how ethnic and cultural pluralism can be reconciled with genuine social, economic, and political equality and self-determination. Neither the theoretical nor practical dimensions of such an arrangement are established or agreed upon. But whatever the difficulties inherent in such a goal, or the probability of its realization, one thing seems certain: the further expropriation and displacement of territorial native peoples does not represent a step in that direction.

Recommendations for Further Research

I will conclude with a brief series of recommendations for ethnohistorical, ethnographic, and other social research that needs to be done in Taos as in other parts of northern New Mexico and southern Colorado. These recommendations are meant to be suggestive and provocative rather than detailed and exhaustive. The research they would involve holds potential substantive, theoretical, and practical value. Although they are couched specifically in terms of research on the Taos area, they are applicable and may be generalized to other community and/or multicommunity areas in the region.

The land grant history of Taos has yet to be comprehensively investigated and written, particularly in relationship to the settlement sequence and history of each village. Each village or community should be focused upon both as an individual—or individuating—entity, and as part of an inclusive multicommunity system. This would apply, in the case of Taos County, to the Questa-Amalia-Costilla and Peñasco-Picuris-Vadito multicommunity areas as well as to the Don Fernando municipal district. The history of each community should be investigated through a combination of archival, documentary, oral-historical, and archaeological methods.[136]

Each settlement's ethnohistoric past should be linked to its ethnographic present. Ideally, ethnographic research would involve ongoing team efforts in which natives would assume active planning and investigatory roles. Given that no single individual in a multiethnic, stratified community such as Taos can have universal access to all of the diverse and frequently embattled segments of local society, the ideal research team would be mixed with respect to ethnicity, age, class background, sex, and origin. This would be particularly important where the focus of inquiry included or had bearing upon interethnic relations.

Two considerations should enter into the design and execution of ethnographic research, particularly when the focus is upon a minority group.[137] First, certainly one—though not the only—criterion of ethnographic accuracy should be whether or not it produces a description in which the natives under study can find more than a fleeting trace of self-recognition. The early ethnographic literature on Mexican Americans has become notorious for its lack of fit between how Mexicanos see themselves and their communities and how they have been described by (mostly Anglo) anthropologists.[138] With few exceptions, it seems to be the case that anthropologists have failed to capture an *emic* or native account of day-to-day Mexicano, Hispano, or Chicano social reality. In this respect, it lags behind the ethnographic literature on Black Americans.[139] The second consideration relates to the first, and has implications for ethnohistorical research as well. It concerns the need to investigate, illuminate, and interpret Hispano behavior not only in terms of the concept of ethnic boundary maintenance but also of resistance, or what Spicer calls the oppositional process. Apart from its organized and overt manifestations, Hispano resistance has assumed myriad covert, oblique, passive, ambiguous, repressed and convoluted, often highly symbolic, forms in northern New Mexico. It has also fluctuated through time. Yet it has not usually been identified as such in the literature. If ethnographic, the research in this case shows an oversight with methodological (including linguistic) causes and dimensions.[140] In general, however, such oversight is perhaps structurally endemic to the dominant perspective in a colonial situation, wherein the invisibility of actual minority resistance may be coupled with an exaggerated if subliminal fear of its sudden or gratuitous outbreak. But however complex the sources of silence or blindness on the matter of how social inequality has shaped face-to-face ethnic interaction in New Mexico, it can become overcome primarily through making this effect itself an explicit focus of study. In short, the proposition that resistance has been a persistent theme or undercurrent in Hispano life since 1847 may help to render much historical and behavioral data into a more coherent picture than has often been perceived.[141]

There are several kinds of problems that historical research and reconstruction could help to illuminate. For all the romance that has been perpetrated about the "unique cultural blend" that developed in Nuevo Mexico, little in fact is known about the everyday nature and character of village or multicommunity life, or about the quality, structure, and extent of face-to-face interethnic relations. While the archival and documentary sources may not justify a descriptively "thick" account of many behavioral and cultural aspects of social history, they may well support a more detailed picture than we have at present of the eighteenth- and nineteenth-century political and household economies in the Taos area. On the one hand, a developing commercial center like Taos should be looked at in terms of the special assets offered by its internal diversity. This diversity was based on a variety of microniches within several watersheds draining into the Taos basin. The ethnic and social composition of village households, and the economic and kinship relations among them, need to be mapped out wherever possible. Similarly, the economic, social, and kinship ties and exchanges between communities, as well as across ethnic boundaries, need to be reconstructed through time to whatever extent made possible by a variety of coordinated research strategies. On the other hand, the dynamics and transformations in Taos must be examined and ultimately explained in terms of their regional and international or global macrosocial contexts. This is particularly necessary with respect to local labor history, which must also be documented and analyzed through time, including the major role out-migration has played for at least the whole of this century. Another important line of inquiry is the evolution and composition of Taos's class structure, which, despite the celebrated "leveling effect" of frontier conditions, we may safely assume was fully operative by the time of the Spanish reconquest, and which for reasons in need of investigation, appears to have accommodated a swift American economic takeover during the Mexican period.[142]

A great deal of research is needed on the twentieth century and especially contemporary Taos, including further documentation and analysis of the economic, political, and cultural development of tourism. At least two questions should help to guide research on tourism: (1) Does or has tourism progressively promote(d) the underdevelopment or nondevelopment of alternative economies (and if so, in what specific ways)? and (2) What further effect, beyond that already discussed in these pages, does the marketing of ethnicity and culture have on specific interethnic and intraethnic politics, and on peoples' awareness of and perception of their own or another's ethnicity?

Finally, in a more applied yet theoretically important vein, two further lines of inquiry are suggested. The history and causes or correlates of pressing social problems, such as today's apparently epidemic incidence of alcoholism across classes among all three ethnic groups, need to be investigated and analyzed comparatively, in order to inform public policy with respect to their treatment. And last but not least: viable and acceptable long-range economic alternatives to Taos's present trajectory need to be discovered.

Notes

1. In keeping with the prevailing trend in the contemporary ethnographic and ethnohistorical literature on the region, the term Hispano will be applied specifically to the subgroup of Mexicanos or subsequently Mexican Americans who settled in the Upper Rio Grande and adjacent regions of northern New Mexico and southern Colorado. The inclusive terms Mexicano (of emic import), Mexican American (etic), and Chicano are also used, the latter in reference to mostly younger, urbanized, and ethnically politicized Mexican Americans. My use of the term homeland derives in part from Spicer's

concept of persistent identity systems (see note 3), and from Nostrand's controversial homeland thesis on Hispanos in New Mexico. Richard Nostrand, "The Hispano Homeland in 1900," *Annals of the Association of American Geographers*, 70, no. 3 (1980): 382–96; see J. M. Blaut and A. Rios-Bustamante, "Commentary on Nostrand's 'Hispanos' and Their 'Homeland,'" and M. Simmons, Fray A. Chavez, D. W. Meinig, and T. Hall, "Rejoinders," in *AAAG*, 74, no. 1 (1984): 157–71. I argue here that the emic or native notion of a homeland, like the evolution of a given population's self-identity as a people, is something that takes place over time and under certain conditions. It is a product of history, of ongoing social interaction and change. My position with respect to the specific issues raised by the heated Hispano homeland debate is developed in the paper, "The Hispano Homeland Debate," presented at a panel discussion of the controversy held during the Western Social Science Association Meeting in April 1985, in Fort Worth. Also see note 18.

2. See Clark Knowlton, "Causes of Land Loss Among the Spanish Americans of Northern New Mexico," in Gilberto Lopez y Rivas, ed., *The Chicanos* (New York: Monthly Review Press, 1973), 111–21; Malcolm Ebright, *The Tierra Amarilla Grant: A History of Chicanery* (Santa Fe: The Center for Land Grant Studies, 1980); John and Christine Van Ness, eds., *Spanish and Mexican Land Grants in New Mexico and Colorado* (Manhattan, Kansas: Sunflower University Press, 1980).

3. Edward Spicer, "Persistent Cultural Systems," *Science,* 174 (1971): 795–800, esp. 797. For a more detailed discussion of the merits and weaknesses of Spicer's model with reference to Hispanos, see S. Rodriguez, "Hispanos in Taos: A Persistent Identity System?" (Paper presented at the annual meeting of the American Society for Ethnohistory, New Orleans, November 1984).

4. Spicer, op. cit. Also see George P. Castille and Gilbert Kushner, eds., *Persistent Peoples* (Tucson: University of Arizona Press, 1981).

5. For various approaches to the proletarianization of Mexicanos after 1847 see, for example, Tomas Almaguer, *Interpreting Chicano History: The 'World System' Approach to Nineteenth Century California* (Berkeley: Institute for the Study of Social Change, Working Papers Series no. 101, 1977); Mario Barrera, *Race and Class in the Southwest* (Notre Dame: University of Notre Dame Press, 1979); Juan Gomez-Quiñones, *Development of the Mexican Working Class North of the Rio Bravo* (Los Angeles: Popular Series No. 2, Chicano Studies Research Center Publications, University of California, Los Angeles, 1982).

6. Fredrik Barth, "Introduction," in *Ethnic Groups and Boundaries* (Boston: Little, Brown and Company, 1969), 19–21.

7. Spicer, "Plural Society in the Southwest," in E. Spicer and R. Thompson, eds., *Plural Society in the Southwest* (Albuquerque: University of New Mexico Press, 1972), 54–55.

8. Michael Hannan, "The Dynamics of Ethnic Boundaries in Modern States," in John Meyer and M. Hannan, eds., *National Development and the World System: Educational, Economic, and Political Change, 1950–1970* (Chicago: University of Chicago Press, 1979), 260.

9. Thomas Hall, "Lessons of Long-Term Change for Comparative and

Historical Study of Ethnicity," *Current Perspectives in Social Theory* 5 (1984): 126.

10. Myra Ellen Jenkins, "Taos Pueblo and Its Neighbors, 1540–1847," *New Mexico Historical Review* 41 (April 1966): 85–114.

11. Spicer, op. cit., 1972.

12. See, for example, Pierre van den Berghe, "Ethnic Pluralism in Industrial Societies: A Special Case?" *Ethnicity* 3 (1976): 242–55.

13. See Hall, this volume, for an in-depth account of the confusing status of Pueblo Indian landownership.

14. John Bodine, "A Tri-Ethnic Trap: The Spanish Americans in Taos," in June Helm, ed., *Spanish-Speaking People in the United States* (Proceedings of the 1968 American Ethnological Society): 145–53. Also see Etsuko Kuroda, "Ethnicity and Ethnic Culture in Crisis: The Struggle for Existence of the Spanish Americans in Taos, New Mexico" (Osaka: The National Museum of Ethnology, 1981).

15. This combines categories of Valene Smith's typology of tourism. See "Introduction" in V. Smith, ed., *Hosts and Guests* (Philadelphia: University of Pennsylvania Press, 1977), 1–13.

16. J. Bodine, "Attitudes and Institutions of Taos, New Mexico: Variables for Value System Expression" (Ph.D. diss., Tulane University, 1967).

17. For sources on Tijerina and the Alianza see: Patricia Bell Blawis, *Tijerina and the Land Grants: Mexican Americans in Struggle for Their Heritage* (New York: International Publishers, 1971). Richard Gardner, *Grito! Reies Tijerina and the New Mexico Land Grant War of 1967* (New York: Bobbs-Merrill Co. Inc., 1970). Michael Jenkins, *Tijerina* (Albuquerque: Paisano Press, 1968). Frances Leon Swadesh, "The Alianza Movement: Catalyst for Social Change in New Mexico," in Helms, ed., op. cit. (see note 14): 162–77. Reies López Tijerina, *Mi Lucha Por La Tierra* (Mexico, D.F.: Fondo de Cultura Economica, 1978).

18. The argument put forth in this paper independently parallels the thesis of John R. Chavez's recent book based on his disseration, *The Lost Land* (Albuquerque: University of New Mexico Press, 1984). Chavez argues historically for Chicanos in general and the Southwest as a whole what this paper argues for Taos and the Rio Arriba ethnographically: that a collective mythos of a lost or stolen homeland, known as "Aztlan," has developed among Chicanos as a people.

19. Dean MacCannell, "Reconstructed Ethnicity: Tourism and Cultural Identity in Third World Communities," in *Annals of Tourism Research* 11 (1984): 376–77.

20. Ibid., 383–85.

21. Ibid.; 388. Also see MacCannell, *The Tourist* (New York: Schocken Books, 1976).

22. J. Bodine, "Taos Pueblo," in Alfonso Ortiz, ed., *Handbook of North American Indians* vol. 9, *Southwest* (Washington, D.C.: Smithsonian Institution, 1979), 257–58.

23. Myra Ellen Jenkins and John Baxter, "Land History of the Pueblo of Taos, 1598–1900" (unpublished manuscript, n.d.), 20–21.

24. See Elsie Clews Parsons, *Taos Pueblo* (New York: Johnson Reprint Corp., 1970; orig. 1936). Bodine, "Taos Pueblo," in Ortiz, ed., *Handbook* esp. 257, 263.

25. See Jenkins and Baxter, "Land History," 22–25. Also Joe Sando, "The Pueblo Revolt," in A. Ortiz, ed., *Handbook*, 194–97.

26. Jenkins and Baxter, "Land History," 31–32.

27. This essay makes no attempt to provide a complete account of the tangled and contradictory land grant history of Taos County. Such a work remains to be written. The reader is referred to Jenkins and Baxter, op. cit., and M. E. Jenkins, "Taos Pueblo and Its Neighbors, 1540–1847," op. cit., and J. J. Bowden, "Private Land Claims in the Southwest," Southern Methodist University (1969, L.L.M. thesis), 885–1031. These are my principal sources on Taos grants. Bowden lists a total of thirty-one grants for Taos, nine of which are only partly inside the county, twenty-three entirely within its boundaries. Victor Westphall lists twenty-six, not including the Pueblo league, in *Mercedes Reales* (Albuquerque, University of New Mexico Press, 1983), Appendix I, 276–77. Ultimately only fourteen were confirmed by Congress and patented. Also see Rowena Martinez, "Land Grants in the Taos Valley" (Taos: Taos County Historical Society Pub. no. 2, n.d.).

28. Jenkins and Baxter, op. cit., 33.

29. Oakah Jones, *Los Paisanos* (Norman: University of Oklahoma Press, 1979), 140–49, 164.

30. See Ramon Gutierrez, "Report on the Taos Valley Population" (6 October 1982), Defendant's Exhibit II, prepared for the La Serna land grant trial, or Kristen Selph vs. Lt. James Alger, et al., January 1983, for a breakdown of the 1796 census report. It lists the placitas by their patron saints' names, including Nuestra Señora de Dolores, which could be either Cañon or El Prado, since until recently NSD was patroness of both. The third largest placita listed is Santa Getrudis; there seems to be no other record and no memory of a chapel or placita in her name in the Taos valley. I suspect it refers to Los Cordovas, whose patron is and has long been San Isidro, but further investigation is needed to determine its identity.

31. Jenkins and Baxter, "Land History," 43. The town, today known simply as Taos, has also been called San Fernando and Fernandez de Taos. Don Fernando was evidently the original name.

32. Richard N. Ellis, "Taos Pueblo," unpublished manuscript on Taos Pueblo legal history of land and water disputes from 1848–1924, n.d.: Part II: 1–3.

33. Gutierrez, "Report," 6.

34. The exact settlement sequence of the Taos area villages has not been definitively determined, and so this account, while broadly accurate, is nevertheless somewhat speculative.

35. David Snow, "Rural Hispanic Community Organization in Northern

New Mexico," Paul Kutsche, ed., *The Survival of Spanish American Villages* (Colorado Springs: Colorado College, 1979), 15: 45–62.

36. John Van Ness, "Hispanic Village Organization in Northern New Mexico: Corporate Community Structure in Historical Comparative Perspective," in Kutsche, ed., *The Survival*, 21–44; also "Hispanos in Northern New Mexico: the Development of Corporate Community and Multicommunity" (Ph.D. diss., University of Pennsylvania, 1979). Ruben Reina, "Town, Community and Multicommunity," *Estudios de Cultura Maya* 5 (1965): 361–90. Francisco Aguilera, *Santa Eulalia's People* (St. Paul: West Publishing Co., 1978).

37. Ramon Gutierrez, "Marriage, Sex, and the Family: Social Change in Colonial New Mexico, 1690–1846" (Ph.D. diss., University of Wisconsin-Madison, 1981).

38. Westphall, *Mercedes Reales*, 65.

39. See David Weber, *The Taos Trappers* (Norman: University of Oklahoma Press, 1970, 1971); also Janet Lecompte, "A Babel-Tongued Multitude on the Upper Arkansas," in Kutsche, ed., *The Survival*, 63–78.

40. See, for example, Nancie Gonzalez, *The Spanish Americans of Northern New Mexico* (Albuquerque: University of New Mexico Press, 1967), 117–18, for speculation as to the constituency of the revolt. Like Twitchell, Gonzalez assumes Padre Martinez to have been an instigator, a view refuted by Fray Angelico Chavez in *But Time and Chance* (Santa Fe: Sunstone Press, 1981), 81–86.

41. Marc Simmons, "History of the Pueblos Since 1821," in A. Ortiz, ed., *Handbook*, 208–9.

42. Roxanne Dunbar Ortiz, *The Roots of Resistance* (Los Angeles: Chicano Studies Research Center and American Indian Studies Center, University of California, Los Angeles, 1980), 93.

43. Knowlton, "Causes of Land Loss Among the Spanish Americans of Northern New Mexico," op. cit.

44. White, Koch, Kelly, and McCarthy, *Land Title Study* (Santa Fe: State Planning Office, 1971): Appendix I: 246–47. They list thirty-two grants for Taos County.

45. Rowena Martinez, op. cit. She lists fourteen grants, including the Ojo Caliente and Sebastian Martin, both of which lie mostly in Rio Arriba County.

46. See, for example, C. Knowlton, "Changing Spanish-American Villages of Northern New Mexico," *The Journal of Mexican American Studies* I, no. 1 (Fall 1970): 36. Olen Leonard, *The Role of the Land Grant* (Albuquerque: Calvin Horn, 1976, orig., 1940), esp. Chap. V.

47. Theodore Rixon, "Report on an Examination of the Taos Forest Reserve, Territory of New Mexico" (U.S. Geological Survey Report, 1905), 13.

48. M. E. Jenkins, "Development Potential of the Taos Pueblo Area in 1906," unpublished manuscript (1983), 7–9.

49. See, for example, Robert Rosenbaum, *Mexicano Resistance in the Southwest* (Austin: University of Texas Press, 1981).

50. See Frank Waters, *To Possess the Land* (Chicago: The Swallow Press, 1973).

51. A railroad did get as far as Taos Junction, roughly ten miles south of town in the gorge, whence it proceeded westward to Tres Piedras. Known as "The Chili Line," this railroad was discontinued in 1941, and never approximated the entrepreneurial potential envisioned in territorial days.

52. Charles Loomis provides some data on wartime out-migration from northern New Mexican villages including some in Taos County, in "Wartime Migration from the Rural Spanish Speaking Villages of New Mexico," *Rural Sociology* 7, no. 4 (1941): 384–95.

53. Simmons, "History of the Pueblos Since 1821," in A. Ortiz, ed., *Handbook*, 214–15.

54. Ibid., 215.

55. Ibid.

56. See, for example, Claire Morrill, *A Taos Mosaic* (Albuquerque: University of New Mexico Press, 1973): 94–97.

57. See Keith Bryant, Jr., "The Atchison, Topeka and Santa Fe Railway and the Development of the Taos and Santa Fe Art Colonies," *The Western Historical Quarterly* 9, no. 4 (October 1978): 437–53.

58. See notes 14, 16.

59. Ronald Grimes, *Symbol and Conquest* (Ithaca: Cornell University Press, 1976).

60. Charles Briggs, *The Wood Carvers of Cordova, New Mexico* (Knoxville: University of Tennessee Press, 1980).

61. Marta Weigle and Kyle Fiore, *Santa Fe and Taos, The Writer's Era* (Santa Fe: Ancient City Press, 1982).

62. The differences between North American and Mexican indianism are as noteworthy as their similarities. Both contained bohemian elements and emerged at broadly comparable stages in national and capitalist development. In the case of modern Mexican indiansim, glorification of the (usually Precolumbian) Indian was and is promoted by an urban mestizo intelligentsia to endorse, paradoxically, a program of forced assimilation, which historically constitutes the very basis of Mexican national identity. In the U.S. Southwest indianism was originally promoted by artists and literati from a conquering society. Like their Mexican contemporaries, they sought and believed they were discovering or forging an authentically American, rather than Eurocentric or Euro-imitative psychocultural identity. In both cases indianism is used to promote tourism. For discussions of Mexican indianism see George Collier, *The Fields of Tztozil* (Stanford: Stanford University Press, 1975), Chap. 9; Judith Friedlander, *Being Indian in Hueyapan* (New York: St. Martin's Press, 1975). For insight into the artistic and bohemian society of mostly pre-World War II Mexican indianism, see Hayden Herrera, *Frida: A Biography of Frida Kahlo* (New York: Harper and Row, 1983).

63. Bodine (1967): 131. Simmons, op. cit., 218–20.

64. J. J. Brody, "The Creative Consumer: Survival, Revival and Invention

in Southwest Indian Arts," in Nelson Graburn, ed., *Ethnic and Tourist Arts* (Berkeley: University of California Press, 1976), 70–84.

65. For examples of the Taos-Santa Fe ethos of bohemian "creative individualism," see above all, Mabel Dodge Luhan's memoirs on Taos: *Lorenzo in Taos* (1932), *Winter in Taos* (1935), *Edge of the Taos Desert: Escape to Reality* (1937). Also see "Taos and Individualism," *New Mexico Quarterly* 21, no. 2 (Summer 1951). For a masterpiece of documentation of the literary circles, see Weigle and Fiore, eds., *Santa Fe and Taos*.

66. See, for example: Raymund Paredes, "The Mexican Image in American Travel Literature 1831–1869," *New Mexico Historical Review* 51 (January 1977): 5–29; "The Origins of Anti-Mexican Sentiment in the United States," *New Scholar* 6 (1977): 139–65. David Weber, "'Scarce More than Apes': Historical Review of Anglo-American Stereotypes of Mexicans," in D. Weber, ed., *New Spain's Far Northern Frontier* (Albuquerque: University of New Mexico Press, 1979), pp. 293–307. Arnoldo De Leon, *They Called Them Greasers* (Austin: University of Texas Press, 1983).

67. Blanche Grant, who edited his autobiography and painted a well-known portrait of him, was an ardent proponent of Kit Carson, and instrumental in producing the special fiesta "Kit Carson Edition" of the *Taos Review* (18 July 1940). See B. Grant, ed., *Kit Carson's Own Story of His Life* (1926).

68. See, for example, the *Taos Review* (8 December 1938).

69. *New Mexico Statistical Abstract* (Albuquerque: Bureau of Business and Economic Research, University of New Mexico, 1979–80 edition), 97.

70. George Sanchez, *Forgotten People* (Albuquerque: Calvin Horn, 1940, 1967), 55.

71. See the *Taos Review*, 1940 (11 January, 9 May, 30 May, 1 August, 31 September). The *Taoseño* (throughout 1940–41, esp. 3 April, 17 April, 31 July, 11 September, 6 October 1941; 30 April 1942). During this same period Hispanos in Ranchitos and El Prado were fighting their eventual ejection from Indian claims. In the 1980's the Rio Costilla Livestock Association became involved in the development of a ski resort on some of the grant lands. In fact the settlers of Costilla Cañon had fought ejectment since shortly after they arrived there around the turn of the century, after having been "kicked off" the Maxwell on the other side of the mountains (personal communication, Marianne Stoller).

72. Two examples: the middle class Anglos who were drafted from Taos became officers in the division sent to Bataan; the Indian women's Red Cross contributions were organized separately.

73. Bodine (1967): 274–308.

74. See, for example, "Taos Campaigns Against Filth," concerning outhouses, *Taos Review* (14 March 1940); or as recently as *The Taos News*, April 1984 issues, concerning the streets.

75. See, for example, Spanish Page editorials by Felix Valdez, in *El Taoseño-Taos Review* (14 March 1940; 12 February, 18 February 1942; 13 May, 12 August 1943; 27 June 1946; 7 August 1947).

76. W. F. Turney and Associates, "Taos County Comprehensive Area-

Wide Plan for Water and Sewer" (Santa Fe: New Mexico Planning Office, November 1966), 55.

77. Mimbres and Associates, "Taos County Comprehensive Planning Program" (December 1978), Working Paper no. 1, "The Land," 45.

78. The figures on the percentage of the population subsisting at a subpoverty level vary from source to source, and even in different reports from the same source. For example, the Bureau of Business and Economic Research (BBER) reports the figure for 1979 at 24.1 percent (*NM Statistical Abstract 1984*), whereas in a more recent update, it is reported at 27.5. According to U.S. Bureau of the Census data for 1970, 35.8 percent of families in Taos were below the poverty level *Census of Population: 1970, General Social and Economic Characteristics, Final Report PC(I)-33, New Mexico*, Table 124 and Appendix B, 13, 29, 30.

79. Estelle Smith, "Cultural Variability in the Structuring of Violence," Thomas Williams, ed., *Psychological Anthropology* (The Hague: Mouton Pubs., 1975): 342–48.

80. Bodine (1967): 185–273.

81. See C. L. Reynolds, "Decision-Making and Cultural Change: the Status of Spanish American Small Farms in Northern New Mexico" (Ph.D. diss., Southern Methodist University, 1975); Reynolds, "Economic Decision-Making: the Influence of Traditional Hispanic Land Use Attitudes on Acceptance of Innovation," *The Social Science Journal* 13, no. 3 (October 1976): 21–34. John Nichols, *If Mountains Die* (New York: Alfred Knopf, 1979), 121–29.

82. J. Nichols, *The Milagro Beanfield War* (New York: Holt, Rinehart and Winston, 1974).

83. Nichols (1979), 129.

84. In 1981 nineteen affidavits were collected which attested to this; see text, 68.

85. *The Taos News* (24 November, 29 December 1983).

86. EID studies for the first full year of operation for the new plant showed some of the worst conditions on record with respect to aquatic biota in the reaches of the river above and below the plant. Studies for 1985, however, indicated that for the first time the pollution problem was under control while biota also showed improvement. See S. Rodriguez, "The Impact of the Ski Industry on the Rio Hondo Watershed," *Annals of Tourism Research*, forthcoming.

87. The filing fee for a protest against a water rights transfer application is $250. Lawyers' and filing fees are usually paid for with funds ditch officers manage to collect from water users. Other sources include occasional fund-raising activities such as bake sales or benefit dances, private donations, and some legal services assistance.

88. Since around 1970 Hispanos have progressed from being officers in Anglo-owned banks (a post-World War II development) to becoming owners of new banks.

89. John Temple and Lynn Wombold, *Population Employment and Income*

for Counties in New Mexico: Historical Data: 1970–1980 and Projections: 1980–2000 (Albuquerque: Bureau of Business and Economic Research, University of New Mexico, January 1983): 213–15, Table 6–3.3: 217. The number of non-agricultural jobs (i.e., manufacturing, construction, trade, services, government, etc., went from 3,519 in 1970 to 6,501 in 1981; see Table 6–3.2: 216.

90. *Environmental Impact Statement for the Proposed Taos Ski Valley Master Development Plan* (U.S. Dept. Agriculture, Forest Service, April 1981), 57.

91. Temple and Wombold (1983), Table 6–3.2: 216; Table 6–3.4: 218.

92. Ibid.

93. Ibid.

94. Ibid.

95. As reported monthly over local radio station KKIT during 1983.

96. In August 1985, Taos reported the third highest unemployment rate in the state. By the end of the year it was second, due to layoffs at the Moly mine, which is due to shut down in early 1986, an economic disaster for the county which promises to drive the unemployment rate to 27 percent to 32 percent. *The Taos News* (8 August 1985; 1 February 1986).

97. Temple and Wombold (1983): Table 6–3.6: 220; Table 6–3.5: 219.

98. In 1985 an Anglo attorney, well-known for service to the Hispanic poor, was elected to the school board.

99. Blanche Grant claims this in *When Old Trails Were New* (Glorietta, NM: The Rio Grande Press, Inc., 1934, 1983), Chap. 29, esp. p. 153. A more recent example is the Martindale case in the late 1970s, when an Oklahoma man shot and killed an unarmed Chicano youth and later successfully requested a change of venue on the grounds that as an Anglo he could not get a fair trial in Taos. In the public schools, some Anglo children, their parents, as well as teachers who fail to receive tenure, complain of "race" or ethnic discrimination by "the Spanish."

100. The 1970 census reported the Spanish language or surnamed population of the county to be 15,109 or 86.3 percent. *New Mexico Statistical Abstract* (Albuquerque: University of New Mexico, 1979–80), 106. According to *The Taos News* (19 March 1981), the 1980 census reckoned Hispanics at 66 percent, with one out of every four residents an Anglo, nearly twice what it had been in 1970. Final BBER 1980 Census figures report Hispanics at 69 percent (13,442), including over 2,000 Mexicans, presumably nationals (Summer Tape I, 1980 NM Census). Reasonably consistent and accurate longitudinal data on ethnic proportions in Taos are hard to come by. Sanchez, op. cit.: 30, reports that in 1938 the Hispanic proportion was 93 percent or 14,229. All this suggests that not only is the Hispanic proportion declining, but its absolute number as well, despite the highest fertility rate (14.35 percent) among all three groups; see *Selected Health Statistics, New Mexico 1979* (Santa Fe: Health & Environment Department), 34.

101. Twining is counted in the tax rolls as part of the Valdez district, but the two are geographically and socially distinct, Valdez proper still being

predominantly Hispano owned and populated. The Hispano-Anglo proportion in San Cristobal is roughly equivalent.

102. "Predominantly" means more than 50 percent Anglo owned. Based on review of 1931–1980 tax rolls.

103. "Anglo" is employed here in its common folk usage, which subsumes a variety of non-Anglo Saxon, non-Hispanic, western European ethnic and national groups.

104. Total federal (50.8 percent), state (6.7 percent), and Indian (4.3 percent) lands come to 61.8 percent of the acreage in Taos County. See Mimbres & Assoc. (1978): Paper no. 1: 31. Also Jerry Williams and Paul McAllister, eds., *New Mexico in Maps* (Albuquerque: University of New Mexico Press, 1979), 116.

105. *The Taos News* (26 September 1985).

106. *The Taos News* (16 August 1985). The average price of a house at this time was $108,000.

107. El Prado adopted a plan with a commercial strip along the highway, whereas farmers, ditch and water officers, and others in Cañon resisted considerable pressure to do the same, and came up instead with a more conservative rural-agricultural plan, closer in spirit to the one developed later by the Tres Valles Special Zoning District.

108. In autumn 1985 the town arranged to buy—or actually to lease—another 2,000 acre-feet of San Juan-Chama water rights from the Bureau of Reclamation, part of the 4,520 acre-feet which had been allocated to the now defunct Indian Camp Dam project. See *The Taos News* (19 September 1985; 26 February 1985). This should help to meet projected demands to the turn of the century. Presumably the lease of San Juan-Chama water will temporarily forestall the need for the city ultimately to condemn all surface water rights in the Taos basin and appropriate them for municipal use, in order to accommodate further growth.

109. This account is based upon 21 months of ethnographic fieldwork in Taos between August 1981 and June 1983, during which time I attended scores of rural zoning meetings in communities around Taos.

110. Simon Tejada, "Historia de Valdez" (WPA Writers' Project Files, State Records Center and Archives, Santa Fe, 25 August 1939), 7.

111. Twining is predominantly "Anglo" owned and populated, more than half by seasonal residents, whereas more than half the land in Des Montes is still Hispano owned, but the greater number of residents is Anglo.

112. By local account, Valdez originally had second priority to Arroyo Hondo, but lost it to Des Montes through some "mishap" during recent adjudication.

113. It is perhaps coincidental but deserving of investigtion that the Ranchos revival followed upon the defeat of Indian Camp Dam. Revival of the fiesta of San Antonio in Valdez took place the spring after the condo war, and involved, significantly, a procession to and blessing of the river. Recent Chicano innovations include Cinco de Mayo festivities, celebrated for the first

Land, Water, and Ethnic Identity 401

time in 1983, replete with a lowrider parade, Danza Azteca, and Corky Gonzales as keynote speaker.

114. These organizers were unaffiliated and independent.

115. It was during the Hacienda protest that I became, more or less fortuitously, resident in Valdez, and involved in the events that unfolded there.

116. This is a pseudonym. All participants on either side of the issue described in this account will remain anonymous.

117. La Lama, a small settlement to the north of San Cristobal, is also included within the Tres Valles district, although its residents were not actively involved in the protest.

118. The complete story of the county commission's remarkable behavior during the condo war cannot be told here, and would in any case be more appropriately part of a discussion of how local government and county politics function in Taos. In recent years both the county commission and school board have been the foci of intense controversies between local factions, interests, and personalities.

119. I assisted in fund-raising efforts, contacted potential supporters, provided public but not easily available information to community members, and donated labor as needed. My decision to do this seemed morally compelled and flowed, on the one hand, from my perception and understanding of the situation as a bi-ethnic native and citizen of Taos, and on the other, from my perception and understanding of the situation as an anthropologist. I believe my actions to be consistent with the 1971 AAA (American Anthropological Association) Statement on Ethics, particularly what I take to be the meaning of Sections 1 and 2d. The methodological and theoretical implications of my involvement will be taken up elsewhere.

120. I gratefully acknowledge Mr. Vigil's permission to include his poem, and also wish to thank both him and Mrs. Vigil for their guidance and help in making the translation. The orthography and Spanish of the poem are New Mexican and Mr. Vigil's.

121. Crandall had filed his condo declaration on 17 May, just forty-eight hours before the new state Condominium Act, containing stricter disclosure requirements, went into effect.

122. By keeping the gallon per day (gpd) limit below 2,000, the Hacienda circumvented the need to publish their permit application, which the EID routinely approved. In principle, one violation was sufficient to revoke the permit, which of course did not, and probably never does, happen. Publicity of these facts after the violation eventually resulted in the arrangement whereby a representative from Valdez, in addition to someone from EID, would monitor Hacienda meter readings.

123. This was done through the caretaker, sent to surrepticiously monitor Valdez zoning meetings at the *escuelita*.

124. Anya Peterson Royce, *Ethnic Identity* (Bloomington: Indiana University Press, 1982), 43–50.

125. John Van Ness, "Spanish American vs. Anglo American Land Tenure

and the Study of Economic Change in New Mexico," *Social Science Journal* 13, no. 3 (October 1976): 46.

126. Ibid., 47–48.

127. Knowlton, "Changing Spanish-American Villages of Northern New Mexico," *Journal of Mexican American Studies* I, no. 1 (Fall 1970): 33.

128. See Florence Kluckhohn and Fred Strodbeck, *Variations in Value Orientations* (Evanston: Row & Peterson, 1961). Evon Vogt and Ethel Albert, eds., *People of Rimrock: A Study of Values in Five Cultures* (New York: Atheneum, 1970). For Chicano critiques of this approach see Octavio Romano, "The Anthropology and Sociology of Mexican Americans," *El Grito* 2, no. 1 (1968): 13–26; and "Social Science, Objectivity, and the Chicanos," *El Grito* 4, no. 1 (Fall 1970): 4–16. Nick Vaca, "The Mexican American in the Social Sciences, 1912–1970," esp. Part II: 1936–1970, *El Grito* 4, no. 1 (Fall 1970): 17–51; and "The Comparative Study of Values in Five Cultures Project and the Theory of Value," *Aztlan* 12, no. 1 (Spring 1981): 89–120.

129. Clyde Eastman, Garrey Carruthers, and James Liefer, *Evaluation of Attitudes Toward Land in North Central New Mexico* 1 (Las Cruces: New Mexico State University Agricultural Experiment Station Bulletin 577, May 1971): 10–11. They employ Knowlton's characterization of Hispano land attitudes found in "Conflicting Attitudes Toward Land Use and Land Ownership in New Mexico," *Proceedings of the Southwestern Sociological Association* 18 (1967): 60–68.

130. Eastman, et al. Ibid.: 1. Eastman follows a similar approach in *Assessing Cultural Change in North Central New Mexico* (Las Cruces: NMSU Agricultural Experiment Station Bulletin 592, January 1972).

131. For a primordialist view of how ethnic or tribal ties impede nation building see Karl Deutsch's "Introduction," in K. Deutsch and W. J. Flotz, eds., *Nation Building* (New York: Atherton Press, 1963). For contrasting views see Edward Shils, "Primordial, Personal, Sacred, and Civil Ties," *British Journal of Sociology* 8 (1957): 130–45, or Clifford Geertz, "The Integrative Revolution: Primoridal Sentiments and Civil Politics in New States," in Geertz, ed., *Old Societies and New States* (Glencoe, Ill.: Free Press, 1963). For more recent discussions incorporating Barth's reactive view of ethnicity as well as world systems theory, see Michael Hannan, "The Dynamics of Ethnic Boundaries in Modern States," in John Meyer and M. Hannan, eds., op. cit. (1970). For an overview of non-Marxist perspectives of ethnicity see Anya Peterson Royce, op. cit. (1982).

132. Spicer suggests that the possession of state power tends to dissipate a persistent identity system, although under "certain rather special conditions" it might reinforce such a system (1971): 797. I suggest that the decisive factor or event in the creation or evolution of Chicano identity has been the psychohistorical experience of the loss of state power and ethnopolitical dominance, which entailed expropriation and ethnic subordination. It is in relation to Spicer's feature of seldom or only temporarily holding state power that the proposed designation of Hispanos as a persistent people is most problematic. This is essentially the problem of how class and ethnicity have, do, and will

interact in New Mexico. More research is needed on the nature and character of the ethnic boundary system during colonial periods. The most promising macrotheoretical framework for diachronic analysis of this problem would probably be Wallerstein's approach. See Immanual Wallerstein, *The Modern World System: Capitalist Agriculture and the Origins of the European World-Economy in the Sixteenth Century* (New York: Academic Press, 1974); *The Capitalist World Economy* (New York: Cambridge University Press, 1979).

133. Spicer (1971), 797. Royce (1982), 44.

134. Royce (1982), 44.

135. Spicer (1971), 798.

136. For a proposed approach along these lines, see P. Kutsche, J. Van Ness, and A. Smith, "A Unified Approach to the Anthropology of Hispanic Northern New Mexico," *Historical Archaeology* 10 (1976): 1–16.

137. It should be clear that "minority" refers to relative power and is therefore a political and not a demographic concept.

138. See Romano, Vaca (note 128), and Americao Paredes, "On Ethnographic Work Among Minority Groups, A Folklorist's Perspective," *New Scholar* 6 (1977): 1–32.

139. See, for example, John Gwaltney, *Drylongso* (New York: Vintage, 1981); Carol Stack, *All Our Kin* (New York: Harper & Row, 1974); Bettylou Valentine, *Hustling and Other Hard Work* (New York: The Free Press, 1978).

140. See Paredes (1977).

141. My use of the term "resistance" here is broader than Rosenbaum's. He distinguishes several kinds of Mexicano response to Anglo conquest and domination, namely withdrawal, accommodation, assimilation, and resistance, by which he specifically means violent resistance. He sees accommodation-assimilation as largely a response by the elite and upwardly mobile, with which I agree, but suggest that these tactics in particular are often ambivalently and ambiguously felt and expressed, and can contain and mask elements of indirect resistance. Perhaps Spicer's oppositional process would appropriately cover what seems a continuum of variously expressed group responses and individual strategies. See Rosenbaum (1981), 14–15.

142. See note 37.

ACKNOWLEDGMENTS

I would like to thank Susan Halci, Sheryl Jimenez, Jonlyn Martinez, Roberta Marquez and Debbie Garcia for their research assistance. Debbie Garcia was funded by the Center for Regional Studies. I appreciate the Center's support for this project.

Cubillos, Herminia L. "Fair Housing and Latinos." *La Raza Law Review* 2 (1988): 49–61. Reprinted with the permission of the University of California Press. Courtesy of Yale University Law Library.

Montejano, David. "The Demise of 'Jim Crow.'" In David Montejano, ed., *Anglos and Mexicans in the Making of Texas, 1836–1986*. (Texas: University of Texas Press, 1987): 262–287, 346–48. Reprinted with the permission of the University of Texas Press. Courtesy of Yale University Cross Campus Library.

Krivo, Lauren J. "Housing Price Inequalities: A Comparison of Anglos, Blacks, and Spanish-Origin Populations." *Urban Affairs Quarterly* 17 (1982): 445–62. Reprinted with the permission of Sage Publications, Inc. Courtesy of Yale University Sterling Memorial Library

Winsberg, Morton D. "Housing Segregation of a Predominantly Middle Class Population: Residential Patterns Developed by the Cuban Immigration into Miami, 1950–74." *American Journal of Economics and Sociology* 38 (1979): 403–18. Reprinted with the permission of the *American Journal of Economics and Society*. Courtesy of Yale University Sterling Memorial Library.

Garcia, John A. "The Voting Rights Act and Hispanic Political Representation in the Southwest." *Publius* 16 (1986): 49–66. Reprinted with the permission of the North Texas State University. Courtesy of *Publius*.

Vigil, Maurilio E. "A New Remedy for an Old Ailment: Cumulative Voting as an Alternative to the Single Member District in Minority Voting Rights." *Latino Studies Journal* 3 (1992): 82–90. Reprinted with the permission of *Latino Studies Journal*. Courtesy of Antoinette Sedillo López.

Guerra, Sandra. "Voting Rights and the Constitution: The Disenfranchisement of Non-English Speaking Citizens." *Yale Law Journal* 97 (1988): 1419–37. Reprinted by permission of The Yale Law Journal Company and Fred B. Rothman & Company. Courtesy of Yale University Law Library.

Garcia, John A. "An Analysis of Chicano and Anglo Electoral Patterns in School Board Elections." *Ethnicity* 6 (1979): 168–83. Article was originally published in *Ethnicity*. Copyright by Abraham H. Miller. Reprinted with the permission of Academic Press, Inc. Courtesy of Yale University Sterling Memorial Library.

Grofman, Bernard and Lisa Handley. "Minority Population Proportion and Black and Hispanic Congressional Success in the 1970s and 1980s." *American Politics Quarterly* 17 (1989): 436–45. Reprinted with the permission of Sage Publications. Courtesy of Yale University Social Science Library.

Guerra, Fernando J. "Ethnic Officeholders in Los Angeles County." *Sociology and Social Research* 71 (1987): 89–94. Reprinted with the permission of the University of Southern California. Courtesy of Yale University Social Science Library.

Subervi-Velez, Federico, Richard Herrera and Michael Begay. "Toward an Understanding of the Role of the Mass Media in Latino Political Life." *Social Science Quarterly* 68 (1987): 185–96. Reprinted from *Social Science Quarterly*, by permission of the authors and the University of Texas Press. Courtesy of Yale University Sterling Memorial Library.

Retana, Robert G. "*Garza v. County of Los Angeles*: Preservation of Minority Group Voting Strength as Justification for Deviation from One Person-One Vote Standard." *La Raza Law Journal* 3 (1990): 51–82. Reprinted with the permission of the University of California Press. Courtesy of Yale University Law Library.

Retana, Robert G. "Case Note Addendum: *Gárza v. County of Los Angeles*." *La Raza Law Journal* 4 (1991): 124–28. Reprinted with the permission of the University of California Press. Courtesy of Yale University Law Library.

Hero, Rodney. "The Election of Hispanics in City Government: An Examination of the Election of Federico Peña as Mayor of Denver." *Western Political Quarterly* 40 (1987): 93–105. Reprinted by permission of the University of Utah, copyright holder. Courtesy of *Western Political Quarterly*.

Welch, Susan, and Lee Sigelman. "A Gender Gap Among Hispanics? A Comparison with Blacks and Anglos." *Western Political Quarterly* 45 (1992): 181–99. Reprinted by permission of the University of Utah, copyright holder. Courtesy of *Western Political Quarterly*.

MacManus, Susan A., Charles S. Bullock III and Barbara P. Grothe. "A Longitudinal Examination of Political Participation Rates of Mexican American Females." *Social Science Quarterly* 67 (1986): 604–12. Reprinted from *Social Science Quarterly,* by permission of the authors and the University of Texas Press. Courtesy of Yale University Sterling Memorial Library.

Lovrich, Nicholas P., Jr., and Otwin Marenin. "A Comparison of Black and Mexican American Voters in Denver: Assertive versus Acquiescent Political Orientations and Voting Behavior in an Urban Electorate." *Western Political Quarterly* 29 (1976): 284–94. Reprinted by permission of the University of Utah, copyright holder. Courtesy of Yale University Sterling Memorial Library.

Cain, Bruce E., and D. Roderick Kiewiet. "Ethnicity and Electoral Choice: Mexican American Voting Behavior in the California 30th Congressional District." *Social Science Quarterly* 65 (1984): 315–27. Reprinted from *Social Science Quarterly*, by permission of the authors and the University of Texas Press. Courtesy of Yale University Sterling Memorial Library.

Vigil, Maurilio E. "Hispanics Gain Seats in the 98th Congress After Reapportionment." *International Social Science Review* 59 (1984): 20–30. Reprinted with the permission of *International Social Science Review*. Courtesy of Yale University Sterling Memorial Library.

Lamar, Howard R. "Land Policy in the Spanish Southwest, 1846–1891: A Study in Contrasts." *Journal of Economic History* 22 (1962): 498–515. Reprinted with the permission of Cambridge University Press. Courtesy of Yale University Sterling Memorial Library.

Rodríguez, Sylvia. "Land, Water, and Ethnic Identity in Taos." In Charles L. Briggs and John R. Van Ness, eds., *Land, Water, and Culture: New Perspectives on Hispanic Land Grants*. (University of New Mexico Press, 1987): 313–403. Reprinted with the permission of the University of New Mexico Press. Courtesy of Yale University Sterling Memorial Library.